iPod® & iTunes®

FOR

DUMMIES®

7TH EDITION

by Tony Bove

WILEY

Wiley Publishing, Inc.

iPod® & iTunes® For Dummies®, 7th Edition

Published by
Wiley Publishing, Inc.
111 River Street
Hoboken, NJ 07030-5774

www.wiley.com

Copyright © 2010 by Wiley Publishing, Inc., Indianapolis, Indiana

Published by Wiley Publishing, Inc., Indianapolis, Indiana

Published simultaneously in Canada

For general information on our other products and services, please contact our Customer Care Department within the U.S. at 877-762-2974, outside the U.S. at 317-572-3993, or fax 317-572-4002.

For technical support, please visit www.wiley.com/techsupport.

Wiley also publishes its books in a variety of electronic formats. Some content that appears in print may not be available in electronic books.

Library of Congress Control Number: 2009936810

ISBN: 978-0-470-52567-8

Manufactured in the United States of America

10   9   8   7   6   5   4   3   2

WILEY

About the Author

Tony Bove is crazy about iPods, iPhones, and iTunes, and not only provides free tips on his Web site (www.tonybove.com) but also took the plunge to develop an iPhone application (*Tony's Tips for iPhone Users*). Tony has written more than two dozen books on computing, desktop publishing, and multimedia, including *iPod touch For Dummies* (Wiley), *iLife '04 All-In-One Desk Reference For Dummies* (Wiley), *The GarageBand Book* (Wiley), *The Art of Desktop Publishing* (Bantam), and a series of books about Macromedia Director, Adobe Illustrator, and PageMaker. Tony also founded *Desktop Publishing/Publish* magazine and the Inside Report on *New Media* newsletter, and he wrote the weekly Macintosh column for *Computer Currents* for a decade, as well as articles for *NeXTWORLD,* the *Chicago Tribune* Sunday Technology Section, and *NewMedia.* Tracing the personal computer revolution back to the 1960s counterculture, Tony produced a CD-ROM interactive documentary in 1996, *Haight-Ashbury in the Sixties* (featuring music from the Grateful Dead, Janis Joplin, and Jefferson Airplane). He also developed the Rockument music site, www.rockument.com, with commentary and podcasts focused on rock music history. As a founding member of the Flying Other Brothers, which toured professionally and released three commercial CDs (*52-Week High, San Francisco Sounds,* and *Estimated Charges*), Tony performed with Hall of Fame rock musicians. Tony has also worked as a director of enterprise marketing for leading-edge software companies, and as a communications director and technical publications manager.

Dedication

This book is dedicated to my sons, nieces, nephews, their cousins, and all their children . . . the iPod generation.

Author's Acknowledgments

I want to thank Jimi Eric Bove for providing technical expertise and performing valuable testing on his iPod touch, and John Paul Bove for iTunes, Windows, and iPhone expertise. I also want to thank Rich Tennant for his wonderful cartoons, and Dennis Cohen for technical expertise beyond the call of duty. And let me not forget my Wiley editors Paul Levesque and John Edwards for ongoing assistance that made my job so much easier. A book this timely places a considerable burden on a publisher's production team, and I thank the production crew at Wiley for diligence beyond the call of reason.

I owe thanks and a happy hour or three to Carole McLendon at Waterside, my agent. And finally, I have Executive Editor Bob Woerner at Wiley to thank for coming up with the idea for this book and helping me to become a professional dummy — that is, a Dummies author.

Publisher's Acknowledgments

We're proud of this book; please send us your comments at http://dummies.custhelp.com. For other comments, please contact our Customer Care Department within the U.S. at 877-762-2974, outside the U.S. at 317-572-3993, or fax 317-572-4002.

Some of the people who helped bring this book to market include the following:

Acquisitions, Editorial, and Media Development

Senior Project Editor: Paul Levesque

Executive Editor: Bob Woerner

Copy Editor: John Edwards

Technical Editor: Dennis Cohen

Editorial Manager: Leah Cameron

Media Development Project Manager: Laura Moss-Hollister

Media Development Assistant Project Manager: Jenny Swisher

Media Development Associate Producers: Josh Frank, Marilyn Hummel, Douglas Kuhn, and Shawn Patrick

Editorial Assistant: Amanda Graham

Sr. Editorial Assistant: Cherie Case

Cartoons: Rich Tennant (www.the5thwave.com)

Composition Services

Project Coordinator: Patrick Redmond

Layout and Graphics: Carl Byers, Ana Carrilo, Joyce Haughey, Christin Swinford, Christine Williams

Proofreaders: John Greenough, Susan Hobbs, Robert Springer

Indexer: Christine Karpeles

Publishing and Editorial for Technology Dummies

    Richard Swadley, Vice President and Executive Group Publisher

    Andy Cummings, Vice President and Publisher

    Mary Bednarek, Executive Acquisitions Director

    Mary C. Corder, Editorial Director

Publishing for Consumer Dummies

    Diane Graves Steele, Vice President and Publisher

Composition Services

    Debbie Stailey, Director of Composition Services

Contents at a Glance

Introduction 1

Part 1: Touching All the Basics 7

Chapter 1: Firing Up Your iPod and iPhone.................................9
Chapter 2: Setting Up iTunes and Your iPod and iPhone 29
Chapter 3: Putting Your Finger on It 39
Chapter 4: Choosing Essential Settings For Daily Operation 57
Chapter 5: Going Mobile 79

Part 11: Filling Up Your Empty Cup 89

Chapter 6: Getting Started with iTunes 91
Chapter 7: Shopping at the iTunes Store 103
Chapter 8: Bringing Content into iTunes 129
Chapter 9: Into the Sync with iTunes 145
Chapter 10: Syncing Mail, Calendars, Contacts, and Bookmarks 161

Part 111: Managing Your Library 177

Chapter 11: Searching, Browsing, and Sorting in iTunes...............179
Chapter 12: Adding and Editing Information in iTunes...................195
Chapter 13: Playing Content in iTunes.......................................207
Chapter 14: Organizing iTunes Content with Playlists....................229
Chapter 15: Gimme Shelter for My Media 239

Part 1V: Playing It Back on Your iPod or iPhone 251

Chapter 16: The Songs Remain the Same 253
Chapter 17: Bring Videos, Books, and Podcasts 279
Chapter 18: Your Pocket Picture Player......................................289

Part V: Touching the Online World 303

Chapter 19: Surfin' Safari 305
Chapter 20: The Postman Always Beeps Once 317
Chapter 21: Using Applications on Your iPod or iPhone 327

Part VI: The Part of Tens 355

Chapter 22: Ten Steps to Recovery 357
Chapter 23: Ten Tangible Tips...365

Index 371

Table of Contents

Introduction *1*

About This Book 2
Conventions Used in This Book 2
And Just Who Are You? 3
A Quick Peek Ahead 4
   Part I: Touching All the Basics 4
   Part II: Filling Up Your Empty Cup 4
   Part III: Managing Your Library 5
   Part IV: Playing It Back on Your iPod or iPhone 5
   Part V: Touching the Online World 5
   Part VI: The Part of Tens 5
   Bonus Chapters 6
Icons Used in This Book 6

Part 1: Touching All the Basics *7*

Chapter 1: Firing Up Your iPod and iPhone **9**

Introducing the iPod and iPhone 10
Comparing iPod Models 11
   Fingering the iPod touch 12
   Twirling the iPod classic 13
   Mano a mano with iPod nano 14
   Doing the iPod shuffle 15
The Innovative iPhone 16
Thinking Inside the Box 18
   Outside the box 18
   Computer and software not included 19
Applying Power 20
   Connecting your iPod or iPhone 20
   Turning it on and off 21
Facing Charges of Battery 23
   Recharging your battery 24
   Saving power 25

Chapter 2: Setting Up iTunes and Your iPod and iPhone **29**

Installing iTunes on a Windows PC 29
Installing iTunes on a Mac 33
Setting Up Your iPod or iPhone 35

Chapter 3: Putting Your Finger on It **39**

Tapping Your iPod touch or iPhone 39
  Sliding to the Home screen 40
  Searching for anything 42
  Checking the status bar 43
  Tons of icons and what do you get? 43
  Touching and gesturing 45
  Rearranging your Home screen pages 45
Tickling the Keyboard on an iPod touch or iPhone 47
  Typing into Notes 47
  Typing numbers and symbols 48
  Editing text and handling word suggestions 49
  Copying (or cutting) and pasting 51
  Setting keyboard options 53
Thumbing through iPod nano and classic Menus 54

Chapter 4: Choosing Essential Settings For Daily Operation **57**

There's No Time Like the Right Time 58
  On an iPod touch or iPhone 58
  On an iPod nano or iPod classic 59
Rock Around the Clocks 61
  Checking the time in Paris and Bangkok 61
  Getting alarmed 63
  Timing your steps (iPod touch and iPhone) 66
  Using the stopwatch 67
  Setting the sleep timer 68
  Using the iPod nano pedometer 69
Setting the Passcode for Your Lock 70
Getting Personal 72
  Adjusting the backlight of your iPod nano or iPod classic 72
  Brightening and wallpapering your iPod or iPhone 73
  Sound effects and fonts 74
  Location, location, location 75
  Setting restrictions on an iPod touch or iPhone 75
Going Online with your iPod touch or iPhone 76
  Turning Wi-Fi on or off 77
  Choosing a Wi-Fi network 77

Chapter 5: Going Mobile **79**

Connecting Headphones and Portable Speakers 79
Playing Car Tunes 81
  Using cassette and power adapters for your car 82
  Integrating an iPod or iPhone with your car stereo 84
Connecting by Wireless Radio 85
Dressing Up Your iPod and iPhone for Travel 86
Using Power Accessories 87

Part II: Filling Up Your Empty Cup 89

Chapter 6: Getting Started with iTunes 91
What You Can Do with iTunes.. 92
Opening the iTunes Window 93
Playing CD Tracks in iTunes.. 97
    Rearranging tracks... 98
    Skipping tracks 99
    Repeating an entire CD... 99
    Displaying visuals 99
Using the iTunes Genius Sidebar 102

Chapter 7: Shopping at the iTunes Store 103
Visiting the iTunes Store... 104
Setting Up an Account.. 106
Cruising the Multimedia Mall 108
    Browsing songs and albums 108
    Power searching.. 111
    Browsing movies, TV shows, music videos, and audio books..... 112
    Browsing and subscribing to podcasts............................ 114
Buying and Downloading Media 116
    Changing other iTunes Store preferences 117
    Resuming interrupted downloads 118
    Redeeming gift certificates and prepaid cards 119
Appearing at the App Store 120
Shopping with your iPod touch or iPhone 122
    Browsing and downloading songs 122
    Browsing and downloading podcasts 124
    Browsing and downloading apps 124
    Updating apps you've downloaded 125
Sharing iTunes Purchases in Your Home Network.................. 126

Chapter 8: Bringing Content into iTunes........................ 129
Adding Music 129
    Changing import preferences and settings 130
    Don't fall into the gaps 134
    Ripping music from CDs.. 136
    Adding music files... 138
Adding Podcasts 139
    Subscribing to podcasts 139
    Updating podcasts... 141
    Scheduling podcast updates 141
Adding Videos... 142

Chapter 9: Into the Sync with iTunes **145**

Syncing with Your iTunes Store Account 146
Choosing What to Sync 150
  Syncing everything but the kitchen 150
  Getting picky about playlists, artists, and genres 151
  Picking and choosing podcast episodes 153
  Choosing movies and TV shows 154
Manually Managing Music and Videos 156
  Copying items directly to your iPod or iPhone 157
  Deleting items on your iPod or iPhone 158
  Autofill it up 159

Chapter 10: Syncing Mail, Calendars, Contacts, and Bookmarks . . .161

Applications to Organize Your Life 162
Syncing Your Personal Info Using iTunes 163
Going MobileMe to Sync Your iPod touch or iPhone 167
  Setting up on a Mac 168
  Setting up in Windows 170
  When you sync upon a cloud 170
Setting Up Mail Accounts on Your iPod touch or iPhone 172
Changing and Deleting Mail Accounts 174

Part III: Managing Your Library **177**

Chapter 11: Searching, Browsing, and Sorting in iTunes 179

Browsing Your Library Content 180
  Browsing by cover art with Cover Flow 182
  Browsing songs by artist and album 184
  Browsing audio books 186
  Browsing podcasts 186
  Browsing movies, videos, and TV shows 186
  Browsing applications and iPod games 187
Displaying Content in List View 188
  Changing the List view options 189
Sorting Content by the List View Options 190
Searching for Content 191
Finding the Content's Media File 192
Showing Duplicate Items 193
Deleting Content 193

Chapter 12: Adding and Editing Information in iTunes 195

Retrieving Song Information from the Internet 196
  Retrieving information automatically 196
  Retrieving information manually 196
Entering Content Information 197

Editing the Information 198
  Editing multiple items at once 199
  Editing fields for a single item.................................... 200
  Adding a rating... 204
Adding Cover Art.. 205

Chapter 13: Playing Content in iTunes 207

Changing the Computer's Output Volume................................... 207
  Adjusting the sound on a Mac....................................... 208
  Adjusting the sound in Windows.................................. 209
Using AirTunes or Apple TV for Wireless Stereo Playback.......... 210
Playing Songs 214
  Grooving with the iTunes DJ 215
  Cross-fading song playback 218
Playing Podcasts.. 219
Playing Audio Books 221
Playing Videos.. 221
  Changing video playback preferences 223
  Playing a video full-screen 223
Adjusting the Sound 225
  Setting the volume in advance 225
  Equalizing the sound 226
  Sound-checking and enhancing the volume................. 227

Chapter 14: Organizing iTunes Content with Playlists. 229

Creating Playlists... 230
  Rearranging and managing playlists 231
  Deleting items from a playlist....................................... 232
Using Smart Playlists... 233
  Creating a smart playlist 233
  Editing a smart playlist 235
Adding a Touch of Genius 235
  Creating a Genius playlist 236
  Playing Genius mixes.. 237

Chapter 15: Gimme Shelter for My Media 239

Burning Your Own Discs 240
  Using recordable CDs and DVDs.................................. 240
  Creating a disc burn playlist.. 241
  Burning a disc.. 244
  Choosing your burn settings 245
Studying Files in an iTunes Library.. 247
  Finding the iTunes library 247
  Locating a media file... 248
  Copying media files... 249
Backing Up an iTunes Library... 249
  Backing up to DVD-Rs or CD-Rs 249
  Backing up to another hard drive................................. 250

Part 1V: Playing 1t Back on Your iPod or iPhone 251

Chapter 16: The Songs Remain the Same 253
Locating Songs on your iPod or iPhone 253
    Going with the Cover Flow.. 254
    Choosing artists and albums 255
    Choosing playlists... 257
    Choosing song titles and more... 258
Controlling Song Playback... 258
    Controlling playback on an iPod touch or iPhone............. 259
    Controlling playback on an iPod classic or iPod nano 260
    Repeating songs 262
    Shuffling song order 263
Playing an iPod shuffle.. 265
    Starting playback 265
    Controlling playback 266
    Using VoiceOver to choose playlists 266
Ordering Playlists On-The-Go 268
    Selecting and playing songs for an On-The-Go playlist.... 268
    Deleting items from an On-The-Go playlist...................... 271
    Clearing an On-The-Go playlist 272
Consulting the iTunes Genius 272
Adjusting and Limiting the Volume 275
Tweaking the Sound 277
    Peaking with the Sound Check 277
    All things being equal(ized) 278

Chapter 17: Bring Videos, Books, and Podcasts. 279
Everything's Coming Up Videos 279
    Playback at your fingertips on an iPod touch or iPhone............. 280
    Scaling the picture on an iPod touch or iPhone 282
    Playback under your thumb on an iPod nano or classic .. 282
YouTube on Your iPod touch or iPhone 283
    Running down a stream: Playback control 284
    Bookmarking and sharing.. 284
    Searching for videos 285
One Chapter at a Time: Audio Books and Podcasts 286
    Finding and playing on an iPod touch or iPhone............. 286
    Finding and playing on an iPod nano or iPod classic..... 287
Playing the FM Radio in an iPod nano 287

Chapter 18: Your Pocket Picture Player 289
Syncing with Photo Albums and Folders..................................... 289
    Transferring pictures to your iPod or iPhone 290
    Syncing saved pictures with iTunes 292

Viewing Pictures and Slideshows 293
    Viewing pictures on an iPod touch or iPhone...........................293
    Viewing pictures on an iPod nano or iPod classic....................296
Shooting Videos with an iPod nano 298
Sharing Pictures with an iPod touch or iPhone..........................299
    Sending a picture by e-mail 299
    Selecting and copying multiple pictures..............................300
    Capturing a screen shot 302

Part V: Touching the Online World 303

Chapter 19: Surfin' Safari 305
Take a Walk on the Web Side with Safari 305
    Go URL own way 306
    Hanging loose with your bookmarks....................................307
    Pearl diving with Google or Yahoo! 309
Let Your Fingers Do the Surfing 310
    Scrolling and zooming 310
    It's all touch and go 310
    Surfing multiple pages 311
    Interacting with pages 312
    Copying text 313
Bookmarking as You Go 314
    Saving a bookmark 314
    Sending a Web link by e-mail 315
Bringing It All Back Home 316

Chapter 20: The Postman Always Beeps Once. 317
Checking E-Mail 318
    The message is the medium 318
    Deleting a message 320
Sending E-Mail 321
Message Settings and Sending Options 323
    What you see is what you got 324
    Return to sender, address unknown....................................325
If Not Push, Then Fetch 325

Chapter 21: Using Applications on Your iPod or iPhone. 327
Checking Your Calendar 328
    A change is gonna come (iPod touch or iPhone) 329
    Yesterday's settings (and today's)...................................332
Using Your Contacts 333
    Orders to sort and display..334
    Soul searchin' on an iPod touch or iPhone 335

Adding, editing, and deleting contacts on an
iPod touch or iPhone...336
Earth, Wind, and Finance on Your iPod touch or iPhone.....................339
Consulting Maps...339
Riding the storms with Weather..344
Tapping your money maker with Stocks......................................345
Recording Voice Memos...347
Recording on an iPod touch or iPhone......................................347
Recording on an iPod nano or iPod classic.................................349
A Day in the Social Life on an iPod touch or iPhone.........................350
Ain't it good to know you've got a Facebook friend........................350
MySpace odyssey...352
Dedicated follower of Twitter...353

Part VI: The Part of Tens.................................. 355

Chapter 22: Ten Steps to Recovery 357
Powering Up and Unlocking...357
Powering Down...358
Stopping a Frozen App...359
Resetting Your iPod or iPhone System......................................359
Resetting iPod or iPhone Settings...360
Checking the Software Version...362
Updating the Software...362
Restoring to Factory Condition..363
Setting Up and Syncing..363
Restoring Settings from a Backup (iPod touch and iPhone)..................364

Chapter 23: Ten Tangible Tips..................................365
Saving the Life of Your Battery...365
Keeping Your Screen Clean...366
Getting Healthy with Nike...366
Rating Your Songs...366
Deleting Apps from Your iPod touch or iPhone..............................367
Deleting Videos and Podcasts from Your iPod touch or iPhone...............368
Measuring Traffic in Maps...368
Turning On International Keyboards on Your iPod touch or iPhone...........369
Drawing Chinese Characters..370
Stopping a Wi-Fi Network from Joining.....................................370

Index.. 371

Introduction

You don't need much imagination to see why so many people are so happy with their iPods and iPhones. Imagine no longer needing to take CDs or DVDs with you when you travel — your favorite music and videos fit right in your pocket and you can leave your precious content library at home.

What's more, this library is stored in electronic form (and easily backed up to other media), so it never deteriorates — unlike CDs, DVDs, and other physical media that may last only a few decades.

When I first encountered the iPod, it came very close to fulfilling my dream as a road warrior — in particular, the dream of filling up a car with music as easily as filling it up with fuel. For example, I use a fully loaded iPod classic with my car, using a custom in-vehicle interface adapter that offers an iPod connector. I use a cassette adapter, or even FM radio transmitter, in a rental car or boat (see Chapter 5). Whether you want to be *On the Road* with Jack Kerouac (in audio book form) or "Drivin' South" with Jimi Hendrix, just fill up your iPod or iPhone and go!

But first, find out about the iTunes application, which is the center of my media universe and the software that manages content on my iPods, my iPhone, and my Apple TV. I bring all my content into iTunes — from CDs, the online iTunes Store, and other sources — and then parcel it out to various iPods, iPhones, and Apple TV for playback. Even though I buy content and apps directly with my iPhone and iPod touch, and occasionally use Apple TV rather than my computer to enter the iTunes Store to rent or buy movies, everything I obtain is automatically synchronized with my main iTunes library. Everything is stored in my main iTunes library on my computer and backed up to another hard drive. I can even burn audio CDs and data DVDs. You can manage all these activities with iTunes.

iTunes was originally developed by Jeff Robbin and Bill Kincaid as an MP3 player called SoundJam MP, and released by Casady & Greene in 1999. It was purchased by Apple in 2000 and redesigned and released as iTunes. Since then, Apple has released numerous updates of iTunes to support new iPods, fix bugs, and add new features to improve your content library and your iPod or iPhone experience. All the important features are covered in this book. iTunes is getting better all the time, and this book gets you started.

About This Book

The publishers are wise about book matters, and they helped me design *iPod & iTunes For Dummies,* 7th Edition, as a reference. With this book, you can easily find the information you need when you need it. I wrote it so that you can read from beginning to end to find out how to use iTunes and your iPod, iPhone, or from scratch. But this book is also organized so that you can dive in anywhere and begin reading the info you need to know for each task.

I didn't have enough pages to cover every detail of every function, and I intentionally left out some detail so that you won't be befuddled with technospeak when it's not necessary. I wrote brief but comprehensive descriptions and included lots of cool tips on how to get the best results from using iTunes and your iPod or iPhone.

At the time I wrote this book, I covered every iPod and iPhone model available and the latest version of iTunes. Although I did my best to keep up for this print edition, Apple occasionally slips in a new model or new version of iTunes between book editions. If you've bought a new iPod, iPhone, that's not covered in the book, or if your version of iTunes looks a little different, be sure to check out the book's companion Web site for updates on the latest releases from Apple, as well as the Tips section of my Web site (www.tony bove.com) for free tips.

Conventions Used in This Book

Like any book that covers computers and information technology, this book uses certain conventions:

- **Choosing from a menu:** When I write "Choose iTunes⇨Preferences in iTunes," you click iTunes on the toolbar and then choose Preferences from the iTunes menu.

  With an iPod classic or iPod nano, when you see "Choose Settings⇨ Brightness from the iPod main menu," you scroll (rotate your finger clockwise around) the click wheel to highlight Settings on the main menu, press the Select button (the center button) to choose Settings, and then highlight and choose Brightness from the Settings menu.

  With an iPod touch or iPhone, when you see "Choose Settings⇨ Brightness from the Home screen," tap Settings on the Home screen and then tap Brightness.

✔ **Sliding, scrolling, and flicking on an iPod touch or iPhone:** When you see "Slide the screen" or "Flick the screen," I mean that you need to use your finger to slide the screen. When I write "Scroll the list on the iPod touch Settings screen," I mean that you should use your finger to slide the list so that it scrolls.

✔ **Clicking and dragging:** When you see "Drag the song over the name of the playlist," I mean that you need to click the song name, hold the mouse button down, and then drag the song with the mouse over to the name of the playlist before lifting your finger off the mouse button.

✔ **Keyboard shortcuts:** When you see ⌘-I, press the ⌘ key on a Mac keyboard along with the _I_ key. (In this case, ⌘-I opens the Song Information window in iTunes.) In Windows, the same keyboard shortcut is Ctrl-I (which means press the Ctrl key along with the _I_ key). Don't worry — I always tell you what the equivalent Windows keys are.

✔ **Step lists:** When you come across steps that you need to do in iTunes or on the iPod or iPhone, the action is in bold, and the explanatory part follows. If you know what to do, read the action and skip the explanation. But if you need a little help along the way, check out the explanation.

✔ **Pop-up menus:** I use the term _pop-up menu_ for menus on the Mac that literally pop up from dialogs and windows; in Windows, the same type of menu actually drops down and is called a drop-down menu. I use the term _pop-up menu_ for both.

And Just Who Are You?

You don't need to know anything about music or audio technology to discover how to make the most of your iPod, iPhone, and iTunes. Although a course in music appreciation can't hurt, these devices and iTunes are designed to be useful even for air-guitar players who barely know the difference between downloadable music and System of a Down. You don't need any specialized knowledge to have a lot of fun while building your digital music library.

However, I do make some honest assumptions about your computer skills:

✔ **You know how to use the Mac Finder or Windows Explorer.** I assume that you already know how to locate files and folders and that you can copy files and folders from one hard drive to another on the computer of your choice: a Mac or a Windows PC.

✔ **You know how to select menus and applications on a Mac or a Windows PC.** I assume that you already know how to choose an option from a menu, how to find the Dock on a Mac to launch a Dock application (or use the Start menu in Windows to launch an application), and how to launch an application directly by double-clicking its icon.

For more information on these topics, see these excellent books, all published by Wiley: *Mac OS X Snow Leopard All-in-One For Dummies* (Mark L. Chambers), *Windows Vista All-in-One Desk Reference For Dummies* (Woody Leonhard), or *Windows XP Gigabook For Dummies* (Peter Weverka).

A Quick Peek Ahead

This book is organized into six parts, and each part covers a different aspect of using your iPod or iPhone and iTunes. Here's a quick preview of what you can find in each part.

Part 1: Touching All the Basics

This part gets you started with your iPod or iPhone: powering it up, recharging its battery, and connecting it to your computer. You install and set up iTunes on your Mac or your Windows PC. You also find out all the techniques of an iPod or iPhone road warrior: setting your alarm and multiple clocks for time zones, keeping time with your stopwatch, changing your display settings, setting the passcode to lock up the device so that others can't use it, and setting restrictions on content and the use of applications. I also describe how to connect an iPod touch or iPhone wirelessly to the Internet with Wi-Fi, how to use your iPod or iPhone on the road with car stereos and portable speakers, and what types of accessories are available.

Part 11: Filling Up Your Empty Cup

This part shows you what you can do with iTunes. To acquire music, you can download it from the iTunes Store or other online services (such as Amazon), record it directly into your computer (using recording software such as GarageBand) and import it into iTunes, or rip audio CDs into iTunes. You can also download podcasts, audio books, movies, TV shows, and music videos from the iTunes Store or import them into iTunes from other sources. You find out how to download applications for the iPod touch or iPhone from the App Store, and how to download music, podcasts, videos, and applications directly to your iPod touch or iPhone. I also show you how to synchronize your iPod or iPhone with your iTunes library on your computer, and with your personal contacts, e-mail accounts, Web bookmarks, and calendars.

Part III: Managing Your Library

This part shows you how to sort the content in your iTunes library by artist, album, duration, date, and other items. You find out how to add and edit iTunes song information, and even fine-tune the sound of each song. You also discover how to arrange songs and albums into iTunes playlists that you can transfer to your iPod or iPhone and burn onto audio CDs. This part also contains crucial information about locating and backing up your iTunes library.

Part IV: Playing It Back on Your iPod or iPhone

I show you how to locate and play all types of content — music, audio books, podcasts, movies, TV shows, and videos — on your iPod, and on the iPod section of your iPhone. You discover how to control playback, adjust the volume, and equalize the sound. I also describe how to synchronize photo albums with your iPod or iPhone and display photo slide shows, as well as how to share images by e-mail and play YouTube videos with your iPod touch or iPhone.

Part V: Touching the Online World

This part describes how to use your iPod touch or iPhone and the Safari application to surf the Web. You also find out how to check and send e-mail, look at your stock portfolio, check the weather in your city and other cities, and display maps and driving directions. I also show how to use your iPod touch or iPhone to locate and communicate with friends on Facebook, MySpace, Twitter, and other social networks and instantly chat with people. You also discover how to enter and edit calendar entries in the Calendar application, and enter and sort contacts in the Contacts application.

Part VI: The Part of Tens

In this book's Part of Tens chapters, I provide initial troubleshooting steps and details about updating and restoring your iPod or iPhone. I also provide useful tips that can help make your iPod, iPhone, and iTunes experience a completely satisfying one.

Bonus Chapters

This book includes a number of bonus chapters on its companion Web site at www.dummies.com/go/ipod7e. Scattered through those chapters you'll find even more great informational nuggets. Topics include the following:

- ✔ Earlier iPod models and the cables for connecting them to your computer
- ✔ Choosing audio encoders and quality settings for importing music
- ✔ Preparing photo libraries, videos, address books, and calendars for your iPod or iPhone
- ✔ Managing multiple iTunes libraries and sharing iTunes libraries over a network
- ✔ Setting up and using Apple TV with iTunes
- ✔ Getting wired for playback and using iPod and iPhone accessories

Icons Used in This Book

The icons in this book are important visual cues for information you need.

Remember icons highlight important things you need to keep in mind.

Technical Stuff icons highlight technical details you can skip unless you want to bring out the technical geek in you.

Tip icons highlight tips and techniques that save you time and energy — and maybe even money.

Warning icons save your butt by preventing disasters. Don't bypass a Warning without reading it. This is your only warning!

On the Web icons let you know when a topic is covered further online at www.dummies.com/go/ipod7e, this book's companion Web site. I also use it to call your attention to specific areas within Apple's site (www.apple.com), and to the free tips section of my site at www.tonybove.com.

Part I
Touching All
the Basics

The 5th Wave   By Rich Tennant

"What I'm doing should clear your sinuses, take away your headache, and charge your iPod."

In this part . . .

*P*art I shows you how to do all the essential tasks with your iPod or iPhone to get you started as quickly as possible.

- ✔ Chapter 1 gets you started with your iPod or iPhone. Here you find out what it can do, how to connect it to power and to your Mac or Windows PC, and how to get the most from your battery.

- ✔ Chapter 2 describes how to install iTunes — including the iPod and iPhone software — on a Mac or Windows PC.

- ✔ Chapter 3 gets you started with a quick tour of the iPod touch and iPhone Home screen, icons, and the on-screen keyboard, and the iPod nano and iPod classic menus and buttons.

- ✔ Chapter 4 sets you up with the right time and date, clocks for different time zones, alarms, the timer, and the stopwatch. You discover how to set a passcode to lock your iPod or iPhone so that no one else can use it. You also find out how to set the display's brightness, turn the sound effects on or off, and set restrictions on an iPod touch or iPhone so that your kids can't jump onto YouTube or download explicit tunes.

- ✔ Chapter 5 describes the accessories you need to listen to tunes whenever you go on the road or stay at the "Heartbreak Hotel."

Chapter 1

Firing Up Your iPod and iPhone

. . . .

In This Chapter

▶ Comparing iPod and iPhone models

▶ Powering up your iPod or iPhone

▶ Using and recharging your battery

. . . .

*i*Pods and iPhones have completely changed the way people play music, audio books, and videos, and new models are changing the way people use computer applications, shoot photos and videos, play games, and use the Internet.

But don't just take my word for it. "It's hard to remember what I did before the iPod," said Grammy Award–winner Mary J. Blige in an Apple press release. "iPod is more than just a music player; it's an extension of your personality and a great way to take your favorite music with you everywhere you go." Lance Armstrong, seven-time Tour de France champion, takes his running shoes and iPod with him everywhere. "I listen to music when I run. Having my music with me is really motivating."

The iPod even plays an important role in Western culture. Pope Benedict XVI has an iPod engraved with his coat of arms. President Barack Obama gave the U.K.'s Queen Elizabeth II an iPod preloaded to play rare songs by Richard Rodgers. And when Bono of U2 gave an iPod shuffle to George H.W. Bush, the former President remarked, "I get the shuffle and then I shuffle the shuffle."

The iPod was first invented for playing music, and you can download entire albums from the iTunes Store and play them on any iPod or iPhone. You can also download movies and TV shows from the iTunes Store and play them on an iPod classic, iPod nano, iPod touch, or iPhone. With an Internet connection, you can download tunes, podcasts (which download automatically when you subscribe to them), and games directly to an iPod touch or iPhone, and also select from a library of over 75,000 applications (known as *apps*) that offer everything from soup to nuts.

This chapter introduces iPods and iPhones and tells you what to expect when you open the box. I describe how to power up your iPod or iPhone and connect it to your computer, both of which are essential tasks that you need to know how to do — your iPod or iPhone needs power, and it needs audio and video, which it gets from your computer.

Introducing the iPod and iPhone

The convenience of carrying music on an iPod or iPhone is phenomenal. For example, the 2GB iPod shuffle can hold 500 songs, which is plenty for getting around town, while the new 160GB iPod classic can hold around 40,000 songs — that's more than eight weeks of nonstop music played around the clock.

A common misconception is that your iPod or iPhone becomes your music and video library. Actually, your iPod or iPhone is simply another *player* for your content library, which is safely stored on your computer. One considerable benefit of using your computer to organize your content is that you can make perfect-quality copies of music, videos, movies, podcasts, and audio books. You can then copy as much of the content as you want, in a more compressed format, onto your iPod or iPhone and take it on the road. Meanwhile, your perfect copies are stored safely on your computer in digital files. These digital files can be copied over and over forever, just like the rest of your information, and they never lose their quality. If you save your content in digital format, you'll never see your songs or videos degrade, and you'll never have to buy the content again.

The iPod and iPhone experience includes *iTunes* (for Mac or Windows), which lets you synchronize content with your iPod and other devices, such as the Apple TV player for your home TV and stereo. Just as importantly, iTunes is the portal to the online iTunes Store, where you can purchase and download content. You also use iTunes to organize your content, make copies, burn CDs, and play disc jockey without discs. I introduce iTunes in Chapter 2.

An iPod is also a data player, and in the case of the iPod touch and iPhone, a complete personal computer that lets you enter data and run applications as well as play content. The current model iPod nano and the iPhone 3GS can also shoot videos, while the iPhone and iPhone 3G can shoot still pictures. You can keep track of your calendar and contacts with an iPod or iPhone, and with an iPod touch or iPhone, you can check and send e-mail, visit your favorite Web sites, get maps, obtain driving directions, check the current weather, and even check your stock portfolio, to name just a few things.

Comparing iPod Models

Introduced way back in the Stone Age of digital music (2001), the iPod family has grown by eight generations as of this writing (see Figure 1-1), including the popular iPod touch, the high-capacity iPod classic, the ultra-slim iPod nano that now includes a video camera, and the tiny iPod shuffle — the iPod you can clip to your belt or wear on your sleeve.

Figure 1-1:
The iPod family includes (left to right) the iPod touch, iPod classic, iPod nano, and iPod shuffle.

Here's a rundown on today's iPod models:

- **The iPod touch:** The iPod touch shares the design characteristics and many of the features of its more famous cousin, the iPhone, with the same multi-touch-sensitive screen (a.k.a. Touchscreen) and Wi-Fi Internet connectivity. (Wi-Fi, which is short for *wi*reless *fi*delity, is a popular connection method for local area networks that I describe in detail in Chapter 4.)

- **The iPod classic:** The original iPod design offers a higher capacity (160GB) than other models.

- **The iPod nano:** The iPod nano comes in a variety of colors and includes a video camera for shooting videos and a motion sensor; you can shake the iPod nano to shuffle your songs!

- **The iPod shuffle:** You can clip the tiniest iPod to your sleeve, and its voice tells you the song title and artist.

To find out more about previous generations of iPods, including detailed information about cables and connections, visit this book's companion Web site. For a nifty chart that shows the differences among iPod models, see the Identifying Different iPod Models page on the Apple iPod Web site (`http://support.apple.com/kb/HT1353`).

Fingering the iPod touch

The iPod touch is much more than a media player. Less than a third of an inch thick and weighing only 4 ounces, the iPod touch is really a pocket computer — it uses a flash memory drive and an operating system that can run applications. Just like the iPhone, it offers the same Touchscreen with icons for launching apps, the same on-screen keyboard for entering information, the same Home button on the front, and the same built-in speaker and volume controls on the left side.

Apple offers the following sizes of iPod touch models as of this writing, and they all use the same battery that offers up to 36 hours of music playback, or 6 hours of video playback:

- **The 8GB model** holds about 1,750 songs, 10,000 photos, or about 10 hours of video.

- **The 32GB model** holds about 7,000 songs, 40,000 photos, or about 40 hours of video. (With 7,000 songs, you would have more than a week of nonstop music played around the clock.)

- **The 64GB model** holds about 14,000 songs, 90,000 photos, or about 80 hours of video.

Like the iPhone, the iPod touch lets you access the Web over a Wi-Fi Internet connection. After it finds one or more networks, the iPod touch lets you choose one to connect to the Internet, and it can remember the settings for that network so that it can automatically choose the same network again.

After you're on Wi-Fi, you can then use the Safari app to browse the Web and interact with Web services, and the Mail app to send and receive e-mail. Stocks, Maps, and Weather are apps that show information from the Internet. You can also use the YouTube app to play YouTube videos on the Web. All these apps are supplied with your iPod touch, and you can download more apps by connecting to Wi-Fi and the Internet as I describe in Chapter 4, and touching the App Store icon, as I describe in Chapter 7.

You also use apps to connect to the Internet in other ways than browsing. For example, popular social networks such as Facebook and MySpace offer apps to connect you with your friends on those services. Google offers an array of services through the Google Mobile app, including the ability to edit documents and spreadsheets, use the Gmail service, and share calendars and photos. The Twitterific app lets you post tweets on Twitter, and the WhosHere and Loopt apps can connect you directly to other iPod touch and iPhone users for chatting.

Many of the apps you'll find listed at the App store are especially designed to take advantage of three distinct features of the iPod touch: its multi-touch display; its accelerometer (which detects acceleration, rotation, motion gestures, and tilt); and its capability to detect its physical location.

For example, Motion X Poker — actually a dice game — uses the accelerometer to let you roll the dice by shaking the iPod touch. The Flick Fishing app senses motion so that you can cast a fishing line with a flick of the wrist. And for really precise motion, try rolling a steel ball over a wooden labyrinth of holes in the free Labyrinth Lite app.

Sensing your iPod touch's location is a very useful feature. The Showtimes app uses your iPod touch's location to show the closest movie theaters to you. The Eventful app uses your location to display local events and venues, and the Lethal app can tell you the dangers that could surround you — the hostile animals, the likelihood of crimes, the prevalence of disease, and the potential for accidents and disasters.

In short, an iPod touch can do nearly everything an iPhone can do, except make cellular-service phone calls, use the 3G data network, shoot pictures, and pinpoint its exact location with the Global Positioning System. Even so, the iPod touch can pinpoint its approximate location with Internet-based Location Services, and you can make phone calls using the Skype app, a Wi-Fi connection, and an external microphone.

Twirling the iPod classic

The eighth-generation iPod classic model uses the same click wheel and buttons as the seventh-, sixth-, and fifth-generation models, combining the scroll wheel with pressure-sensitive buttons underneath the top, bottom, left, and right areas of the circular pad of the wheel. As of this writing, Apple provides a slim, 4.9-ounce 160GB model in black or gray.

The eighth-generation 160GB model holds about 40,000 songs, 25,000 photos, or about 200 hours of video, and its battery offers up to 36 hours of music playback, or 6 hours of video playback. The seventh-generation 120GB model holds about 20,000 songs or about 150 hours of video.

Mano a mano with iPod nano

The iPod nano, pencil thin and only 1.5 inches wide by 3.5 inches high, weighs only 1.3 ounces. Its curved, all-aluminum design and fine array of colors make it the most fashionable iPod.

This mini marvel (see Figure 1-2) offers a 2-inch color LCD that crisply shows iPod menus, album artwork, and video in either vertical or horizontal orientation, and includes a motion sensor so that you can rotate it quickly to change orientation and shake it to shuffle songs. Apple offers an 8GB model that holds about 2,000 songs or up to 8 hours of video (or 7,000 photos) and a 16GB model that holds about 4,000 songs or up to 16 hours of video (or 14,000 photos).

As part of the eighth-generation of the iPod family, the fifth-generation iPod nano includes a video camera and a built-in microphone, as well as an FM tuner for listening to radio and a pedometer to keep track of your footsteps.

Figure 1-2: iPod nano can shoot videos as well as play audio and video content.

Each model offers a battery that can play up to 24 hours of music — all day and all of the night — or 4 hours of video.

The earlier-generation iPod nano models are the smallest that can serve up videos, podcasts, photos, and musical slide shows as well as your personal calendar and contacts. Each model uses the same style of click wheel and buttons as the iPod classic. Unlike the smaller iPod shuffle, the iPod nano models are full-featured iPods with loads of accessories tailored specifically for it.

Doing the iPod shuffle

If the regular iPod models aren't small enough to fit into your lifestyle, try the ultra-tiny 2GB or 4GB iPod shuffle (see Figure 1-3), which is only 1.8 inches tall and 0.3 inches thin. Its built-in clip lets you attach it to almost anything. It has no display, but that's actually a good thing because this design keeps the size and weight to a minimum.

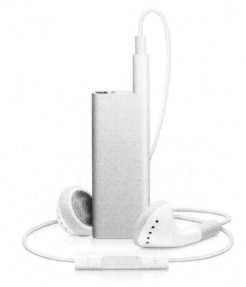

Figure 1-3: An iPod shuffle is so small that its controls are on the earbud cable.

For the third-generation of this tiny iPod, Apple moved its controls to the right earbud cord (refer to Figure 1-3) so that you can navigate through your songs easily without looking at the controls. A single button click starts music playing, and a single click pauses the music that's already playing. Click twice to go to the next track or three times to go to the previous track. You can use the earbud control while running, driving, skiing, snowboarding, or even skydiving.

Another cool feature makes it even easier to use these earbud controls: The iPod shuffle talks to you with the VoiceOver feature. Press and hold the center button to hear the title and artist of the song, or hold it longer until you hear a tone, and then release to hear the names of playlists. After hearing the playlist you want, click once to select it (if you copied over multiple playlists, as I describe in Chapter 9). VoiceOver even tells you whether your battery needs charging.

The 2GB iPod shuffle holds about 500 songs, and the 4GB iPod shuffle holds about 1,000 songs, assuming an average of 4 minutes per song, using the AAC format at the High Quality setting for adding music (as described in Chapter 8). The battery is the same for both models, offering up to 12 hours of power between charges.

 Unlike other iPods, iPod shuffle can't play tunes in the highest-quality Audio Interchange File Format (AIFF) or Apple Lossless formats, which consume a lot of storage space. See Chapter 8 for details on adding music to your iTunes library.

 To find out more about audio encoding formats, and about converting music from one format to another, visit the Tips section of the author's Web site at www.tonybove.com.

The Innovative iPhone

The iPhone, which includes all the features of an iPod touch, can not only phone home, but also monitor all your e-mail and browse the Internet with a full-page display, using a Wi-Fi network when it senses one. The Touchscreen (see Figure 1-4) provides a rich set of icons for launching apps, and includes a full on-screen keyboard for entering text, numbers, and special symbols. And the iPhone is no slouch when it comes to acting like an iPod: It can play music, audio books, videos (such as TV shows, music videos, and even feature-length movies), and even podcasts. You can also display photos and slide shows set to music.

The 8GB iPhone 3G, (introduced in July 2008), is slimmer and more powerful than the original iPhone, adding fast 3G data wireless technology, GPS mapping, and the capability for enterprises to push virtual private network (VPN) and Wi-Fi configurations out to all their iPhones in the field. The iPhone 3GS, introduced in June 2009 in 16GB and 32GB models, offers faster 3G data service, a higher-resolution camera for photos that also shoots videos, as well as voice control and longer battery life. Both incorporate flash memory just like an iPod touch, iPod shuffle, or iPod nano. The iPhone 3.5-inch, widescreen, multi-touch display offers 480-x-320–pixel resolution at 160 dots per inch for crisp video pictures, and it can display multiple languages and characters simultaneously.

The iPhone 3GS built-in rechargeable lithium-ion battery offers up to 12 hours of talk time using 2G or 5 hours using 3G (with 300 hours on standby); the iPhone 3G offers the same except only 10 hours of talk time using 2G. The iPhone 3GS also offers up to 9 hours browsing the Internet on Wi-Fi or 5 hours using 3G, up to 10 hours playing video, and up to 30 hours playing music. The iPhone 3G offers 6 hours of Wi-Fi, 5 hours of 3G, 7 hours of video, and 24 hours of music. Both offer Bluetooth for using wireless headphones and microphones when making phone calls.

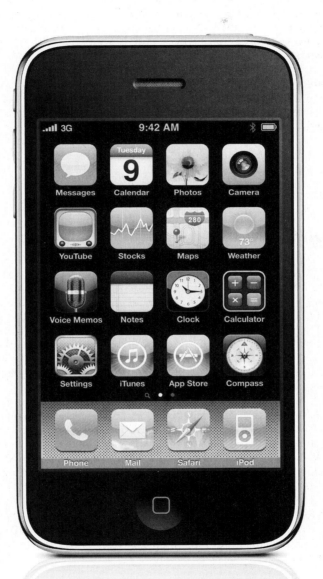

Figure 1-4:
The iPhone
3GS
includes
all the
features
of an iPod
touch and
can also
phone home
and shoot
videos.

Thinking Inside the Box

Don't destroy the elegantly designed box while opening it. Before going any further, check the box and make sure that all the correct parts came with your iPod or iPhone. Keep the box in case, heaven forbid, you need to return the iPod or iPhone to Apple — the box ensures that you can safely return it for a new battery or replacement.

The iPod touch, iPod classic, iPod nano, and iPhone are each supplied with

- Stereo headphones (often called *earbuds*)
- A dock adapter fitted for the optional Apple Universal Dock (not included)
- A Dock Connector–to–USB cable

The cable connects your iPod or iPhone (or its dock) to your computer or to the AC power adapter using a USB (Universal Serial Bus) connection — a way of attaching things to computers and bussing data around while providing power. The cable has a USB connector on one end and a flat dock connector on the other end to connect either to a dock or directly to an iPod or iPhone.

The iPod shuffle comes with earbuds and a special cable to connect to a power adapter or your computer. Older iPod shuffle models come with earbuds and a special smaller dock to connect to a power adapter or your computer.

The iPhone also comes with a power adapter for recharging the battery. You will want to get a power adapter for your iPod (not in the box but available from the Apple Store) if you want to use AC power, rather than your computer, to supply power to recharge your iPod.

Outside the box

There are a few things you may want to have around that are not in the box. For example, even though you don't really need an AC power adapter or dock — you can connect the iPod or iPhone directly to your computer to recharge your battery — a power adapter or dock is useful for keeping the battery charged without having to connect the iPod or iPhone to your computer.

The earbuds supplied with your iPod or iPhone may not suit your tastes, but you can find a hundred other headphone products that might. You can get all kinds of accessories, including headphones, speakers, the Apple Universal Dock, other docks, and AC power adapters, from the online Apple Store (www.apple.com/store), the physical Apple Store, or other stores such as Amazon.com and Fry's. Docks of various sizes, shapes, and functions are also available from vendors such as Belkin, Monster, and Griffin.

Computer and software not included

You still need a computer and iTunes to manage the content on your iPod or iPhone. These things are not in the box, obviously.

You've seen requirements before — lots of jargon about MB (megabytes), GB (gigabytes), GHz (gigahertz), and RAM (random access memory), sprinkled with names like Intel, AMD, and Mac OS X. Skip this section if you already know that your iPod or iPhone works with your computer and you already have iTunes. But if you don't know whether it will work, and you don't have iTunes yet, read on.

You need the following:

✔ **A PC or Mac to run iTunes:** On a PC, iTunes version 9 requires Windows XP (with Service Pack 2) or a 32-bit edition of Windows Vista, running on a 1-GHz Intel or AMD processor with a QuickTime-compatible audio card and a minimum of 512MB of RAM; 1GB is required to play HD-quality videos, an iTunes LP, or iTunes Extras from the iTunes Store. You need a DirectX 9.0–compatible video card with 32MB of video RAM (64MB recommended) to watch video, and a 2-GHz Intel Core 2 Duo or faster processor to play HD-quality videos, an iTunes LP, or iTunes Extras. 64-bit editions of Windows Vista require the iTunes 9 64-bit installer, available for downloading from the iTunes download page.

With a Mac, iTunes version 9 runs on all versions of Mac OS X Leopard and Snow Leopard or newer versions, and on the older Mac OS X Tiger version 10.4.11 or newer version. You need a 500-MHz processor or better (Intel or PowerPC) and at least 512MB of RAM; 1GB of RAM is required to play HD-quality videos, an iTunes LP, or iTunes Extras from the iTunes Store. You also need an Intel PowerPC G5 or a 1-GHz PowerPC G4 or faster processor, with 16MB of video RAM, to play videos, and a 2-GHz Intel Core 2 Duo or faster processor to play HD-quality videos, an iTunes LP, or iTunes Extras.

✔ **USB connection:** You need support for USB 2.0 (also called a *high-powered USB*) for iPod classic, iPod nano, iPod shuffle, iPod touch, iPhone, and sixth- and fifth-generation iPods. However, you can use FireWire (IEEE 1394) with older iPod models.

For details about using USB or FireWire cables, visit this book's companion Web site.

✔ **iTunes:** Make sure that you have the current version of iTunes — use the Automatic Update feature, which I describe in Chapter 2, to keep your iTunes software up to date. You can also download iTunes for Windows or the Mac from the Apple site (www.apple.com/itunes/download); it's free. See Chapter 2 for instructions.

Older iPod models, still available in stores and online, might include versions of iTunes on CD-ROM as old as version 4.5, which is fine because version 4.5 works. (It just doesn't have all the features of the current version.) You can download a newer version at any time to replace it.

✔ **QuickTime:** QuickTime comes with iTunes. The iTunes installer for the PC installs the newest version of QuickTime for Windows (version 7.6.2 as of this writing), replacing any older version you might have. Macs have QuickTime preinstalled (version 7.6.2 as of this writing), and Mac OS X automatically updates QuickTime if you use the Software Update feature of System Preferences on the Apple menu.

✔ **Internet connection:** Apple recommends a broadband Internet connection to buy content and stream previews from the iTunes Store, although it is possible with a dialup connection. At a minimum, you need some kind of Internet connection to download iTunes itself.

✔ **CD-R or DVD-R drive:** Without a disc burner, you can't burn your own discs. On a PC, you need a CD-R or DVD-R drive. On a Mac, you need a Combo or Super Drive to burn your own discs.

Applying Power

All iPod and iPhone models come with essentially the same requirement: power. You can supply power to your iPod or iPhone (and charge your battery at the same time) by using the provided cable and your computer, or you can use an optional AC power adapter that works with voltages in North America and many parts of Europe and Asia. (See Chapter 5 for information about plugging into power in other countries.)

Connecting your iPod or iPhone

On the bottom of the iPod touch, iPod classic, iPod nano, or iPhone, you find a large connection called the Dock Connector. The Dock Connector mirrors the connection on the end of a dock — your iPod or iPhone fits snugly in a dock, and the dock offers the Dock Connector for your computer.

To connect your iPod or iPhone to your computer, plug the flat connector of the cable into the iPod or iPhone Dock Connector (or the connector on the dock holding your iPod or iPhone) and then plug the USB connector on the other end of the cable into the USB port on your computer.

The iPod shuffle is supplied with a special USB cable that plugs into the headphone connection of the iPod shuffle and draws power from the USB connection on the computer or from a USB power adapter. Plug one end of the included cable into the headphone connection of iPod shuffle and the other end into a USB 2.0 connection on your computer or power adapter.

Older iPod shuffle models are supplied with a mini-dock with a USB cable attached — insert your iPod shuffle into the mini-dock, and connect the unattached end of the cable to a USB 2.0 connection on your computer or power adapter.

Do you want your iPod or iPhone to stand upright? Just connect it to an Apple or a third-party dock and then use the cable supplied with your iPod or iPhone to connect the dock to your computer or power adapter. The dock keeps your iPod or iPhone in an upright position while connected and also provides connections for a home stereo or headphones. Some docks offer built-in speakers. A dock can be convenient as a base station when you're not traveling with your iPod or iPhone because you can slip it into the dock without connecting cables. You can pick up a dock at an Apple Store, order one online, or take advantage of third-party dock offerings.

You can connect the USB end of the supplied cable to either the Apple (or third-party USB) power adapter for power, or to the computer's USB 2.0 port for power. As soon as you connect it to the computer, iTunes starts up and begins syncing the iPod or iPhone (see Chapter 9). After syncing, the computer continues to provide power through the USB 2.0 port to the iPod or iPhone.

Why USB 2.0? What happened to 1.0? Most PCs and all current Macs already have USB 2.0, which is all you need to provide power and to sync an iPod or iPhone with your computer. Although you can use a low-speed USB 1.0 or 1.1 connection to sync your iPod or iPhone, it's slower than molasses on a subzero morning for syncing.

To find out more about previous generations of iPods, including detailed information about USB and FireWire cables and connections, visit this book's companion Web site.

Don't use another USB device in a chain, and don't use a USB hub to connect your iPod or iPhone unless the hub is a *powered* hub — a hub with a separate power source, in other words. Note that many USB keyboards (such as current Apple keyboards) that offer USB connections don't provide power to the iPod or iPhone.

Turning it on and off

Touch any button to turn on an iPod nano or iPod classic. To turn off an iPod nano or iPod classic, press and hold the Play/Pause button. To keep an iPod nano or iPod classic from turning on by accident, you can lock it with the Hold switch on the top (or on the bottom next to the dock connection on early iPod nano models). The Hold switch locks the iPod buttons so that you don't accidentally activate them — slide the Hold switch so that it exposes an orange layer underneath. To unlock the buttons, slide the Hold switch so that it hides the orange layer underneath.

To turn on an iPod shuffle, slide the three-way switch to expose the green layer underneath. To turn it off, slide the three-way switch to hide the green layer. Older iPod shuffle models provide an On/Off switch, located on top next to the word OFF. Slide this switch away from OFF to turn it on, or toward OFF to turn it off. With the three-way switch or On/Off switch, iPod shuffle models don't need a Hold switch.

To turn on the iPod touch or iPhone, press the Sleep/Wake (On/Off) button on top, or the Home button on the front. The screen shows the message `Slide to unlock` — slide your finger across this message to unlock your iPod touch or iPhone.

To put an iPod touch or iPhone to sleep, press the Sleep/Wake (On/Off) button. This reduces the power consumption to a tiny trickle (just enough to allow the software to respond to a quick touch, and in the case of the iPhone, to respond to phone calls). Putting the iPod touch or iPhone to sleep also locks its controls just like a Hold switch.

To awaken the iPod touch or iPhone again, press the Sleep/Wake (On/Off) button or Home button.

You can turn the iPod touch or iPhone completely off by holding down the Sleep/Wake (On/Off) button for about two seconds, until you see the Slide to Power Off slider; then slide your finger across the slider to turn it off. You can then turn it back on by pressing and holding the Sleep/Wake (On/Off) button. To save battery power, you should plug the iPod touch or iPhone into AC power or your computer before turning it back on from a completely off state. (For battery details, see the next section in this chapter.)

If your iPod nano or iPod classic shows a display but doesn't respond to your button-pressing, don't panic. Just check the Hold switch and make sure that it's set to one side so that the orange layer underneath disappears (the normal position).

You might notice that an iPod classic or iPod nano display turns iridescent when it gets too hot or too cold, but this effect disappears when its temperature returns to normal. iPods can function in temperatures as cold as 50 degrees and as warm as 95° F (Fahrenheit), but they work best at room temperature (closer to 68° F).

If you leave your iPod or iPhone out in the cold all night, it might have trouble waking from Sleep mode, and it might even display a low-battery message. Plug the iPod or iPhone into a power source, wait until it warms up, and try it again. If it still doesn't wake up or respond properly, try resetting the iPod or iPhone, as I describe in Chapter 22.

Facing Charges of Battery

You can take a six-hour flight from New York City to California and listen to your iPod the entire time — and, with some models, listen all the way back on the return flight — without recharging. All current iPod models use the same type of built-in, rechargeable lithium-ion (Li-Ion) battery with the following power specs:

✔ The iPod shuffle offers 10 hours of music-playing time.

✔ The iPod nano offers 24 hours of music-playing time or 4 hours of video or photo display with music.

✔ The iPod classic offers 36 hours of music playback or 6 hours of video or photo display with music.

✔ The iPod touch offers 36 hours of music-playing time, or 6 hours of video, browsing the Internet using Wi-Fi, or displaying photo slide shows with music.

✔ The iPhone models offer up to 30 hours of music-playing time, 10 hours of video-playing time, or 6 hours of photo display with music. However, depending on your network settings, practical battery time can vary widely. The iPhone models can operate for 300 hours on standby (waiting for calls) if you do nothing else with them. You also find different power requirements for different networks:

  • All iPhone models offer the AT&T 2G network in the United States for calling and data transfer, and give you about 10 hours of talk time (12 hours on an iPhone 3GS).

  Note that the iPhone 3G offers both 2G and 3G modes for calling and data transfer, and gives you about 5 hours of talk time in 3G mode. You can turn off 3G to use 2G by choosing Settings➪General➪Network and tapping the On button for the Enable 3G option.

  • The iPhone 3GS offers 9 hours of browsing the Internet using Wi-Fi (the iPhone 3G offers 6 hours), and both the iPhone 3G and 3GS offer 5 hours of browsing using 3G.

To find out more about the batteries in previous generations of iPods, visit this book's companion Web site.

Keep in mind that playback battery time varies depending on how you use your iPod or iPhone — if you mix Web browsing and picture-taking with video playback on an iPod touch or iPhone, you'll have less battery time than if you just played music.

Recharging your battery

The iPod or iPhone battery recharges automatically when you connect it to a power source. For example, it starts charging immediately when you insert it into a dock that's connected to a power source (or to a computer with a powered USB connection). It takes only four hours to recharge the battery fully for all models, and only three hours for an iPod nano or iPod shuffle.

Need power when you're on the run? Look for a power outlet in the airport terminal or hotel lobby and plug in your iPod with your AC power adapter — the iPod nano battery fast-charges to 80 percent capacity in 1.5 hours, and the other models and iPhone fast-charge in 2 hours. After the fast-charge, the battery receives a trickle charge until fully charged.

Don't fry your iPod or iPhone with some generic power adapter. Use *only* the power adapter from Apple or a certified iPod adapter, such as the power accessories from Belkin, Griffin, Monster, XtremeMac, and other vendors.

A battery icon with a progress bar in the upper-right corner of the iPod or iPhone display indicates how much power is left. When you charge the battery, the battery icon displays a lightning bolt. The battery icon is completely filled in when the battery is fully charged, and it slowly empties into just an outline as the battery is used up.

You can use your iPod or iPhone while the battery is charging, or you can disconnect it and use it before the battery is fully charged.

You can check the battery status of an iPod shuffle by turning it on or by connecting it to your computer. You can check the battery status without interrupting playback by quickly turning the iPod shuffle off and then on again. The tiny battery status light next to the headphone connector tells you how much charge you have:

- ✔ **Green:** The iPod shuffle is fully charged (if connected to a computer) or charged at least 50 percent.

- ✔ **Orange:** The iPod shuffle battery is still charging (if connected to a computer) or is as low as 25 percent. If the iPod shuffle is connected to your computer and blinking orange, this means that iTunes is synchronizing it — don't disconnect the iPod shuffle until it stops blinking.

- ✔ **Red:** Very little charge is left, and you need to recharge it.

If no light is visible, the iPod shuffle is completely out of power, and you need to recharge it to use it.

On the newest iPod shuffle models, you can click and hold the center button to hear the VoiceOver feature tell you your battery status: "full," "75 percent," "50 percent," "25 percent," or "low."

In iTunes, the battery icon next to your iPod shuffle's name in the Devices section of the Source list shows the battery status. The icon displays a lightning bolt when the battery is charging and a plug when the battery is fully charged.

The iPod's or iPhone's built-in, rechargeable battery is, essentially, a life-or-death proposition. After it's dead, it can be replaced, but Apple charges a replacement fee plus shipping. If your warranty is still active, you should have Apple replace it under the warranty program (which may cost nothing except perhaps shipping). Don't try to replace it yourself unless you don't mind invalidating the warranty.

Keeping an iPod or iPhone in a snug carrying case when charging is tempting but also potentially disastrous. An iPod or iPhone needs to dissipate its heat, and you could damage the unit by overheating it and frying its circuits, rendering it as useful as a paperweight. To get around this problem, you can purchase one of the heat-dissipating carrying cases available in the Apple Store. Alternatively, MARWARE (www.marware.com) offers a variety of sporty cases for about $30 to $40. See Chapter 5 for more on accessories.

If you don't use your iPod or iPhone for a month, even if it is connected to power and retaining a charge, it can still become catatonic. Perhaps it gets depressed from being left alone too long. At that point, it may not start — you have to completely drain and recharge the battery. To drain the battery, disconnect your iPod or iPhone from power for 24 hours. Then, to fully recharge the battery, connect it to power for at least 4 hours without using it (or longer if you are using it).

Saving power

The iPod classic and older models include a hard drive, and whatever causes the hard drive to spin causes a drain on power. iPod nano, iPod shuffle, iPod touch, and iPhone models use a flash drive, which uses less power but still uses power when playing content. The iPod touch and iPhone also use power accessing the Internet, running applications, and in the case of the iPhone, making and receiving calls and using Bluetooth devices. Keeping these activities to a minimum can help you save power.

Maintaining battery mojo

You have several ways to keep your battery healthy. I recommend a lean diet of topping off your iPod or iPhone battery whenever it is convenient.

Using and recharging 100 percent of battery capacity is called a *charge cycle.* You can charge the battery many times, but there is a limit to how many full-charge cycles you can do before needing to replace the battery.

Each time you complete a charge cycle (100 percent recharge), it diminishes battery capacity slightly. Apple estimates that the battery loses 20 percent of its capacity (meaning it holds 80 percent of the charge) after 400 full-charge cycles. Recharging your battery when it's only half empty does not count as a full-charge cycle, but as half a charge cycle. That means you can use half its power one day and then recharge it fully, and then use half the next day and recharge it fully again; this would count as one charge cycle, not two.

It's a good idea to *calibrate* the battery once soon after you get your iPod or iPhone. That is, run it all the way down (a full discharge) and then charge it all the way up (which takes four hours for an iPod touch, iPhone, or iPod classic, or three hours for an iPod nano or iPod shuffle). Although this doesn't actually change battery performance, it does improve the battery gauge so that the gauge displays a more accurate reading. This calibration occurs anyway if you fully recharge the battery, but if you've never done that, you can calibrate it by disconnecting the iPod or iPhone from power for 24 hours to make sure that the battery is empty, and then fully recharging the battery.

Lithium-ion batteries typically last three years or more and are vulnerable to high temperatures, which decrease their life spans considerably. Don't leave your iPod or iPhone in a hot place, such as on a sunny car dashboard, for very long.

For a complete description of how Apple's batteries work, see the Apple Lithium-Ion Batteries page at `www.apple.com/batteries`.

If you use the AIFF or WAV formats for adding music to your iTunes library, don't use them with your iPod or iPhone. AIFF and WAV take up way too much space on the iPod or iPhone and fill the cache too quickly, causing skips when you play them and using too much battery power because the hard drive or flash drive is accessed more often. (See Chapter 8 for details on adding music.)

To find out more about audio encoding formats and about converting music from one format to another, visit the Tips section of the author's Web site at `www.tonybove.com`.

The following are tips on saving power while using your iPod or iPhone:

  ✔ **Pause.** Pause playback when you're not listening to music or watching video. Pausing (stopping) playback is the easiest way to conserve power, especially with an iPod shuffle.

✔ **Lock it (with the iPod touch or iPhone).** Press the Sleep/Wake button on top of the iPod touch or iPhone to immediately put it to sleep and lock its controls to save battery power. You can set your iPod touch or iPhone to automatically go to sleep by choosing Settings⇨General⇨Auto-Lock from the Home menu, and choosing 1 Minute, 2 Minutes, 3 Minutes, 4 Minutes, or 5 Minutes (or Never, to prevent automatic sleep).

✔ **Hold it (with the iPod classic or iPod nano).** Flip the Hold switch on iPod classic and iPod nano models to the locked position (with the orange layer showing underneath) to make sure that controls aren't accidentally activated. You don't want your iPod playing music in your pocket and draining the battery when you're not listening.

✔ **Back away from the light.** Turn down the brightness on an iPod touch or iPhone by choosing Settings⇨Brightness and dragging the brightness slider to the left. Use the backlight sparingly on iPod classic and iPod nano models. Select Backlight Timer from the iPod Settings menu to limit backlighting to a number of seconds, or set it to Off. (Choose Settings from the main menu.) Don't use the backlight in daylight if you don't need it.

✔ **Forget where you are (with an iPod touch or iPhone).** Turn off Location Services if you aren't using apps that need it. Choose Settings⇨General from the Home screen, and touch On for the Location Services option to turn it Off. See Chapter 4 for details.

✔ **Let the postman ring twice (with an iPod touch or iPhone).** Check e-mail less frequently. You may want to change Push and Fetch settings to be less frequent. See Chapter 20 for details.

✔ **Turn off 3G (with an iPhone 3G or iPhone 3GS).** Turn off 3G in any areas that don't offer a strong 3G signal: Choose Settings⇨General⇨Network and tap the On button for the Enable 3G option to turn it off. You can still make and receive calls with the 2G network, but the iPhone will stop using so much power continually searching for 3G.

✔ **Tune out Bluetooth (with an iPhone).** Turn off Bluetooth (choose Settings⇨General⇨Bluetooth and touch the On button to turn it off) if you're not using a Bluetooth device.

✔ **Drop in from the Internet (with an iPod touch or iPhone).** Turn off Wi-Fi when not browsing the Internet: Choose Settings⇨Wi-Fi and touch the On button to turn it off.

✔ **Turn it off completely.** To turn an iPod nano or iPod classic completely off, press and hold the Play/Pause button. To turn off an iPod shuffle, slide the switch to the off position, hiding the green layer underneath the switch. You can turn the iPod touch or iPhone completely off by holding down the Sleep/Wake (On/Off) button for about two seconds, until you see the Slide to Power Off slider; then slide your finger across the slider to turn it off. You can then turn it back on by pressing and holding the Sleep/Wake (On/Off) button.

Keep in mind that starting up an iPod touch or iPhone that was completely turned off takes quite a bit of power — more than if it woke from sleep. If you do turn it off, plug it into AC power or your computer before turning it back on.

✔ **You may continue.** Play songs continuously without using the iPod or iPhone controls. Selecting songs and using Previous/Rewind and Next/ Fast Forward require more energy. Also, turn off your iPod or iPhone equalizer (EQ) if you don't need it (see Chapter 16).

Always use the latest iPod and iPhone software, and update your software when updates come out. Apple constantly tries to improve how your iPod and iPhone models work, and many of these advancements relate to power usage.

Chapter 2

Setting Up iTunes and Your iPod and iPhone

In This Chapter

▶ Installing iTunes on a Windows PC

▶ Installing iTunes on a Mac

▶ Setting up your iPod and iPhone

*A*n iPod or iPhone without iTunes is like a CD player without CDs. Sure, you can use utility programs from sources other than Apple to put music, podcasts, and videos on an iPod. But iTunes gives you access to the vast online iTunes Store and App Store, and it's excellent for managing content on your computer and synchronizing your content library and personal information with your iPod or iPhone.

This chapter explains how to set up your iPod or iPhone with iTunes on a Mac or for Windows. iTunes includes the iPod and iPhone software, which provides the intelligence inside the device. iTunes is no slouch in the intelligence department either because it immediately recognizes the type of iPod or iPhone you have and installs the correct software.

Installing iTunes on a Windows PC

Setting up iTunes is a quick and easy process. The most up-to-date version of iTunes as of this writing is version 9. However, software updates occur very rapidly, so you may end up installing a newer version by the time you read this. (If you already have iTunes installed, see Chapter 22 for instructions on updating it.)

The CD-ROMs supplied with older iPods offer older versions of iTunes and iPod software. You should visit the Apple Web site to download the most up-to-date version of iTunes, which recognizes all iPod and iPhone models.

Before installing iTunes, make sure that you're logged on as a Windows administrator user. Quit all other applications before installing, and be sure to disable any antivirus software.

The iTunes installer also installs the newest version of QuickTime, replacing any older version you might have. *QuickTime* is the Apple multimedia development, storage, and playback technology. Although Windows users aren't required to use QuickTime beyond its use by iTunes, QuickTime is a bonus for Windows users because it offers digital video playback.

To install iTunes for Windows, follow these steps:

1. **Download the iTunes installer from the Apple site.**

   Browse the Apple Web site (`www.apple.com/itunes`), and click the Download iTunes Free button, as shown in Figure 2-1. Follow the instructions to download the installer to your hard drive. (A crucial step here is picking a location on your hard drive to save the installer and *remembering* that location.)

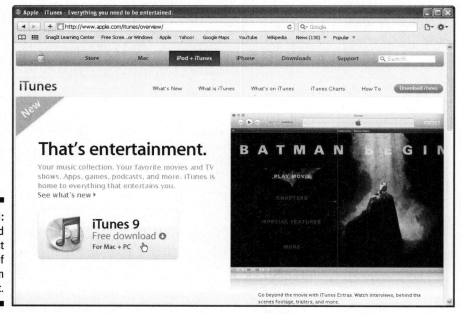

Figure 2-1: Download the newest version of iTunes from the Internet.

2. **Run the iTunes installer.**

   Double-click the iTunesSetup.exe file to install iTunes. At the Welcome screen, click the Next button. Apple's license agreement appears in the installer window. Feel free to scroll down to read the agreement if that's something you tend to do. You must select the option to accept the agreement, or the installer goes no further.

3. **Select the option to accept the terms of the license agreement and then click the Next button.**

   After clicking Next (which is active only if you accept), the installer displays the iTunes installation options, as shown in Figure 2-2.

Figure 2-2:
Choose
iTunes
installation
options.

4. **Choose your iTunes installation options.**

   You can turn the following options on or off (as shown in Figure 2-2):

   - *Add iTunes and QuickTime Shortcuts to My Desktop:* You can install shortcuts for your Windows desktop for iTunes and the QuickTime player.

   - *Use iTunes as the Default Player for Audio Files:* I suggest turning this option on, allowing iTunes to be the default audio content player for all audio files it recognizes. If you're happy with your audio player, you can deselect this option, leaving your default player setting unaffected.

5. **Choose the default language for iTunes.**

   The installer assumes that you want English (U.S.), so if you want to use a different language, you need to select it from the drop-down menu.

6. **Choose the destination folder for iTunes.**

   By default, the installer assumes that you want to store the program in the Program Files folder of your C: drive. If you want to use a different folder, click the Change button to use Windows Explorer to locate the desired folder.

7. **Click the Install button to finish.**

   After you click Install, the installer finishes the installation and displays the Complete dialog.

8. **Click the Finish button.**

   Restarting your Windows PC after installing software is always a good idea.

iTunes and QuickTime are now installed on your PC. To start using iTunes, double-click the iTunes desktop shortcut or use your Start menu to locate iTunes and launch it.

The first time you launch iTunes, yet another Apple license agreement appears. You must click the Agree button to continue (or cancel). After clicking Agree, iTunes displays the iTunes Setup Assistant — to get started, click the Next button.

The Setup Assistant displays two options: Add MP3 and AAC Files, and Add WMA Files (this applies only to non-copyright protected WMA files). Select either or both options to copy music files to the iTunes library. WMA file copies are converted to the AAC format (see Chapter 8 for descriptions of these formats). The original files are left intact and in place (you can delete them later if you don't need them as backup copies). After selecting (or not selecting) these options, click the Next button to continue.

The Setup Assistant then asks whether you want to keep your music folder organized. Choose Yes to keep the iTunes Music Folder organized, and click the Next button to continue. (For more information on how the iTunes Music Folder works, see Chapter 15.) The Setup Assistant then displays a screen that explains how album artwork is downloaded (you need an iTunes Store account — see Chapter 7); click the Next button to continue. Finally the Setup Assistant asks whether you want to go directly to the iTunes Store. Choose Yes to go directly to the store or No to go directly to your iTunes library, and click the Finish button.

Installing iTunes on a Mac

As a Mac user, you should already have iTunes installed because all Macs sold since 2003 come preinstalled with iTunes and Mac OS X. The most up-to-date version of iTunes as of this writing is version 9.

The version of iTunes that's provided with the Mac might be the newest version; then again, it might not be. If iTunes displays a dialog with the message that a new version of iTunes is available and asks whether you would like to download it now, choose Yes to download the new version. Mac OS X not only downloads iTunes but also installs it automatically — after asking you for the administrator's password, of course.

 You can set your Mac to automatically download the latest version of iTunes when it becomes available. Choose Preferences from the iTunes menu, click the General tab, and select the Check for Updates Automatically check box at the bottom of the General preferences to turn it on.

 You can also set your Mac to check for all system software and Apple applications (including iTunes). Choose System Preferences from the Apple menu, and then choose Software Update from the System Preferences window. Select the Check for Updates check box to turn it on, and select Daily, Weekly, or Monthly from the pop-up menu. You can also click the Check Now button to check for a new version immediately. If one exists, it appears in a window for you to select. Click the check mark to select it, and then click the Install button to download and install it.

If you want to manually install iTunes on your Mac or manually upgrade the version you have, browse the Apple Web site (www.apple.com/itunes) to get it. You can download iTunes for free. Follow these steps:

1. **Download the iTunes installer from the Apple site.**

   Browse the Apple Web site (www.apple.com/itunes), select the Mac OS X version you have installed on your computer, and then click the Download iTunes button. Your browser downloads the iTunes installer disk image file iTunes.dmg to your hard drive. After your browser downloads the file, locate the file in the Finder.

2. **Open the iTunes installer disk image.**

   Double-click the iTunes.dmg file to mount the iTunes installation drive.

3. **Double-click the iTunes.mpkg file to unpack the installer package.**

   The iTunes.mpkg file is a package that contains all the elements of the iTunes software and the installation program. After double-clicking this package file, a dialog appears that asks whether the installer can run a special program to check your computer.

4. **Click the Continue button to run the special program.**

   The installer needs to run a program to check your computer and make sure that it's capable of running iTunes. After it runs the program, the installer displays the Introduction page.

5. **Click the Continue button, read the Read Me page, and click Continue again.**

   The installer displays important Read Me information about the latest iTunes features. If you like, click the Save button to save the page as a document or click Print to print it. Click Continue to continue to the license agreement.

6. **Read the license agreement, and click the Continue button to go to the second page. Click the Agree button and then click Continue again.**

   To read the entire agreement, you'll need to scroll down. You must choose to accept the agreement by clicking the Agree button, or the installer goes no further. After clicking Agree, the installer displays the Select a Destination page.

7. **(Optional) Before you click the Agree button, you can click the Save button to save the license agreement as a document or click Print to print it.**

8. **Select the Mac OS X startup drive as the destination volume and then click the Continue button.**

   The installer asks for the *destination* volume (hard drive), which must be a Mac OS X startup drive. Any other drive is marked by a red exclamation point, indicating that you can't install the software there. iTunes is installed in the Applications folder on the Mac OS X startup drive, and the iPod Software Updater is installed in the Utilities folder inside the Applications folder.

9. **Click the Install (or Upgrade) button to proceed with the installation.**

   After clicking Install, Mac OS X asks for the system administrator password. Supply your password, and click the OK button.

10. **Click the Close button when the installer finishes.**

You can now launch iTunes by double-clicking the iTunes application or clicking the iTunes icon on the Dock.

The first time you launch iTunes, yet another Apple license agreement appears. You must click the Agree button to continue (or cancel). After clicking Agree, iTunes displays the iTunes Setup Assistant — to get started, click the Next button.

The Setup Assistant displays the option to Add MP3 and AAC Files; select this option to copy music files to the iTunes library. (See Chapter 8 for descriptions of these formats.) The original files are left intact and in place; feel free to delete them if you don't need them as backup copies. After selecting (or not selecting) this option, click the Next button to continue. The Setup Assistant then asks whether you want to keep your music folder organized. Choose Yes to keep the iTunes Music Folder organized, and click the Next button to continue. (For more information on how the iTunes Music Folder works, see Chapter 15.) The Setup Assistant then displays a screen that explains how album artwork is downloaded (you need an iTunes Store account — see Chapter 7); click the Next button to continue. Finally the Setup Assistant asks whether you want to go directly to the iTunes Store. Choose Yes to go directly to the store or No to go directly to your iTunes library, and click the Finish button.

Setting Up Your iPod or iPhone

When you connect a new iPod or iPhone for the first time, iTunes displays the Register and Set Up screen. Follow these steps to set up your iPod or iPhone:

1. **With iTunes open, connect your iPod or iPhone to the computer with a USB cable.**

   iTunes recognizes your iPod or iPhone and opens the Register and Set Up screen to get you started.

2. **Click the Continue button (or click the Register Later button to skip the registration process).**

   iTunes displays the software license agreement. You can scroll down to read it if you want. You must choose to accept the agreement, or the installer goes no further.

3. **Select the option to accept the terms at the end of the license agreement and then click the Continue button.**

   After clicking Continue (which is active only if you accept), iTunes lets you register your iPod or iPhone with Apple online so that you can take advantage of Apple support. iTunes displays a screen for entering your Apple ID; a membership ID for the MobileMe (formerly .Mac) service is also valid. If you purchased your iPod or iPhone directly from Apple or have an Apple iTunes Store account, you already have an Apple ID. Enter that ID and password and then click the Continue button to swiftly move through the registration process — Apple automatically recognizes your purchase. If you bought your iPod or iPhone elsewhere or you don't have an Apple ID or MobileMe ID, select the I Do Not Have an Apple ID radio button and then click the Continue button to get to the page for entering your iPod or iPhone serial number and your personal information. Fields marked with an asterisk (*) are required, such as your name and e-mail address.

If you don't already have an iTunes Store account, the Setup Assistant is going to ask you to set up such an account now, as part of your iPod or iPhone setup. Chapter 7 has all the details on setting up an iTunes Store account.

4. **Click the Continue button to advance through each screen in the registration process and then click the Submit button at the end to submit your information.**

After clicking Submit, iTunes checks to see if you have ever backed up an iPod touch or iPhone before. If you've synced an iPod touch or iPhone previously as I describe in Chapter 9 (and you haven't deleted its backup as I describe in Chapter 22), iTunes displays a dialog that gives you the choice of restoring the settings from the previously backed-up iPod touch or iPhone, or setting up the iPod touch or iPhone as new. If appropriate, choose the option to restore the settings and then click the Continue button to finish setting up your iPod touch or iPhone. If you choose to set it up as new, continue following these steps.

5. **(iPod touch or iPhone only) If you've synced an iPod touch or iPhone previously on the same computer, iTunes asks if you want to use its settings.**

6. **Enter a new name for your iPod or iPhone.**

iTunes displays a screen that lets you enter a name for your iPod or iPhone, as shown in Figure 2-3 for an iPod touch, and Figure 2-4 for an iPod nano.

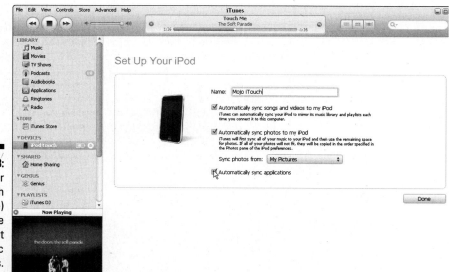

Figure 2-3: Give your iPod touch (or iPhone) a name and set automatic options.

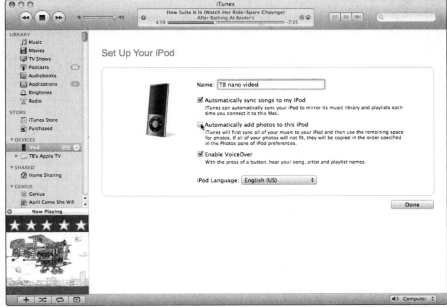

Figure 2-4:
Give your
iPod nano
a name
and set
automatic
options.

7. **Set the automatic options, and then click the Done button (on a Mac) or the Finish button (in Windows).**

When it comes to setting automatic options, here's the deal:

- *Automatically Sync Songs and Videos:* If you want to copy your entire iTunes music and video library to your iPod or iPhone, leave the Automatically Sync Songs and Videos option selected. This option creates a mirror image of your music and video library on the iPod or iPhone, including all playlists and audio files. (You can always change this setting later; see Chapter 9.) If your iPod or iPhone can't hold your entire library, iTunes chooses songs for you, based on your ratings and how often you've played the songs. (To find out how to add ratings, see Chapter 12.) If you want to control which portion of your library to copy to the iPod or iPhone, deselect this option and turn to Chapter 9 for synchronization details.

- *Automatically Choose Songs for an iPod Shuffle:* If you leave the Automatically Choose Songs for My iPod option selected, iTunes copies a random selection of songs to your iPod shuffle. You can always choose to sync your iPod shuffle with a different selection as I describe in Chapter 9.

- *Automatically Add Photos:* Select this option (all iPods and iPhones except the iPod shuffle) to copy all the photos in your photo library to your iPod or iPhone. (See Chapter 18 for information about synchronizing and playing photo libraries.) Leave it deselected if you want to transfer photos later. On a Windows PC you can choose the Pictures folder or choose another folder in the Sync Photos From pop-up menu (refer to Figure 2-3).

- *Automatically Sync Applications:* Select this option (iPod touch and iPhone only) to copy all applications in your iTunes library to your iPod touch or iPhone.

- *Enable VoiceOver:* Select this option to enable the VoiceOver kit, which is supplied with the iPod nano and iPod shuffle. VoiceOver tells you the name of the song you're playing (as well as your battery status) and lets you choose from a spoken menu of playlists. See Chapter 16 for details.

After finishing setup, your iPod or iPhone name appears in the iTunes Source pane (the left column) under the Devices subheading (refer to Figure 2-3).

If you chose the option to automatically synchronize your songs and videos, your iPod or iPhone quickly fills up with music and videos from your iTunes music library.

Don't want to add songs or videos now? If you deselect the automatically synchronize option, you can still add songs and videos later, along with podcasts and audio books — either manually or automatically, as I describe in Chapter 9.

After setting up your iPod or iPhone (and syncing if you chose the sync options), disconnect the iPod or iPhone from your computer by *ejecting* it. To eject your iPod or iPhone, click the Eject button next to the iPod or iPhone name (refer to Figure 2-3) in the Devices section of the Source pane. You can then connect the iPod or iPhone to its dock or power adapter to continue recharging its battery.

Although you can leave your iPod or iPhone connected to the computer, using the computer as a source of power, I don't recommend doing that because it will synchronize whenever you start iTunes. Also, if you use a laptop running on a battery, the iPod or iPhone quickly drains the laptop battery.

After ejecting the iPod or iPhone, wait for its display to show the main menu or the OK to disconnect message. You can then disconnect the iPod or iPhone from the computer. Never disconnect an iPod or iPhone before ejecting it because such bad behavior might cause it to freeze and require a reset. (If that happens, see Chapter 22 for instructions.)

Chapter 3

Putting Your Finger on It

In This Chapter

▶ Touching and gesturing on an iPod touch or iPhone

▶ Typing on the iPod touch or iPhone

▶ Thumbing through iPod menus

The iPod is all about convenience. Apple designed the iPod classic and iPod nano models to be held in one hand so that you can perform simple operations by thumb. Even if you're all thumbs when pressing small buttons on tiny devices, you can still thumb your way to iPod heaven.

With the iPod shuffle, Apple took convenience a step further — the controls are on the earbud cord so that you can tuck the tiny device somewhere on your clothing and control it without looking at it. Its VoiceOver feature complements this arrangement by announcing each song, so you can quickly jump around.

With an iPod touch or iPhone, your fingers do the walking. You can make gestures, such as flicking a finger to scroll a list quickly, sliding your finger to scroll slowly or drag a slider (such as the volume slider), pinching with two fingers to zoom out of a Web page in Safari, or pulling apart with two fingers (also known as *unpinching*) to zoom in to the page to see it more clearly.

This chapter gives you a quick tour of the iPod and iPhone models, including the menus of an iPod classic or iPod nano, the iPod shuffle controls, and all the touch-and-gesture tricks to make your iPod touch or iPhone dance and sing. I also give you a complete tour of the most unique feature of the iPod touch and iPhone: the on-screen keyboard.

Tapping Your iPod touch or iPhone

The iPod touch or iPhone responds to tapping, flicking, and sliding your finger(s), among other gestures (such as shaking, tilting, two-finger tapping, and so on). One tap is all you need to run an app or select something, but sometimes you have to slide your finger to scroll the display and see more selections.

Sticky fingers are not recommended. To clean your iPod touch or iPhone, make sure to unplug all cables and turn it off. (See Chapter 1.) Use a soft, slightly damp, lint-free cloth to wipe your iPod touch or iPhone clean. — see Chapter 23 for cleaning tips.

Sliding to the Home screen

The first message you see on an iPod touch or iPhone display (besides the time of day and the date) is `Slide to unlock` — to get started, you have to unlock the iPod touch or iPhone by sliding your finger across the message. After the unit is unlocked, your Home screen appears in all its glory. (See Figure 3-1.)

There's no place like Home — it's the screen where you start. Everything is available from the Home screen at the touch of a finger:

- ✔ To access your music on an iPod touch, tap the Music icon in the bottom row; on an iPhone, tap the iPod icon in the bottom row (which offers music and videos).

- ✔ To access your videos on an iPod touch, tap the Videos icon in the bottom row; on an iPhone, tap the iPod icon in the bottom row.

- ✔ Tap the Photos icon to view your photos on an iPod touch or iPhone.

- ✔ Tap the Calendar icon to view your calendars on an iPod touch or iPhone.

- ✔ Tap the Contacts icon to view your contacts on an iPod touch or iPhone.

- ✔ Tap the iTunes icon to access the iTunes Store on an iPod touch or iPhone.

- ✔ Tap the App Store icon to access the App Store on an iPod touch or iPhone.

After tapping an icon, a new screen appears with selections and icons. (Tapping Music on an iPod touch, for example, brings up Artists, Songs, Albums, and so on.) The multitouch interface changes for each app. Press the physical Home button below the screen at any time to go to back to the Home screen.

Apps you download from the App Store (as I describe in Chapter 7) show up as icons on your Home screen. You can also save Web "clips" (page references) to your Home screen as icons that take you directly to those Web pages (as I describe in Chapter 19). When you add enough apps and Web clips so that they no longer all fit on the first page of the Home screen, the iPod touch or iPhone automatically creates more Home screen pages to accommodate them. (See the section "Rearranging your Home screen pages," later in this chapter, to find out how to customize your icons and Home screen pages.)

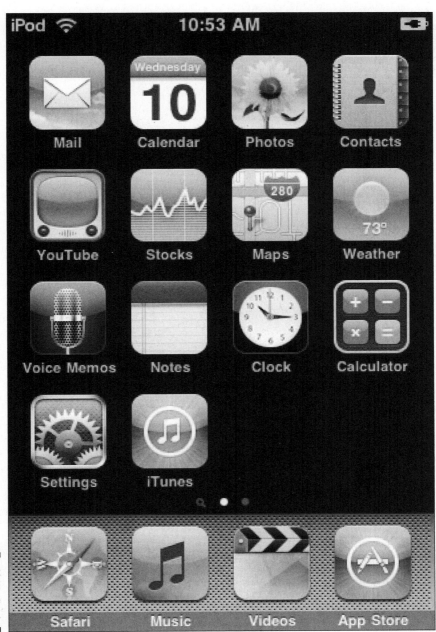

Figure 3-1:
The iPod touch Home screen.

The bottom row of the Home screen (refer to Figure 3-1) is called the *dock*. The number of dots above the dock shows the number of Home screen pages you have, and also indicates which page you're viewing. To switch to another Home screen page, flick with your finger left or right, or tap to the left or right of the row of dots.

Searching for anything

A tiny magnifying glass icon for searching (introduced with the iPhone 3.0 software) appears to the left of the dots above the dock on the Home screen. Tap this icon, or flick with your finger to the right, to show the Search screen (see Figure 3-2). The Search function is similar to the Spotlight universal search feature available in Mac OS X. You can then type in a search term and immediately see suggestions.

Figure 3-2: The iPod touch Search screen.

Search looks through contacts, calendars, e-mail (the To, From, and Subject fields, but not the message content), the content (songs, videos, podcasts, and audio books), the text in the Notes app, and text messages on an iPhone. Tap a contact, calendar entry, e-mail, note, or text message suggestion to open it, or tap the song, video, podcast, or audio book suggestion to play it.

Checking the status bar

The iPod touch or iPhone shows its current state in the status bar at the top of the screen (refer to Figure 3-1). The icons mean the following:

- **iPod:** Just in case you forgot you had an iPod touch in your hands (very existential). On an iPhone, you see the cascading bars of cell-phone service coverage.

- **Wi-Fi:** This icon says that the iPod touch or iPhone is connected to a Wi-Fi network. If the network offers Internet access (all commercial ones do), you're on the Internet (or at least on it as far as the commercial service's log-in screen — you may have to purchase access and log into the service). The more arcs you see in the icon, the stronger the connection to the network. To find out more about setting up Wi-Fi with Internet in your home, see Chapter 4.

- **Network activity:** This icon twirls to show that data is traveling from the network to your iPod touch or iPhone (or vice versa). (Not visible in Figure 3-1.)

- **VPN:** If you have special network settings that access a virtual private network (VPN), this icon shows up to tell you that you are connected to it. See Chapter 4 for details. (Not visible in Figure 3-1.)

- **Lock:** You see this icon whenever the iPod touch or iPhone is locked. (The `Slide to unlock` message also appears on the screen.) (Not visible in Figure 3-1.)

- **Play:** This icon tells you that a song, audio book, or podcast is playing (in case you didn't know — maybe you took your headphones off). (Not visible in Figure 3-1.)

- **Alarm:** This icon appears if you set an alarm. See Chapter 4 for details. (Not visible in Figure 3-1.)

- **Battery:** The Battery icon shows the battery level or charging status. It's completely filled in when the battery is fully charged, and it slowly empties into just an outline as the battery is used up. A lightning bolt appears inside the icon when the device is recharging, and a plug appears inside it when the iPod touch or iPhone is connected to power.

Tons of icons and what do you get?

You get flexible apps and a key to the Net! The iPod touch or iPhone Home screen (refer to Figure 3-1) offers the following icons:

- **Safari:** Use the Safari Web browser.

- **Phone:** Use the phone functions (iPhone only).

- **Mail:** Check and send e-mail.

- **Calendar:** View your calendar.

- **Contacts:** View your contacts (on the first Home screen page of an iPod touch, or the second Home screen page on the iPhone).

- **YouTube:** List and select videos from YouTube.

- **Stocks:** Check the prices for financial stocks, bonds, and funds.

- **Maps:** View maps and get driving directions.

- **Weather:** View the weather in multiple cities.

- **Clock:** View multiple clocks and use the alarm clock, timer, and stopwatch.

- **Compass:** View a compass showing your direction (iPhone 3GS only).

- **Calculator:** You can use your iPod touch or iPhone as a regular calculator for adding, subtracting, multiplying, dividing, and so on. Also, if you hold the iPod touch or iPhone horizontally, it becomes a scientific calculator.

- **Notes:** Add text notes.

- **Settings:** Adjust settings for Wi-Fi, sounds, brightness, Safari, and other apps, as well as apply other settings for the iPod touch or iPhone itself.

- **Music (iPod touch):** Select playlists, artists, songs, albums, and more (including podcasts, genres, composers, audio books, and compilations). The Music icon also offers Cover Flow browsing, as I describe in Chapter 16.

- **Videos (iPod touch):** Select videos by type (movies, music videos, TV shows, or video podcasts).

- **iPod (iPhone):** Select playlists, artists, songs, videos, and more (including podcasts, genres, composers, audio books, and compilations). The iPod icon also offers Cover Flow browsing, as I describe in Chapter 16.

- **Photos:** Select photos by photo album or select individual photos in the Photo Library.

- **Camera:** Snap a photo (iPhone only), or shoot video (iPhone 3GS only).

- **Voice Memos:** Record using the built-in microphone (iPhone only) or the Apple earbud microphones (iPhone or iPod touch).

- **App Store:** Go to Apple's online App Store to download other Apple and third-party apps.

- **iTunes:** Go to the iTunes Store to purchase content.

You find one more icon for an app that you can activate in Settings, if you have the appropriate Nike shoes and the Nike+ iPod Sport Kit, sold separately. See Chapter 23 for details.

Touching and gesturing

With the iPhone or iPod touch, it's touch and go. These models respond to gestures you make with your fingers:

- **Drag with your finger:** Scroll up or down lists slowly.
- **Flick up or down:** Swipe your finger quickly across the surface to scroll up or down lists quickly.
- **Touch and hold:** While scrolling, touch and hold to stop the moving list.
- **Flick from left to right or right to left:** Quickly swipe your finger across the screen to change screens or application panes (Home screens, Cover Flow when browsing music, Weather, and other apps).
- **Single tap:** Select an item.
- **Double tap:** Zoom in or out with Safari, Maps, and other applications.
- **Two-finger single tap:** Zoom out in Maps.
- **Pinch:** Zoom out.
- **Unpinch:** Zoom in.

Need to practice your tapping? Try Tap Tap Revenge, a rhythm game that plays music while requiring you to tap each of the colored balls when they reach the line at the bottom of the screen. If you tap the ball on the beat, you gain points; if not, it counts as a miss. You can also activate a revenge mode to score more points by shaking the iPod touch or iPhone after setting a winning streak of 50 beats.

Rearranging your Home screen pages

You can rearrange your iPod touch or iPhone app icons, create additional Home screen pages, and customize these pages. Touch and hold any icon until all the icons begin to wiggle. (That's right; it looks like they're doing the Cha-cha-cha.) Then drag a wiggling icon to the right edge of the screen until a new page appears. You can flick to return to the original Home screen page and drag more wiggling icons to the new page. You can create up to nine Home screen pages.

Press the Home button under the screen to go to back to the first Home screen page. To go to any other Home screen page, tap one of the dots above the dock on any Home screen page — for example, to go to Home screen page 4, tap the fourth dot.

While the wiggling icons are doing their show, you can also rearrange them. Drag the wiggling icons into new positions, and the other icons move to accommodate, creating a new arrangement.

TIP

You can also delete apps you downloaded from the App Store by tapping the circled X that appears inside the icon as it wiggles.

To stop all that wiggling, press the Home button, which saves your new arrangement and pages.

To reset your Home screen to the default arrangement, thereby cleaning up any mess you may have made on your Home screens, tap Settings on the Home screen and then tap General. On the General screen, drag your finger to scroll the list to Reset and then tap Reset. On the Reset screen, tap Reset Home Screen Layout. (In the future, I make it easier for you by abbreviating instructions like these to the more manageable Settings⇨General⇨Reset⇨ Reset Home Screen Layout.)

Shake, rattle, and roll

Your iPod touch or iPhone can sense motion using a built-in accelerometer. When you rotate it from a vertical view (portrait) to a horizontal view (landscape), the accelerometer detects the movement and changes the display accordingly. This happens so quickly that you can control a game with these movements.

For example, Pass the Pigs is a dice game in which you shake three times to roll your pigs to gain points. In the Labyrinth game, you tilt your iPod touch or iPhone to roll a ball through a wooden maze without falling through the holes. And you can shake, rattle, and roll your way around the world in Yahtzee Adventures as you rack up high scores.

And if that's too tame for you, try Chopper, a helicopter game in which you need to complete your mission and return to base while avoiding enemy fire from tanks and bazooka-wielding madmen. You tilt the iPod touch or iPhone to fly, and you touch the screen to drop bombs or fire the machine gun.

Xhake Shake lets you shake, flip, rub, and tap your iPod touch or iPhone to challenge your hand-eye responses. And for scrolling practice, try Light Bike (loosely based on the Disney movie *Tron*) in which you scroll to maneuver a light bike from a third-person perspective against three computer-controlled light bikes. And infants can join the fun: Silver Rattle shows a screen that changes color and rattles with every shake. Big Joe Turner would be proud.

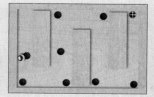

Tickling the Keyboard on an iPod touch or iPhone

One trick that's sure to amaze your friends is the ability to whip out your iPod touch or iPhone and type notes, contact information, calendar entries, map locations, stock symbols, e-mail messages, and Web site addresses (and even cell-phone text messages on an iPhone). You can also make selections for pop-up menus that appear on Web pages. You can do all this with the on-screen keyboard.

You may want to start practicing on the keyboard with just one finger, and as you get used to it, try also using your thumb. Tap a text entry field, such as the URL field for a Web page in Safari (as I describe in Chapter 19) or the text of an e-mail message (as I describe in Chapter 20), and the on-screen keyboard appears.

Typing into Notes

You can practice your technique using the Notes app. Tap Notes on the Home screen and the on-screen keyboard appears, as shown in Figure 3-3. (If you've already saved notes, a list of notes appears — tap the + button in the upper-right corner to type a new note.)

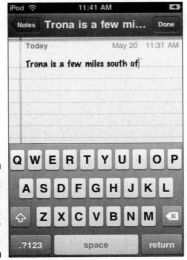

Figure 3-3: The on-screen keyboard for typing.

Tap the keys, and as you type, each letter appears above your thumb or finger. If you tap the wrong key, slide your finger to the correct key. The letter isn't entered until you lift your finger from the key.

You can start a new sentence quickly by double-tapping the spacebar to insert a period followed by a space. The keyboard automatically capitalizes the next word after you type a period, a question mark, or an exclamation point.

To enable caps lock (locking the keyboard to uppercase letters), choose Settings⇨General⇨Keyboard and then tap the Off button next to Enable Caps Lock to turn it on. (Tap it again to turn it off.) You can then double-tap the Shift key to turn on caps lock (uppercase letters). The Shift key turns blue, and all letters you type are uppercase. Tap the Shift key again to turn caps lock off.

To save your note, tap Done in the upper-right corner. A list of Notes appears with a date attached to each note. You can also delete a note by choosing the note and tapping the Trash icon at the bottom of the note. Notes can be synchronized back to your computer's e-mail program — see Chapter 10.

You can e-mail notes to others (and also transfer notes to your computer by e-mailing them to an e-mail address you receive e-mail with on your computer). Choose the note from the Notes screen and tap the letter icon at the bottom of the note to display a ready-made e-mail message that contains the text of your note — all you need to do is enter the e-mail address. See Chapter 20 for details on sending the message.

Typing numbers and symbols

To enter numbers, symbols, or punctuation, tap the .?123 key at the lower-left corner of the keyboard (refer to Figure 3-3). This changes the keyboard layout to numbers, as shown in Figure 3-4 (left side). To return to the alphabetical keys, tap the ABC key.

To enter symbols with the keyboard, tap the .?123 key for the number layout (refer to Figure 3-3) and then tap the #+= key (refer to Figure 3-4, left side) to change the layout to symbols, as shown in Figure 3-4 (right side).

Here's a trick you can use to switch to the numeric keyboard layout and back to alphabetical layout automatically to type a number and continue typing letters: Touch and hold down the .?123 key and then slide your finger over the keyboard to the number you want. Release your finger to select the number. The keyboard immediately reverts back to alphabetical keys so that you can continue typing letters.

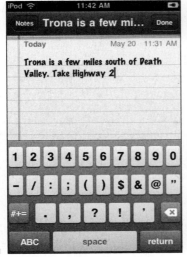 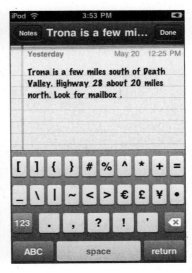

Figure 3-4: The keyboard layout for numbers (left) and for symbols (right).

TIP

Need to use an accent mark? For instance, the word *café* should really have an accent mark over the *e,* and there may even come a day when you need to include a foreign word or two in a note — lycée or Autowäsche or también, for example. Although you can switch the language for the keyboard (as I describe in Chapter 23), you can also include an accent mark over a vowel by using the English keyboard. Hold your finger on a vowel (such as *e*) to show a row of keys that offer variations on the letter. Slide your finger over the row to highlight the variation you want and then release your finger to select it.

Editing text and handling word suggestions

Yes, you can edit your mistakes. To edit text in an entry field, touch and hold to see the circular magnifier, which magnifies portions of the text view as shown in Figure 3-5.

Before releasing your finger, slide the magnifier to the position for inserting text. You can then tap keys to insert text, or you can use the backspace key — the key sporting the X — to remove text.

The intelligent keyboard automatically suggests corrections as you type, as shown in Figure 3-6 (some languages only). You don't need to accept the suggested word — just continue typing. If you do want to accept it, tap the spacebar, a punctuation mark, or the Return key. Your iPhone or iPod touch fills in the rest of the word.

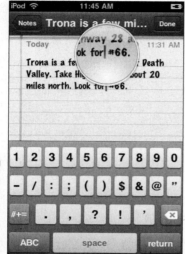

Figure 3-5:
Touch and
hold for the
circular
magnifier.

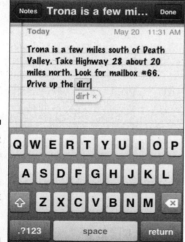

Figure 3-6:
The
keyboard
suggests
the correct
word for a
typo.

To reject the suggested word, finish typing the word or tap the x next to the suggestion to dismiss it. Each time you reject a suggestion for the same word, your iPod touch keeps track and eventually adds the word you've been using all along to its dictionary. The iPod touch includes dictionaries for English, English (UK), French, French (Canada), German, Japanese, Spanish, Italian, and Dutch. The appropriate dictionary is activated automatically when you select a particular international keyboard. (See Chapter 23 for details about international keyboards.)

You can turn off suggestions by choosing Settings⇨General⇨Keyboard from the Home screen and tapping On for Auto-Correction. (On changes to Off when you tap it.)

You don't have to turn suggestions off if you just want to temporarily make them go away. To keep suggestions from appearing, start by typing a special symbol (such as $ or &), a numeral (such as 0). Then touch and hold to see the magnifier for inserting text, and drag the insertion point to be right before this symbol or numeral, so that you'll be inserting text before it. Release and start typing. The keyboard won't suggest anything because it won't know what you mean — there are no words in its dictionary that end with these symbols or numerals. Don't use punctuation symbols such as a period, comma, parentheses or quotes, or even the @ symbol because the keyboard knows that they're used after words.

Copying (or cutting) and pasting

If you've upgraded your iPod touch or iPhone to version 3.0 of the software or newer, you can copy or cut a chunk of text and paste it into another app — for example, you can copy a paragraph from a note in Notes and paste it into an e-mail message in Mail.

Double-tap a word to select it for copying or cutting. The word appears selected with handles on either end of the selection and a Cut/Copy/Paste bubble above it, as shown in Figure 3-7 (left side). You can then tap Cut (to cut the text) or Copy (to copy the text) in preparation for pasting it elsewhere.

You can also select the nearest word, or the entire text, by touching an insertion point. The Select/Select All/Paste bubble appears (refer to Figure 3-7, center). Tap Select to select the nearest word (left or right of the insertion point) or Select All to select all the text, and the Cut/Copy/Paste bubble appears (refer to Figure 3-7, right side).

To make a more precise selection, double-tap a word as previously described and then drag one of the handles by sliding your finger. A rectangular magnifier appears, as shown in Figure 3-8 (left side), which magnifies portions of the text view so that you can drag the handle more precisely. When you remove your finger to stop dragging, the Cut/Copy/Paste bubble appears (refer to Figure 3-8, right side). You can then tap Cut or Copy.

To paste the text you just cut or copied, open a note (or create a new note) in Notes, create a new e-mail message, or open any app that lets you enter text. (For details on creating a new e-mail message, see Chapter 20.) Touch an insertion point for pasting the text. The circular magnifier appears (as shown in Figure 3-9, left side), which magnifies portions of the text view so that you can mark the insertion point precisely. When you remove your finger, the Cut/Copy/Paste bubble appears (refer to Figure 3-9, center), or if text is already in the message, the Select/Select All/Paste bubble appears. Either way, you can then tap Paste to paste the text at that point (refer to Figure 3-9, right side).

Figure 3-7: Double-tap a word to cut or copy it with the Cut/Copy/ Paste bub-ble (left). Or, tap an inser-tion point and select all the text (center) to cut or copy it with the Cut/Copy/ Paste bubble (right).

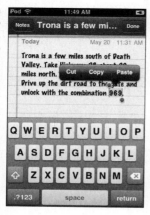
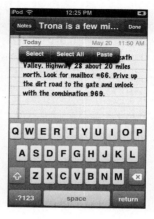
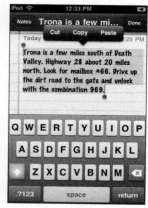

Figure 3-8: Drag a handle to extend the selection for cutting or copying (left) and then release your finger to complete the selection (right).

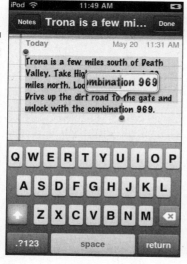
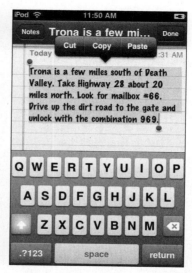

Figure 3-9:
Touch an
insertion
point (left),
release to
complete
the selec-
tion (center),
and then
tap Paste;
the pasted
text appears
(right).

You can use Copy, Cut, and Paste in Safari to copy portions of a Web page
(see how in Chapter 19), in Mail to copy portions of an e-mail message (see
Chapter 20), or even in Calendar to copy the details of an event (see Chapter 21).

Setting keyboard options

To set keyboard options, choose Settings⇨General⇨Keyboard from the
Home screen. The Keyboard settings screen appears, with options for Auto-
Correction, Auto-Capitalization, Enable Caps Lock, and the Shortcut for
inserting a period, as shown in Figure 3-10.

Figure 3-10:
Change
settings
for the
on-screen
keyboard.

Tap On to turn off Auto-Correction if you don't want the keyboard to suggest typing corrections.

Auto-Capitalization automatically capitalizes the next word after you type a period, question mark, or exclamation point (punctuation that ends a sentence). It also automatically capitalizes after you tap the Return key. The assumption is that you're starting a new sentence or new line of text that should begin with a capital letter. Tap On to turn this feature off if you want; tap Off to turn it back on.

To turn on caps lock (locking the keyboard to uppercase letters), tap the Off button next to Enable Caps Lock. (Tap it again to turn it off.) You can then double-tap the Shift key to turn on caps lock (uppercase letters). The Shift key turns blue, and all letters you type are uppercase. Tap the Shift key again to turn caps lock off.

The shortcut for inserting a period is to double-tap the spacebar, which inserts a period followed by a space. The assumption is that you want to finish a sentence and start the next one. Tap On to turn this feature off if you want; tap Off to turn it back on.

To find out how to turn on and use multiple international keyboards, see Chapter 23.

Thumbing through iPod nano and classic Menus

The circular click wheel on iPod classic and iPod nano models makes scrolling through an entire music collection quick and easy. With your finger or thumb, scroll clockwise on the wheel to scroll down a list or counterclockwise to scroll up. As you scroll, options on the menu are highlighted. Press the Select button at the center of the wheel to select whatever is highlighted in the menu display.

The main menu for iPod classic and iPod nano models offers the following selections:

✔ **Music:** Select playlists, artists, albums, songs, genres, composers, or audio books. You can also select Cover Flow to browse by cover art or choose Search to search for a song or album title or artist (as I describe in Chapter 16). On an iPod nano you can also select Genius Mixes, which appear if you follow my instructions in Chapter 16.

- ✔ **Videos:** Select videos by video playlist or by type (movies, music videos, or TV shows) as I demonstrate in Chapter 17. On an iPod nano you can also select Camera Videos — the videos you shoot with the iPod nano camera See Chapter 18 for details.

- ✔ **Photos:** Select photos by photo album or select all photos in the Photo Library (as I show in Chapter 17).

- ✔ **Podcasts:** Select podcasts by title and then select podcast episodes. Find out more in Chapter 19.

- ✔ **Radio:** Select the built-in FM radio in the iPod nano to listen to local stations, as I describe in Chapter 17 and radio regions for the iPod nano built-in FM radio (see Chapter 17).

- ✔ **Video Camera:** Select the built-in video camera in the iPod nano to shoot videos — it's incredibly easy, as I show in Chapter 18.

- ✔ **Extras:** View the clock, set time zones for clocks, set alarms and the sleep timer, use the stopwatch, use the iPod nano fitness features, and view contacts and your calendar, as I show in Chapter 4.

- ✔ **Settings:** Adjust menu settings, the backlight timer, the clicker, the date and time, and so on (see Chapter 4). You can also set the iPod's EQ (see Chapter 16). and radio regions for the iPod nano built-in FM radio (see Chapter 17).

- ✔ **Shuffle Songs:** Play songs from your music library in random order.

- ✔ **Now Playing:** This selection appears only when a song is playing — it takes you to the Now Playing display.

The iPod classic or iPod nano click wheel has pressure-sensitive buttons underneath the top, bottom, left, and right areas of the circular pad that tilt as you press them. These buttons on the iPod classic or iPod nano do various tasks for song, podcast, audio book, and video playback. Here they are, in clockwise order from the top:

- ✔ **Select:** Press the Select button at the center of the wheel to select whatever is highlighted in the menu display.

- ✔ **Menu:** Press once to go back to the previous menu. Each time you press, you go back to a previous menu until you reach the main menu.

- ✔ **Next/Fast Forward:** Press once to skip to the next item. Press and hold Next/Fast Forward to fast-forward.

- ✔ **Play/Pause:** Press to play the selected item. Press Play/Pause when the item is playing to pause the playback.

- ✔ **Previous/Rewind:** Press once to start an item over. Press twice to skip to the previous item (such as a song in an album). Press and hold to rewind.

The buttons and click wheel on the iPod classic or iPod nano can do more complex functions when used in combination:

- **Turn on the iPod.** Press any button.

- **Turn off the iPod.** Press and hold the Play/Pause button.

- **Reset the iPod.** You can reset the iPod if it gets hung up for some reason. (For example, it might get confused if you press the buttons too quickly.) See Chapter 22 for instructions on how to reset your iPod.

- **Change the volume.** While playing a song (the display reads Now Playing), adjust the volume by scrolling the click wheel. Clockwise turns the volume up; counterclockwise turns the volume down. A volume slider appears on the iPod display, indicating the volume level as you scroll.

- **Skip to any point in a song, video, audio book, or podcast.** While playing an item (the display reads Now Playing), press and hold the Select button until the progress bar appears to indicate where you are, and then scroll the click wheel to move to any point in the song. Scroll clockwise to move forward and counterclockwise to move backward. Press the Select button again to see lyrics for the song (if available). Find out more about using these controls in Chapter 16.

To discover advanced iPod and iPhone techniques, such as customizing your menus, visit the Tips section of the author's Web site at www.tonybove.com.

Chapter 4

Choosing Essential Settings For Daily Operation

In This Chapter

▶ Setting the time, date, clock, alarm, timer, and stopwatch
▶ Changing the brightness, wallpaper, sound effects, and other settings
▶ Locking your iPod or iPhone with a combination passcode
▶ Connecting your iPod touch or iPhone with Wi-Fi networks

You may think Apple designed the iPod just for listening to music or watching videos, but those thoughtful engineers crammed a lot more features into their invention. You can use your iPod or iPhone as a timekeeper to help you keep track of your personal life — setting an alarm, using the stopwatch, and displaying clocks of different time zones for traveling. And if you worry that your iPod or iPhone might fall into the wrong hands, consider setting a combination lock.

This chapter shows you how to do all this and more with your iPod, including setting the backlight, the click sound, and even the display font. I show you how to check your calendar and your contacts on an iPod classic or iPod nano.

I also cover settings that are specific to the iPod touch and iPhone: setting the brightness of the display, choosing the *wallpaper* (a stylin' background when it's locked), knowing your location, and placing restrictions on downloading and playing content. You also find out how to connect an iPod touch or iPhone to a Wi-Fi network for Internet access.

There's No Time Like the Right Time

Your iPod may already be set to the correct time, date, and time zone (based on the computer you connected it to for setup). If not, you can set it yourself. You can also set an iPhone to set the time automatically from its cell-phone network, or have an iPod touch set the time from the Internet. You can even set how the time appears in the status bar at the top of the screen.

On an iPod touch or iPhone

To set the date and time for an iPod touch or iPhone, follow these steps:

1. **Choose Settings⇨General⇨Date & Time from the Home screen.**

   The Date & Time screen appears with the 24-Hour Time, Time Zone, and Set Date & Time options, and time zone support for your calendar.

2. **(Optional) Tap the Off button for the 24-Hour Time option to turn it on and show military time.**

   With the 24-hour display, 11 p.m. is displayed as 23:00:00 and not 11:00:00. To turn off the 24-Hour Time option, tap the On button.

3. **iPhone only: Turn off Set Automatically to set the time and date manually.**

   The Set Automatically option is turned on by default for the iPhone to set the time and date automatically using its cell-phone network. If this is okay with you, skip to Step 10 (you're done). If not, touch the On button to turn the Set Automatically option off so that you can set the time and date manually. After turning off the Set Automatically option, two new options appear: Time Zone and Set Date & Time.

4. **Tap the Time Zone option to set the time zone.**

   The on-screen keyboard appears; see Chapter 3 for instructions on how to use it. Type the name of the city you're in (or, if you're in the middle of nowhere, the nearest big city) and then tap the Return button on the keyboard. Your iPod touch or iPhone looks up the time zone for you.

5. **Tap the Date & Time button in the upper-left corner of the display to finish and return to the Date & Time menu.**

6. **Tap the Set Date & Time option.**

   Tapping the Date field brings up a slot-machine-style date wheel, as shown in Figure 4-1.

7. **Slide your finger over the wheel to select the month, day, and year.**

   Slide until the selection you want appears in the gray window on the slot-machine wheel.

8. **Tap the Time field to bring up a time wheel.**

   Slide your finger over the wheel to set the hour, minutes, and AM or PM.

Figure 4-1:
Slide the
wheel of
fortune
to set the
month, day,
and year
(left) and
time (right).

9. **Tap the Date & Time button in the upper-left corner of the display (refer to Figure 4-1) to finish and return to the Date & Time menu.**

10. **Tap the General button in the upper-left corner to return to the General screen.**

On an iPod nano or iPod classic

To set the date and time on an iPod nano or iPod classic, follow these steps:

1. **Press the Menu button until you see the iPod main menu.**

2. **Choose Settings⇨Date & Time.**

   The Date & Time menu appears, with selections for setting the date, time, time zone, 24-hour clock, and the Time in Title option, which displays the time in the iPod display's menu title bar.

3. **(Optional) Choose Time Zone.**

   Skip this step and the next step if the time zone already set is correct. After choosing Time Zone, a map appears with a red dot set to your current time zone on the map.

4. **(Optional) Scroll to choose a time zone and press Select.**

   Skip this step if the time zone is correct; otherwise, move the red dot to another zone by scrolling the click wheel — the red dot jumps from one region of the map to another, and the time zone appears below the map. Press the Select button to choose a zone. After selecting it, the Date & Time menu appears again.

5. **Choose Date from the Date & Time menu.**

   The Date display appears with the month field highlighted.

6. **Change the field setting by scrolling the click wheel.**

   Scroll clockwise to go forward and counterclockwise to go backward.

7. **Press the Select button after scrolling to the appropriate setting.**

   The next field is now highlighted.

8. **Repeat Steps 6 and 7 for the day and year.**

   After you finish scrolling and then selecting the Year field, the Date & Time menu appears automatically.

9. **Choose Time from the Date & Time menu.**

   The Time display appears with the Hour field highlighted.

10. **Change the field setting by scrolling the click wheel.**

    Scroll clockwise to go forward and counterclockwise to go backward.

11. **Press the Select button after scrolling to the appropriate setting.**

    The next field is now highlighted.

12. **Repeat Steps 10 and 11 for minutes and AM/PM.**

    After finishing the AM/PM field, the Date & Time menu appears again.

To show military time (so that 11 p.m. is displayed as 23:00), choose the 24-Hour Clock option in the Date & Time menu and press the Select button to turn it on. The option changes from 12-hour to 24-hour. To switch back, press the Select button again.

To display the time on the menu title bar of an iPod classic or iPod nano, scroll to the Time in Title option in the Date & Time menu and then press the Select button to turn this option on. To stop showing the time on the menu title bar, press the Select button again to toggle it to Off.

Rock Around the Clocks

You can always know what time it is — just look at the time on the Home screen of an iPod touch or iPhone, or on the main menu title bar of an iPod classic or iPod nano. But you can also know what time it is in *other* time zones by displaying multiple clocks. Your iPod and iPhone even let you set an alarm and run a stopwatch.

Checking the time in Paris and Bangkok

You can display clocks with different time zones, which is useful for traveling halfway around the world (or calling someone who lives halfway around the world).

To create clocks on an iPod touch or iPhone, tap the Clock icon on the Home screen and then tap the World Clock icon along the bottom of the display. It takes only two steps to add a clock:

1. **Touch the plus (+) button in the upper-right corner of the display.**

   The on-screen keyboard appears with a text entry field.

2. **Type a city name on the keyboard, and tap Return (or tap Cancel next to the text entry field to cancel).**

   The iPod touch or iPhone looks up the city's time zone to display the clock. (For details on how to use the on-screen keyboard, see Chapter 3.)

The initial clock and any clocks you add sport a daytime face (white background and black hands) from 6 a.m. to 5:59 p.m., as shown in Figure 4-2, and a nighttime face (black background with white hands) from 6 p.m. to 5:59 a.m.

To remove a clock, tap the Edit button in the upper-left corner of the display (refer to Figure 4-2) and then tap the circled minus (–) button next to the clock to delete it.

Figure 4-2:
Add more
clocks for
other time
zones.

To create more clocks, edit the clocks, or delete additional clocks with an iPod nano or iPod classic, follow these steps:

1. **Choose Extras⇨Clocks from the main menu, and highlight a clock.**

   One or more clocks appear (depending on how many you have created), showing the present time and location. If you have more than one clock and you want to edit one of them, scroll the click wheel to highlight the clock you want to edit.

2. **Press the Select button on the iPod to select the clock.**

   The Add and Edit options appear, along with a Delete option if you have more than one clock.

3. **Scroll the click wheel to select Add, Edit, or Delete and press the Select button.**

   If you select Add or Edit, a list of geographical regions appears in alphabetical order, from Africa to South America. If you select Delete, the clock is deleted, and you can skip the following steps.

4. **Scroll the Region list, choose a region, and press the Select button.**

   The City menu appears with a list of cities in the region in alphabetical order.

5. **Scroll the City list, choose a city, and then press the Select button.**

   You return to the list of clocks. You now have added a new clock (or edited a clock if you selected the Edit option).

Getting alarmed

Time is on your side with your iPod or iPhone. You can set *multiple* alarms to go off on different days and set a variety of tones and sounds for your alarms that play through its speaker. On an iPod nano or iPod classic, you can even assign a playlist to an alarm to play through external speakers or headphones.

To set alarms on an iPod touch or iPhone, follow these steps:

1. **Tap the Clock icon on the Home screen, and tap the Alarm icon along the bottom of the display.**

2. **To add an alarm, tap the plus (+) button in the upper-right corner of the display.**

   The Add Alarm screen appears, as shown in Figure 4-3, with options and a slot-machine-style wheel for setting the alarm time.

Figure 4-3:
Add an
alarm.

3. **Slide your finger over the wheel to set the hour and minute, and AM or PM.**

   Slide until the selection you want appears in the gray window on the slot-machine wheel.

   Now you can set some optional features, or you can skip to Step 8 and be done with it.

4. **(Optional) Tap the Repeat option to set the alarm to repeat on other days.**

   You can set it to repeat every Monday, Tuesday, Wednesday, Thursday, Friday, Saturday, and/or Sunday. (You can select multiple days.)

5. **(Optional) Tap the Sound option to select a sound for the alarm.**

   A list of sounds appears; touch a sound to set it for the alarm.

6. **(Optional) Tap the On button to turn off the Snooze option, or tap it again to turn it back on.**

   With the Snooze option, the iPod or iPhone displays a Snooze button when the alarm goes off, and you tap Snooze to stop the alarm and have it repeat in 10 minutes (so that you can snooze for 10 minutes).

7. **(Optional) Tap the Label option to enter a text label for the alarm.**

   The label helps you identify the alarm in the Alarm list.

8. **Tap the Save button in the upper-right corner to save the alarm.**

When the alarm goes off, your iPod or iPhone displays the message You have an alarm (and the date and time), along with the Snooze button if the Snooze option is turned on (refer to Step 6). Slide your finger to unlock the iPod touch or iPhone to stop the alarm's sound, or tap the Snooze button to stop the alarm temporarily and let it repeat 10 minutes later. (When it goes off again, slide the unlock slider to turn it off — don't tap the Snooze button again; you're late for work!)

To delete an alarm on an iPod touch or iPhone, tap the Clock icon on the Home screen and tap the Alarm icon along the bottom of the display. In the Alarm list, tap the alarm you want to trash and then tap the Edit button in the upper-left corner of the display. The alarm appears with a circled minus (–) button next to it; tap this button and then tap the red Delete button that appears to delete the alarm.

An iPod nano or iPod classic can do more than play a beep sound for the alarm — you can set a playlist, which you can hear by connecting the iPod to speakers or a stereo (or headphones, if you sleep with headphones on). To set an alarm on an iPod classic or iPod nano, follow these steps:

1. **Choose Extras⇨Alarms from the main menu.**

   The Create Alarm and Sleep Timer options appear on the Alarms main menu.

2. **Choose Create Alarm, and press the Select button.**

   The Alarms submenu appears.

3. **Highlight the Alarm option, and press the Select button to turn it on.**

4. **Choose Date from the Alarms submenu.**

   The Date display appears with the month field highlighted.

5. **Change the field setting by scrolling the click wheel.**

   Scroll clockwise to go forward and counterclockwise to go backward.

6. **Press the Select button after scrolling to the appropriate setting.**

   The next field is now highlighted.

7. **Repeat Steps 5 and 6 for the day and year.**

   After you finish scrolling and then selecting the Year field, the Alarms submenu appears automatically.

8. **Choose Time from the Alarms submenu.**

   The Time display appears with the Hour field highlighted.

9. **Change the field setting by scrolling the click wheel.**

   Scroll clockwise to go forward and counterclockwise to go backward.

10. **Press the Select button after scrolling to the appropriate setting.**

    The next field is now highlighted.

11. **Repeat Steps 9 and 10 for minutes and AM/PM.**

    After finishing the AM/PM field, the Alarms submenu appears again.

12. **Choose Repeat from the Alarms submenu, and choose a repeat multiple.**

    You can choose to set the alarm to go off once, every day, weekdays, weekends, every week, every month, or every year. After choosing a repeat multiple, the Alarms submenu appears again.

13. **Choose Sounds from the Alarms submenu and choose a tone or a playlist.**

    The Tones and Playlists options appear. Choose Tones to select a beep, or set Tones to none (no sound) if you want the iPod to display the alarm without making a sound. Choose Playlists to select a playlist. After choosing a tone or a playlist, the Alarms submenu appears again.

14. **Choose Label from the Alarms submenu to set a label to identify this alarm.**

    You can set labels for your alarms so that you can identify them easily in the Alarms main menu. Select a label from the prepared list, which includes labels such as Wake Up, Work, Class, Appointment, and so on. After choosing a label, the Alarms submenu appears again.

15. **Press Menu to return to the Alarms main menu, which now includes your new alarm with its label in a list of alarms under the Sleep Timer heading.**

You can create as many alarms, at different dates and times, as you need. To delete an alarm, select the alarm from the list on the Alarms main menu. The Alarms submenu appears with a list of options. Choose Delete.

When the alarm goes off, your iPod classic or iPod nano displays an alarm message along with the Dismiss and Snooze buttons. Choose Dismiss or Snooze by scrolling the click wheel and then select it by pressing the Select button. Dismiss stops the alarm's sound, whereas Snooze stops the sound temporarily and repeats it 10 minutes later.

Timing your steps (iPod touch and iPhone)

You can set an hour-and-minute timer for anything — baking cookies, baking CDs, or baking in the sun on the beach. The timer built into the Clock app on your iPod touch or iPhone will continue running even when playing music or videos or running other apps. You might want to use a timer to see whether a set of activities — playing songs, playing videos, selecting from menus, and running apps — occurs within a specific time. (If you need to use seconds as well as minutes and hours, try using the stopwatch, which I describe in the next section.)

To use the timer, follow these steps:

1. **Tap the Clock icon on the Home screen.**

   The Clock display appears.

2. **Tap the Timer icon along the bottom of the Clock display.**

   The timer wheel for minutes and hours appears, along with the Start button.

3. **Flick the timer wheel to set the timer in hours and minutes.**

4. **Tap the When Timer Ends button and then tap a sound to use when the timer is up.**

5. **Tap Set in the upper-right corner of the display to set the sound (or Cancel in the upper-left corner to cancel the sound).**

6. **Tap Start to start the timer.**

The timer runs backward. You can touch Cancel to cancel the timer or wait until it runs out. When it runs out, the iPod touch plays the sound (if a sound is set) and presents an OK button. Tap OK to stop the sound.

Using the stopwatch

You can use a stopwatch with a lap timer for timing exercises, jogging, racing laps, seeing how long it takes the bus to travel across town, or finding out how long your friend takes to recognize the song you're playing. Whatever you want to measure with accurate time to the tenth of a second, the stopwatch is ready for you.

Even while you're running the stopwatch, you can still use the iPod or iPhone to play music, videos, audio books, and podcasts. When you play a video, the stopwatch continues to count as usual; when you switch back to the stopwatch display, the video automatically pauses.

To use the stopwatch on an iPod touch or iPhone, follow these steps:

1. **Tap the Clock icon on the Home screen, and tap the Stopwatch icon along the bottom of the display.**

   A stopwatch appears with Start and Reset buttons and 00:00.00 (minutes, seconds, and fractions of seconds) as the stopwatch counter.

2. **Tap the Start button to start counting.**

   The stopwatch starts counting immediately; the left button changes to Stop and the right button changes to Lap, as shown in Figure 4-4.

Figure 4-4: After tapping Start (left) and after tapping Lap (right).

3. **(Optional) Tap the Lap button to mark each lap.**

   Tap the Lap button to record each lap. Repeat this step for each lap — Clock creates a list of lap times.

4. **Tap the Stop button to stop counting.**

   The counter stops counting. The left button changes to Start, and the right button changes to Reset. You can resume the count from where you left off by tapping Start, or you can start the count again from zero by tapping Reset.

To use the stopwatch on an iPod classic or iPod nano, follow these steps:

1. **Choose Extras⇨Stopwatch from the main menu.**

   A stopwatch appears with the Play/Pause icon.

2. **Press the Select button to start counting.**

   The stopwatch starts counting immediately.

3. **(Optional) Press the Select button to mark each lap.**

   Press the Select button to record the current lap time while counting resumes accurately for the next lap. Repeat this step for each lap.

4. **Press the Play/Pause button to stop counting, and then press the menu button.**

   The Stopwatch menu appears. The menu now includes the Current Log option to show the lap timings for the stopwatch session. Also included are previous stopwatch session logs. The iPod saves the stopwatch results in a session log for convenience, so you don't have to write them down.

5. **Select Resume to resume counting or New Timer to start a new stopwatch session.**

   You can resume the stopwatch session from where you left off, or you can start a new stopwatch session.

6. **(Optional) Read your stopwatch logs by choosing Current Log or the date of a previous log on the Stopwatch menu.**

7. **(Optional) Delete your stopwatch logs by choosing Clear Logs on the Stopwatch menu.**

Setting the sleep timer

As you can with a clock radio sleep timer, you can set your iPod or iPhone to play music or videos for a while before going to sleep.

To set the timer on the iPhone or iPod touch as a sleep timer, first follow the instructions in the section "Timing your steps (iPod touch and iPhone)" earlier in this chapter. Then touch the When Timer Ends button, and touch Sleep iPod at the top of the list to put the iPod touch or iPhone to sleep when the timer ends. Touch Set in the upper-right corner of the display to set the Sleep iPod option (or Cancel in the upper-left corner to cancel). Finally, touch Start to start the timer. You can then play music or videos until the timer ends and the iPod touch or iPhone automatically goes to sleep.

To set the sleep timer on an iPod classic or iPod nano, choose Extras from the main menu; then choose Alarms➪Sleep Timer. A list of intervals appears, from 0 (Off) to 120 minutes (2 hours). You can select a time amount or the Off setting (at the top of the list) to turn off the sleep timer. After the iPod shuts itself off or you turn it off, the preference for the Sleep Timer is reset to the default status, Off.

Using the iPod nano pedometer

A pedometer counts each step you take by detecting the motion, measuring your progress and motivating you to exercise more. The iPod nano offers a pedometer that uses the built-in accelerometer to keep track of your steps. For more accurate results, keep the iPod nano in your pocket or in the iPod nano Armband while using the pedometer. Even so, pedometers also record movements other than walking, such as bending to tie one's shoes, or shakin' your booty, so don't expect complete accuracy.

To use the pedometer for the first time, follow these steps:

1. **Choose Extras➪Fitness➪Settings➪Weight from the iPod nano main menu.**

   Before using the pedometer, you should set it to your correct weight. The Choose Weight screen appears with the weight in large numbers on the display.

2. **Set your correct weight.**

   Scroll the click wheel to set the correct weight. Then press the Select (center) button. The Settings menu appears.

3. **Select Pedometer and press the Select button to change it to either Manual or Always On.**

   You can turn on the pedometer whenever you want to (Manual), or set the pedometer to Always On so that the pedometer counts all the steps you take all the time.

4. **Select Daily Step Goal in the Settings menu, and choose the number of steps.**

   You can create a daily step goal, None (for no goal), or a Custom goal (to set your own number of steps).

5. **Choose the screen orientation for the pedometer.**

   Choose Screen Orientation in the Settings menu, and then choose Vertical, Left (left side of the screen in horizontal orientation), or Right (right side of the screen in horizontal orientation). Then press Menu to go back to the Fitness menu.

That's it. Now you are ready to use the pedometer. Choose Extras⇨>Fitness⇨ Pedometer to turn it on, unless you have already set it to be always on (in Step 3 above). The Pedometer menu item appears in the main menu when the pedometer is on, so you can easily choose it to turn it off. The preview panel below the main menu shows your step count when you scroll the click wheel to highlight Pedometer in the menu.

To view your workout history, choose Extras⇨Fitness⇨History, and scroll the click wheel and press Select to select a date from the calendar, or press Next/Fast-forward or Previous/Rewind to go forward or backward by month in the calendar and then select a date. After pressing the Select button, your workout history appears. If you have more than one workout session on the selected date, scroll the click wheel and press Select to choose a session. The iPod nano pedometer displays your step goal, workout duration, start and end times, calories burned, and totals for the week and month. You can even view a bar graph by rotating the iPod nano to landscape mode.

Setting the Passcode for Your Lock

You can set a four-digit combination passcode for the iPod nano, iPod classic, iPod touch, or iPhone to lock it and thereby prevent others from navigating through your content. *Note:* The lockup works only when your iPod or iPhone is not attached to a computer.

An iPod touch or iPhone locks itself when it goes to sleep, and as you already know, you have to slide your finger over the unlock message to wake it up. But you can also set this passcode to keep the iPod touch or iPhone protected from access after waking up — so that you need to supply the passcode.

If you're playing music when your iPod nano or iPod classic is locked, the music continues playing — and you can even use the Play/Pause button to pause and resume playback — but if you set a passcode, no one can navigate the iPod nano or iPod classic or even change the volume without providing the passcode.

To conserve power, you can force your iPod touch or iPhone to go to sleep by pressing the Sleep/Wake (On/Off) button — but you'll still need the passcode (if you set one) to use it after waking it up. Similarly, you can force an iPod classic or iPod nano to go to sleep by pressing the Play/Pause button, but you'll still need the passcode to unlock it. When the iPod or iPhone awakens, it remembers everything — including its passcode.

Don't bother to call Apple to see whether the company can unlock your iPod or iPhone for you. If you can't enter the correct passcode, or attach it to the computer you set it up on, your only recourse is to restore the iPod or iPhone to its factory conditions — see Chapter 22.

Dont forget this passcode! Use a four-digit number that's easy to commit to memory.

To set a passcode for your iPhone or iPod touch, follow these steps:

1. **Choose Settings⟿General⟿Passcode Lock from the Home screen.**

   The Set Passcode display appears.

2. **Enter a four-digit passcode by tapping numbers on the calculator-style.**

3. **Enter the same passcode number again to confirm the passcode.**

   After reentering the passcode, the Passcode Lock menu appears with the Turn Passcode Off, Change Passcode, and Require Passcode options.

4. **Select the Passcode option you want to use.**

   You can turn off the passcode, change it, or set the Require Passcode option to Immediately, After 1 Minute, After 5 Minutes, After 15 Minutes, After 1 Hour, or After 4 Hours.

5. **When you're done, tap General to return to the General menu.**

To unlock a passcode-locjed iPod touch of iPhone, you must enter the same passcode, or restore the iPod touch or iPhone to its original factory settings, as I describe in Chapter22. (Restoreing erases everthing — this is, of course, a measure of last resort.) The passcode screen with four spaces and a numeric keypad appears immediately after you slide the "Slide to unlock" message After correctly entering the combination of numbers for the numeric keypad, the iPod touch of iPhone unlocks.

To set a passcode (a.k.a. combination lock) for your iPod classic or iPod nano, follow these steps:

1. **Choose Extras⟿Screen Lock⟿Lock.**

   The Screen Lock icon appears with your combination lock set to zeros.

2. **Select the first number of the passcode by scrolling the click wheel.**

   While you scroll with your iPod, the first digit of the passcode changes. You can also press the Previous/Rewind or Next/Fast Forward button to scroll through numbers.

3. **Press the Select button to pick a number.**

   This sets your choice for the first number and moves on to the next number of the passcode. Repeat this step for each number of the passcode. When you pick the last number, the message Confirm Combination appears.

4. **Confirm the passcode**

   Repeat Step 2 and 3 for each number of the passcode to confirm. After confirming, your iPod is locked.

On a locked iPod nano or iPod classic, the lock icon appears if you press any key. To unlock the iPod after locking it, press any button and then repeat Steps 2 and 3 to enter each number of the passcode. After correctly entering the passcode, the iPod nano or iPod classic unlocks and returns to the last viewed screen.

To reset the passcode, first unlock the iPod, and then choose Extras⇨ Screen ⇨Reset Combination, and then repeat Steps 2 through 4. To turn off the lock, reset the combination to all zeroes.

If you don't know the passcode, attach the iPod nano or iPod classic to the computer you used to set it up and synchronize it with iTunes. When you disconnect it after synchronizing with iTunes, the iPod nano or iPod classic is no longer locked with a passcode.

Getting Personal

Your future might be so bright that you gotta wear shades, but your iPod or iPhone display might not be bright enough. From the Settings menu, you can change the timer for the backlight on iPod classic and iPod nano models, and set the brightness of the display on all models, as well as set the contrast of the black-and-white displays of older models. Choose the Settings menu from the main menu of an iPod classic, nano, or older model, or from the Home screen of an iPod touch or iPhone.

You have plenty of other settings to consider to give your iPod or iPhone a personal touch. Besides wallpapering the display of your iPod touch or iPhone, you can set keyboard clicks and alert sounds to indicate that e-mail has arrived, that something in your calendar needs attention, and so on.

If you share your iPod touch or iPhone with children or adults that act like children, you may want to place restrictions that prevent explicit music from the iTunes Store from being displayed in playlists, prevent the use of apps such as YouTube, or stop any access to the iTunes Store or App Store. Your iPod touch or iPhone can let you do that, too.

Adjusting the backlight of your iPod nano or iPod classic

The iPod classic, iPod nano, and older iPods use a display backlight that turns on when you press a button or use the click wheel and then turns off after a short amount of time. You can set the backlight on iPod classic and iPod nano models to remain on for a certain interval of time. From the main menu, choose Settings⇨General⇨Backlight on an iPod nano, or

Settings⇨Backlight on an iPod classic. A menu appears, giving you the options of 2 seconds, 5 seconds, 10 seconds, 15 seconds, 20 seconds, 30 seconds, and Always On. Select one by scrolling to highlight the selection and then press the Select button.

Using the backlight drains an iPod battery; the longer you set the interval, the more frequently you need to recharge the battery.

To set the backlight to *always* be on, choose Always On. If you want the backlight to *always* be off, choose Always Off. If you set it to always be off, the backlight doesn't turn on automatically when you press any button or use the click wheel — and the display is much darker, of course.

To adjust the brightness of an iPod classic or nano, choose Settings⇨Brightness from the main menu. The Brightness screen appears with a slider that shows the brightness setting, which ranges from low (a quarter-moon icon) to high (a bright sun icon). Scroll clockwise to increase the brightness (toward the bright sun) and counterclockwise to decrease the brightness (toward the moon).

Brightening and wallpapering your iPod or iPhone

To adjust the brightness of an iPod touch or iPhone, first tap the Settings icon on the Home screen and then tap Brightness, which is near the top of the Settings screen. The Brightness screen appears with a slider that shows the brightness setting, which ranges from low (a dim sun icon) to high (a bright sun icon). Slide the brightness slider's knob with your finger to the right to increase the brightness (toward the bright sun) and to the left to decrease the brightness (toward the dim sun). Of course, the brighter the screen, the more power is drawn from the battery.

While you're at it, why not wallpaper your display? You can make your iPod touch or iPhone display a stylish background when it's locked. You can also put up photos or other images from your photo library as your wallpaper.

It's not like you'll see it often — the iPod touch or iPhone displays the wallpaper image only when you first press the Sleep/Wake button or Home button to wake it up. After you swipe with your finger to unlock your iPod touch or iPhone, the wallpaper is replaced by the Home screen or whatever app you were last running.

To set the wallpaper, choose Settings⇨General⇨Wallpaper from the Home screen. You can then choose from among stylish built-in wallpaper images by tapping the Wallpaper button.

You can also choose from the photo library you synchronized with your iPod touch or iPhone by tapping Photo Library, or you can choose photos saved on your iPod touch or iPhone by tapping Saved Photos. (For more about photos, see Chapter 18.)

Tap a thumbnail to select the image for your wallpaper, or tap the Wallpaper button in the upper-left corner to return to the Wallpaper menu. After tapping an image, your iPod touch or iPhone displays the Move and Scale screen, which lets you optionally pan the image by dragging your finger, and optionally zoom in or out of the image by pinching and unpinching with your fingers. Tap the Set Wallpaper button to set the image as your wallpaper or tap Cancel to cancel.

To set the brightness level on an iPod nano, choose Settings⇨General⇨Brightness; on an iPod classic, choose Settings⇨ Brightness. You can then scroll the click wheel clockwise to increase brightness, or counter-clockwise to decrease brightness.

Sound effects and fonts

Don't want to hear the iPod touch or iPhone keyboard click as you type, or the snap noise as you swipe your finger over the "unlock" message? You can set which events can trigger sound effects as well as the volume of the sound effect. Choose Settings⇨General⇨Sounds from the Home screen. You can then turn the alert on or off and click sounds for new mail, sent mail, calendar alerts, locking and unlocking, and using the on-screen keyboard. Tap On to turn off each option or vice versa.

The click wheel of an iPod nano makes a clicking sound you can hear through headphones or the tiny speaker. On an iPod classic, you can hear the click wheel sound only through the tiny speaker.

You can turn the click wheel sound off with an iPod classic by choosing Settings from the main menu, or in an iPod nano by choosing Settings⇨General, and then selecting Clicker once so that Off appears next to it on the right. Selecting Clicker again turns it back on.

You can change the click wheel sound with an iPod nano so that you can hear it on your headphones only, on the tiny speaker only, both, or not at all. Choose Settings⇨General and then select Clicker once to cycle through its settings one at a time: Off, Speaker, Headphones, or Both.

The iPod nano can display its menu text in two different font sizes: standard and large. To set the font size, choose Settings⇨General⇨Font Size and then select Standard or Large.

You can set the minimum font size for Mail messages with an iPod touch or iPhone to increase readability — for details on Mail message settings, see Chapter 20.

Location, location, location

Perhaps nothing is more personal than your physical location. With Location Services, iPod touch and iPhone apps like Maps (and lots of third-party apps like Showtimes, Eventful, WhosHere, Loopt, and various travel apps) can grab this physical location information and use it to help you find things closer to you. For example, the Maps app can find your location on the map, which is very useful for getting directions (see Chapter 21).

An iPhone can tell you where you are in the physical world with the utmost precision. The iPhone 3G and iPhone 3GS offer the Global Positioning System (GPS), which uses orbiting satellites to pinpoint your location in a range of 10 to 100 meters. The earlier-model iPhone and the iPod touch can triangulate their location with scary precision as well, even though these models don't offer GPS — they leverage the most extensive Wi-Fi reference database in the world. You need to be connected to Wi-Fi to use Location Services on an iPod touch (see the section "Going Online with your iPod touch or iPhone," later in this chapter).

You can turn Location Services on or off by choosing Settings⇨General from the Home screen and then tapping the Off button for Location Services to turn it on, or the On button to turn it off.

After turning it off, your iPod touch or iPhone prompts you to turn it back on if you run an app that makes use of Location Services (such as Maps).

To conserve battery power, turn off Location Services if you aren't using applications that make use of it.

Setting restrictions on an iPod touch or iPhone

If you need to, you can set restrictions for an iPod touch or iPhone that

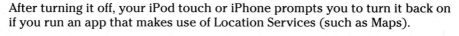

- ✔ Prevent explicit music from the iTunes Store from being displayed in playlists
- ✔ Prevent the use of apps such as YouTube
- ✔ Stop access to the iTunes Store or App Store

Choose Settings⇨General from the Home screen and then tap Restrictions to see the Restrictions screen. Tap Enable Restrictions and then set up a restrictions passcode (which is separate from your Passcode Lock passcode). Enter a four-number passcode by touching numbers on the calculator-style keypad. (If you change your mind, tap the Cancel button to cancel the operation.) Then enter the same passcode number again to confirm the passcode, and the restrictions are enabled and appear ready for you to change.

Set the restrictions you want by tapping each control's On switch to turn it off. By default, all controls are on, which means that usage is allowed (not restricted). Turn off a control to restrict its use.

If you restrict access to Safari, YouTube, the Camera (on an iPhone), the iTunes Store, and/or the App Store (for installing apps), those icons are removed from the Home screen so that they can't be accessed. If you turn off Location, location data is no longer provided to applications. Restricted content does not appear when accessing the iTunes Store. To access the icons and the restricted content, you need to turn off the restrictions first (or turn off all restrictions).

To turn off all restrictions, choose Settings⇨General⇨Restrictions and then enter the passcode. Tap Disable Restrictions and then reenter the passcode. Your iPod touch or iPhone is now free. Be careful out there!

Going Online with your iPod touch or iPhone

To surf the Web, check e-mail, or use the iTunes Store or App Store (or any other app that uses the Internet) on your iPod touch or iPhone — or to use Location Services on your iPod touch or earlier-model iPhone — you must first join a Wi-Fi network that's connected to the Internet.

An iPod touch or iPhone can join Wi-Fi networks at home, at work, or at Wi-Fi hotspots around the world. Although some public Wi-Fi networks are free, others require logging in first, and still others require logging in and supplying a credit card number. Still others are detected but locked — if you select a locked network, a dialog appears asking for a password.

If you don't have Wi-Fi at home but you do have a broadband Internet connection (such as cable or DSL), I recommend buying an AirPort Express or AirPort Extreme, available in the Apple Store — you can then connect your Internet connection to the AirPort to extend Internet access over Wi-Fi. AirPort Express is powerful enough to run a home Wi-Fi network yet portable enough to take on the road and use in hotel rooms that offer Internet connections, and it even plays music from your iTunes library through speakers connected to it. AirPort Extreme offers a stronger antenna for greater range, and lets up to 50 users connect to Wi-Fi at once, with shared printing and storage and Ethernet connections — perfect for a large family or small business. You can give your network a unique name, which appears in the list of networks on your iPod touch or iPhone when it is in range of the network.

Turning Wi-Fi on or off

To turn Wi-Fi on, choose Settings⇨Wi-Fi from the Home screen to display the Wi-Fi Networks screen. Tap the Off button for the Wi-Fi setting to turn it on (tap it again to turn it off).

When Wi-Fi is turned on, your iPod touch or iPhone detects and automatically acquires a Wi-Fi signal you've used before, or it can detect one or more signals in the area and present them in a list for you to choose. The list of available Wi-Fi networks appears below the Wi-Fi setting, as shown in Figure 4-5.

If your iPod touch or iPhone isn't already connected to Wi-Fi, it's set by default to look for networks and ask whether you want to join them whenever you use something that requires the network (such as Safari, Weather, YouTube, Mail, and so on). You can stop your iPod touch or iPhone from looking and asking: Scroll down to the end of the list of Wi-Fi networks on the Wi-Fi Networks screen and then tap the On button for the Ask to Join Networks option to turn it off. You can still join networks manually, but you won't be interrupted with requests to join networks.

You should turn off Wi-Fi if you're not using it to save battery power and to keep your iPhone or iPod touch from automatically receiving e-mail. Choose Settings⇨Wi-Fi and then tap the On button for the Wi-Fi setting to turn it off.

Choosing a Wi-Fi network

You can scroll the list of networks on the Wi-Fi Networks screen to choose one. (Refer to Figure 4-5.) You can scroll quickly by flicking your finger or scroll slowly by dragging up or down, but however you scroll, you choose a Wi-Fi network by tapping its name. Networks are named by their administrators. (If you set up your own home Wi-Fi, you get to name yours whatever you want.)

When connected to a Wi-Fi network, your iPod touch or iPhone displays the Wi-Fi icon in the status bar at the top of the display. This also indicates the connection strength — the more arcs you see in the icon, the stronger the connection.

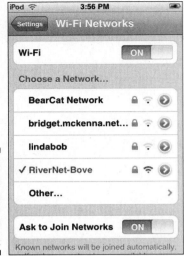

Figure 4-5:
Enable Wi-Fi
and then
choose a
Wi-Fi
network.

If a Lock icon appears next to the Wi-Fi network name (refer to Figure 4-5), it means that the network is locked and you need a password. When you select a locked network, the iPod touch or iPhone displays an Enter Password screen and the on-screen keyboard. Tap out the password using the keyboard. (For details on how to use the on-screen keyboard, see Chapter 3.) Tap Join to join the network or tap Cancel in the upper-right corner to cancel joining.

To join a Wi-Fi network that requires either a credit card or an account for you to log into, select the network and then use Safari to open the network's Web page. (For more on using Safari, see Chapter 19.) The first Web page you see is typically the login page for the service (for example, a commercial Wi-Fi service or a hotel service). Follow the instructions in Chapter 19 for interacting with Web pages.

Your iPod touch or iPhone remembers your Wi-Fi connections and automatically uses one when it detects it within your range. If you've used multiple Wi-Fi networks in the same location, it picks the last one you used.

You can also stop your iPod touch or iPhone from automatically joining a Wi-Fi network — such as a paid or closed Wi-Fi service that somehow got hold of your iPod touch or iPhone and won't let you move on to other Web pages without typing a password. See Chapter 23 for this tip.

Chapter 5

Going Mobile

In This Chapter

▶ Connecting headphones and using portable speakers

▶ Using adapters and mounts to play your iPod or iPhone in a car

▶ Using an integrated iPod/iPhone car stereo interface

▶ Playing your iPod or iPhone on FM radios by using wireless adapters

▶ Protecting your iPod or iPhone with carrying cases

▶ Using power accessories on the road

*P*ut on "Eight Miles High" by the Byrds while cruising in a plane at 40,000 feet. Watch the "Lust for Life" music video by Iggy Pop on a bus heading out of Detroit. Ride the rails listening to "All Aboard" by Muddy Waters, followed by "Peavine" by John Lee Hooker. Or cruise on the autobahn in Germany with Kraftwerk. When you go mobile with your iPod or iPhone, it provides high-quality sound and excellent picture quality no matter how turbulent the environment.

If you can't plug your iPod or iPhone into a power source while it's playing, you can use the battery for quite a while before having to recharge. You can find all the accessories that you need to travel with an iPod or iPhone in the Apple Store at www.apple.com. This chapter is all about using your iPod or iPhone on the road with accessories.

Connecting Headphones and Portable Speakers

Apple designed the iPod and iPhone to provide excellent sound through headphones. From the headphone/line-out connection, though, the iPod or iPhone can also play music through portable speaker systems. The speaker systems must be self-powered or able to work with very little power (just like headphones do) and allow audio to be input via a 3.5mm, stereo mini-plug connection.

Looking at specs, you'll notice that iPod and iPhone models include a small amplifier that's plenty powerful enough to deliver audio through the headphone/line-out connection. All current models, including the iPod shuffle, have a frequency response of 20 to 20,000 Hz (hertz), which provides distortion-free music at the lowest or highest pitches. (In this case, hertz has nothing to do with rental cars. A *hertz* is a unit of frequency equal to one cycle per second.) At pitches that produce frequencies of 20 cycles per second or 20,000 cycles per second (and everything in between), the iPod or iPhone responds with distortion-free sound.

If headphones aren't your thing, you can even wear an iPod shuffle inside a headband (and keep it relatively dry no matter how much you, um, create your own moisture). Thanko (`http://thanko.jp/voniasports`) offers the Vonia sports headband that uses *bone conduction* — a hearing aid technology that conducts "Good Vibrations" through the bones of your skull, directly into your inner ear. The sound can be surprisingly clear and crisp, although it won't be in stereo because the sound seems to come from inside your head.

Portable speaker systems typically include built-in amplifiers and a volume control, and they usually offer a stereo mini-plug that you can attach directly to the iPod or iPhone headphone/line-out connection or to a dock headphone/line-out connection. Some portable speaker systems, such as the DLO Portable Speakers from DLO (`www.dlo.com`), or the Bose SoundDock Portable digital music system (`www.bose.com`, see Figure 5-1), provide a convenient dock connection for playing audio. To place the external speakers farther away from the iPod or iPhone, use a stereo mini-plug extension cable, which is available at most consumer electronics stores. These cables have a stereo mini-plug on one end and a stereo mini-socket on the other.

Figure 5-1:
The Bose SoundDock Portable speaker system.

When using a portable speaker system equipped with volume controls, set your iPod or iPhone volume to about half or three-quarters and then raise or lower the volume of your speaker system.

When you travel, take an extra pair of headphones (or earbuds) and a splitter cable, which are available in any consumer electronics store. The Monster iSplitter is available in the Apple Store. That way, you can share music with someone on the road.

For a portable stereo system that offers big sound on a rechargeable battery and is perfect for environments like the beach or a boat, check out the i-P23 speaker systems from Sonic Impact (www.si5.com). It includes universal adapters for all dockable iPod and iPhone models, and an audio input connection for connecting your computer or an audio player. The double-duty case is a durable cover that acts as a speaker cabinet for both speakers, to give the speakers better bass response.

Playing Car Tunes

I always wanted to be able to fill up a car with music just as easily as filling it up with fuel, without having to carry dozens of cassettes or CDs. With an iPod or iPhone, an auto-charger to save on battery power, and a way to connect the iPod or iPhone to your car's stereo system, you're ready to pump music. (Start your engine and queue up "Getting in Tune" and then "Going Mobile" by The Who.) You can even go one step further and get a new BMW, Toyota, or similarly equipped car that offers an iPod or iPhone dock cable installed and integrated into the car's stereo system so that you can control the iPod or iPhone from your car stereo — including handy controls on the steering wheel.

Here are your options when it comes to linking your iPod or iPhone to a car stereo:

- ✔ **Use your cassette player.** Use a standard cassette adapter and an iPod power adapter for your car's lighter socket. This method works even with rental cars (as long as they're supplied with cassette players). For a semipermanent installation, you can add a car mount to keep your iPod or iPhone secure. Cassette adapters offer medium quality that's usually better than wireless adapters.

- ✔ **Buy or lease a car that offers an iPod-ready stereo or AUX input.** BMW, Mercedes-Benz, Toyota, Honda, and many other auto companies offer models that are iPod-ready, and you can use your iPhone with them and control the iPod or iPhone from your car stereo's head unit.

This method offers the best sound quality. Some offer a connector for the iPod or iPhone that uses the dock connection, whereas others offer AUX (auxiliary) line-in audio input — you can connect a mini-plug cable directly to the iPod or iPhone headphone connection and then to the AUX input. You can then get a power adapter for your car's lighter socket, or plug directly into a 110-volt socket if your vehicle offers one.

✔ **Use your radio and a wireless adapter.** Use a wireless adapter that plays your iPod or iPhone as if it were a station on your FM radio dial. Some car mounts offer built-in wireless adapters. This might be your only inexpensive choice if you don't have a cassette deck. *Note:* Wireless adapters might not work well in cities where FM stations crowd the radio dial.

✔ **Install an iPod/iPhone interface.** Install an iPod or iPhone interface for your car stereo that offers high-quality, line-in audio input and power. After you install this interface, thread the iPod/iPhone dock cable into the glove box so that you can plug the cable into your iPod or iPhone, hide the iPod or iPhone in the glove box, and control the iPod or iPhone from your car stereo's head unit. Toyota offers an integration kit for plugging an iPod into the car glove box and using either the steering wheel or usual audio system controls.

Using cassette and power adapters for your car

Until you get an iPod-ready car, a car stereo with a mini-socket for AUX (auxiliary) line-in audio input (also called a *stereo-in connection*), or an iPod connection — or get one installed — you can use a cassette-player adapter to connect with your car stereo. (I describe wireless connectivity later, in the section "Connecting by Wireless Radio.") These wireless connectivity solutions provide lower sound quality than iPod interface installations or stereo-in connections but are inexpensive and work with most cars.

Many car stereos have a cassette player, and you can buy a cassette adapter — the Sony CPA-9C Car Cassette Adapter, for example — from most consumer electronics stores. The cassette-player adapter looks like a tape cassette with a mini-plug cable (which sticks out through the slot when you're using the adapter). Adapters work with most front-loading and side-loading cassette decks — it's the same shape as a cassette — as long as the cable doesn't prevent its loading.

First connect the mini-plug cable directly to the iPod or iPhone headphone connection. Then insert the adapter into the cassette player, being careful not to get the cable tangled inside the player.

One inherent problem with this approach is that the cable that dangles from your cassette player looks unsightly. You also might have some trouble ejecting the adapter if the cable gets wedged in the cassette-player door. Overall, though, this method is the best for most cars because it provides better sound quality than most wireless methods.

Although some new vehicles (particularly SUVs and cars such as the Toyota Matrix mini–station wagon) offer 110-volt power outlets you can use with your Apple-supplied battery charger, most cars offer only a lighter/power socket that requires a power adapter to use with your iPod or iPhone. Be careful to pick the right type of power adapter for your car's lighter/power socket.

Belkin (www.belkin.com) offers the Auto Kit for $39.99, and it includes a car power adapter with a convenient socket for a stereo mini-plug cable (which can connect directly to a car stereo if the stereo has a mini-socket for audio input). The adapter includes a volume-adjustable amplifier to boost the sound coming from the iPod or iPhone before it goes into the cassette adapter or car stereo. If you don't need the extra volume control, you can get a less expensive car power adapter, the Mobile Power Cord for iPod, for $19.99 from Belkin.

Even with a cassette adapter and power adapter, you have at best a clumsy solution that uses one cable (power) from a power adapter to the iPod or iPhone, and another cable (audio) to your car stereo cassette adapter. Attached to these wires, your iPod or iPhone needs a secure place to sit while your car moves because you don't want it bouncing around.

You can fit your iPod or iPhone securely in position in a car without getting a custom installation. The TuneDok ($29.99) from Belkin (www.belkin.com) holds your iPod or iPhone securely and fits into your car's cup holder. The TuneDok ratcheting neck and height-adjustment feature lets you reposition the iPod or iPhone to your liking. The cable-management clip eliminates loose and tangled cables, and the large and small rubber base and cup fit most cup holders.

MARWARE (www.marware.com) offers an inexpensive solution for both car use and personal use. The $6 Car Holder attaches to the dashboard of your car and lets you attach an iPod or iPhone that's wearing one of the MARWARE Sportsuit covering cases. (See the section "Dressing Up Your iPod and iPhone for Travel," later in this chapter.) The clip on the back attaches to the Car Holder.

ProClip (www.proclipusa.com) offers mounting brackets for clip-on devices. The brackets attach to the dashboard, and you can install them in seconds. After you install the bracket, you can use different custom holders for the iPod or iPhone models or for cell phones and other portable devices.

Integrating an iPod or iPhone with your car stereo

Premium car manufacturers are introducing cars that are *iPod-ready*, including an iPod interface for the car stereo system that uses the dock connector cable that's compatible with all iPod and iPhone models. For example, BMW offers such a model with audio controls on the steering wheel. Mercedes-Benz, Volvo, MINI Cooper, Nissan, Alfa Romeo, and Ferrari all also offer iPod-ready models. In addition, car stereo manufacturers (such as Alpine and Clarion) offer car audio systems with integrated iPod interfaces; see Figure 5-2.

Figure 5-2:
An iPod-integrated car stereo installation.

If you can't afford an iPod-ready car, you can opt for a custom installation of an iPod interface for your existing car stereo and car power (such as using a custom cable interface for a CD changer, which a skilled car audio specialist can install in your dashboard). For example, Dension (www.dension.com) offers the Gateway series of products for controlling iPod and iPhone models and auxiliary devices in a car.

Connecting by Wireless Radio

A wireless music adapter lets you play music from your iPod or iPhone on an FM radio with no connection or cable. However, the sound quality might suffer a bit from radio interference. I always take a wireless adapter with me whenever I rent a car because even if a rental car has no cassette player (ruling out the use of my cassette adapter), it probably has an FM radio.

You can use a wireless adapter in a car, on a boat, or even on the beach with a portable radio. I even use it in hotel rooms with a clock radio.

To use a wireless adapter, follow these steps:

1. **Set the wireless adapter to an unused FM radio frequency.**

   Some adapters offer only one frequency (typically 87.9 MHz). Others offer you a choice of several frequencies: typically 88.1, 88.3, 88.5, and 88.7 MHz. Some even let you pick any FM frequency. If given a choice, choose the frequency and set the adapter according to its instructions. Be sure to pick an unused frequency — a frequency that's being used by an FM station in range of your radio is sure to interfere with your iPod signal.

2. **Connect the wireless adapter to the iPod or iPhone headphone/line-out connector or to the line-out connector on an iPod car dock.**

   The wireless adapter acts like a miniature radio station, broadcasting to a nearby FM radio. (Sorry, you can't go much farther than a few feet, so no one else can hear your Wolfman Jack impersonation.)

3. **Tune to the appropriate frequency on the FM dial.**

   Tune any nearby radio to the same FM frequency that you chose in Step 1.

You need to set the adapter close enough to the radio's antenna to work, making it impractical for home stereos. You can get better-quality sound by connecting to a home stereo with a cable.

Don't be surprised if the wireless adapter doesn't work as well in cities — other radio stations might cause too much interference.

Here are a few wireless adapters I have no trouble recommending:

- ✔ **TRAFFICJamz** ($19.99) from Newer Technology (www.newertech.com) is both a charger and a transmitter that works with all model iPods.
- ✔ **iTrip family of FM transmitters,** including iTrip Auto SmartScan ($59.99) from Griffin Technology (www.griffintechnology.com), which automatically finds the three clearest frequencies wherever you are and saves them for you as presets.

- ✔ **TuneCast Auto with ClearScan for iPhone and iPod** ($79.99) from Belkin (www.belkin.com) quickly scans and finds the best FM frequency with one push of a button.

- ✔ **Monster iCarPlay Wireless** ($79.95) from Monster Cable (www.monster cable.com) offers a power adapter as well as excellent-quality playback for a wireless radio unit. You can select radio frequencies of 88.1, 88.3, 88.5, 88.7, 88.9, 89.1, 89.3, or 89.5 MHz. Although a bit more expensive, I prefer it for its sound quality.

- ✔ **TransDock micro with IntelliTune** ($69.99) from Digital Lifestyle Outfitters (www.dlo.com) scans for open FM frequencies automatically and sports a cool dial for adjusting your settings and manually tuning the frequency.

Dressing Up Your iPod and iPhone for Travel

The simple protective carrying cases supplied with some iPod and iPhone models just aren't as stylin' as the myriad accessories that you can get for dressing up your iPods and iPhones for travel. You can find different types of protective gear — from leather jackets to aluminum cases — in many different styles and colors. Apple offers access to hundreds of products from other suppliers on its Accessories page (www.apple.com/ipod/accessories.html) — follow the "Shop" links to go directly to Apple's online store to view product details and make purchases. Some are designed primarily for protecting your iPod or iPhone from harm; others are designed to provide some measure of protection while also providing access to controls.

On the extreme end of the spectrum are hardened cases that are ready for battlefields in deserts or jungles — the Humvees of iPod protective gear, if you will. Matias Corporation (http://matias.ca/armor) offers versions of the sturdy Matias Armor case ($29.95) for each iPod and iPhone model, which offers possibly the best protection against physical trauma on the market. Your iPod or iPhone rests within a hard, resilient metal exoskeleton that can withstand the abuse of bouncing down a flight of metal stairs without letting your iPod or iPhone pop out.

Business travelers can combine personal items into one carrying case. The Leather Folio ($29.99) cases from Belkin (www.belkin.com) for iPod classic and iPod touch models are made from fine-grain leather that even Ricardo Montalban would rave about. The cases can also hold personal essentials, such as business and credit cards. The HipCase cases ($29.99) from DLO (www.dlo.com) let you stash credit cards and other essentials along with your iPod, and the HipCase includes a sturdy, leather-covered belt clip.

On the sporty side, MARWARE (www.marware.com) offers the Sportsuit Convertible cases ($12.99) for iPod and iPhone models, with a patented belt-clip system, offering interchangeable clip options for use with the MARWARE Car Holder or with an armband or belt. The neoprene case has vulcanized rubber grips on each side and bottom for a no-slip grip as well as plastic inserts for impact protection, offering full access to all the device's controls and connections while it's in the case.

Using Power Accessories

If you want to charge your iPod or iPhone battery when you travel abroad, you can't count on finding the same voltage that exists in your home country. However, you still need to use your Apple power adapter, or your computer, to recharge your iPod or iPhone — basically, you need to plug something into some outlet somewhere. Fortunately, power converters for different voltages and plugs for different outlets are available in most airport gift shops, but the worldly traveler might want to consider saving time and money by getting a travel kit of power accessories from the Apple Store or from a consumer electronics store.

I found several varieties of power converter kits for world travel in my local international airport, but they were pricey — check your local Radio Shack or consumer electronics store first, or try Amazon.com. Most kits include a set of AC plugs with prongs that fit different electrical outlets around the world. You can connect the Apple power adapter for iPod and iPhone to these adapters. The AC plugs typically support outlets in North America, Japan, China, the United Kingdom, Continental Europe, Korea, Australia, and Hong Kong. You should also include at least one power accessory for use with a standard car lighter, such as car chargers from Belkin (www.belkin.com), Kensington (www.kensington.com), or Newer Technology (www.newertech.com).

One way to mitigate the battery blues is to get an accessory that lets you use replaceable alkaline batteries — the kind that you can find in any convenience store — in a pinch. The TunePower Rechargeable Battery Pack for iPod ($79.99) from Belkin (www.belkin.com) lets you power an iPod Classic or older-model iPod with standard AA alkaline replaceable batteries even when your internal iPod battery is drained.

The mophie Juice Pack Air Case and Rechargeable Battery for iPhone 3G ($79.95, available in the Apple Store) is a unique power accessory that doubles as an iPhone hard-shell case. With its rechargeable external battery concealed inside the protective form-fitting case, it drains its own battery before it moves on to the one in your iPhone, conserving your iPhone battery power.

Part II

Filling Up Your Empty Cup

The 5th Wave   By Rich Tennant

JERRY AND LYLE ATTEMPT TO LOAD THE NEWEST VERSION OF "TOAST," CD BURNING SOFTWARE

Okay, I've got the Sunbeam firewired to the iMac. Try putting the CD in the slot again.

In this part . . .

Part II shows you how to how to fill up your iPod or iPhone with extreme content and killer apps using iTunes.

- Chapter 6 gets you started with iTunes on a Mac or Windows PC.

- Chapter 7 covers the online iTunes Store. You set yourself up with an account and then download music, videos, TV shows, movies, podcasts, and audio books, as well as applications for the iPod touch or iPhone. You also find out how to download tunes and applications directly to your iPod touch or iPhone.

- Chapter 8 describes how to get music, audio books, videos, and podcasts into your iTunes library from other sources, including CDs and the Internet.

- Chapter 9 describes synchronizing your iPod, iPhone, or iPod shuffle with your iTunes library, as well as how to manually manage the contents of an iPod, iPod shuffle, or iPhone.

- Chapter 10 describes automatically synchronizing your iPod or iPhone with calendars and contacts using iTunes and MobileMe. It also covers managing and synchronizing e-mail accounts on your iPod touch or iPhone.

Chapter 6

Getting Started with iTunes

In This Chapter

▶ Finding out what you can do with iTunes

▶ Playing music tracks on a CD

▶ Skipping and repeating music tracks

▶ Displaying visuals while playing music

▶ Getting suggestions from the Genius sidebar

More than half a century ago, jukeboxes were the primary and most convenient way for people to select the music they wanted to hear and share with others, especially newly released music. Juke joints were hopping with the newest hits every night. You could pick any song to play at any time, but you had to insert a coin and pay for each play. Radio eventually supplanted the jukebox as the primary means of releasing new music to the public, and the music was free to hear — but you couldn't choose to play any song you wanted at any time.

Today, using iTunes, you not only have a digital jukebox *and* a radio in your computer, but you also have online access to millions of songs, with most songs available for download for 99 cents each and entire albums available for download at less than the list price of a CD.

Connect your computer to a stereo amplifier in your home (through wires or Apple TV), or connect speakers to your computer, and suddenly your computer is the best jukebox in the neighborhood. Connect your computer to a television, and you have a full multimedia environment in your home, all controlled by iTunes. And after you've organized your content in iTunes, you can put it all on your iPod or iPhone to carry your jukebox with you.

This chapter gives you an overview of what you can do with iTunes, and you get started in the simplest way possible: using iTunes to play music tracks on a CD. You can use iTunes just like a jukebox, only better — you don't have to pay for each song you play, and you can play some of or all the songs on an album in any order.

What You Can Do with iTunes

You can download songs or entire albums, audio books, TV shows, movies, and other videos from the iTunes Store directly into your iTunes library (as I describe in Chapter 7), or you can copy these items from other sources (including audio CDs) into your iTunes library (as I describe in Chapter 8). You can also subscribe to *podcasts* that transfer audio or audio/video episodes, such as weekly broadcasts, automatically to your iTunes library from the Internet or through the iTunes Store. You can even use iTunes to listen to Web radio stations and add your favorite stations to your music library. After you store the content in your iTunes library, you can play it on your computer and transfer it to iPod, Apple TV, and iPhone models. You can also use your computer to burn the audio content onto an audio CD or copy audio and video files onto other hard drives or DVD data discs as backups.

Transferring songs from a CD to your computer is referred to as *ripping* a CD (to the chagrin of the music industry old-timers who think that users intend to rip off music without paying for it). Ripping an entire CD's worth of songs is quick and easy, and track information, such as artist name and title, arrives automatically over the Internet for most commercial CDs. (You can add the information yourself for rare CDs, custom-mix CDs, live CDs, and others that are unknown to the database.)

You can also add video files to your iTunes library in a couple of ways: by choosing content from the iTunes Store (such as TV shows, feature-length high-definition movies, music videos, and even free movie trailers) or by downloading standard video files in the MPEG-4 format from other sources on the Internet. You can also create your own videos with a digital camcorder (or cameras built into computers, such as the iSight camera included with MacBooks) and copy them to iTunes.

Although you can't use iTunes to transfer video content from a DVD, you can use other software to convert DVDs to digital video files, and you can transfer video content from older VHS players. Visit the Tips section of the author's Web site at www.tonybove.com for more info.

As if that weren't enough, iTunes gives you the power to organize content into playlists, as I describe in Chapter 14. (You can even set up dynamic, smart playlists that reflect your preferences and listening habits.) iTunes even has a built-in equalizer with preset settings for all kinds of music and listening environments, with the added bonus of being able to customize and save your own personalized settings with each item of content.

The Mac and Windows versions of iTunes are virtually identical, with the exception that dialogs and icons look a bit different between the two operating systems. You also find a few other differences, mostly related to the different operating environments. The Windows version lets you import unprotected Windows Media (WMA) songs; the Mac version, like most Mac applications, can be controlled by AppleScript programs and Automator workflows. Nevertheless, as Apple continues to improve iTunes, the company releases upgrades to both versions at the same time, and the versions are free to download.

Opening the iTunes Window

You can run iTunes anytime (with or without an iPod, iPhone, or Apple TV) to build and manage your library of music, audio books, podcasts, Web radio stations, TV shows, and other videos. You don't have to connect your iPod or iPhone until you're ready to transfer content to it (as I describe in Chapter 9).

When you launch iTunes, your library and other sources of content appear. Figure 6-1 shows the iTunes window on a PC running Windows, showing the Column Browser (to browse by artist) and the Artwork Column (to show album covers). You can also click the column headings in the List pane to sort your library by artist, album title, or any of the other view options.

The Mac and Windows versions of iTunes offer the same functions and viewing options, including the *cover browser* (also known as Cover Flow). Figure 6-2 shows the iTunes window on the Mac with the cover browser open, displaying the cover art for albums. Both versions also offer the Genius Sidebar (shown in Figure 6-1, but hidden in Figure 6-2) and the Speakers pop-up menu for choosing a speaker system.

iTunes offers multiple views of your library and your sources for content, as well as controls for organizing, importing, and playing content, as follows:

✔ **Source pane:** Displays the source of your content, handily divided into the following sections:

• *Library:* Includes your music, movies, TV shows, podcasts, audio books, applications and games, ringtones, and all available radio stations.

• *Store:* Includes the iTunes Store and your Purchased or Downloads list (if you've purchased items or have recently downloaded items).

• *Devices:* Includes audio CDs and any iPods (such as *Mojo iTouch* in Figure 6-1), iPhones, and Apple TV devices (such as TB's Apple TV in Figure 6-2) that are connected to your computer.

• *Eject button:* This button appears next to the name of an audio CD, iPod, or iPhone in the Source pane. Clicking the Eject button, um, *ejects* a CD or an iPod or iPhone. However, whereas a CD actually pops out of some computers, iPods and iPhones act like hard drives, and ejecting them simply removes *(unmounts)* the drives from the system so that you can disconnect them.

- *Shared*: Includes iTunes libraries on your home network that you can share iTunes Store content with, as I describe in Chapter 7.

- *Genius*: Includes Genius mixes and your Genius playlists, which I describe in Chapter 14.

- *Playlists:* Includes the automatic tune-selector iTunes DJ (see Chapter 13 for details) and the Genius and your own playlists (see Chapter 14 for more info).

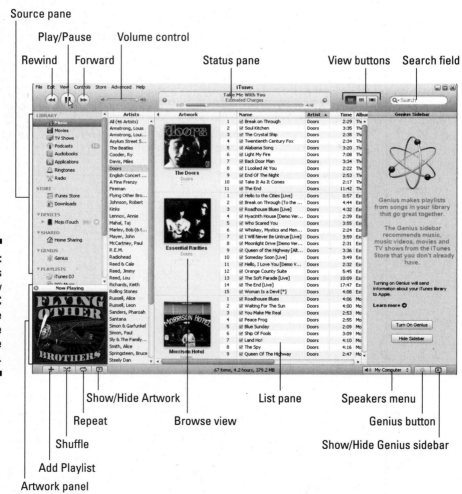

Figure 6-1:
The iTunes window on a PC showing the List pane in Browse view.

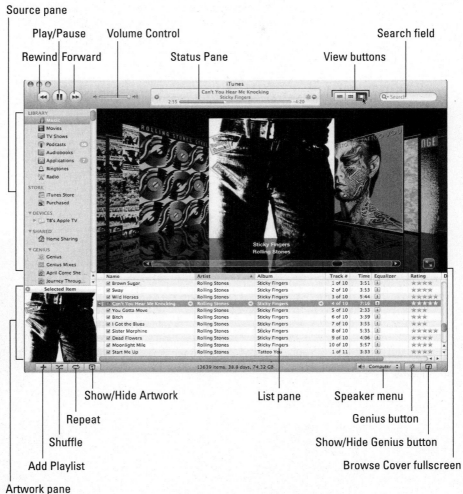

Source pane

Play/Pause   Volume Control

Rewind Forward   Status Pane   View buttons   Search field

Figure 6-2:
The iTunes
window on
a Mac with
the cover
browser
open.

Show/Hide Artwork   List pane   Speaker menu

Repeat   Genius button

Shuffle   Show/Hide Genius button

Add Playlist   Browse Cover fullscreen

Artwork pane

✔ **Cover browser:** Also called Cover Flow, the cover browser lets you flip through your cover art to choose songs. (Refer to Figure 6-2.) You can use the slider to move swiftly through your library, or you can click to the right or left of the cover in the foreground to step forward or backward in your library.

✔ **List pane:** Depending on the source that's selected in the Source pane under Library, Store, Devices, Shared, Genius, or Playlists, the List pane (refer to Figure 6-1) displays the content from that source. For example, choosing an iPod in the Devices section displays the iPod content in the List pane, while choosing Music in the Library section displays the music in your iTunes library.

- ✔ **Column Browser and Artwork Column:** To see these views, click the leftmost View button for List view (refer to Figure 6-1) and then choose either View⇨Show Column Browser or View⇨Show Artwork Column. To hide the Artwork Column, click the tiny left arrow to the left of the Artwork Column heading or choose View⇨Hide Artwork Column; to hide the Column Browser, choose View⇨>Hide Column Browser.

- ✔ **View buttons:** The three buttons near the upper-right corner change your view of the List pane to show items in a list, cover art thumbnail images in a grid, or the cover browser.

- ✔ **Search field:** Type in this field to search your library. You can also use the Search field to peruse a playlist or to look within the iTunes Store.

- ✔ **Status pane:** When content is playing, you can see the artist name, piece title (if known), and the elapsed time displayed in this pane. When synchronizing, you see a progress bar. If more than one operation is happening at the same time (such as playing music and synchronizing), you can see either status display by clicking the tiny right arrow in the status pane.

- ✔ **Player buttons — Forward/Next, Play/Pause, and Previous/Rewind:** Use these buttons to control the playback of content in iTunes.

- ✔ **Volume control:** You can change the volume level in iTunes by dragging the volume control slider in the upper-left section of the iTunes window to the right to increase the volume or to the left to decrease it. The maximum volume of the iTunes volume slider is the maximum set for the computer's sound, which you set separately. See Chapter 13 for more about setting volume levels on your computer.

- ✔ **Playlist buttons — Add, Shuffle, Repeat:** Use these buttons to add playlists, and randomly shuffle or repeat playback of playlists.

- ✔ **Show/Hide Artwork button:** Use this button to display or hide artwork (either your own or the artwork supplied with purchased songs and videos).

- ✔ **Speakers pop-up menu:** Use this pop-up menu near the lower-right corner of the iTunes window to select a different speaker system than the computer's speakers (see Chapter 6). This pop-up menu appears only if you choose Preferences (from the iTunes menu on a Mac or the Edit menu in Windows), click the Devices tab, and turn on the Look for Remote Speakers Connected with AirTunes option. If iTunes locates such speakers, the pop-up menu appears.

- ✔ **Genius button:** The Genius button, located in the lower-right corner of the iTunes window to the left of the Show/Hide Genius Sidebar button, generates a Genius playlist of songs from your library that go great with the song you selected. The Genius button appears gray unless you have selected a song — see Chapter 14 for details. After clicking the Genius button, the Genius playlist appears and is automatically selected in the Source pane in the Playlists section.

✔ **Show/Hide Genius Sidebar button:** Use this button to display or hide the Genius Sidebar.

✔ **Genius Sidebar:** The Genius Sidebar (refer to Figure 6-1) makes suggestions for what to get from the iTunes Store based on what you've selected. You have obligation to buy anything, and you can dispense with it if it bothers you — you can open or close the Genius Sidebar by clicking the boxed-arrow Show/Hide Genius Sidebar button in the lower-right corner of the iTunes window. (See the section "Using the iTunes Genius Sidebar," later in this chapter, for details.)

If you don't like the width of the Source pane, you can adjust it by dragging the vertical bar between the Source and List panes. You can also adjust the horizontal bar between the song listing in the List pane and the Column Browser. To resize the iTunes window on a Mac, drag diagonally from the lower-right corner. In Windows, drag the edges of the window horizontally or vertically.

Playing CD Tracks in iTunes

iTunes needs content. You can get started right away by ripping music from CDs into your library, as I describe in Chapter 8. For more instant gratification, though, you can play music right off the CD without importing it. Maybe you don't want to put the music into your library. Maybe you just want to hear it first, as part of your Play First, Rip Later plan.

To play a CD, insert any music CD — or even a CD-R that someone burned for you — into your computer. After you insert the CD, iTunes displays a dialog that asks whether you want to import the CD into your library right now — you can click the Yes button to import now or the No button to do nothing yet. Click No for now.

If you're connected to the Internet, iTunes accesses the Gracenote CDDB for song information while you are answering the import question so that after you click Yes or No, iTunes presents the track information for each song automatically, as shown in Figure 6-3. (*Gracenote CDDB* is a song database on the Internet that knows the track names of most commercial CDs but not those of homemade mix CDs. You can read about Gracenote CDDB and editing song information in Chapter 12.)

When you play a CD in iTunes, it's just like using a CD player. To play a CD from the first track, click the Play button. (If you clicked somewhere else after inserting the disc, you might have to click the first track to select it before clicking the Play button.) The Play button then turns into a Pause button, and the song plays.

Figure 6-3:
CD track
info appears
after iTunes
consults the
Internet.

When the song finishes, iTunes continues playing the songs in the list in sequence until you click the Pause button (which then toggles back into the Play button) or until the song list ends. You can skip to the next or previous song by using the arrow keys on your keyboard or by clicking the Forward button or the Back button (next to the Play button). You can also double-click another song in the list to start playing it.

You can press the spacebar to perform the same function as clicking the Play button; pressing it again is just like clicking the Pause button.

The Status pane above the list of songs tells you the name of the artist and the song title as well as the elapsed time of the track. When you click the artist name, the artist name is replaced by the album name. The time on the left of the slider is the elapsed time; the time on the right is the duration of the song. When you click the duration, it changes to the remaining time; click it again to return to the song's duration.

Eject a CD by clicking the Eject icon next to the CD name in the Source pane or by choosing Controls⇨Eject Disc. You can also right-click the CD name and choose Eject from the contextual menu that appears.

Rearranging tracks

You can rearrange the order of the tracks to automatically play them in any sequence you want, similar to programming a CD player. When you click the up arrow at the top of the first column in the List pane (refer to Figure 6-3), it changes to a down arrow, and the tracks appear in reverse order.

To change the order of tracks that you're playing in sequence, just click and hold the track number in the leftmost column for the song; then drag it up or down in the list. You can set up the tracks to play in a completely different sequence.

Skipping tracks

To skip tracks so that they don't play in sequence, deselect the check box next to the song names. iTunes skips deselected songs when you play the entire sequence.

To remove all check marks from a list, press ⌘ on a Mac or Ctrl in Windows while clicking a check mark. Select an empty check box while pressing ⌘ or Ctrl to add check marks to the entire list.

Repeating an entire CD

You can repeat an entire CD by clicking the Repeat button, which you can find below the Source pane on the left side of the iTunes window (or by choosing Controls⇨Repeat All). When it's selected, the Repeat button shows blue highlighting. Click the Repeat button again to repeat the current song (or choose Controls⇨Repeat One). The button changes to include a blue-highlighted numeral 1. Click it once more to return to normal playback (or choose Controls⇨Repeat Off).

The Shuffle button, located to the left of the Repeat button, plays the songs on the CD in random order, which can be fun. You can then press the arrow keys on your keyboard or click the Back and Forward buttons to jump around in random order.

Displaying visuals

The visual effects in iTunes can turn your iTunes window into a light show that's synchronized to the music in your library. You can watch a cool display of eye candy while the music plays — or leave it on like a lava lamp.

Choose View⇨Show Visualizer to display visual effects (or press ⌘-T on a Mac or Ctrl-T in Windows). An animation appears in the iTunes window and synchronizes with the music. Choose View⇨Hide Visualizer (or press ⌘-T on a Mac or Ctrl-T in Windows) to turn off the visual effects.

iTunes offers two visualizers: The iTunes Visualizer has a simulated 3D look that includes spheres, ribbons, and lights that pulsate to the beat and tempo of the song you're playing. The Classic Visualizer, with a 2D look, has been part of the application since the beginning. To switch from the iTunes Visualizer to the Classic Visualizer, choose View⇨Visualizer⇨Classic Visualizer. To switch back to the new one, choose View⇨Visualizer⇨iTunes Visualizer.

You can tweak the Classic Visualizer a bit by changing the Visualizer options. Choose View⇨Visualizer⇨Classic Visualizer and then choose View⇨ Visualizer⇨Options to open the Visualizer Options dialog, as shown in Figure 6-4.

Figure 6-4:
Set options
for visual
effects.

The Visualizer Options dialog offers the following options that affect the animation (but not the performance of iTunes when it's playing music):

✔ **Display Frame Rate:** Choosing this option displays the frame rate of the animation along with the animation so that you can tell whether it is going faster or slower than normal video (30 fps).

✔ **Cap Frame Rate at 30 fps:** Choosing this option keeps the frame rate at 30 fps (frames per second) or lower to keep animation from moving too fast.

✔ **Always Display Song Info:** Choosing this option displays the song name, artist, and album for the song currently playing, along with the animation.

✔ **Use DirectX (Windows only) or Use OpenGL (Mac only):** You can choose to use DirectX on a Windows PC or OpenGL on a Mac to display very cool animation with faster performance. These are the most widely used standards for three-dimensional graphics programming.

✔ **Faster but Rougher Display:** When you use this option, animation plays faster but with rougher graphics. Select this option if your animation plays too slowly.

Choosing View⇨Full Screen (or pressing ⌘-F on a Mac or Ctrl-F in Windows) while showing the visualizer sets the visual effects to fill the entire screen. When displaying the full-screen visual effects, you can click the mouse button or press Escape (Esc) to stop the display and return to iTunes.

The Preferences dialog in iTunes lets you set the visualizer to always display full-screen. Choose iTunes➪Preferences on a Mac or Edit➪Preferences in Windows, click the Advanced tab (in Windows), and select the Display Visualizer Full Screen option, as shown in Figure 6-5, to always display the visualizer in full-screen mode.

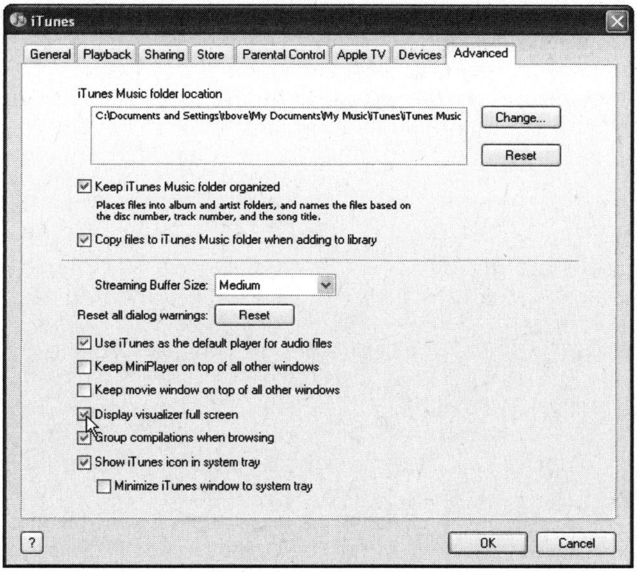

Figure 6-5:
Set the
visualizer
to always
display full-
screen.

While the animated visual effects play, press Shift-/ (as if you're typing a question mark) to see a list of keyboard functions. Depending on the visual effect, you might see more choices of keyboard functions by pressing Shift-/ again.

You can enhance iTunes with plug-ins that provide even better visuals. For example, SpectroGraph from Dr. Lex displays a spectrogram of the music, and Cover Version from imagomat displays the album cover artwork. You can find them — and many other enhancements — at Apple's software download site (www.apple.com/downloads/macosx/ipod_itunes).

After installing an iTunes plug-in, you can switch from one plug-in to another by choosing View➪Visualizer to see the submenu of plug-ins (including iTunes Visualizer and Classic Visualizer, supplied with iTunes).

Using the iTunes Genius Sidebar

If you display the iTunes Genius Sidebar (refer to Figure 6-1), which shows up next to the List pane, it makes suggestions on what to buy from the iTunes Store based on the song or video you've selected. (This is not the same guy as the Genius button that creates a playlist from your library based on the song you select, or the Genius Mixes that iTunes creates automatically for you — see Chapter 14 for details on these geniuses.)

The Genius Sidebar will try to skip songs or videos that are already in your library to show you content you might want to buy. But it's not perfect — sometimes it doesn't recognize that you already have the song or video (especially if you ripped the song from a CD).

iTunes informs the online store about the songs and videos you select whenever the Genius Sidebar is open. It then shows you content that other iTunes users purchased when they purchased the content you're playing. You can click any item in the Genius Sidebar to go right to the iTunes Store page for that item. See Chapter 7 for details about using the iTunes Store.

The Genius Sidebar operates only if you give it permission and if you already have an iTunes Store account. (To open an account, see Chapter 7.) When you first start iTunes, the sidebar is not yet turned on. (Refer to Figure 6-1.) To turn it on, click the Turn On Genius button, enter your Apple ID and password for your iTunes Store account, and click the Continue button. If you don't have an account yet, select the Create a New iTunes Store Account option, and choose your country from the country pop-up menu. Then click Continue. See Chapter 7 for further instructions on creating an account.

If the Genius Sidebar can't find the content you're playing, it offers choices that are simply in the same genre. If you don't have an iTunes Store available for your country, you see the U.S. store, just as Chuck Berry once sang, "Anything you want, we got right here in the U.S.A."

Chapter 7

Shopping at the iTunes Store

· ·

In This Chapter

▶ Setting up an account with the iTunes Store

▶ Previewing and buying songs, TV shows, movies, and audio books

▶ Browsing, previewing, and downloading podcasts

▶ Buying music, podcasts, and apps directly with your iPod touch or iPhone

· ·

*W*hen Apple announced its online music service, Steve Jobs remarked that other services put forward by the music industry tend to treat consumers like criminals. The Apple CEO had a point. Record labels dragged their feet for years, experimenting with online sales and taking legal action against online sites that allowed free downloads and music copying. Consumers and the industry both needed a solution. Apple did the research on how to make a service that worked better and was easier to use, and the company forged ahead with the iTunes Store.

By all accounts, Apple has succeeded in offering the easiest, fastest, and most cost-effective service for buying content online. You can purchase or rent movies, including HD movies, and you can purchase TV shows, music videos, applications, and games to play on your iPod or iPhone.

The iTunes Store includes the App Store, which offers free and commercial iPod touch and iPhone applications by the thousands. You can find apps in just about every category you can think of, including gaming, social networking, sports, business, and more. The store also includes games for the iPod nano and iPod classic.

You can also download free or commercial content and apps directly to an iPod touch or iPhone. The music and podcast sections of the iTunes Store and the entire App Store are available right at your fingertips. This chapter shows you how to sign in and take advantage of what the iTunes Store has to offer.

The iTunes Store also offers parental controls that let you disable various sections as well as limit the purchase of various content based on MPAA/TV ratings. To learn more about managing your iTunes Store account, visit this book's companion Web site.

Visiting the iTunes Store

You can visit the iTunes Store on your computer by connecting to the Internet and using iTunes. You can also click an iTunes Store link on Apple's Web site, or a similar link on any other Web sites that are iTunes affiliates with songs for sale (such as www.rockument.com). The link automatically launches of iTunes and opens the iTunes Store.

As of this writing, the iTunes Store offers millions of songs you can freely copy and play on other devices for 69 cents, 99 cents, or $1.29. Until recently, many of the songs were copy-protected — you could only play them on up to five different authorized computers and use them on iPods, iPhones, or Apple TVs. Now, all songs and albums are provided in the "iTunes Plus" format that offers higher sound quality *without* copy protection. You can play iTunes Plus songs on any player that supports the AAC format and on an unlimited number of computers, and you can burn an unlimited number of CDs with them. The copy-protected songs you purchased before can now be updated to the iTunes Plus format (for a fee).

To learn more about updating your songs to the iTunes Plus format, visit this book's companion Web site.

You can buy audio books as well as episodes and entire seasons of TV shows, and you can purchase them in advance, so you see them immediately. First-run movies are available for rent or purchase. iTunes also offers tons of free content in the form of *podcasts,* which are similar to syndicated radio and TV shows, but you can download and play them at your convenience on your computer and on your iPod, iPhone, and Apple TV. iTunes even offers free lectures, language lessons, and audio books with educational content in its iTunes U section.

To learn more about renting movies from the iTunes Store, visit this book's companion Web site.

Like with most online services, the music that you buy online isn't as high in audio quality as music on a commercial CD, although most people can't tell the difference when playing the music on car stereos or at low volume. The quality of the music sold in the iTunes Store is comparable with the quality you get when ripping CDs or importing songs using the MP3 or AAC format. You also get song information, such as artist, song titles, the album title, and cover artwork. The iTunes Store also offers albums with an immersive visual experience (referred to as iTunes LP)) that includes liner notes, pictures, video, animation, and lyrics. Some albums are provided with the electronic equivalent of a complete jewel case booklet that you can print yourself.

To find out more about audio encoding formats, and why iTunes uses them to reduce the space the music occupies on the hard drive or flash memory of your iPod or iPhone, visit this book's companion Web site.

The iTunes Store is part of iTunes version 4 and newer, but you should be using the newest version of iTunes; I describe how to get it in Chapter 2.

If you already have your iTunes program open, you have at least three choices when it comes to opening the iTunes Store:

- ✔ **Click iTunes Store in the Store section of the Source pane.** The iTunes Store home page opens, as shown in Figure 7-1.

- ✔ **Click any link in the Genius Sidebar.** The iTunes Store home page opens and automatically switches your Source pane selection to iTunes Store. The Genius Sidebar offers suggestions based on the music you select in your library; see Chapter 6 for details.

- ✔ **Follow a content link in iTunes.** Click the *content link* (the gray-circled arrow next to a song or video title, an artist name, or an album title) to go to an iTunes Store page related to the song or video, artist, or album. iTunes searches the iTunes Store based on the item you selected. If nothing closely related turns up, at least you end up in the iTunes Store, and you might even find music you like that you didn't know about.

The iTunes Store uses the iTunes List pane to display its wares. You can check out content to your heart's content, although you can't buy content, download free content, or rent movies unless you have an iTunes Store account set up.

The iTunes Store also provides tabs and buttons on a black bar above the List pane. The left and right triangle buttons work just like the Back and Forward buttons of a Web browser, moving back a page or forward a page, respectively. The button with the Home icon takes you to the iTunes Store home page. (Refer to Figure 7-1.)

Back

Forward Home Sign In tab

Figure 7-1:
The iTunes
Store home
page.

Setting Up an Account

One important task that you must do in iTunes on your computer is set up your iTunes Store account. You need an account to download free or commercial content and apps to your computer as well as to use the iTunes Store and App Store apps on your iPod touch or iPhone. To create an iTunes Store account, follow these steps:

1. **In iTunes, click the iTunes Store option in the Store section of the Source pane, or click a music link or Genius Sidebar link.**

   The iTunes Store home page appears (refer to Figure 7-1), replacing the List pane.

2. **Click the Sign In tab in the upper-right area of the window to either create an account or sign in to an existing account.**

   When you're logged in to an iTunes account, the account name appears in place of the Sign In tab.

   After you click the Sign In tab, iTunes displays the account sign-in dialog, as shown in Figure 7-2.

If you already set up an account with the iTunes Store with the MobileMe (formerly .Mac) service or with other Apple services (such as the Apple Developer Connection), you're halfway there. Type your ID and password and then click the Sign In button. Apple remembers the personal information that you put in previously, so you don't have to reenter it every time you visit the iTunes Store. If you forgot your password, click the Forgot Password button, and iTunes provides a dialog so that you can answer your test question. If you answer correctly, iTunes e-mails your password to you.

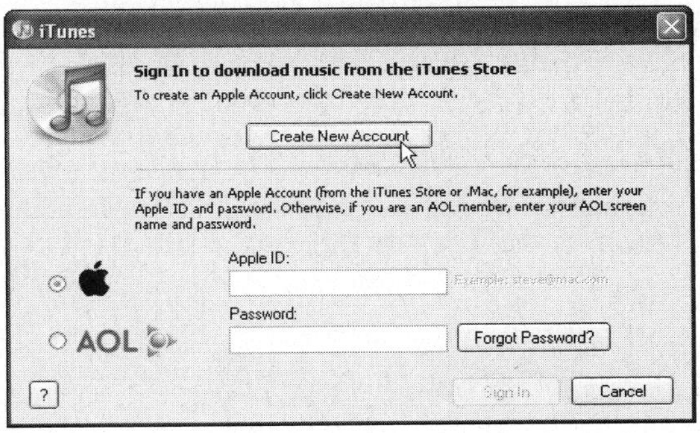

Figure 7-2:
The sign-in dialog for the iTunes Store.

3. Click the Create New Account button.

iTunes displays a new page that welcomes you to the iTunes Store.

4. Click the Continue button on the iTunes Store welcome page.

After you click Continue, the terms of use appear with the option at the end to agree to the terms. If you don't select the option to agree, iTunes continues to display the terms until you agree or click the Cancel button.

5. Select I Have Read and Agree to the iTunes Terms and Conditions and click the Continue button.

iTunes displays the personal account information page of the setup procedure, with text fields to enter your e-mail address, password, and other information.

6. Fill in your personal account information.

Type your e-mail address into the Email Address field. Make up a password, and enter it twice — in the Password field and in the Verify field. Then enter a question and answer that you can easily remember (in case you forget your password). Finally, enter your birth date and options for receiving e-mail from Apple. Don't forget the password you made up — you need it to access the store from your iPod touch or iPhone as well as from your computer or another computer.

7. **Click the Continue button and then enter your credit card information.**

   The entire procedure is secure, so you don't have to worry. The iTunes Store keeps your personal information (including your credit card information) on file, and you don't have to type it again.

8. **Click the Continue button to finish the procedure.**

   The account setup finishes and returns you to the iTunes Store home page. You can now use the iTunes Store to purchase and download content to play in iTunes and use on any iPod, iPhone, or Apple TV.

Select a country from the My Store pop-up menu at the bottom of the iTunes Store page to choose online stores in other countries. For example, the iTunes Store in France displays menus in French and features hit songs and TV shows for the French market. If you've set up your account in only one country (such as the United States), you have to set an account up again for the country you're switching to, in order to purchase content in that country's store. You can set up multiple accounts in multiple countries, and Apple takes care of credit card transactions and currency conversions

Cruising the Multimedia Mall

The iTunes Store home page is loaded with specials and advertisements to peruse. You can preview any song in the iTunes Store for up to 30 seconds. Some movies offer one-minute previews and movie trailers you can view for free, and TV shows and audio books can offer up to 90 seconds. If you have an account set up, you can buy and download content immediately, including movies for rent. I don't know of a faster way to purchase or rent content from the comfort of your home.

Browsing songs and albums

To look at music in more depth, choose the Music tab in the black bar above the List pane. (Refer to Figure 7-1.) You can also pick a music genre by clicking the down-arrow button that appears next to the Music tab when you click it. iTunes displays more panels of advertisements and specials for music lovers, including iTunes LP albums that include liner notes, lyrics, videos, and other features.

After selecting an advertisement for an iTunes LP album, for example, the album's page appears with a description and other links, as shown in Figure 7-3.

Figure 7-3:
An iTunes
Store page
showing an
iTunes LP
album.

Do you want to copy a link to an iTunes Store item, share it with friends, add it to your wish list, or send it as a gift? Click the down-arrow button attached to the Buy Song or Buy Album button (refer to Figure 7-3) and choose the option to Gift This Song (or Album), Add to Wish List, Tell a Friend (by e-mail, albums or entire pages), Copy Link (so that you can Paste it in a text file or message), Share on Facebook, or Share on Twitter.

What if you're looking for particular music in a particular genre? You can browse the iTunes Store by genre and artist name in a method similar to browsing your iTunes library.

To browse the iTunes Store, choose View➪Show Column Browser, or click the Browse link in the Quick Links Column on the right side of the iTunes Store home page. iTunes displays the store's offerings categorized by type of content (such as Music), and it displays music by genre and subgenre — and within each subgenre, by artist and album. Select a genre in the Genre column, then a subgenre in the Subgenre column, then an artist in the Artist column, and finally an album in the Album column, which takes you to the list of songs from that album that are available to preview or purchase, as shown in Figure 7-4.

To see more information about the album that it came from, click the content link (one of the gray-circled arrow buttons in the List pane):

✔ Clicking the arrow in the Artist column takes you to the artist's page of albums.

✔ Clicking the arrow in the Album column takes you to the album page.

✔ Clicking the arrow in the Name column takes you to album page with the song highlighted.

Figure 7-4: Browse the iTunes Store for music by genre, artist, and album.

My only complaint about browsing by artist is that artists are listed alphabetically by first name. For example, you have to look up Lou Reed under *Lou* and not *Reed.*

To preview a song, click the song title in the List pane and then click the Play button (or press the spacebar) or double-click the song.

By default, the previews play on your computer off the Internet in a stream, so you might hear a few hiccups in the playback. Each preview lasts about 30 seconds. Just when you start really getting into the song, it ends. If the song is irresistible, though, you can buy it on the spot — for details, see the section "Buying and Downloading Media," later in this chapter.

Power searching

If you're looking for DMB's "That Song That Jane Likes" or know specifically what to search for, type it into the Search field in the upper-right corner of the iTunes window; this lets you search the iTunes Store for just about anything. You can type part of a song title or artist name to quickly display results from the iTunes Store in the List pane.

If you're serious about your content, and you truly desire the power to search for exactly what you want, click the Power Search link in the Quick Links column on the right side of the iTunes Store home page (or choose Store⇨Search).

The Power Search page appears, as shown in Figure 7-5. You can choose the type of content to search through by choosing from a pop-up menu under the page title at the top: All Results (search all types), Music, Movies, TV Shows, Applications, Audiobooks, Podcasts, or iTunes U (part of the iTunes Store that offers free lectures, language lessons, and audio books).

For example, choose Music to power-search only for music and music videos (refer to Figure 7-5). The entry fields for Artist, Composer, Song, Album, and Genre appear. You can fill in some of or all these fields, or just fill in part of any field if that's all you know.

Celebrities tell all (and so can you)

Do you want to be influenced? Do you want to know what influenced some of today's celebrities and buy what they have in their record collections? Choose the Music tab at the top of the iTunes Store page in the List pane to go to the Music page. Scroll down the Music page, and click a celebrity name in the Celebrity Playlists section of the More in Music column on the right — to go to that celebrity's page. A typical celebrity playlist offers about an album's worth of songs from different artists. You can preview or buy any song in the list, or follow the music links to the artist or album page.

The Music page advertises some of the celebrity playlists, but a lot more are available. To see all the celebrity playlists, go to the More in Music pane column on the right side of the Music page and click the Celebrity Playlists link. You arrive at the Celebrity Playlists page. You can use the Sort By pop-up menu in the upper-right corner to sort the list by Most Recent or by Title.

You can also be influenced by other buyers and do a little influencing yourself. Go to the Music page, and click the iMix link in the More to Explore column at the bottom right corner of the page to check out playlists that have been contributed by other consumers and published in the iTunes Store. iMixes offer 30-second previews of any songs in the iMix playlists.

To find out how to publish your own iMix playlist, visit this book's companion Web site.

After you fill in as much as you know, click the Search button in the top right corner. Albums, movies, music videos, and other items found appear in the upper part of the page, while songs appear below in a list.

Figure 7-5: Use Power Search to refine your search in the iTunes Store.

Browsing movies, TV shows, music videos, and audio books

The uncool thing about video stores — besides the weird people who hang out in them — is the lack of a comfortable way to preview videos before you buy them. Instead, go to the iTunes Store online to preview movies and TV shows before you buy them (and before you rent a movie) — and then go ahead and buy or rent them from the iTunes Store. Most shows offer 30 seconds of previewing time, and many movies offer trailers that are even longer.

To find TV shows, movies, music videos, or audio books, do one of the following:

✔ Click the TV Shows, Movies, or Audiobooks tab in the black bar at the top of iTunes Store page in the List pane. You can also click the down-arrow button next to each tab to browse by genre. The iTunes Store displays advertisements for the most popular items. Click an item, such as an audio book or movie, to go to its page.

✔ Click the Music tab, and then click the down-arrow button next to the Music tab and then select Music Videos from the pop-up menu.

✔ Browse the iTunes Store by clicking the Browse link in the Quick Links column on the right side of the iTunes Store home page (or by choosing View⇨Show Column Browser). Select Audiobooks, Movies, Music Videos, or TV Shows from the iTunes Store column and then do one of the following to display the item's page and list of contents:

    • *For an audio book,* pick a genre from the Genre column and then pick an author from the Author/Narrator column.

    • *For a movie,* pick a genre from the Genre column.

    • *For a music video,* pick a genre from the Genre column and then pick an artist from the Artist column.

    • *For a TV show,* pick a genre in the Genre column, then a TV show in the TV Shows column, and finally a season of episodes in the Season column.

To preview a TV show, movie, or music video, click the title in the List pane and then click the Play button (or press the spacebar). (Movies, music videos, and TV shows are all just videos on the computer, so I use the term *videos* from now on.)

The video plays in the iTunes window, in the Artwork pane in the lower-left corner of the iTunes window, in a separate window, or full-screen, depending on your playback settings. (See Chapter 13 for details.) If the Artwork pane isn't visible, click the Show/Hide Artwork button to display it. Click the iTunes Play/Pause, Forward/Next, and Previous/Rewind buttons to control playback, and use the iTunes volume slider to control the volume, just like with songs. For more details about playing videos in iTunes, see Chapter 13.

Most movie pages offer a View Trailer button to view the theatrical trailer for the movie (as shown in Figure 7-6), as well as the Buy HD Movie button for the high-definition (HD) version, if available, and the Buy Movie button for the non-HD version (or the Pre-Order button to pre-order the movie before release). Many (but not all) offer a Rent Movie button to rent the movie.

To learn more about renting movies from the iTunes Store, visit this book's companion Web site.

Clicking the View Trailer button does the obvious — it plays the movie trailer. At any time, though, you can return to the movie page by clicking Close Preview under the lower-right corner of the trailer picture.

Audio books can be even more entertaining than movies and certainly easier to consume while driving or walking. The Audiobooks tab at the top of the iTunes Store page takes you to the Audiobooks page. Click an advertisement, thumbnail, or title, or click the circled arrow next to the title in a list of titles, to go to the specific audio book's page. Then click the Preview button to preview the audio book. Use the Play/Pause button to pause and resume playback.

Figure 7-6:
The movie's page has buttons to view its trailer or pre-order it

You can double-click the iTunes Store option in the Store section of the Source pane to open the iTunes Store in a separate window. With two windows, you can use the first window to search for and play content in your library while using the second to browse the iTunes Store and purchase and download a video. The first window stops playing content when you use the second window to preview a song or video.

Browsing and subscribing to podcasts

Podcasting is a popular method of publishing audio and video shows to the Internet, enabling people to subscribe to a feed and receive the shows automatically. Similar to a tape of a radio broadcast, you can save a podcast episode and play it back at your convenience, both in iTunes on your computer and on your iPod. You can also burn an audio podcast episode to an audio CD or MP3 CD. A podcast episode can be anything from a single song to a commentary-hosted radio show; a podcaster, like a broadcaster, provides a stream of episodes over time. Thousands of professional and amateur radio and video shows are offered as podcast episodes. Video podcasts are also called *videocasts* or *vodcasts*.

The iTunes Podcast page in the iTunes Store lets you browse, find, preview, and subscribe to podcasts, many of which are free. You don't need an account to browse the iTunes Store and subscribe to free podcasts.

To find podcasts in the iTunes Store, do one of the following:

✔ **Click the Podcasts tab in the black bar at the top of the iTunes Store page in the List pane.** The iTunes Store displays the Podcast page, with advertisements for popular podcasts and a list of Top Podcasts in the far-right column. You can click the down-arrow button next to the Podcasts tab to choose specific categories.

You can also get to the Podcast page by clicking Podcasts in the iTunes Source pane and then clicking Podcast Directory at the bottom of the List view.

✔ **Browse all podcasts in a particular category.** Click the Browse link in the Quick Links column on the right side of the iTunes Store home page (or choose View➪Show Column Browser) and then select Podcasts in the iTunes Store column. Select options from the Category column and Subcategory column.

✔ **Search for a podcast by name or keyword.** You can type a search term into the Search iTunes Store field in the upper-right corner of the iTunes window to find any podcasts or other content items that match. You can also use the Power Search feature, described earlier in this chapter in the section "Power searching."

After you select a podcast, the iTunes Store displays the podcast's specific page in the iTunes Store, as shown in Figure 7-7, with all available podcast episodes in the List pane.

Figure 7-7: The podcast page for a video podcast (videocast) with the Subscribe button and list of episodes.

To select, play, and subscribe to a podcast, follow these steps:

1. **Choose a podcast in the iTunes Store.**

   The iTunes Store offers a description, a Subscribe button to receive new podcasts, and a link to the podcast's Web site for more information. The page also lists the most recent podcast episodes, with a Get Episode button next to each one. You can click the *i* icon on the far-right listing margin to display separate information about each podcast episode.

2. **To preview the podcast, click an episode title and then click the Play button or press the spacebar.**

   You can play a preview of any episode in the list. iTunes plays the episode for about 90 seconds, just like a Web radio station streaming to your computer. To jump ahead or play the entire episode, you must first subscribe to the podcast. By subscribing, you enable automatic downloading of episodes to your computer.

3. **Click the Subscribe button on the podcast page to subscribe to the podcast.**

   In typical Apple fashion, iTunes first displays an alert to confirm that you want to subscribe to the podcast.

4. **Click the OK button to confirm.**

   iTunes downloads the podcast to your computer and switches to Podcasts in the Library section of the Source pane. iTunes displays your newly subscribed podcast in the List pane. See Chapter 13 for details on playing podcasts in iTunes.

5. **(Optional) Get more episodes of the podcast.**

   When you subscribe to a podcast, you get the current episode. However, a podcast probably has past episodes still available. To download previous episodes, click the Get Episode button next to each episode (refer to Figure 7-7) to download it.

You can play the podcast, incorporate it into playlists, and make copies and burn CDs as much as you like. See Chapter 8 for details on subscribing to, deleting, and updating podcasts.

Buying and Downloading Media

As you select multimedia content, you can purchase the items and download them to your computer immediately. All you need to do is click the Buy button, whether the item is a song, an album, a TV show episode, or an audio book.

For example, if you select a song in the List pane, click the Buy Song button in the far-right column for the song. (You might have to scroll your iTunes Store window to see the far-right column.) When you select a TV show episode, click the Buy Episode button in the far-right column. You can also click the Buy Album button.

The iTunes Store may prompt you to log in to your account after you click the Buy button (unless you just recently logged in). It then displays a warning dialog to make sure that you want to buy the item, and you can then complete your purchase by clicking the Buy button, or cancel. After clicking the Buy button, iTunes downloads the item and, after downloading, it appears in your iTunes library. You can continue buying items while downloading, and since you've already logged in, the iTunes Store complies immediately without asking again for a password. The iTunes Store keeps track of your purchases over a 24-hour period and charges you for a total sum rather than for each single purchase.

You can see the list of all the items that you purchased by selecting the Purchased playlist under the iTunes Store option in the Source pane. The List pane changes to show the items you purchased.

Each time you buy content, you get an e-mail from the iTunes Store with the purchase information. It's nice to know right away what you bought.

Changing other iTunes Store preferences

You can change iTunes Store preference settings by choosing iTunes⇨ Preferences on the Mac or by choosing Edit⇨Preferences in Windows. In the Preferences window, click the Store button. The Store Preferences pane appears as shown in Figure 7-8. You can set the following features:

- ✔ Automatically check for available downloads from the iTunes Store, such as downloads that were not completed and new episodes for a podcast subscription.

- ✔ Automatically download prepurchased content, such as an iTunes Pass for TV show episodes. As the episodes become available, iTunes automatically downloads them.

- ✔ Automatically download missing album artwork from the iTunes Store for albums and songs you've imported from other sources (such as audio CDs).

- ✔ Use the full iTunes window for the iTunes Store (rather than just the List pane) so that you can see more of the store choices.

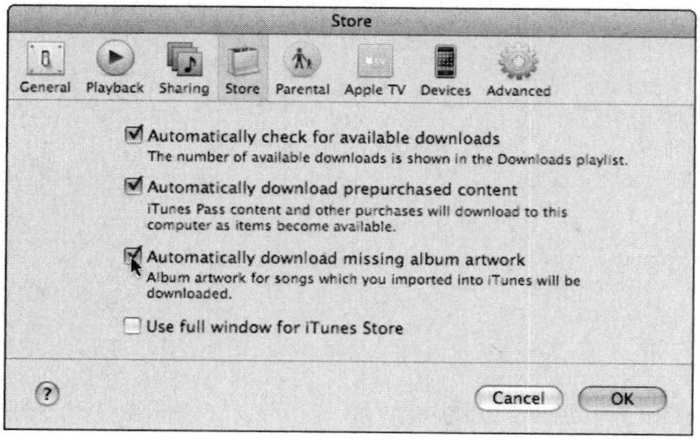

Figure 7-8:
Change
preferences
for the
iTunes
Store.

Store

General Playback Sharing Store Parental Apple TV Devices Advanced

☑ Automatically check for available downloads
The number of available downloads is shown in the Downloads playlist.

☑ Automatically download prepurchased content
iTunes Pass content and other purchases will download to this computer as items become available.

☑ Automatically download missing album artwork
Album artwork for songs which you imported into iTunes will be downloaded.

☐ Use full window for iTunes Store

(?)   (Cancel) (OK)

Resuming interrupted downloads

All sales are final; you can't return the digital merchandise. However, the download must be successful — you have to receive it all — before the iTunes Store charges you for the purchase. If for any reason the download is interrupted or fails to complete, your order remains active until you connect to the iTunes Store again.

iTunes remembers to continue the download when you return to iTunes and connect to the Internet. If, for some reason, the download doesn't continue, choose Store➪Check for Available Downloads to continue the interrupted download. You can also use this command to check for any purchased content that hasn't downloaded yet.

While downloading from the iTunes Store, you can select Downloads in the Store section of the Source pane, as shown in Figure 7-9, to see the progress of your downloads, and to pause and resume (or cancel) any particular download. You can also prioritize the order of downloading by dragging items into a different order.

For the impatient viewers, the iTunes Store lets you start watching a video or movie before it finishes downloading. Click Downloads in the Store section of the Source pane as you're downloading and double-click the item to watch it. The download continues as you watch from the beginning.

If your computer's hard drive crashes and you lose your information, you also lose all your digital content — you have to purchase and download that content again. However, you can mitigate this kind of disaster by backing up your iTunes library. You can also burn your songs, including purchased songs, to an audio CD, an MP3 CD, or a data DVD, as I describe in Chapter 15.

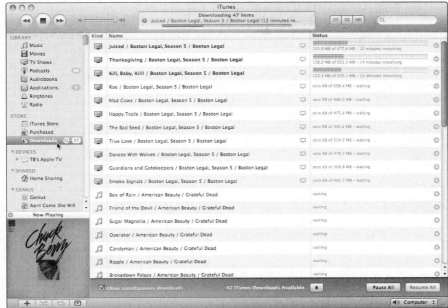

Figure 7-9:
Check the
progress of
your
downloads.

To find out more about backing up your iTunes library, visit this book's companion Web site.

Redeeming gift certificates and prepaid cards

If you're the fortunate recipient of an iTunes Store gift certificate, all you need to do is use iTunes to go to the iTunes Store and set up a new account — if you don't already have one. Recipients of gift certificates can set up new accounts without having to provide a credit card number. As a recipient of a gift, you can simply choose None for the credit card option and use the gift certificate as the sole payment method.

You can receive gift certificates on paper (delivered by snail mail) or by e-mail. You can also receive a prepaid card with a fixed balance. To redeem a certificate, go to the Quick Links column on the right side of the iTunes Store home page and click the Redeem link to go to the Redeem page. In the Redeem Code section of the Redeem page, type the number printed on the certificate or supplied in the e-mail and click the Redeem button to credit your account. If you haven't signed in to your account yet or you have no account, iTunes displays the sign-in dialog; for information about setting up an account, see the "Setting Up an Account" section, earlier in this chapter.

If you use Apple's Mail program or access your MobileMe (formerly .Mac) e-mail through the Safari Web browser, you can redeem a gift certificate that was sent by e-mail by clicking the Redeem Now button at the bottom of the e-mail message. This button launches iTunes with the iTunes Store option selected in the Source pane and displays the Redeem page with the certificate's number automatically filled in. Click the Redeem button to credit your account.

The *balance* of your gift certificate (how much you have left to spend) appears right next to your account name in the iTunes Store window and is updated as you make purchases.

Appearing at the App Store

Got an iPod touch or iPhone? You can get loads of free and commercial applications (called *apps*) that run on your iPod touch or iPhone just like the built-in Maps and Weather apps. Click the App Store tab in the black bar at the top of the iTunes Store page (refer to Figure 7-1) to find the apps. The App Store page appears, as shown in Figure 7-10.

Figure 7-10: iPod touch and iPhone apps in the App Store section of the iTunes Store.

Click an app's icon to go to the information page for that app, which may also contain reviews and a slide show depicting the app in all its glory. The information page offers the Buy App button (to purchase and download a commercial app) or the Get App button (to download a free app). Click the Buy App or Get App button to download the app to your iTunes library.

Downloaded apps appear in the Applications section of your iTunes library — click Applications in the Library section of the Source pane to see their icons. If you don't see Applications in the Source pane, choose iTunes➪Preferences (Mac) or Edit➪Preferences (Windows), click the General tab at the top of the Preferences window, select the Applications option from the list of options for the Show heading, and click the OK button. The Applications item then appears in the Source pane in the Library section.

When an app you downloaded is updated, iTunes informs you — the message `Update Available` appears at the bottom of the Applications section with an arrow link that takes you to the My Apps Update page in the iTunes Store, with icons of the apps to update. Click the Get Update button next to each app to download the update, which automatically replaces the previous version of the app.

The iTunes Store also offers colorful "click wheel" games to play on your iPod classic or nano (or seventh-, sixth-, or fifth-generation iPods) — all kinds of games, from Mini Golf, Monopoly, and Mahjong to the classic Tetris and Cubis 2. You can even play the wildly popular Japanese puzzle Sudoku. The games play on iPods that can play videos — not in iTunes itself. However, you can see a preview of the game while browsing the iTunes Store.

To find the iPod games, click the the App Store tab in the black bar at the top of the iTunes Store page, and then click the down-arrow button next to the App Store tab to see the pop-up menu; choose iPod Games from the menu. iTunes displays the iPod Games page with thumbnail icons for each game. Click the game's icon to go to the game's page. Click the Preview button on the game's page to see a preview of the game. Use the iTunes Play button, just as you would for a song, to play the game preview. At any time, click the Close Preview button to return to the game's page.

Shopping with your iPod touch or iPhone

The music and podcast sections of the iTunes Store, and the entire App Store, are both available right at your fingertips on your iPod touch or iPhone. You can search for, browse, and preview songs and albums; make purchases; and download music and apps directly to your iPod touch or iPhone. Whatever you buy on your iPod touch or iPhone is automatically copied to your iTunes library the next time you synchronize it with your computer, as I describe in Chapter 9.

Be sure to use iTunes to set up an iTunes Store account first if you don't already have one, and then sign in to the account, as I describe in the section "Setting Up an Account," earlier in this chapter — and you'll need to remember your password. Then sync your iPod touch or iPhone to iTunes as I describe in Chapter 9. After syncing your iPod touch or iPhone so that it has your account information, you shouldn't have to bother with it again, and you'll be able to download items from the iTunes Store and App Store on your iPod touch or iPhone from then on.

To use the iTunes Store and App Store on your iPod touch, you must first join a Wi-Fi network that's connected to the Internet (see Chapter 4 for details). As for the iPhone, you can use either the 3G network or Wi-Fi. Be sure you have an iTunes Store account set up (see the section "Setting Up an Account," earlier in this chapter).

Browsing and downloading songs

To go to the iTunes Store on an iPod touch or iPhone, tap the iTunes icon on the Home screen. The store screen appears with Music, Videos, Podcasts (see the next section), Search, and More icons along the bottom, as shown in Figure 7-11 (left side). Tap any song to hear a preview.

Here's the lowdown on the icons:

✔ **Tap the Music icon** to see featured music, as shown in Figure 7-11 (left side). The screen displays New Releases, Top Tens, and Genres buttons along the top. To search through genres, tap the Genres button and choose a genre.

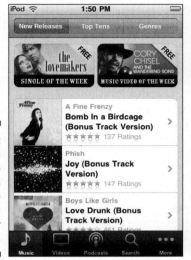

Figure 7-11:
The iTunes Store (left) and App Store (right) on an iPod touch or iPhone.

- ✔ **Tap the Videos icon** to see featured movies, TV shows, and music videos.

- ✔ **Tap the Podcasts icon** to . . . er, well, I explain that one in the next section.

- ✔ **Tap the Search icon** to search the store and then tap the entry field to bring up the on-screen keyboard. Type the search term and tap the Search button to search the store.

- ✔ **Tap the More icon** for more choices, including Audiobooks, iTunes U, and Downloads, which shows you the progress of your downloads from the store.

To buy a song, tap the price and then tap Buy Now. Enter your password, and tap OK.

Purchased songs are added to a Purchased playlist on your iPod touch or iPhone, and they're included in your Purchased playlist in iTunes. iTunes automatically syncs songs and albums purchased on your iPod touch or iPhone to your iTunes library when you connect it to your computer so that you have a backup if you manage to delete purchases from the iPod touch or iPhone.

Some albums offer bonus content, such as liner notes, which are downloaded to your iTunes library on your computer, but not to your iPod touch or iPhone. An alert appears on your iPod touch or iPhone if you've previously purchased one or more songs from an album. Tap Buy if you want to purchase the entire album, or tap Cancel if you want to buy the remaining songs on the album individually.

If you lose your network connection or turn off your iPod touch or iPhone while downloading, the download pauses and then resumes when you reestablish connection with the Internet. If you go back to your computer, iTunes can complete the download operation to your iTunes library. To make sure that you received all your downloads from purchases on your iPod touch or iPhone, use iTunes on your computer and choose Store➪Check for Available Downloads.

Browsing and downloading podcasts

If you'll recall, podcasts are audio and video episodes designed to be downloaded to your iPod touch or iPhone. Most podcast episodes are free. On the store screen, tap the Podcasts icon to see podcasts available for downloading from the iTunes Store directly to your iPod touch or iPhone.

You can also view categories of podcasts by tapping Categories in the upper-right corner of the Podcasts screen, or you can see the top ten in each category by tapping Top Tens at the top of the screen.

After selecting a podcast, a list of episodes appears. Tap the Free button (or Buy button for paid podcasts) next to an episode, enter your password, and then tap OK to start downloading the podcast episode. To return to the iTunes Store music screen, tap Music in the upper-left corner of the screen that lists the podcast episodes.

Browsing and downloading apps

To use the App Store, tap the App Store icon on the Home screen. The Store screen appears with Featured, Categories, Top 25, Search, and Updates icons along the bottom (refer to Figure 7-11, right side). The following list tells you what's what when it comes to the icons:

- ✔ **Tap the Featured icon** and then tap the What's Hot button at the top to see the most popular apps based on downloads, or tap the New button to see featured new apps.

- ✔ **To browse by category,** tap the Categories icon on the bottom menu and then tap a category, such as Games, to see a list of all games by popularity.

- ✔ **Tap the Top 25 icon** on the bottom menu and then tap Top Paid to see the top 25 paid apps by popularity, or tap Top Free to see the top 25 free apps.

- ✔ **Tap the Search icon** to search the store, and tap the entry field to bring up the on-screen keyboard. (See Chapter 3 for details on how to type.) Type the search term and tap Search to search the store. Suggestions pop up right away; for example, if you search for *Tony* in the App Store, my app "Tony's Tips for iPhone Users Manual" appears in the list of suggestions.

- ✔ **Tap the Updates icon** . . . wait, forget I said that. I cover that icon in the *next* section, so check that out if you want details.

To view information and to purchase and download an app, tap the app in the list that appears after tapping the Featured, Categories, Top 25, or Search icon. You can then scroll the display to see more information about the app, or you can tap the Featured, Categories, Top 25, or Search icon in the upper-left corner to return to those lists.

You can also tap the Tell a Friend button at the bottom of the app's information screen to send the app information in an e-mail. See Chapter 20 for details on how to send the e-mail.

To download an app, tap the Price button (for a paid app) or Free button (for a free app). The Price or Free button changes to the Install button. Tap Install and then enter your password and tap OK.

Your iPod touch or iPhone displays the Home screen with the icon for the new app as it loads. As soon as the Loading message is replaced by the name of the app, the app is ready to be tapped.

Updating apps you've downloaded

The App Store on your iPod touch or iPhone notifies you if any of your apps have been updated — a number appears in the Updates icon along the bottom row of icons. You should update an app when an update is available because updates fix bugs and introduce new features you may want.

Tap the Updates icon to see the list of updated apps. To update an app, tap the app in the list to see the app's information screen and then tap the Update button. The Update button changes to the Install button. Tap Install and then enter your password and tap OK.

The update replaces the previous version of the app as it loads into your iPod touch or iPhone. As soon as the Loading message is replaced by the name of the app, the icon is ready to be tapped.

Sharing iTunes Purchases in Your Home Network

A family member in your home just bought an album from the iTunes Store that you would like to have in your computer's iTunes library as well, so that you can sync it to your iPod. Rather than painstakingly copying the music files from computer to computer or changing your sync options, you can use the Home Sharing feature to share the purchased content. With Home Sharing, you can browse the iTunes libraries of up to five authorized computers in your house, copy over from those libraries anything you want, and automatically add new purchases made on any of the computers to your own library.

Home Sharing is linked to a single iTunes Store account, which is perfect if you use one account for family purchases. In order to share purchased content that is copy-protected, such as movies and TV shows, you must first choose Store⇨Authorize Computer, and enter your account and password for each computer's iTunes library whose purchased content you want to share (up to five computers can be authorized at once). You can share non-protected content without authorizing the computers. (To deauthorize a computer, choose Store⇨Deauthorize Computer.)

To learn more about managing your iTunes account, including authorizing and deauthorizing computers, visit this book's companion Web site.

To turn on Home Sharing, click Home Sharing in the Source pane, and sign into your iTunes account. Do the same for each computer's iTunes library that you want to share.

After signing into your account in Home Sharing, and after signing into your account on another computer's iTunes library in Home Sharing, the other computer's library appears below Home Sharing in the Shared section the Source pane, as shown in Figure 7-12. Click the other computer's shared library ("Tony's PC Library" in Figure 7-12) to view the other library in the List pane.

You can show all the items in the shared library, or just the items that are *not* in your library so that you can see what you're missing — choose All Items or Items Not in My Library from the Show pop-up menu in the bottom left corner of the List pane (refer to Figure 7-12).

To import an item from the shared library to your library, select the item in the shared library, and then click the Import button in the bottom right corner of the List pane (refer to Figure 7-12). You can also drag items, albums, and artists directly over the Library section of the Source pane to copy them to your library.

Figure 7-12:
Share
another
iTunes
library on
your home
network
with Home
Sharing.

You can set up Home Sharing so that purchases made with the shared iTunes library on other computers are automatically copied to your iTunes library. Click Settings in the lower right corner of the List pane (refer to Figure 7-12), and then select the content categories for automatic transfer: Music, Movies, TV Shows, Audiobooks, and Applications.

To stop sharing a library on another computer, click the Eject button next to the library name ("Tony's PC Library" in Figure 7-12), or choose Controls➪ Disconnect "*library name*" (or press Cmd-E on a Mac or Ctrl-E in Windows).

To learn more about the network-sharing features of iTunes, including sharing content with other libraries on a network, visit this book's companion Web site.

Chapter 8

Bringing Content into iTunes

. . . .

In This Chapter

▶ Setting your music importing preferences

▶ Ripping music from CDs and adding music files

▶ Subscribing to podcasts on Web sites

▶ Adding video files to your library

. . . .

*I*f iPods and iPhones were spaceships, iTunes would be the space station they dock with to get supplies. iTunes is the central repository of all content. You can bring your music from audio CDs into iTunes to preserve the music forever in digital format and play the music on your iPod, iPhone, or Apple TV without having to fumble for discs. You can import sound and video files downloaded from the Internet into iTunes to keep all your content organized and to take it with you in your iPod or iPhone.

In this chapter, I show you not only how to import music from audio CDs, but also how to import music, videos, and podcasts from Web sites into your iTunes library.

Adding Music

Bringing music tracks from a CD into iTunes is called *ripping* a CD (audio programmers *do* have a sense of humor). *Ripping,* in technical terms, is extracting the song's digital information from an audio CD. In common terms, ripping includes compressing the song's digital information and encoding it in a particular sound file format (such as AAC or MP3, explained later in this chapter).

How easy is it to rip a CD? Pop an audio CD into your CD-ROM/DVD drive, and unless you've changed your preferences (as described in the following section), you'll see the message in Figure 8-1. Click the Yes button to rip your CD into iTunes and, without further ado, your CD tracks are absorbed into your iTunes library.

Figure 8-1:
Click Yes to
rip your CD
into iTunes
automati-
cally or No
to set
preferences
or edit song
information
first.

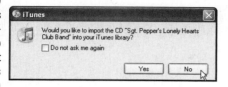

Before ripping, you may want to edit the song information, as I describe in Chapter 12 or set the Gapless Album option, which I describe in "Don't fall into the gaps" in this chapter. If this is your first time ripping a CD, you may want to set your import settings more precisely to improve sound quality or to reduce the amount of disk space occupied by songs. If you want to edit the song information, set the Gapless Album option, or change import settings, click the No button to stop the import operation and make your changes first. Then start the rip, as I describe in the section "Ripping music from CDs," later in this chapter.

The import settings affect sound quality as well as hard drive space on both the computer and the iPod or iPhone, and compatibility with other types of players and computers. After setting them, your import settings stay the same until you change them again. Read on to find out about changing your import preferences and settings before ripping.

Changing import preferences and settings

To change your import preferences and settings or change the way iTunes rips — whether it rips right away, asks first, or automatically ejects afterward — follow these steps:

1. **Choose iTunes⇨Preferences⇨General on a Mac or Edit⇨Preferences⇨ General in Windows.**

   The iTunes Preferences dialog opens, showing the General preferences, including the When You Insert a CD pop-up menu and the Import Settings button.

2. **Choose what action iTunes should take for the When You Insert a CD option in the General preferences.**

Choose one of the following actions on the pop-up menu for when you insert an audio CD, as shown in Figure 8-2:

- *Show CD:* iTunes does nothing else. This setting is ideal if you regularly edit the song information first, as I describe in Chapter 12.

- *Begin Playing:* See Chapter 6 for details on playing CDs.

- *Ask to Import CD:* iTunes displays the dialog that asks whether you want to import the CD (refer to Figure 8-1).

- *Import CD:* iTunes uses the current import settings and automatically imports the CD. Don't use this setting unless you're sure that the import settings are already set to your liking.

- *Import CD and Eject:* iTunes automatically imports and then ejects the CD, making way for the next one. This option is useful for importing a batch of CDs. Don't use this setting unless you're sure that the import settings are already set to your liking.

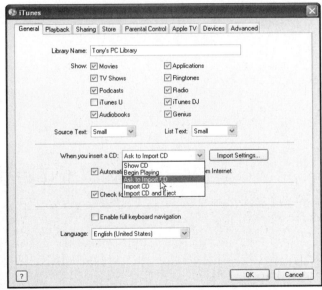

Figure 8-2:
Set the appropriate action for iTunes after a CD is inserted.

3. **Select the Automatically Retrieve CD Track Names from Internet check box.**

   This option is selected by default, but make sure that the box is checked. iTunes automatically grabs the song titles, artist names, album titles, and so on directly from the Internet database of songs, as I describe in Chapter 12. If you don't want to use an Internet connection at this time, you can grab this information later, as I explain in Chapter 12.

4. **Click the Import Settings button in the General preferences.**

   The Import Settings dialog appears, as shown in Figure 8-3.

5. **Make your changes, guided by my suggestions that follow, and then click the OK button.**

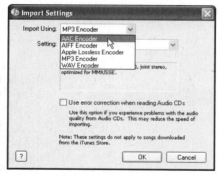

Figure 8-3: Change your import settings for ripping CDs.

The Import Settings dialog offers the following choices:

- **Import Using:** Set this pop-up menu to choose the import encoder. This choice is perhaps the most important, and I describe it in more detail later in this section.

- **Setting:** This offers different settings depending on your choice of encoder. For example, in Figure 8-4, the AAC Encoder is already selected, and I'm in the process of choosing the iTunes Plus setting, which is the quality setting for music available in the iTunes Store. Set this pop-up menu to the iTunes Plus or High Quality setting for most music, or choose Custom to choose a custom setting. The Spoken Podcast setting is for lower-quality voice recordings. See below for more information about encoders and settings and how they affect quality and file size.

- **Use Error Correction When Reading Audio CDs:** Although you'll reduce importing speed, select this check box to use error correction if you have problems with audio quality or if the CD skips. (Not every skipping CD can be imported even with error correction, but it might help.)

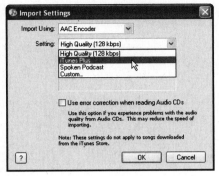

Figure 8-4:
Change the
quality
setting
for the
encoder you
chose for
importing.

For a quick and pain-free ripping session, choose from among the following encoders in the Import Using pop-up menu, based on how you plan to use the music:

- **AAC Encoder:** I recommend AAC for almost all music. (However, AIFF, Apple Lossless, or WAV is better if you plan to burn another audio CD at the highest quality with the songs you ripped, and MP3 is the only format to use for MP3 CDs and other MP3 players.) For music, choose the High Quality or iTunes Plus settings from the Setting pop-up menu.

- **AIFF Encoder:** Use AIFF if you plan to burn the song to an audio CD using a Mac (use WAV for Windows), or use it with a DVD project. AIFF offers the highest possible quality, but it takes up a lot of space (about 10MB per minute). Choose the Automatic option from the Setting pop-up menu for best results. Don't use the AIFF format for songs that you intend to transfer to your iPod or iPhone, or to an MP3 CD; convert them first to AAC or MP3.

  You can rip a CD as many times as you want, and use a different encoder each time, as long as you modify the album name or song title to identify each version. For example, you might rip *Sgt. Pepper's Lonely Hearts Club Band* with the AAC encoder for use in your iPod or iPhone. You might then rip it again after changing the encoder to the higher-quality Apple Lossless or AIFF encoder, using a different album name (such as Sgt. Pepper-2), for burning onto an audio CD. After burning the CD, you can delete Sgt. Pepper-2 to reclaim the hard drive space.

- **Apple Lossless Encoder:** Use the Apple Lossless encoder for songs that you intend to burn onto audio CDs as well as for playing on an iPod or iPhone. The files are just small enough (about 60–70 percent of the size of the AIFF versions) that they don't hiccup on playback.

- **MP3 Encoder:** Use the MP3 format for songs that you intend to burn on MP3 CDs or that you intend to use with MP3 players or your iPod or iPhone — it's universally supported. If you use MP3, I recommend choosing the Higher Quality option from the Setting pop-up menu.

✔ **WAV Encoder:** WAV is the high-quality sound format that's used on PCs (like AIFF on Macs), but it also takes up a lot of space (about 10MB per minute). Use WAV if you plan on burning the song to an audio CD or using WAV with PCs. Choose the Automatic option from the Setting pop-up menu for best results. Don't use WAV for songs that you intend to transfer to your iPod or to an MP3 CD; use MP3 instead.

To find out more about audio encoding formats, how to adjust custom settings to reduce space and increase audio quality, and how to convert songs from one format to another (and what problems to look out for when doing so), visit this book's companion Web site.

Don't fall into the gaps

Some CDs — particularly live concert albums, classical albums, rock operas (such as The Who's *Tommy*), and theme albums (such as *Sgt. Pepper's Lonely Hearts Club Band* by The Beatles) — are meant to be played straight through, with no fading between the songs.

Fortunately, you can turn on the Gapless Album option for multiple songs or for an entire album. With the Gapless Album option set in iTunes, songs play seamlessly one to the next. You can also play these songs seamlessly on your iPod or iPhone (including seventh-, sixth-, and fifth-generation models).

To turn on the Gapless Album option for an entire CD before importing it, follow these steps:

1. **Click the No button if the import dialog appears (to postpone importing).**

2. **Select the CD title in the Source pane.**

   The CD title appears in the Source pane under Devices.

3. **Choose File⇨Get Info.**

   The CD Info dialog opens, as shown in Figure 8-5.

4. **Select the Part of a Gapless Album check box and then click the OK button.**

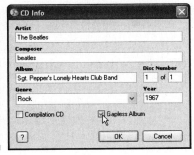

Figure 8-5:
Select the
Gapless
Album
option for
an entire
album.

To turn on the Gapless Album option for multiple songs on the CD but not the entire CD, follow these steps:

1. **Follow Steps 1 and 2 in the preceding list.**

2. **Select the songs in the List pane.**

   From the album, select the songs that you want to play continuously (such as the first two songs of *Sgt. Pepper*).

   To select multiple songs, click the first one, press and hold ⌘ on a Mac or Ctrl in Windows, and click each subsequent song. To select consecutive songs, click the first one, hold down the Shift key, and click the last one.

3. **Choose File⇨Get Info and then click the Yes button in the warning dialog about editing multiple items.**

   The Multiple Item Information dialog opens.

4. **Click the Options tab to see the Options pane, as shown in Figure 8-6.**

5. **Select Yes from the Gapless Album pop-up menu.**

   After choosing Yes on the pop-up menu, a check mark appears next to the Gapless Album option to indicate that it has changed.

6. **Click the OK button to close the Multiple Item Information dialog and update the options for the selected songs.**

For older iPod models, or as an alternative to using the Gapless Album option, you can use the Join Tracks option when ripping a CD to join the tracks in your iTunes library so that they play seamlessly on an iPod or iPhone. To join tracks, select the tracks and choose Advanced⇨Join CD Tracks. You can join tracks only when ripping a CD, not afterward.

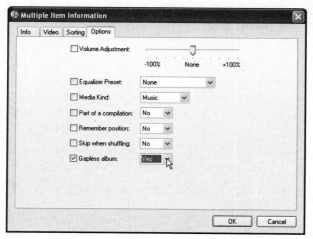

Figure 8-6:
Select the
Gapless
Album
option for
multiple
tracks.

Ripping music from CDs

After changing your import settings and preferences, you're ready to rip. To rip a CD, follow these steps:

1. Insert an audio CD into your computer.

The songs appear in the List pane as generic, unnamed tracks at first. If your computer is connected to the Internet *and* you've turned on the option to automatically retrieve song information from the Internet *and* the CD is in the Gracenote CDDB database (described in Chapter 12), iTunes automatically retrieves the track information.

A dialog appears asking whether you want to import the CD, with Yes and No buttons.

2. Click Yes to import (and skip to Step 5) or No to set options first.

Click the No button to set preferences and import settings as described in the previous section, to set songs to be skipped, or if you see unnamed tracks rather than the proper track, artist, and album names in the List pane. If all you need to change are the import settings, click the Import Settings button in the lower right corner of the List pane.

If the first attempt at retrieving song information doesn't work and you see unnamed tracks, check your connection to the Internet first. If everything is fine with your connection, stop the importing operation and then choose Advanced➪Get CD Track Names to try again to get the track information. If you don't want to connect to the Internet or if your CD isn't recognized by the Gracenote database, you can type in the track information yourself (see Chapter 12).

3. (Optional) Deselect the check boxes next to any songs on the CD that you don't want to import.

iTunes imports only the songs that have check marks next to them; when you remove the check mark next to a song in the List pane, iTunes skips that song.

Be sure to set your import settings and the Gapless Album option to your liking before actually ripping the CD.

4. Click the Import CD button.

The Import CD button appears next to the Import Settings button in the lower-right corner of the List pane. The status display shows the progress of the operation. To cancel, click the small *x* next to the progress bar in the status display.

iTunes displays an orange, animated waveform icon next to the song that it's importing. When iTunes finishes importing each song, it replaces the waveform icon with a check mark, as shown in Figure 8-7. (On a color monitor, the check mark is green.) iTunes chimes when it finishes the import list.

Figure 8-7: iTunes shows a check mark to indicate that it's done ripping the song.

5. When all the songs are imported, eject the CD by clicking the Eject button next to the disc name in the Devices section of the Source pane.

You can also choose Controls⇨Eject Disc to eject the disc. Mac users can press the Eject button on the upper-right corner of the Mac keyboard.

Adding music files

If you already have music or other audio files — MP3, AAC, AIFF, or WAV files — that you downloaded or copied to your hard drive, you can simply drag them over the Library section of the Source pane, or the List pane, of the iTunes window to bring them into your library. If you drag a folder or disk icon, all the audio files that it contains are added to your iTunes library (and if you drag it into the Playlists section of the Source pane, a playlist is created — see Chapter 14 for details). You can also choose File⇨Add to Library on a Mac, or File⇨Add File to Library and File⇨Add Folder to Library on a Windows PC, as an alternative to dragging.

When you add an audio file to your iTunes library, a copy is placed inside the iTunes Media folder without changing or deleting the original file; that is, as long as you have your iTunes preferences set for Copy Files to iTunes Media Folder When Adding to Library. (This is the default setting, which you can find on the Advanced tab of the iTunes Preferences dialog.) See Chapter 15 for details on storing music in your iTunes Media folder.

If you have files in another folder or on another hard drive and you want to add them to the iTunes library without copying the files to the iTunes Media folder, you can copy a link to the original files without copying the files. To copy only links to song files and not copy the actual files when you add songs, you can turn off the default copy files option by doing the following:

1. **Choose iTunes⇨Preferences (Mac) or Edit⇨Preferences (Windows).**

2. **Click the Advanced tab in the iTunes Preferences dialog.**

3. **Turn off the Copy Files to iTunes Media Folder When Adding to Library setting.**

You can check out the contents of your iTunes Media folder by using the Finder on a Mac or Windows Explorer on a Windows PC, as I describe in detail in Chapter 15.

MP3 CDs are easy to add because they're essentially data CDs. Simply insert them into your CD-ROM drive, open the CD in the Finder, and drag and drop the MP3 audio files into the iTunes window — no need to rip, in other words. Downloaded audio files are even easier — just drag and drop the files into iTunes. If you drag a folder or CD icon, all the audio files it contains are added to your iTunes library.

Adding Podcasts

A *podcast* can be anything from a single song or video to a radio or TV show — an audio podcast is an MP3 audio file, and a video podcast is a video file (see "Adding Videos" in this chapter for technical details).

You can add podcasts to your iTunes library by subscribing to them in the iTunes Store (as I describe in breathtaking detail in Chapter 7) or by subscribing to them directly from Web sites that host them. Similar to a recording of a radio broadcast, you can save and play a podcast at your convenience — both in iTunes on your computer and on your iPod, iPhone, and Apple TV.

The podcast producer uses Really Simple Syndication (RSS) technology — the same technology used to distribute blogs and news feeds across the Internet — to publish the podcast. RSS feeds are typically linked to an RSS or an eXtensible Markup Language (XML; the language of RSS) button. With a feed reader, aggregator application, or browser plug-in, you can automatically check RSS-enabled Web pages and display updated stories and podcasts. RSS version 2, the most popular version for podcasting, is supported directly by some Web browsers, including Apple's Safari for Mac OS X and Windows.

With iTunes, you can play a podcast, incorporate it into playlists, make copies, and burn it onto CD as much as you like.

Subscribing to podcasts

The Podcasts section of the iTunes Store offers access to many thousands of podcasts, but more than a million podcasts exist, many of which are available only on their respective Web sites. The iTunes Store makes it easy to subscribe to podcasts, so check there first — turn to Chapter 7 to see how to find and subscribe to podcasts in the iTunes Store.

By *subscribing,* I mean simply listing the podcast in your iTunes Podcasts pane so that new episodes are downloaded automatically. It's like a magazine subscription that's updated with a new issue every month or so. You don't have to register or fill out any form. You don't have to provide an e-mail address or any other information. Your copy of iTunes automatically finds new podcast episodes and downloads them to your computer.

The easiest way to subscribe to a podcast is through the iTunes Store. However, if you can't find a podcast in the store and you know how to find its Web site, open your browser and go to that Web site. Some Web sites also offer an iTunes button to click to go directly to the iTunes Store to subscribe to the podcast.

If you don't see an iTunes button, you can still subscribe to a podcast directly from iTunes by grabbing information from its Web site first. Follow these steps:

1. **In your browser, Control-click (Mac) or right-click (Windows or Mac) the podcast's RSS2 link on the Web page.**

   Look for the RSS version 2 link on the Web page.

2. **Copy the podcast's RSS2 link:**

   - *Safari:* Choose Copy Link.

   - *Firefox or Internet Explorer:* Choose Copy Link Location.

3. **In iTunes, choose Advanced⇨Subscribe to Podcast.**

   The Subscribe to Podcast dialog opens.

4. **Paste the RSS2 link into the dialog that appears by choosing Edit⇨Paste and then click the OK button.**

   As an alternative, you can also press ⌘-V on a Mac or Ctrl-V in Windows.

   When you paste it, the link should look something like this:

   ```
   http://www.rockument.com/blog/?feed=RSS2
   ```

   iTunes downloads the podcast to your computer and switches to the Podcasts selection in the Source pane.

5. **Click the *i* icon to see information about the podcast.**

   You can click the *i* icon on the far-right podcast listing margin to display separate information about the podcast's newest episode.

6. **Select the podcast and then click the Play button.**

   You can now play the podcast just like a song or video in your iTunes library. You can use the iTunes playback controls to fast-forward, rewind, or play the podcast from any point. The blue dot next to a podcast means that you haven't played it yet. As soon as you start listening to or watching a podcast, the dot disappears. You can even drag podcast episodes into a playlist, as I describe in Chapter 14, and then burn that playlist onto a CD, as I describe in Chapter 15.

If the podcaster embedded a photo in an audio podcast file or included a link to a video from the file, the photo or video content appears in the Artwork pane.

Updating podcasts

Many podcast feeds provide new material on a regular schedule. iTunes can check these feeds automatically and update your library with new podcast episodes. You can, for example, schedule iTunes to check for new podcast episodes — such as news, weather, traffic reports, and morning talk shows — before you wake up and automatically update your iPod or iPhone. When you get up, you have new podcast episodes to listen to in your iPod or iPhone.

To check for updates manually, select Podcasts in the Library section of the Source pane and then click the Refresh button in the lower-right corner of the Podcasts pane, which appears if podcasts need to be updated. All subscribed podcast feeds are updated immediately when you click Refresh, and iTunes downloads the most recent (or all) episodes, depending on how you set your podcasts preferences to schedule podcast updates.

Scheduling podcast updates

To change your podcast settings so that iTunes can check for new podcasts automatically, click the Settings button at the bottom of the Podcasts pane to display the Podcast Settings dialog, as shown in Figure 8-8.

Figure 8-8:
Set iTunes to automatically check for, download, and keep podcast episodes.

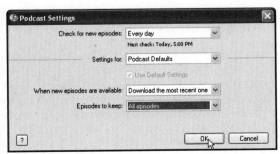

You can change the settings for each podcast separately by choosing the podcast in the Settings For pop-up menu. The settings are as follows:

- ✔ **Check for New Episodes:** Choose to check for podcasts every hour, day, week, or manually — whenever you want.

- ✔ **Settings For:** Choose which podcast in your iTunes library you are scheduling updates for, or choose Podcast Defaults to apply these settings to all podcasts in your library.

- ✔ **When New Episodes Are Available:** You can download the most recent one (useful for news podcasts), download all episodes (useful for podcasts you might want to keep), or nothing so that you can use the Refresh button to update manually as you need.

- ✔ **Episodes to Keep:** Choose to keep all episodes, all unplayed episodes, the most recent episodes, or previous episodes (refer to Figure 8-8).

Keeping unplayed episodes is a useful way to organize your news podcasts. If you've played an episode (or a portion of it), you likely don't need it anymore, but you probably do want to keep the ones you haven't played yet. With this setting, iTunes automatically deletes the ones you've played.

If you copy podcasts automatically when synchronizing your iPod or iPhone, as I describe in Chapter 9, don't set the Episodes to Keep pop-up to All Unplayed Episodes — use All Episodes instead. This is why: If you listen to part of a podcast episode on your iPod or iPhone and then synchronize your iPod or iPhone, the podcast episode disappears from iTunes (because it is no longer unplayed). But don't worry; the episodes are still out there on the Internet. You can always recover them by choosing Download All for the When New Episodes Are Available option.

Adding Videos

Besides purchasing and downloading videos from the iTunes Store, as I describe in nearly orgasmic detail in Chapter 7, you can also download video files (files that end in `.mov`, `.m4v`, or `.mp4`) from the Internet, or copy them from other computers and bring them into iTunes. From iTunes, you can sync them to your iPod, iPhone, and Apple TV after converting them into a format that looks best for those devices.

To convert a video for use with an iPod or iPhone, select the video (see Chapter 11 for browsing instructions) and choose Advanced⇨Create iPod or iPhone Version. To convert a video for use with Apple TV, choose Advanced⇨Create Apple TV Version. The selected videos are automatically copied when you convert them, leaving the originals intact.

To find out more about bringing videos from other sources into iTunes and converting videos for use with iPods, iPhones, and Apple TV, visit the Tips section of the author's Web site (www.tonybove.com).

You can drag a video file into iTunes just like an audio file. Drag each video file from the Mac Finder or Windows Desktop to the Library section of the Source pane, or directly to a playlist in the Playlists section of the Source pane, or to the List pane. The video files that you import into iTunes show up in the Movies section of your iTunes library — click Movies in the Library section of the Source pane to see them.

Video files are organized in folders and stored in the iTunes Media library on your hard drive just like audio files. You can find the video file's location on your hard drive and its type by selecting the video and choosing File⇨Get Info.

Chapter 9

Into the Sync with iTunes

*i*Tunes is the all-knowing, all-powerful synchronizer, the software you use to put content and your iTunes Store account information on your iPod or iPhone.

Synchronizing your iPod or iPhone with iTunes means keeping it up to date with all or part of your iTunes library — matching it song for song, movie for movie, and so on. The sync operation also keeps an iPod touch or iPhone up to date with your iTunes Store account information so that you can download items from the iTunes Store or App Store directly to your iPod touch or iPhone.

If you make changes in iTunes after syncing the iPod or iPhone, those changes are automatically made in the iPod or iPhone when you sync again. Your iPod or iPhone mirrors all the content of your iTunes library, or as much of the content as will fit — and iTunes can make assumptions if the entire library won't fit, or give you options to be more selective, as I describe in this chapter.

You also use iTunes to sync Apple TV, which lets you play your iTunes library content on an HDTV audio-video system. To find out more about Apple TV, visit this book's companion Web site.

When you first set up your iPod or iPhone, you can choose the option to sync your entire iTunes library automatically. From that point on, your iPod or iPhone synchronizes with your entire library automatically, right after you connect it to your computer. (See Chapter 2 for details on setting up your iPod or iPhone.)

The full, everything-but-the-kitchen-sync approach works well if your combined iTunes library and photo library are small enough to fit in their entirety on your iPod or iPhone. For example, if your iTunes and photo libraries combined are less than 29GB and you have a 32GB iPod touch, sync everything. (You can see the size of your iTunes library in GB, or *gigabytes,* at the bottom of the iTunes window in the center.) Syncing everything copies your entire library, and it's just as fast as copying individual items (if not faster) because you don't have to select the items to copy.

If your iTunes library has more content than your iPod, iPhone, or Apple TV can hold, you can make decisions about which parts to sync. You can select options to synchronize music, TV shows, movies, and so on. For example, you can copy all your songs and audio books, but only some of your TV shows, none of your movies, and only the podcasts you haven't heard yet.

This chapter also describes how to copy songs, videos, podcasts, and audio books directly to your iPod or iPhone using the manual method. You can even combine automatic syncing with manual methods to build your iPod or iPhone library as you see fit.

If you store photos in an iPhoto library (on a Mac) or in a program (such as Adobe Photoshop Album in Windows), you can set up your iPod, iPhone, or Apple TV with the option to copy your entire photo library. See Chapter 18 for details.

Syncing with Your iTunes Store Account

You can sync your iPod touch or iPhone with your iTunes Store account information in advance, so that you don't have to manually sign in with your iPod touch or iPhone before downloading from the iTunes Store or App Store.

To manually sign in or create an account on your iPod touch or iPhone, choose Settings⇨Store and touch Sign In or Create New Account. If your iPod touch or iPhone is already synced with your account, the View Account button appears in place of Sign In.

If you were signed in to your iTunes Store account when you initially set up and synced your iPod touch or iPhone, the store account information was also synchronized. If not, or if you want to resync your store information, visit the iTunes Store and sign in to your account first, before syncing your iPod or iPhone.

You don't have to buy anything; just signing in to the store provides all the info you need for syncing an iPod touch or iPhone with the iTunes Store account. (If you haven't set up your iTunes Store account yet, flip back to Chapter 7, do the deed, and then sign in by clicking the Sign In tab in the upper-right area of the iTunes window.)

After signing into your account, go ahead and follow the steps in the next sections to sync your iPod or iPhone — "Copying Everything", "Choosing What to Sync", or "Manually Managing Music and Videos".

After syncing to your account, your iPod touch or iPhone will always sync any purchased content or apps you download directly to it with your iTunes library whenever you connect it to your computer — that way you don't lose any content or apps if, heaven forbid, something happens to your iPod touch or iPhone.

Copying Everything

Follow these steps to sync all the content in your iTunes library to an iPod or iPhone:

1. **Connect the iPod or iPhone and select its name when it appears in the Devices section of the Source pane.**

   iTunes displays the sync options to the right of the Source pane, with the Summary page (under the Summary tab) open. The Summary page shows how much space on the device is occupied by content and how much is still free. (See Figure 9-1.)

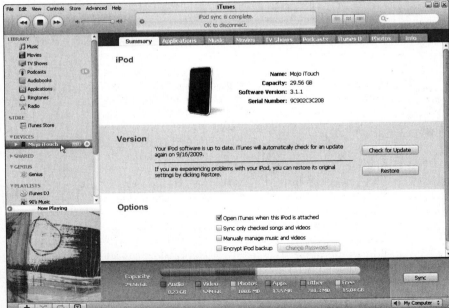

Figure 9-1: The Summary page for an iPod touch offers sync options.

2. **If the iPod or iPhone isn't already synchronizing, click the Sync button in the lower-right corner to synchronize it.**

   Most likely your iPod or iPhone is already set to automatically synchronize with iTunes after connecting it. After clicking the Sync button (or if iTunes is automatically syncing), the iTunes Status pane tells you that iTunes is syncing the iPod or iPhone.

   If you haven't made any sync selections, the default is to copy everything in your iTunes library to your iPod or iPhone. (Only the music, audio books, and audio podcasts in your library are copied to an iPod shuffle.)

   If your iPod or iPhone is not set to automatically synchronize, or even if synchronization is going on, you can select content to sync, as I describe later in this chapter, and click Apply to start re-syncing again with the new settings.

3. **Wait for the synchronization to finish and then click the Eject button next to the iPod or iPhone name in the Source pane.**

   You should always wait until the iTunes Status pane (at the top) displays that the synchronization is complete.

4. **Disconnect your iPod or iPhone from your computer.**

   That's it. Your iPod or iPhone is now synchronized.

Your iTunes library is the main library for your content, while the library in your iPod or iPhone is like a satellite holding some or all of the same content. If you make changes in your iTunes library after syncing the iPod or iPhone, those changes are automatically made in the iPod or iPhone when you sync again — unless you manually manage content, as I describe in "Manually Managing Music and Videos" in this chapter. That means if you delete an album or video from your iTunes library, that album or video is also deleted from your iPod or iPhone the next time you sync. You can delete items directly from your iPod or iPhone without changing your iTunes library — see "Deleting items on your iPod or iPhone" in this chapter.

You probably don't need to know anything else in this chapter about synchronizing your iPod or iPhone with content — unless your iTunes library and additional photo library are too large to fit, or if you want to be more selective about which content to synchronize.

iTunes backs up your synchronization settings for each iPod or iPhone that you connect from the last time when you synchronized the device.

Photos you've organized in an iPhoto library (on a Mac) or in a program (such as Adobe Photoshop Album in Windows) are also copied over. See Chapter 18 for details.

If your iTunes library is too large to fit on your iPod or iPhone, iTunes decides which songs and albums to include by using the ratings that you set for each song. (To find out how to set ratings, see Chapter 12.) If your iPod or iPhone already has photos on it, iTunes asks whether you want to delete them to gain more space. After clicking the Yes or No button, iTunes tries its best to fit everything. If it has to cut something, though, it skips copying new photos and displays the message Some photos were not copied.

You can squeeze more songs onto an iPod shuffle if you convert them to a lower-bit-rate format — and you can do this on the fly. If you've imported songs into iTunes at higher-bit-rate formats or with encoders such as iTunes Plus, Apple Lossless, or WAV (see Chapter 8 for details), you can set iTunes to automatically convert songs to 128-kbps AAC files while syncing with the iPod shuffle. The songs are not changed in your iTunes library. To do this, connect your iPod shuffle to your computer, click its name in the Devices section of the Source pane to show the Summary page sync options, and select the Convert Higher Bit Rate Songs to 128 kbps AAC option (which appears only for an iPod shuffle). As a result, the songs take up less space on the iPod shuffle than they occupy in your iTunes library.

If you're still short of space even after skipping photos, iTunes displays a warning about the lack of free space, and it asks whether you want to disable podcast synchronization and let iTunes create a selection of songs in a playlist based on ratings and playback counts in iTunes. (See Chapter 14 for details on using playlists.)

- **If you click the Yes button,** iTunes creates a new playlist (titled "*Your device name* Selection," as in "My iPod touch Selection") and displays a message telling you so. Click the OK button, and iTunes synchronizes your iPod or iPhone using the new playlist. iTunes also sets your iPod or iPhone to synchronize music automatically by playlist, as I describe in the next section.

- **If you click the No button,** iTunes updates automatically until it fills your iPod or iPhone without creating the playlist.

From that point on, your iPod or iPhone synchronizes with your iTunes library automatically, right after you connect it to your computer. If you add or delete content in your iTunes library, that content is added or deleted in the iPod or iPhone when you sync again.

To prevent an iPod or iPhone from automatically synchronizing, press ⌘-Option (Mac) or Ctrl-Alt (Windows) while you connect the device; then keep pressing until the iPod or iPhone name appears in the iTunes Source pane. You can then change the iPod or iPhone sync setting to manually manage music and videos, as I describe later in this chapter.

If you connect an iPod or iPhone previously linked to another computer to *your* computer, iTunes displays a message warning you that clicking the Yes button replaces the iPod or iPhone content with the content from your computer's library. If you don't want to change the content on the iPod or iPhone, click No. If you click Yes, iTunes erases the iPod or iPhone and synchronizes it with your computer's library. To avoid this warning, first set the iPod or iPhone sync settings to manually manage music and videos, as I describe later in this chapter, on the computer the iPod or iPhone was previously synced.

Choosing What to Sync

If you have a massive music library that doesn't fit on your iPod or iPhone, you can go the selective route, choosing which content to automatically sync with your iTunes library. By synchronizing selectively, you can still make your iPod or iPhone match at least a subset of your iTunes library. If you make changes to that subset in iTunes, those changes are automatically made in the device when you synchronize again.

You don't have to sync to one massive library in iTunes — you can create several subsets of your main library (sublibraries) so that each sublibrary could be small enough to fit on a certain type of device. For example, you might create a sublibrary for a 32GB iPod touch and another sublibrary for a 16GB iPod nano. Before connecting a device, you could switch to its corresponding sublibrary within iTunes and then synchronize automatically.

To find out how to manage multiple iTunes libraries, visit the Tips section of the author's Web site (www.tonybove.com).

Syncing everything but the kitchen

You can decide which items you *don't* want to synchronize and simply not include them by first *deselecting* them one by one in your iTunes library. (If you have a large iTunes library, this may take some time — you may find it easier to synchronize by playlists, artists, and genres, as I show in the next section.)

By default, all content items are selected — a check mark appears in the check box next to the item. To deselect an item in your iTunes library, click the check box next to the item so that the check mark disappears. To reselect an item, just click the check box again.

You can quickly select (or deselect) an entire album by showing the Browser (choose View➪Show Column Browser) and selecting the album. Then press ⌘ (Mac) or Ctrl (Windows) while selecting (or deselecting) a single song in the album in the List pane.

After you deselect the items you don't want to transfer, connect your iPod or iPhone to your computer and select its name when it appears in the Devices section of the Source pane (refer to Figure 9-1). Then select the Sync Only Checked Songs and Videos check box. The Sync button changes to Apply — click the Apply button.

iTunes restarts synchronization and deletes from the iPod or iPhone any items in the library that are deselected, to save space, before adding back in the items in the iTunes library that are selected. That means the items you deselected are now *gone* from your iPod or iPhone — replaced by whatever items were selected. Of course, the items are still in your iTunes library. Wait for the synchronization to finish and then click the Eject button next to the iPod or iPhone name in the Source pane.

Getting picky about playlists, artists, and genres

You can include just the items that are defined in playlists, including Genius playlists, and/or just specific artists. Syncing by playlists, artists, and genres is a great way of syncing vast amounts of music without syncing the entire library. (To find out how to create playlists, see Chapter 14.)

For example, you can create four playlists that contain all essential rock, folk, blues, and jazz albums, and then select all four, or just one, two, or three of these playlists to sync with your iPod or iPhone, along with everything by specific artists (such as Frank Zappa, who doesn't fit into these categories). You can even include audio books in your playlists, or create a playlist of just audio books, to sync with your iPod or iPhone.

After connecting your iPod or iPhone to your computer, select its name when it appears in the Devices section of the Source pane (refer to Figure 9-1). Then click the Music tab of the sync options. The Music sync options page appears, as shown in Figure 9-2.

Figure 9-2:
Synchronize
only the
selected
playlists,
artists, and
genres.

By default, the Entire Music Library option is checked, unless you are manually managing music as I describe later in this chapter. To change your sync options, select the Sync Music check box.

If you were manually managing music, a message appears asking if you are sure that you want to sync music — all content already on your iPod or iPhone will be replaced. Click the Sync Music button (or Cancel to cancel) to return to the Music sync options page.

To choose playlists, artists, and genres to sync with the iPod or iPhone, click the Selected Playlists, Artists, and Genres option at the top of the Music sync options page (refer to Figure 9-2). You can then select each playlist from the Playlists list, each artist from the Artists list, and (if you scroll the Music sync options page) each genre from the Genres list. You can choose any number of playlists, artists, and genres. (In Figure 9-2, I selected the Music Videos and Recently Added smart playlists along with a few artists.)

Finally, click the Apply button to apply changes and click the Sync button if synchronization hasn't already started automatically.

iTunes copies only what you've selected in the Playlists, Artists, and Genres sections of the Music sync options page. If you also select the Include Music Videos check box (as I do in Figure 9-2), iTunes includes music videos listed in the playlists (except, of course, for an iPod shuffle, which doesn't play video). For an iPod touch or iPhone, you can also select the Include Voice Memos check box to sync your voice memos from the Voice Memo app with iTunes. (See Chapter 21 for details on using Voice Memo.)

You can also automatically fill up the rest of your iPod or iPhone free space with random songs (after syncing your selected playlists, artists, and genres) by selecting the Automatically Fill Free Space With Songs option. iTunes randomly chooses the music as I describe in the latter part of the "Copying Everything" section. If you select the Sync Only Checked Songs and Videos check box on the Summary page of the iPod or iPhone sync options (refer to Figure 9-1), only selected items are copied. iTunes ignores items that are not selected, even if they're listed in the chosen playlists for synchronization.

Picking and choosing podcast episodes

You can get picky about which podcast episodes should be copied during synchronization. Clicking the Podcasts tab of the sync pages presents options for choosing podcast episodes to include. (You can include audio podcasts to sync with an iPod shuffle, but not video podcasts.)

Connect your iPod or iPhone to your computer, and select its name when it appears in the Devices section of the Source pane (refer to Figure 9-1). Then click the Podcasts tab. The Podcasts sync options page appears, as shown in Figure 9-3. Click the Sync Podcasts option at the top.

The Podcast sync options let you choose unplayed or recently added episodes (as shown in Figure 9-3). Select the Automatically Include ____ Episodes Of ____ check box; choose a modifier from the first pop-up menu, such as All Unplayed or 10 Most Recent; and then choose All Podcasts or Selected Podcasts from the second pop-up menu. If you chose Selected Podcasts, you can select a podcast in the Podcasts column below these options, and then select specific episodes in the Episodes column (which may already be selected depending on your choices in the pop-up menus).

For example, in Figure 9-3, I'm synchronizing the 10 most recent episodes of selected podcasts — I've already selected The Flying Other Brothers-Music Podcast (2 new episodes out of 3), and I'm selecting the Social Folk Roots of California Rock episode of the Rockument podcast.

Finally, click the Apply button to apply changes, and click the Sync button if synchronization hasn't already started automatically.

Choosing movies and TV shows

Movies and TV shows take up a lot of space, so if you limit the movies and TV episodes you synchronize with your iPod or iPhone, you gain extra space for more music, audio books, podcasts, and photos. (This section doesn't apply to the iPod shuffle, which doesn't play movies or TV shows.)

To get choosy about movies, connect your iPod or iPhone to your computer, and select its name when it appears in the Devices section of the Source pane (refer to Figure 9-1). Then click the Movies tab of the sync options. The Movies sync options page appears as shown in Figure 9-4. You see the Movies sync options page for an iPod, as shown in Figure 9-4, or the Video sync options for an iPhone — scroll the Video sync options page to see the Movies section.

Select the Sync Movies check box (as shown in Figure 9-4). Select the Automatically Include _____ Movies check box; choose a modifier from the pop-up menu, such as All, All Unwatched, or 10 Most Recent Unwatched. If you choose any option other than All, you can then select specific movies from the list below the option. For example, in Figure 9-4 I'm automatically including 1 Most Recent movie along with the selected movie *Jacob's Ladder.*

Figure 9-4:
Synchronize
the selected
movies only
(iPod).

To pick only the TV episodes you want, click the TV Shows tab of the sync options. The TV Shows sync options page appears, as shown in Figure 9-5.

Select the Automatically Include ____ Episodes Of ____ check box; choose a modifier from the first pop-up menu, such as All, All Unwatched, or 5 Most Recent; and then choose All Shows or Selected Shows from the second pop-up menu. If you chose Selected Shows, you can select a show in the Shows column below these options, and then select specific episodes in the Episodes column (which may already be selected depending on your choices in the pop-up menus).

For example, in Figure 9-5, I'm synchronizing all episodes of selected shows whether I've watched them or not — but I'm also selecting only two episodes of Star Trek: The Original Series and deselecting the other episodes, in order to get only the episodes I want.

Finally, click the Apply button to apply changes and click the Sync button if synchronization hasn't already started automatically.

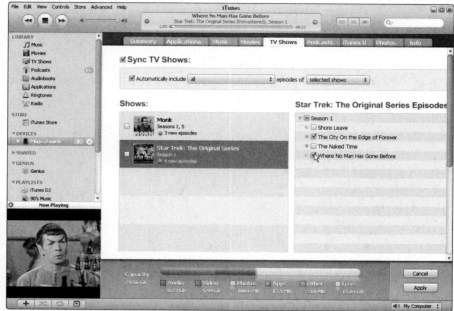

Figure 9-5:
Synchronize
only
selected
TV show
episodes.

Manually Managing Music and Videos

If your entire library is too big for your iPod or iPhone, you may want to copy individual items directly. By setting your iPod or iPhone to manually manage music and videos, you can add content to your iPod or iPhone directly via iTunes, and you can delete content as well. You can even copy some songs or videos from another computer's iTunes library without deleting any content from your iPod or iPhone.

To set your iPod or iPhone to manually manage music and videos, first connect it to your computer. Then follow these steps:

1. **Select the iPod or iPhone name in the Devices section of the iTunes Source pane.**

   After selecting the name, the Summary page appears, displaying the iPod or iPhone sync options (refer to Figure 9-1).

2. **Select the Manually Manage Music and Videos check box (on an iPod shuffle, select Manually Manage Music).**

   iTunes displays a message for iPod nano and iPod classic models (and older models) warning you that manually managing music and videos also requires manually ejecting the iPod or iPhone before each disconnect

3. **Click the OK button for the warning, and click the Apply button to apply the change.**

Don't disconnect your iPod or iPhone while managing music and videos manually. You have to eject it first, as spelled out in the next section. If you don't, you may find that it doesn't work properly and needs to be restored, as I describe in Chapter 22.

Copying items directly to your iPod or iPhone

After setting your iPod or iPhone to manually manage music and videos, you can select and drag music and videos — songs, albums, audio books, music videos, movies, and TV shows — to your iPod or iPhone name in the Source pane. (Similarly, after setting an iPod shuffle to manually manage music, you can select and drag music, audio books, and audio podcasts to the iPod shuffle.)

You can drag the media from its section in the iTunes library or from an existing playlist, or drag an entire playlist. To do so, follow these steps:

1. **In the iTunes Source pane, select the source of your media.**

    You might select Music in the Library section, for instance, or a playlist in the library.

    You can select music in your library using List, Grid, or Cover Flow view (see Chapter 11 for browsing details), or select songs in a playlist.

2. **Drag items (such as one or more songs or an album) directly from your iTunes library or playlist over the iPod or iPhone name in the Devices section of the Source pane.**

    You can drag an individual songs or an entire album from Cover Flow view, List view, or Grid view (as I do in Figure 9-6). When you drag an album cover or album title, all the songs in the album are copied. If you drag a playlist name from the Source pane to the iPod or iPhone name, all the songs associated with the playlist copy along with the playlist itself.

3. **Wait for the copying to finish and then click the Eject button next to the iPod or iPhone name in the Source pane to eject it.**

4. **Disconnect your iPod or iPhone from your computer.**

Figure 9-6:
Drag an
album from
the Artwork
Column in
the iTunes
library to
an iPod
or iPhone
to copy
the entire
album.
(My iPod
touch is
called Mojo
iTouch.)

Deleting items on your iPod or iPhone

When you manually manage music and videos on an iPod or iPhone (or manage music on an iPod shuffle), you can also delete content from the iPod or iPhone. Set the option to manually manage music and videos (if it isn't set that way already) and then follow these steps:

1. **In the Source pane, click the triangle to the left of the iPod or iPhone name to expand its library.**

   The iPod or iPhone library appears in the Source pane with Music, Movies, TV Shows, and other sections, followed by playlists. The library is indented underneath the iPod or iPhone name.

2. **Click any content type in the iPod or iPhone library to see the items.**

   The content items appear in the iTunes List pane to the right of the Source pane.

3. **Select an item and press Delete/Backspace or choose Edit⇨Delete.**

   iTunes displays a warning to make sure that you want to do this; click the OK button to go ahead or the Cancel button to stop. If you want to delete a playlist, select the playlist underneath the iPod or iPhone name in the Source pane and then press Delete/Backspace or choose Edit⇨Delete.

Like in the iTunes library (as I describe in Chapter 14), if you delete a playlist, the songs listed in the playlist aren't deleted. They're still on your iPod or iPhone unless you delete the songs directly from the iPod or iPhone library.

Autofill it up

You can also automatically fill your iPod or iPhone while managing music and videos manually. Autofill randomly picks songs from your entire iTunes library or from a playlist you select in the iTunes Source pane.

Autofill is especially useful for copying random songs to an iPod shuffle every time you connect it to your computer. Eventually, you can shuffle through everything in your library if you so wish by randomly autofilling your iPod shuffle every time you sync.

Set the option to manually manage music on the iPod shuffle or to manage music and videos on the iPod or iPhone (if it isn't set that way already). Then follow these steps:

1. **In the Source pane, click the triangle to the left of the iPod or iPhone name to expand its library.**

   The iPod or iPhone library appears in the Source pane.

2. **Select Music under the iPod or iPhone name in the Devices section of the Source pane.**

   The music on your iPod or iPhone appears in the List pane, along with the Autofill pane along the bottom, as shown in Figure 9-7.

3. **Choose your source of music from the Autofill From pop-up menu.**

   Choose either a playlist, as I did in Figure 9-7 (the Purchased smart playlist), the Genius option (which I describe in Chapter 14), or Music for the entire music library. If you choose a playlist or Genius, Autofill uses only the playlist or the Genius feature as the source to pick random songs. After choosing your source of music, iTunes creates a playlist and displays it in the List pane.

4. **(Optional) Click the Settings button to set options and then click the OK button.**

   After clicking the Settings button, the Autofill Settings dialog appears. You can choose to replace all the items on the iPod or iPhone, to choose items randomly, or to choose higher rated items more often. If you don't select to replace all items, iTunes adds the items without replacing existing content. Click the OK button to close the Autofill Settings dialog.

Figure 9-7:
Autofill your
iPod or
iPhone from
an iTunes
playlist.

5. **Click the Autofill button to start copying songs.**

   iTunes copies the contents of the Autofill playlist to your iPod or iPhone.

6. **Wait for the copy operation to finish and then click the Eject button.**

   Always wait until the iTunes Status pane (at the top) tells you that the copying is finished.

You can click the Autofill button repeatedly to create different random playlists. When you get one you like, select all its contents and choose File➪New Playlist from Selection to create a new playlist that contains the songs generated by Autofill. The next time you connect your iPod or iPhone, select this new playlist from the Autofill From pop-up menu and then click the Autofill button to load the music from the playlist to your iPod or iPhone.

Chapter 10

Syncing Mail, Calendars, Contacts, and Bookmarks

In This Chapter

▶ Using iTunes to sync calendars and contacts with an iPod or iPhone

▶ Using iTunes to sync e-mail accounts, notes, and bookmarks with an iPod touch or iPhone

▶ Using MobileMe to sync an iPod touch or iPhone over the Internet

▶ Setting up e-mail accounts on your iPod touch or iPhone

*Y*ou may choose an iPod classic to play music and videos on the road, but you may also find it useful for viewing the personal information — contacts, appointments, and events — that you manage on your home or office computer. The iPod classic, nano, and older models offer *one-way* synchronization of personal information from your computer to the iPod. (The iPod shuffle doesn't hold personal information, so this chapter isn't relevant for it.)

The iPod touch or iPhone can take care of all aspects of your digital life: It can send and receive e-mail, keep track of your calendar, sort your contacts, and save bookmarks to all your favorite Web sites as you browse them. You can also add personal info directly to your iPod touch or iPhone, and synchronize that information back with your computer, which is *two-way* synchronization.

If you're a road warrior, you may want to fill your iPod or iPhone with your personal information. This chapter shows you how.

Applications to Organize Your Life

You already manage your contacts, calendars, e-mail, and Web bookmarks with applications on your computer. Now you can use iTunes to synchronize your iPod classic or iPod nano with these calendars and contacts, or your iPod touch or iPhone with these calendars, contacts, e-mail accounts, and bookmarks.

If you're a Mac user, you have it easy: You can use the Address Book application to manage your contacts, iCal for calendars, Mail for e-mail, and Safari for Web bookmarks. All these applications are provided free with Mac OS X. You can also sync contacts from Microsoft Entourage, Yahoo! Address Book, and Google Address Book, and sync calendars from Entourage.

If you're a Windows user, you can sync your contacts with Microsoft Outlook 2003 or 2007, Yahoo! Address Book, Google Address Book, Windows Address Book (Outlook Express), or Vista Contacts. You can sync calendars with Outlook and sync bookmarks with Microsoft Internet Explorer or Apple's Safari for Windows.

The iPod touch and iPhone can also use the Exchange ActiveSync protocol to sync e-mail, calendars, and contacts with Microsoft Exchange Server 2003 Service Pack 2 or Exchange Server 2007 Service Pack 1. For many e-mail accounts, the settings automatically appear, like magic.

If you signed up for Apple's MobileMe service (formerly the .Mac service, now www.me.com), you can automatically keep your iPod touch or iPhone synchronized along with several computers and other iPod touch and iPhone models, all at once, with the latest e-mail, bookmarks, calendar entries, and contacts, as I describe in the section "Going MobileMe to Sync Your iPod touch or iPhone," later in this chapter.

What's cool about "cloud computing" Web services like MobileMe, Microsoft Exchange, and Yahoo! Mail is that their e-mail services *push* e-mail messages to your computer and your iPod touch or iPhone so that they arrive immediately, automatically. Other types of e-mail account services let you *fetch* e-mail from the server — you must first select the account in Mail on your iPod touch or iPhone before it can actually retrieve the e-mail.

You probably already know how to manage your calendar activities and your contacts on your computer. In fact, you're probably knee-deep in contacts, and your calendars look like they were drawn up in the West Wing. If not, visit the tips section of my Web site (www.tonybove.com) for advice on using MobileMe and on adding and editing contacts and calendar information on your Mac (with Address Book and iCal) or Windows computer (with Outlook). You can also find out how to use third-party utilities to manage personal information on your iPod touch or iPhone.

Syncing Your Personal Info Using iTunes

You use iTunes to synchronize an iPod classic or iPod nano with calendars and contacts on your computer.

With an iPod touch or iPhone, you can sync your personal information in three ways: using iTunes or using MobileMe (if you purchase the MobileMe service) or Microsoft Exchange. You can switch between these methods anytime you want. If you set up the iPod touch or iPhone to sync contacts, calendars, or bookmarks with MobileMe or Microsoft Exchange, syncing for those items is turned off in iTunes. MobileMe and Microsoft Exchange get their write-ups in the next section, and this section tackles the iTunes method.

To synchronize your iPod or iPhone with contacts, calendars, e-mail accounts, and bookmarks by using iTunes, follow these steps:

1. **Connect the iPod or iPhone, and select its name when it appears in the Devices section of the Source pane.**

   iTunes displays the iPod or iPhone sync options to the right of the Source pane, with the Summary page (under the Summary tab) open.

2. **Click the Info tab for an iPod touch or iPhone, or the Contacts tab for an iPod classic or iPod nano (or older model).**

   The Info sync options page appears for the iPod touch or iPhone (see Figure 10-1 for an iPod touch), offering the Contacts, Calendars, Web Browser, Notes, Mail Accounts, and Advanced sections. (At the top is a link to the MobileMe service if you are not already using it for syncing.)

   If you have an iPod classic, nano, or older model, what you see is the Contacts and Calendars synchronization options page, as shown in Figure 10-2.

3. **Select the option to synchronize contacts.**

   On a Mac: Select the Sync Address Book Contacts check box (shown in Figure 10-2). With an iPod touch or iPhone, you also have the option to sync with Yahoo! Address Book — click the Configure button to enter your login information. An option to sync with Microsoft Entourage appears for the iPod touch, iPhone, iPod nano, or iPod classic if you have that application on your Mac.

   On a Windows PC: Select the Sync Contents With option and choose Yahoo! Address Book, Windows Address Book, Google Contacts, or Outlook from the pop-up menu (refer to Figure 10-1).

4. **Select the All Contacts option, or select the Selected Groups option and choose which groups to synchronize.**

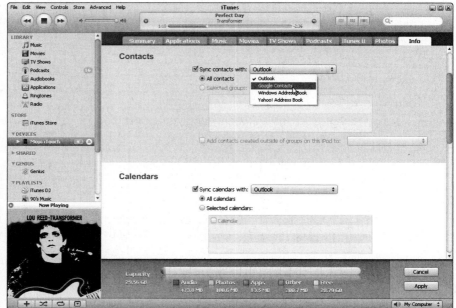

Figure 10-1:
Synchronize contacts and calendars with an iPod touch (or iPhone).

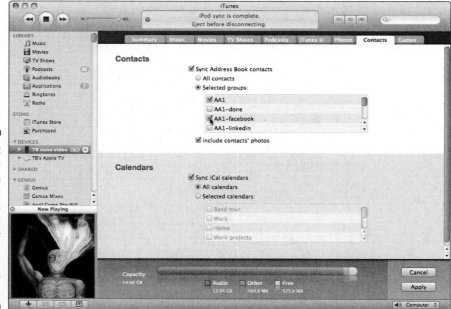

Figure 10-2:
Synchronize contacts and calendars with an iPod nano (or iPod classic or older model).

You can synchronize all contacts or just selected groups of contacts (such as the AA1 and AA1-facebook groups selected in Figure 10-2). To choose groups, select the check box next to each group in the list; scroll the list to see more groups.

If you make changes on an iPod touch or iPhone, iTunes automatically keeps all contacts you've selected synchronized with your computer's application.

5. **Scroll the page and select the option to synchronize calendars.**

   On a Mac, select the Sync iCal Calendars check box (shown in Figure 10-2); an option to sync with Microsoft Entourage also appears if you have the application on your Mac. On a Windows PC, select the Sync Calendars With option and choose Outlook from the pop-up menu (refer to Figure 10-1).

6. **Select the All Calendars option. (Alternatively, if you're using iCal with Mac OS X, select the Selected Calendars option and choose the calendars to synchronize.)**

   In Windows, you can synchronize all calendars with Microsoft Outlook, but you don't have the option to sync only selected calendars. (The Selected Calendars option is grayed out.) With iCal in Mac OS X, you can synchronize all calendars or just those you select. To choose specific calendars, select the check box next to each calendar in the list.

   The iPod touch and iPhone include the Do Not Sync Events Older Than *xx* Days option, in which you can set the *xx* number of days.

   Unless you are using an iPod touch or iPhone, you can skip to Step 12.

7. **Select the calendar to use for new events entered into your iPod touch or iPhone (Mac OS X only).**

   If you're using Mac OS X and iCal, you should set the calendar to use for new events you create on your iPod touch or iPhone. Choose a calendar name in the Put New Events into the Calendar option. When you create a new event on your iPod touch or iPhone (as I describe in Chapter 21) and sync it to your computer, the new event appears in this calendar. This affects only new events — events you modify on your iPod touch or iPhone retain their calendar information from before.

   Because you can't select individual calendars with Outlook in Windows, this option is grayed out — all events you create on an iPod touch or iPhone synchronize with the Outlook main calendar.

8. **To synchronize Web bookmarks with your iPod touch or iPhone, scroll down to the Web Browser section and select the Sync Bookmarks option.**

   On a Mac running OS X, the option is Sync Safari Bookmarks; on a Windows PC, iTunes selects Internet Explorer or Safari for this option, depending on which one is your default browser.

9. **To synchronize notes on your computer with an iPod touch or iPhone, scroll down to the Notes section.**

   You can sync the notes you create in the Notes app on your iPod touch or iPhone with the Mail application on a Mac or with Outlook on a Windows PC. Select the Sync Notes option; on a Windows PC, choose Outlook from the pop-up menu for the Sync Notes With option.

10. **To synchronize e-mail accounts with an iPod touch or iPhone, scroll down to the Mail Accounts section and select the Sync Selected Mail Accounts option.**

    Mail Accounts, as shown in Figure 10-3, appears below the Notes and Calendars sections on the Info sync options page. On a Mac, select the Sync Selected Mail Accounts option. On a Windows PC, choose Outlook or Outlook Express from the pop-up menu for the Sync Selected Mail Accounts From option.

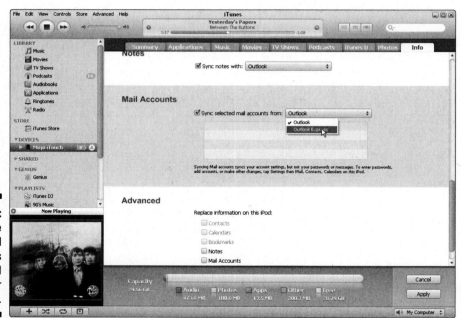

Figure 10-3: Synchronize e-mail accounts with an iPod touch (or iPhone).

11. **Choose the e-mail accounts you want to sync with your iPod touch or iPhone.**

    After selecting the Sync Selected Mail Accounts option in Step 10, a list of e-mail accounts appears in the box below. To choose accounts, select the check box next to each account in the list; scroll the list to see more e-mail accounts.

12. **Click the Apply button to apply the changes. (Alternatively, click the Cancel button to cancel the changes.)**

    iTunes starts to synchronize your iPod or iPhone.

13. **Wait for the sync to finish and then click the Eject button next to the iPod or iPhone name in the Source pane to eject the iPod or iPhone.**

    Wait until the iTunes Status pane (at the top) displays the message Sync is Complete.

After setting the synchronization options, every time you connect your iPod or iPhone, iTunes automatically synchronizes it with your personal sync options.

Synchronizing an e-mail account to your iPod touch or iPhone copies *only* the e-mail account setup information; the messages are retrieved by the iPod touch or iPhone over the Internet. Whether the messages in your inbox appear on your iPod touch or iPhone *and* on your computer depends on the type of e-mail account you have and how you've configured it.

If you select a calendar or a group of contacts to be synchronized on a Mac and later want to remove that particular calendar or group of contacts, deselect the calendar (see the preceding Step 6) or the group (see the preceding Step 4) and then click the Apply button to resynchronize. iTunes synchronizes only the group of contacts and calendars selected, removing from the iPod or iPhone any that aren't selected.

iTunes also offers Advanced options at the bottom of the Info page for the iPod touch or iPhone (refer to Figure 10-3). Use these options to sync your iPod touch or iPhone from scratch to replace all contacts, calendars, notes, mail accounts, or bookmarks. You can choose which ones you want to replace by selecting the check box next to each option. iTunes replaces the information once, during the next sync operation. After that operation, these Advanced options are automatically turned off.

Going MobileMe to Sync Your iPod touch or iPhone

MobileMe synchronizes MobileMe e-mail accounts, along with contacts, calendars, and bookmarks, on a Web server — also known as *the cloud*. You can then keep your iPod touch or iPhone synchronized to the cloud wirelessly, without having to connect it to your computer.

The place to start organizing your information is usually your computer. However, if you've already entered contacts and calendars on your iPod touch or iPhone, sync your contacts and calendars on your iPod touch or iPhone with iTunes first, as I describe in the previous section. Then sync your computer with MobileMe, and then your iPod touch or iPhone with MobileMe.

Make sure that the information you synchronize the very first time to MobileMe is the correct, complete information. You should synchronize your primary source — typically your computer — with MobileMe *before* synchronizing your iPod touch or iPhone.

MobileMe first makes its appearance when you set up your iPod touch or iPhone: An advertisement appears with buttons to try MobileMe. If you skipped the ad (like many people do), you can go back and try MobileMe by following these steps:

1. **Connect the iPod touch or iPhone to your computer and select its name when it appears in the Devices section of the Source pane.**

   iTunes displays the sync options to the right of the Source pane, with the Summary page (under the Summary tab) open.

2. **Click the Info tab.**

   The Info sync options page appears, offering the MobileMe setup button.

3. **Click the Set Up Now button.**

   iTunes jumps to your browser to open the MobileMe setup page on the Apple Web site. Here you can find out all about MobileMe, click the Free Trial button, or log in if you already have an account. Apple also provides step-by-step instructions for setting up MobileMe on your computer and syncing with your iPod touch or iPhone — or you can read all about it in the next few sections.

After setting up your MobileMe account on a Mac or Windows PC as described in the next sections, you turn on your MobileMe account on your iPod touch and iPhone, as I describe in section "Setting Up Mail Accounts on Your iPod touch or iPhone," later in this chapter.

Setting up on a Mac

Setting up MobileMe is easy on a Mac: When you sign in to MobileMe for the first time, MobileMe automatically configures Mac OS X Mail on your Mac to send and receive e-mail from your MobileMe account and to synchronize contacts from Address Book and calendars from iCal. If you already set up your iPod touch or iPhone with a Mac and MobileMe service, automatic synchronization should already be set up on that Mac.

If not, you can set up a Mac to sync with MobileMe at any time. Follow these steps:

1. **Choose System Preferences from the Apple menu, choose MobileMe, click the Account tab, and sign in.**

   If you see the .Mac logo instead (for older versions of Mac OS X), select .Mac and sign in. Follow the on-screen instructions, if they appear.

2. **Click the Sync tab.**

   The Sync options for MobileMe appear, as shown in Figure 10-4.

Figure 10-4:
Sync
options for
MobileMe
on a Mac.

3. **Select the Synchronize with MobileMe check box and then choose a sync interval from the pop-up menu. (Refer to Figure 10-4.)**

   For the most frequent updates, choose Automatically to sync with MobileMe every 15 minutes.

4. **Select the check boxes to choose information to sync with MobileMe.**

   You can choose to sync just contacts, calendars, bookmarks, or mail accounts, or all of them. (You can also sync other items, such as Dashboard Widgets, Dock Items, Keychains, and Mail Rules and Signatures, for use with other Macs, but these are not synced to your iPod touch or iPhone.)

5. **Click the Sync Now button.**

   The sync commences. To make sure that your data has synced, go to www.me.com, log in, and click the Contacts and Calendar icons along the top row of icons on the left.

Setting up in Windows

Download and install on your PC the latest version of MobileMe Control Panel for Windows, available from `http://support.apple.com/downloads`. MobileMe Control Panel is required to set up and manage MobileMe syncing and manage iDisk settings on a Windows PC.

To set up a Windows PC to sync with MobileMe or to check your sync settings or sync immediately, follow these steps:

1. **From the Windows Start menu, open Control Panel and choose MobileMe Control Panel.**

   The MobileMe panel appears with tabs along the top.

2. **Click the Account tab for the Account pane (if it isn't already visible) and log in with your MobileMe member name and password if you aren't already logged in.**

3. **Click the Sync tab.**

   The sync options appear, as shown in Figure 10-5.

4. **Select the Sync with MobileMe check box and then select a sync interval.**

   For the most frequent updates, choose Automatically to sync with MobileMe every 15 minutes.

5. **Select the check boxes to sync your contacts, calendars, and bookmarks, and then use the drop-down lists to choose which Windows applications you want to use when syncing with these items.**

6. **Click the Sync Now button.**

   The sync starts. To make sure that your data has synced, go to `www.me.com`, log in, and click the Contacts and Calendar icons along the top row of icons on the left.

If you use Microsoft Outlook in conjunction with Microsoft Exchange Server, MobileMe won't sync contacts or calendars with Outlook — use Exchange Server instead. See the section "Setting Up Mail Accounts on Your iPod touch or iPhone," later in this chapter.

When you sync upon a cloud

If your contacts or calendar entries show up in duplicate or triplicate in your computer or on your iPod touch or iPhone, as if they were stuck inside of MobileMe with the memory blues again, you probably need to overwrite the data in the MobileMe cloud.

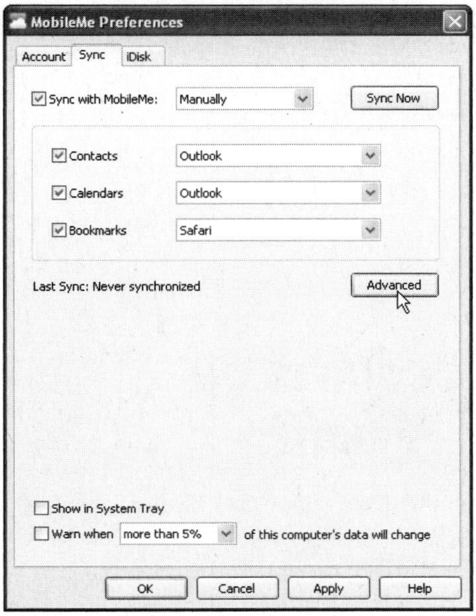

Figure 10-5:
Sync
options for
MobileMe
on a
Windows
PC.

Selecting items to synchronize may not overwrite all the data in the cloud. To overwrite the data stored in the cloud with the data on your computer, open MobileMe (in System Preferences on a Mac or Control Panel in Windows), click the Sync tab, and then click the Advanced button. (Refer to Figure 10-4 for a Mac or Figure 10-5 for Windows.) Select the computer you are syncing from in the list at the top and then click Reset Sync Data.

In the dialog that appears, choose an option from the Replace pop-up menu:

✔ On a Mac, you can choose All Sync Info, or Bookmarks, Calendars, or Contacts. (The other choices on the pop-up menu — Key Chains, Mail Accounts, and so on — don't copy over to the iPod touch or iPhone but are useful for keeping other computers synchronized.)

✔ In Windows, you can choose All Sync Info, or Bookmarks, Calendars, or Contacts.

After choosing an option from the Replace pop-up menu, click the arrow underneath the Cloud icon to change the animation so that the data arrow points from the computer to the cloud. Finally, click the Replace button.

This action replaces the data in the MobileMe cloud with the data on your computer. You can also use these steps to go in reverse — replace the data on your computer with the data in MobileMe. To do this, click the arrow so that the animation points the arrow from the cloud to the computer.

Your iPod touch or iPhone can receive pushed e-mail, contacts, calendars, and bookmarks from the MobileMe cloud over a Wi-Fi connection as long as it is awake (meaning that the screen is on or the device is connected to your computer or to a power adapter).

Changes you make to contacts, calendars, and bookmarks in your iPod touch or iPhone are synchronized to the Web server at www.me.com. You can also go to www.me.com and access your information directly with your Web browser.

Setting Up Mail Accounts on Your iPod touch or iPhone

To set up a Mail account on your iPod touch or iPhone, including a MobileMe e-mail account (with contacts, calendars, and bookmarks) or a Microsoft Exchange account, follow these steps:

1. **Choose Settings⇨Mail, Contacts, Calendars from the Home screen.**

   The Mail, Contacts, Calendars settings screen appears, with the Accounts section at the top, as shown in Figure 10-6 (left side).

2. **Tap the Add Account button and then tap the account type from the list of account types that appears.**

   Your choices are Microsoft Exchange, MobileMe, Gmail, Yahoo! Mail, AOL, or Other, as shown in Figure 10-6 (right side). After tapping the account type, the New Account screen appears for Exchange, MobileMe, Gmail, Yahoo! Mail, and AOL accounts, and the Other screen appears for Other accounts.

3. **Enter your account information as follows:**

   Generally speaking, you'll need to enter your name, username, password, and optional description by tapping next to a field's name (such as Name or Address) to display the keyboard. Then use the keyboard to enter the information and tap Return on the keyboard to finish entering. As you tap Return, the next field appears ready for you to enter information, until you reach the last field. Tap Return to finish entering information.

   • *MobileMe, Gmail, Yahoo! Mail, or AOL:* Enter your name, username, password, and an optional description on the New Account screen, and then tap Save in the upper-right corner to save account information. Your iPod touch or iPhone verifies the account; if the account can't be verified, the message `Cannot Get Mail` appears, indicating that the username or password is incorrect. Tap OK and try Steps 2 and 3 again (or tap Cancel to cancel). If the account is verified, you're done for a Gmail, Yahoo! Mail, or AOL account and you can skip the rest of these steps — the Mail, Contacts, Calendars settings screen appears with the new account listed in the Accounts section. For MobileMe, your iPod touch or iPhone displays your account's settings screen.

- *Microsoft Exchange:* Enter your name, username, domain (optional), password, and an optional description on the New Account screen, and then tap Next in the upper-right corner to save the account information and move on to the Exchange account's settings screen. Microsoft's Autodiscovery service kicks in to check your username and password to determine the address of the Exchange server. If it can't find the server's address, a dialog appears for you to enter it — enter the complete address in the Server field and tap Save.

- *Other:* Tap Add Mail Account on the Other screen for an IMAP (Internet Message Access Protocol) or POP (Post Office Protocol) account. The New Account screen appears; enter your name, username, password, and an optional description, and then tap Save in the upper-right corner to save the account information. The iPod touch or iPhone searches for the account on the Internet and displays the New Account settings screen.

Figure 10-6:
Tap Add Account (left) to see the list of account types (right).

4. **Set your mail account settings on the New Account settings screen as follows:**

   • *MobileMe or Exchange:* Turn on any of or all the items you want to sync: Mail, Contacts, Calendars, and Bookmarks (MobileMe only). If you sync contacts, calendars, or bookmarks using your MobileMe or Exchange account, syncing them in iTunes is turned off. Any contacts, calendars, and bookmarks on your iPod touch or iPhone are replaced by the MobileMe or Exchange account versions. You can always return to the account setting's screen to turn them off to enable syncing with iTunes. For Exchange, you can set how many days of e-mail you want to sync to your iPod touch or iPhone. Tap Save in the upper-right corner to finish and save your settings.

   • *Other:* Tap IMAP or POP on the New Account settings screen, depending on the type of e-mail account you have — ask your e-mail service provider if you don't know. Then enter or edit the account information, including your user name and password for incoming and outgoing mail. (You get this information from your service provider if you don't know it.) Tap Save in the upper-right corner to finish and save your settings. The Mail, Contacts, Calendars settings screen appears with the new account listed in the Accounts section.

5. **When the Sync or Cancel warning appears for MobileMe or Exchange accounts, tap Sync (or Cancel).**

   When you tap the Sync button, MobileMe or Exchange overwrites any existing contacts, calendars, and bookmarks on your iPod touch or iPhone (or the subset of these that you chose in Step 4). The Mail, Contacts, Calendars settings screen appears with the new account listed in the Accounts section.

6. **Tap Fetch New Data, and tap Off for Push to turn it on (if it isn't already on).**

   That's it! Your iPod touch or iPhone syncs automatically from this point on, with data pushed or fetched from the e-mail account depending on your push and fetch settings. (For details, see Chapter 20.)

Changing and Deleting Mail Accounts

You can temporarily turn off a Mail account on your iPod touch or iPhone, change its settings, or delete it from your iPod touch or iPhone.

Changes you make to Mail accounts on your iPod touch or iPhone are *not* transferred back to your computer when you synchronize, so it's safe to make changes without affecting e-mail account settings on your computer.

To turn off a Mail account in your iPod touch or iPhone temporarily, or change account settings, choose Settings⇨Mail, Contacts, Calendars from the Home screen and then touch the account in the Accounts section to see that account's settings screen. You can then change your account's settings, including the items that are synced to your iPod touch or iPhone with a MobileMe or Microsoft Exchange account.

To delete the account, scroll down and tap Delete Account. Deleting a Mail account from an iPod touch or iPhone doesn't delete the e-mail account itself or its settings on your computer.

It's way beyond the scope of this book to explain all the e-mail account and advanced options. Grab your network administrator or Internet service provider and offer free coffee in exchange for help. If you don't have anyone to turn to, visit the Tips section of my Web site (www.tonybove.com) for tips on using MobileMe and other e-mail accounts, and for changing e-mail account settings on your iPod touch or iPhone.

Part III
Managing Your Library

The 5th Wave   By Rich Tennant

"It's like any other pacemaker, but it comes with an internal iPod docking accessory."

In this part . . .

Visit this part to find out how to organize the content in your iTunes library, add song information as well as ratings, build playlists, burn CDs, and make a backup of your library.

✔ Chapter 11 describes how to browse your iTunes library, change the List view options, sort your content, and search for songs, artists, albums, music videos, audio books, movies, TV shows, applications, and games.

✔ Chapter 12 describes how to add information, artwork, and ratings for each content item and then edit the info in iTunes.

✔ Chapter 13 describes how to play music, audio books, videos, and podcasts in your iTunes library.

✔ Chapter 14 shows you how to build playlists (including smart playlists) of songs and entire albums in iTunes.

✔ Chapter 15 is a guide to burning audio CDs, MP3 CDs, and data CDs and DVDs, as well as copying media files and making backup copies of your iTunes library.

Chapter 11

Searching, Browsing, and Sorting in iTunes

In This Chapter

▶ Browsing your iTunes library

▶ Changing options for viewing your content

▶ Sorting content by view options

▶ Searching for content in the library

▶ Finding pesky duplicates

▶ Deleting items from the library

*Y*ou rip a few CDs, buy some songs and movies from the iTunes Store, and you're hooked. You keep adding more and more content to your library and forget how to find items you added last month. It's time to discover how to organize your content and navigate your iTunes library.

The iTunes library can hold an unlimited number of files, depending on how much space you have on your hard drive. But even if you keep your iTunes library down to the size of what fits on your iPod or iPhone, you still have a formidable collection at your fingertips. If your content collection is getting large, organize it to make finding songs, audio books, podcasts, and videos easier. After all, finding U2's "I Still Haven't Found What I'm Looking For" is a challenge, even in a library that fits on an 8GB iPod nano.

This chapter shows you how to search, browse, and sort your iTunes library. You can find any content item in seconds. You can also change the viewing options to make your library's display more useful, such as displaying songs sorted by artist, album, genre, or other attributes, or sorting TV shows by season or episode.

Browsing Your Library Content

As you know, the iTunes window provides the List pane on the right side and the Source pane on the left side (refer to Chapter 6 for figures showing Mac and Windows versions). The List pane offers a view of your library and content, depending on which sources of content you choose in the Source pane on the left side. The choices in the Source pane are as follows:

✔ **Library section:** Select Music, Movies, TV Shows, Podcasts, Audiobooks, Applications, Ringtones, or Radio. By default, iTunes doesn't display iTunes U. To see iTunes U, or to change the options listed in the Library section, choose iTunes⇨Preferences (Mac) or Edit⇨Preferences (Windows), click the General tab at the top of the Preferences window, and select or deselect the Show options depending on what you want to display. Click the OK button to accept the changes.

  • *Music:* Lists the entire library of songs and music videos purchased, downloaded, ripped, or copied into the library.

  • *Movies:* Lists the movies downloaded from the iTunes Store and movie files you've added to your library.

  • *TV Shows:* Lists TV shows downloaded from the iTunes Store. (This list includes video files you've imported and then changed to TV Show in the Media Kind popup of the Options pane of the Info dialog — see Chapter 12 for details on adding or changing the content information.)

  • *Podcasts:* Lists the podcasts you've subscribed to. (See Chapter 8 for details on subscribing to and browsing podcasts.)

  • *Audiobooks:* Lists the audio books downloaded from the iTunes Store or from Audible.com or other sources. (This list includes audio files you've ripped or imported and then changed to Audiobook in the Media Kind popup of the Options pane of the Info dialog — see Chapter 12 for details on adding or changing the content information.)

  • *Applications:* Lists the iPod touch and iPhone applications downloaded from the App Store or iTunes Store, and iPod games downloaded from the iTunes Store.

  • *Ringtones:* Lists the ringtones downloaded from the iTunes Store or from other sources, as well as those created in GarageBand on a Mac and added to your iTunes library.

- *Radio:* Lists the Web radio stations you can play. Radio station content is streamed to your computer but not stored in your library.

- *iTunes U:* Courseware, lectures, and other items downloaded from or subscribed to in the iTunes U section of the iTunes Store.

✔ **Store section:** The iTunes Store (see Chapter 7).

✔ **Devices section:** Your iPod, iPhone, and Apple TV appear listed here when connected, as well as an audio CD when inserted into your computer. When you select a device such as an iPod, iTunes displays the summary page with synchronization options. See Chapter 9 for details on navigating the library on an iPod set for managing content manually.

✔ **Shared section:** Shared iTunes libraries on your home network appear here, as I describe in Chapter 7.

✔ **Genius section:** The Genius Mix and any Genius playlists you generate appear in this section. See Chapter 14 for details on using the Genius Mix and Genius playlists.

✔ **Playlist section:** Smart playlists and regular playlists appear in this section. Also appearing in this section is iTunes DJ, which lets you continually change a playlist of random songs. See Chapter 13 for details on iTunes DJ, and Chapter 14 for the player's guide to playlists.

Overwhelmed by all the content in the List pane? Try browsing. iTunes offers three View buttons in the upper-right corner for browsing your content in the List pane:

✔ **List** (the left button, or choose View⇨As List) shows items in a list. You've seen this before in Chapter 6.

✔ **Grid** (the center button, or choose View⇨As Grid) shows thumbnail cover art images in a grid, as shown in Figure 11-1. Select a thumbnail of an album to select the album. Double-click a thumbnail to display a list of albums with an artwork column.

✔ **Cover Flow** (the right button, or choose View⇨As Cover Flow) shows the cover browser, also known as Cover Flow, as described in the next section.

In List view, choose View⇨Show Column Browser to show the browser, which displays columns you can browse to easily find items. The browser appears in the top part of the List pane (peek ahead to Figure 11-3 to see it). To make the browser disappear and see your content in a full list, choose View⇨Hide Column Browser. You can also display songs in a list with the album cover art by choosing View⇨Show Artwork Column. (Turn this off by choosing View⇨Hide Artwork Column.)

Figure 11-1:
Browse
music in the
List pane
as a grid of
cover art.

Browsing by cover art with Cover Flow

Does viewing a cover whet your appetite for the music, story, or video inside? Of course it does. Covers provide a context that simply can't be put into words or conveyed by sound. One fantastic innovation of iTunes is how it integrates cover art from albums, books, podcasts, and videos with your library so that you can flip through your content to find items based on the artwork. Figure 11-2 shows the iTunes window using Cover Flow view to display the Music portion of the iTunes library.

To select Cover Flow, click the rightmost of the three View buttons in the upper-right corner of the iTunes window. You can also show the cover browser by choosing View➪As Cover Flow.

Cover Flow lets you flip through your cover art to select music, movies, TV shows, podcasts, and audio books. (The cover browser doesn't work with ringtones or radio stations.) Just drag the slider to scroll swiftly through your library or click to the right or left of the cover art in the foreground to move forward or backward, respectively. When you scroll or click through cover art, the content items in the List pane also change. Double-click the foreground cover art to start playing the first item — whether it's an album's first song, a movie, the first chapter of an audio book, or the first episode of a TV show.

Click the Browse Full-Screen button to display Cover Flow, um, full-screen. You can still click a cover to select an album, click within each cover to move forward and backward, and use the cover browser's slider to navigate your library. iTunes also offers a volume control slider to set the audio volume while browsing full-screen cover art. Press Esc (Escape) or click the Browse Full-Screen button (with its arrows pointing inward) in the lower-right corner of the display to stop displaying the cover browser full-screen and return to the iTunes window.

To fill your library automatically with cover art, get yourself an iTunes Store account (if you don't already have one). Log in to your account; then choose Advanced⇨Get Album Artwork. iTunes grabs the cover art not only for content downloaded from the iTunes Store — including movies, TV shows, audio books, and podcasts — but also for CDs you ripped, provided that the albums are also available in the iTunes Store. Even if you downloaded or ripped only one song of an album, you get the album's cover art for that song.

Browse Full-Screen

Figure 11-2:
Browse
music using
Cover Flow
view.

You can also get your cover art from other places that sell CDs, audio books, and DVDs (including Amazon.com) or even scan it from the actual CDs, DVDs, or books. You can then add cover art from a scanned or downloaded image file to any content item in your iTunes library, as I describe in Chapter 12. The optimal size for cover art is 300 x 300 pixels.

Browsing songs by artist and album

To select List view, click the leftmost of the three View buttons in the upper-right corner of the iTunes window. You can also choose View⇨As List.

To browse music in your library in List view, select Music in the Source pane in the Library section. The List view shows the title of each song in the Name column, the artist or band name in the Artist column, and the title of the album in the Album column. To browse the list, choose View⇨Show Column Browser. To hide the browser, choose View⇨Hide Column Browser. Browser.

The Column Browser in List view organizes music content into Genres, Artists, Albums, Composers, and Groupings columns — you can choose which columns to display by choosing View⇨Column Browser and selecting each category to show (or deselecting each category to remove). For example, in Figure 11-3, I show the Genres, Artists, and Albums columns, and I also display the Artwork Column by choosing View⇨Show Artwork Column. (Turn this off by choosing View⇨Hide Artwork Column.)

The Column Browser appears in the leftmost column by default or if you choose View⇨Column Browser⇨On Left (as described in Chapter 6). The Genres, Artists, and Albums columns appear from left to right, with the song list in the far right column. When you select an album, iTunes displays only the songs for that album in the far right column.

You can switch the Column Browser to appear in the top part of the List pane, as shown in Figure 11-3, if you choose View⇨Column Browser⇨On Top. This view is useful if your display is not very wide.

Select a genre in the Genres column to see artists in that genre in the Artists column, or select All at the top of the column to see all artists for all genres. When you select an artist in the Artists column (refer to Figure 11-3), the album titles appear in the Album column (on the right). When you select an album, iTunes displays only the songs for that album in the List pane below the Column Browser.

Figure 11-3:
Select an artist to see the list of albums for that artist.

To see more than one album from an artist at a time, press ⌘ (Mac) or Ctrl (Windows) while clicking each album name.

After selecting an album in the Albums column, the songs in the List pane are listed in the proper album track order, just as the artist, producer, or record label intended.

If you don't get track information from the Internet for each song on a CD that you're ready to rip (as I show dramatically in Chapter 6), or if you don't add the track information yourself via the content item's information dialog (as I describe in wondrous detail in Chapter 12), iTunes displays only a blank space for the artist and album name along with Track 01 and so on for each track. That makes browsing for a song or artist by name difficult, to say the least.

To see all the songs in the library in the browser, select All at the top of each of the columns — Genres, Artists, and Albums. You can also switch to Grid (refer to Figure 11-1) or to Cover Flow view (refer to Figure 11-2) to show the album cover art.

Browsing audio books

If you don't see Audiobooks in the Library section of the Source pane, choose iTunes⇨Preferences (Mac) or Edit⇨Preferences (Windows), click the General tab at the top of the Preferences window, select the Audiobooks option next to the Show heading, and click the OK button. The Audiobooks option then appears in the Source pane in the Library section.

To browse the audio books in your library, select Audiobooks in the Source pane. You can browse audio book titles and authors with the Column Browser in List view, or browse cover art in Grid or Cover Flow view. The List view shows the title of each book with its part number (long books typically have multiple parts) in the Name column and the author's name in the Authors column. If you add the Albums column heading to the Column Browser or to List view (as I describe in the section "Changing the List view options," later in this chapter), the title of the book appears in the Albums column.

Browsing podcasts

To browse podcasts, select Podcasts in the Library section of the Source pane. You can browse podcast episodes with the Column Browser in List view, or browse cover art in Grid or Cover Flow view. You can then see the episodes of a podcast by clicking the podcast, and in List view, clicking the triangle next to the podcast name. For details on playing episodes, see Chapter 13.

The List view shows the title of each podcast and its episodes in the Podcast column. The mysterious blue dot next to a podcast means that you haven't played one or more episodes of the podcast yet. (The same blue dot appears next to each unplayed episode.) As soon as you start listening to or watching a podcast, the dot turns into a half-moon until you complete the episode (accompanied by the theme of *The Twilight Zone*).

You can click the *i* icon on the far-right podcast listing margin in List view to display separate information about the podcast's newest episode.

Browsing movies, videos, and TV shows

To browse movies, select Movies in the Library section of the Source pane. Any video files you add to your library from sources other than the iTunes Store are classified as movies — but you can change their media type as I describe in Chapter 12 so that, for example, a video shows up as a TV show rather than a movie. You can also find in the Movies listing those movies and short films you downloaded from the iTunes Store.

You can browse movies, TV shows, and videos with the Column Browser in List view, or browse cover art in Grid or Cover Flow view. The Grid view (as shown in Figure 11-4) and the Cover Flow view show the first key frame of the movie or the box cover art for the movie.

You can browse TV shows by selecting TV Shows in the Library section of the Source pane. The List view shows the episode title, show title, and season number. The Column Browser in List view organizes TV shows by Genres, Shows, and Seasons. The Grid and Cover Flow views show the promotional cover art for the TV show.

Browsing applications and iPod games

The applications you download for your iPod touch or iPhone, along with the games you download for your iPod classic or iPod nano (or older model iPod), show up in the Applications section of your iTunes library. Applications for the iPod touch and iPhone are available in the App Store, and games for the iPod nano, iPod classic, and older models are in the iTunes Store (see Chapter 7 for glorious details). And although you can't run the applications or play the games in iTunes, you can browse the list of applications and games you downloaded.

If you don't see Applications in the Library section of the Source pane, choose iTunes⇨Preferences (Mac) or Edit⇨Preferences (Windows), click the General tab at the top of the Preferences window, select the Applications option from the list of options for the Show heading, and click the OK button. The Applications option then appears in the Source pane in the Library section.

To browse iPod touch or iPhone applications, or iPod classic and iPod nano "click wheel" games, select Applications in the Source pane. Applications are classified by genre according to the App Store categories, and these genres appear in the Genre category in List view. The iPod Games genre refers to any "click wheel" games you download for your iPod classic or iPod nano (or older model iPod). The applications in Grid view are separated into two sections: one for iPhone and iPod touch Apps, and the other for iPod Games. The Grid and Cover Flow views show the promotional cover art for the application.

In case you're a closet gamer without an iPod touch or iPhone, visit this book's companion Web site for details on how to play games on your iPod classic or iPod nano.

Figure 11-4:
Browse
and play
movies in
your iTunes
library in
Grid view.

Displaying Content in List View

To display your content in the List pane as a list, click the left View button
(refer to Figure 11-1) or choose View⇨As List. Choose View⇨Show Column
Browser to show the Column Browser in List view, or choose View⇨Hide
Column Browser to hide it. You can also display cover art in List view by
choosing View⇨Show Artwork Column, or hide the cover art by choosing
View⇨Hide Artwork Column.

iTunes displays a playlist as a song list in the List pane, even if it includes
other content items. The column headings for playlists have different
meanings for the following types of content:

- ✔ **Songs and music videos:** The Name is the title of the song; the Artist is
  the band, artist, or performer. The Album is the title of the CD or vinyl
  record on which the song appeared. For music videos, the Name is
  typically the title of a song in the music video.

- ✔ **Podcasts:** The Name is the title of the podcast episode (as in "Ballad
  Roots of California Folk-Rock"), the Artist is the name of the podcast
  author (as in Tony Bove) or producer (such as Chicago Public Radio),
  and the Album is the name of the podcast (as in *Rockument*).

✔ **Audio books:** The Album is typically the book's title (as in *Fear and Loathing in Las Vegas*), and the Name is typically the title of one of the parts (as in *Fear and Loathing in Las Vegas*–Part 1 of 3).

✔ **TV shows:** The Name is the name of the TV show episode (as in "Mr. Monk and the Airplane"), the Artist is the name of the show (as in *Monk*), and the Album is the season (as in *Monk,* Season 1).

Changing the List view options

iTunes lets you customize the List view in the List pane for each type of content. For music, the list starts out with the Name, Art, Time, Artist, Album, Genre, Rating, and Play Count columns. You might have to drag the horizontal scroll bar along the bottom of the song list to see all these columns. You can display more, less, or different information in your song list.

Customize your List view in the following ways:

✔ **Make a column wider or narrower.** While you move your cursor over the divider between two columns, the cursor changes to a vertical bar with opposing arrows extending left and right; you can click and drag the divider to change the column's width.

✔ **Change the order of columns.** Click a column heading and drag the entire column to the left or right.

You can't change the position of the Name column and the narrow column to its left, which displays indicators and shows the playlist order.

✔ **Add or remove columns.** You can add or remove any column except Name and the playlist order:

    a. Select the type of content in the Source pane in the Library section (Music, Movies, TV Shows, , iTunes U, Podcasts, Audiobooks, Ringtones, or Radio) and choose View⇨View Options.

    b. Select the columns that you want to appear in the list from the View Options dialog (as shown in Figure 11-5 for Music).

You can also change which columns are visible by Control-clicking (on a Mac) or right-clicking (in Windows) any column heading in the list in either Browse view or List view.

Enabling the Kind column in the View Options dialog can help you keep track of different kinds of files, such as songs encoded as AIFF, AAC, or MP3 or videos encoded in QuickTime or MPEG.

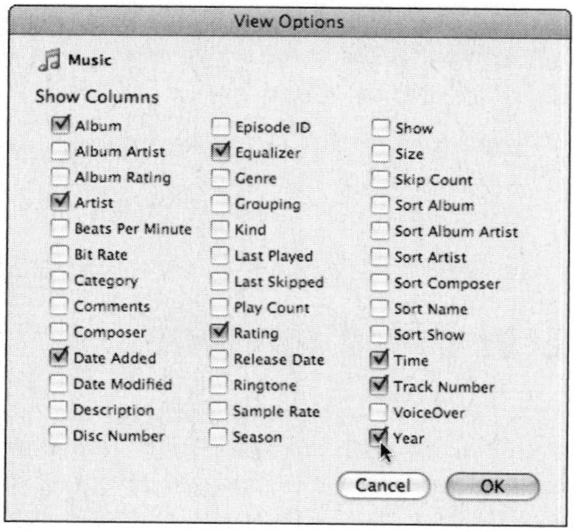

Figure 11-5:
Change the
viewing
options for
music in List
view.

View Options

♫ Music

Show Columns

☑ Album   ☐ Episode ID   ☐ Show
☐ Album Artist   ☑ Equalizer   ☐ Size
☐ Album Rating   ☐ Genre   ☐ Skip Count
☑ Artist   ☐ Grouping   ☐ Sort Album
☐ Beats Per Minute   ☐ Kind   ☐ Sort Album Artist
☐ Bit Rate   ☐ Last Played   ☐ Sort Artist
☐ Category   ☐ Last Skipped   ☐ Sort Composer
☐ Comments   ☐ Play Count   ☐ Sort Name
☐ Composer   ☑ Rating   ☐ Sort Show
☑ Date Added   ☐ Release Date   ☑ Time
☐ Date Modified   ☐ Ringtone   ☑ Track Number
☐ Description   ☐ Sample Rate   ☐ VoiceOver
☐ Disc Number   ☐ Season   ☑ Year

(Cancel)   (OK)

Sorting Content by the List View Options

With just a little know-how, you can use the List view options to sort the
listing of content items. You can sort items not only by name or album but
also by composer, the date the items were added to the library, or other
information that you can add to an item (as I describe in Chapter 12).

At the very least, you can sort the content by the column headings you now
use in the List view. You can also add other column headings to your List
view (as I describe in the previous section) and sort with them.

For example, clicking the Time heading reorders the items by their duration
in *ascending order,* from shortest to longest. If you click the Time heading
again, the sort is in *descending order,* which is reversed, starting with the
longest item. You can sort by any column heading, such as Artist, Album,
Track, Date Added, and Ratings.

You can tell whether the sort is in ascending or descending order by the
little arrow indicator in the heading. When the arrow points up, the sort is in
ascending order; when pointing down, it's in descending order.

You can always sort a list using the old standby, alphabetical order. Click
the Artist heading to sort the items in the list by artist name in alphabetical
order (arrow pointing up). Click it again to sort the list in reverse alphabetical order (arrow pointing down).

iTunes also lets you sort the song list via the Album column. Each time you
click Album, the heading cycles through each of the following options:

> ✔ **Album,** which sorts alphabetically by album title.
>
> ✔ **Album by Artist,** which groups albums by artist and then lists them alphabetically.
>
> ✔ **Album by Year,** which groups albums by artist and then lists them chronologically by year (set in the Song Information dialog).

iTunes keeps track of the songs, audio books, and podcasts you skip — not to be polite, just to be useful. You can use this feature to sort the Music and Audiobooks lists of your library in List view, thereby making it easier to select and delete the items you skip.

Searching for Content

Because your iTunes library will most likely grow, you might find the usual browsing and scrolling methods that I describe earlier in this chapter too time-consuming. Let iTunes find your content for you!

If you want to search the entire library with the Column Browser open in List view, select All at the top of the Genres and Artists columns to browse the entire library before typing a term in the Search field. Or, if you prefer, choose View➪Hide Browser to show the List view without the browser. (For a peek at what that looks like, see Figure 11-6.)

Locate the Search field — the oval field in the upper-right corner — and follow these steps:

1. **Click in the Search field and enter several characters of your search term.**

   Use these tips for successful searching:

   • *Specify your search* with a specific title, artist, or album.

   • *Narrow your search* by typing more characters. Using fewer characters results in a longer list of possible songs.

   • *Case doesn't matter, nor do whole words.* The Search feature ignores case. For example, when I search for *miles,* iTunes finds a long list that includes "Eight Miles High," "Forty Miles of Bad Road," and "She Smiles like a River," as well as everything by Miles Davis.

2. **Look through the results, which display while you type.**

   The search operation works immediately, as shown in Figure 11-6, displaying any matches in the Name, Artist, and Album columns.

3. **Scroll through the search results and then click an item to select it.**

To back out of a search so that the full list appears again, you can either click the circled X in the Search field (which appears after you start typing characters) or delete what you typed. You then see the entire list in the List pane, just like before you began your search. All the items are still there and remain there unless you explicitly remove them. Searching manipulates only your view of the items.

Figure 11-6: Search for anything by typing any part of the name, artist, album, or title.

Finding the Content's Media File

Getting lost in a large library is easy. While you browse your library, you might want to return quickly to view the current item playing. While your file plays, choose View⇨Go to Current Song (or press ⌘-L on a Mac or Ctrl-L in Windows as a shortcut). iTunes shows you the item that's playing.

You can also show the location of the media file for any content item. This trick comes in handy when you want to open the media file's folder. On a Mac, choose File⇨Show in Finder (or press ⌘-R); in Windows, choose File⇨Show in Windows Explorer (or press Ctrl-R). iTunes gives control to the operating system (Mac or Windows), which displays the folder that contains the media file.

Showing Duplicate Items

Because your library will grow, you'll probably want to check for duplications. Some songs that appear on artist CDs also appear on compilation or soundtrack CDs. If you rip them all, you could have duplicate songs that take up space on your hard drive. You might even have duplicate videos and audio books.

On the other hand, maybe you want to find different versions of the same song by the same artist. Even when the songs appear on different albums, iTunes can quickly find all the songs with the same title by the same artist.

To show duplicate items in the list, choose File⇨Show Duplicates. iTunes displays all the duplicate items in the List pane in the order of the last sort. (For example, if you last sorted by Album, the items appear in Album order.) If you're using the Column Browser in List view, you see all the duplicate items in artist order. Click the artist to see the duplicate items specifically for that artist.

To stop showing duplicate items and return to your previous view, click the Show All button below the list of duplicates.

Deleting Content

Deleting content might seem counterproductive when you're trying to build your iTunes library, but sometimes you just have to do it. For example, you might want to delete the following:

- **Versions of songs:** You might have ripped a CD twice — say, once in AIFF format to burn the songs onto another CD and once in AAC format for your library and iPod or iPhone. You can delete the AIFF versions in your library after burning your CD (see Chapter 15 for burning instructions).

  Items from playlists: You can delete items from playlists yet keep the items in your library. When you delete an item from a playlist, the item is simply deleted from the list — not from the library. You can delete entire playlists as well without harming the content in the library. You have to select a media category in the Library section in the Source pane first, to delete content from the library. (See Chapter 14 for more information about playlists.)

> ✔ **Anything you are embarrassed to have in your library or simply don't want.**
>
> You can select any content item and remove it from your iTunes library. You then have a choice of keeping the item's file on your hard drive in the same folder, or transferring it to the Trash (on a Mac) or Recycle Bin (on a Windows PC) to delete it entirely.

To delete a song, iTunes lecture, video, audio book, application, or an entire album or artist, select the media type (Music, Movies, TV Shows, Podcasts, iTunes U, Audiobooks, Applications, Ringtones, or Radio) and then select the item (or select an artist for the artist's entire *oeuvre,* or an album to select the entire album). Press Delete/Backspace (or choose Edit➪Delete) to delete.

You can select a single TV show episode and then choose Edit➪Delete All to delete all episodes.

You can select a single episode of a podcast and then choose Edit➪Delete All to delete all episodes but keep the podcast itself so that you are still subscribed to the podcast. If you delete the podcast, you remove it from your library, and you have to resubscribe to it to get it back. If you delete an episode, you can get it back by clicking the Get button next to the episode.

Deleting a content item from the iTunes library removes the item from your library, but it doesn't remove it from your hard drive until you agree. In the first warning dialog that appears, click the Remove button to remove the selected items from the library or click the Cancel button. iTunes then displays a second warning about moving the files that are still in the iTunes Music folder to the Trash (Mac) or Recycle Bin (Windows). You can click the Move to Trash button on a Mac, or the Move to Recycle Bin button in Windows, to trash the item. Click Keep File to keep it in your music folder, or click Cancel to cancel the operation.

If you choose to move content to the Trash or Recycle Bin, the content is not yet deleted from your hard drive — you can recover the files by copying them out of the Trash or Recycle Bin, or you can empty them to delete them permanently.

You can delete multiple items in one clean sweep. Press Shift while you click a range of items. Alternatively, press ⌘ (Mac) or Ctrl (Windows) when you click individual items to add them to the selection. Then press Delete/Backspace (or choose Edit➪Delete).

Chapter 12

Adding and Editing Information in iTunes

In This Chapter

▶ Retrieving information online

▶ Editing information for each content item

▶ Adding information, cover art, comments, and ratings

*O*rganization depends on information. You expect your computer to do a lot more for you than just store a song with *Track 01* as the only identifier. Not only can iTunes retrieve the song's track information from the Internet, but it can also find the cover art for you.

Adding all the information for your iTunes content seems like a lot of trouble, but you can get most of the information automatically from the Internet — and without all that pesky typing. Adding track information is important because you certainly don't want to mistakenly play Frank Zappa's "My Guitar Wants to Kill Your Mama" when trying to impress your classical music teacher with the third movement of Tchaikovsky's *Pathétique Symphony,* do you? And because videos you make yourself or convert from other sources don't have this automatic information, you have to enter *some* description to tell them apart.

This chapter shows you how to add information to your content library in iTunes and edit it for better viewing so that you can organize your content by artist, album name, genre, composer, and ratings. You can then use this information to sort your content in List view or Browse view by clicking the column headings. This chapter also describes how to add cover art for navigating your library with Cover Flow.

Retrieving Song Information from the Internet

Why bother entering information if someone else has already done it for you? You can easily get information about most music CDs from the Internet (that is, assuming you can connect to the Internet). The online database available for iTunes users holds information for millions of songs on commercial CDs and even some bootleg CDs.

Retrieving information automatically

When you pop a commercial music CD into your computer running iTunes, iTunes automatically looks up the track information for that CD on the Internet and fills in the information fields (name, artist, album, and so on). You don't need to do anything to make this happen. You can also edit the information after iTunes fills in the fields.

If your computer doesn't access the Internet automatically, you might want to turn off this automatic information retrieval. (You can always retrieve the information manually, as I describe in the next section.) To turn off the retrieval of track information, follow these steps:

1. **Choose iTunes⇨Preferences (Mac) or Edit⇨Preferences (Windows).**

   The iTunes Preferences dialog appears with buttons along the top.

2. **Click the General tab (if it's not already selected).**

   The General preferences appear.

3. **Deselect the Automatically Retrieve CD Track Names from Internet option.**

   With this option turned on, iTunes connects to the Internet automatically and retrieves the track information. When turned off, iTunes doesn't retrieve the information, but you can retrieve it manually. (Cue the next section!)

Retrieving information manually

You can connect manually to the Internet at any time (for example, by using a modem connection) and retrieve the song information when you're ready to use it. After you connect to the Internet, choose Advanced⇨Get CD Track Names.

Using the Gracenote database

The first time I popped a commercial music CD into a computer, song information appeared like magic. iTunes automatically displayed the song names, album title, and artist names. How did it know? This information isn't stored on a standard music CD in digital form, but iTunes has to recognize the disc somehow.

The magic is that the software knows how to reach out and find the information on the Internet — in the Gracenote CDDB service. CDDB stands for (you guessed it) *CD Database*. The site (www.gracenote.com) hosts CDDB on the Web and searches for music CDs by artist, song title, and other methods. The iTunes software already knows how to use this database so you don't have to!

Gracenote recognizes an audio CD by taking into account the number, sequence, and duration of tracks. (This is how the database recognizes CD-Rs that are burned with the identical songs in the same order.) The database keeps track of information for most of the music CDs that you find on the market.

The database doesn't contain any information about personal or custom CDs unless people submit information to the database about such CDs. You can submit information about your personal or custom CDs by using iTunes: Type the information for each track while the audio CD is in your computer and then choose Advanced➪Submit CD Track Names. The information that you enter is sent to the Gracenote CDDB site, where the good people who work tirelessly on the database check out your information before including it. In fact, if you spot a typo or something erroneous in the information that you receive from the Gracenote CDDB, you can easily correct it. Just use the Submit CD Track Names command to send the corrected version back to the Gracenote site. The good folks at Gracenote appreciate the effort.

Entering Content Information

You have to enter the information for certain media, including CDs that aren't known by the Gracenote CDDB, custom CD-Rs, and videos and audio books that you bring into iTunes from sources other than the iTunes Store. No big deal, though; just follow these steps:

1. **Click directly in the information field (such as Artist).**

2. **Click again so that the mouse pointer toggles to an editing cursor — but not so quickly that the track starts playing.**

3. **Type text directly into the information field.**

After grabbing the song information from the Internet or typing it, iTunes keeps track of the information for the CD even if you just play the CD without importing it. The next time you insert the CD, the song information is automatically filled in.

Editing the Information

Retrieving ready-made song information from the Internet is a great help, but you might not always like the format it comes in. Maybe you want to edit artist and band names or other information the way I do — I like to list solo artists by last name rather than by first name. (Gracenote CDDB lists artists by first name.) For example, I routinely change *Miles Davis* to *Davis, Miles*.

Other annoyances sometimes occur when bands feature *The* at the beginning of their names, such as The Who, The Band, The Beatles, and The Beach Boys. Even though these names sort correctly (in alphabetical order, under their proper names), I dislike having *The* before the band name, so I routinely remove it.

You might also want to change the information that is supplied by the iTunes Store for the movies, TV shows, music videos, audio books, and podcasts you download. And if you obtain your content from other sources, you might need to add information for the first time.

You can edit the content information by clicking directly in the specific track's field (such as the Artist field) and then clicking again so that the mouse pointer toggles to an editing cursor. You can then select the text and type over it — or use the Copy, Cut, and Paste commands on the Edit menu — to move tiny bits of text around within the field. As you can see in Figure 12-1, I changed the Artist field to *Beck, Jeff*.

Figure 12-1:
Click inside
a field to
edit the
information.

You can edit the Name, Artist, Album, Genre, and Ratings fields in the list. However, editing this information by choosing File➪Get Info is easier. Keep reading to find out why.

Editing multiple items at once

Editing in the content list is fine if you're editing the information for one item, but typically you need to change all the tracks of an audio CD. For example, if a CD of songs by Bob Dylan is listed with the artist as *Bob Dylan,* you might want to change all the songs at once to *Dylan, Bob.* Changing all the information in one fell swoop is fast and clean, but like most powerful shortcuts, you need to be careful because it can be dangerous.

Follow these steps to change a group of items at once:

1. **Select a group of content items by clicking the first item and then pressing Shift while you click the last item.**

   All the items between the first and last are highlighted. You can extend a selection by Shift-clicking other items or add to a selection by ⌘-clicking (Mac) or Ctrl-clicking (Windows). You can also remove items already selected by ⌘-clicking (Mac) or Ctrl-clicking (Windows).

2. **Choose File⇨Get Info or press ⌘-I (Mac) or Ctrl-I (Windows).**

   A warning message displays:

   ```
   Are you sure you want to edit information for multiple
   items?
   ```

   Speed-editing the information in multiple items at once can be dangerous for your library organization. If, for example, you change an informational snippet for one item in a selected group (the song or movie title, for example), the corresponding snippet for all items in the selected group is going to change as well! Be careful about what you edit when using this method.

3. **Click the Yes button to edit information for multiple items.**

   The Multiple Item Information dialog appears, as shown in Figure 12-2.

4. **Edit the field you want to change for all the items.**

   When you edit a field, a check mark appears automatically in the check box next to the field. iTunes assumes that you want that field changed in all the selected items. Make sure that no other check box is selected except the ones for the fields that you want.

5. **Click the OK button to make the change.**

   iTunes changes the field for the entire selection of items.

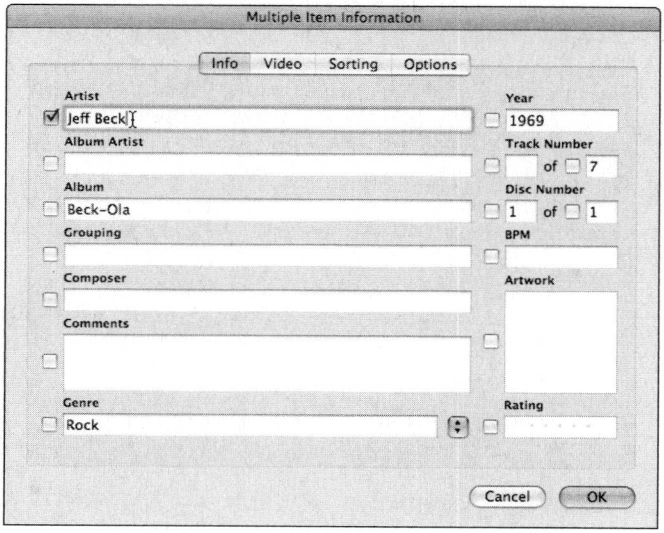

Multiple Item Information

| Info | Video | Sorting | Options |

Artist
☑ Jeff Beck

Album Artist
☐

Album
☐ Beck-Ola

Grouping
☐

Composer
☐

Comments
☐

Genre
☐ Rock

Year
☐ 1969

Track Number
☐   of ☐ 7

Disc Number
☐ 1 of ☐ 1

BPM
☐

Artwork
☐

Rating
☐

Cancel   OK

Figure 12-2: Change the field info for multiple items at once.

iTunes offers both Artist and Album Artist fields for a song so that you can include the album artist name if it's different — such as the artist name for a compilation album that features songs by different artists (for example, Eric Clapton's *Crossroads* box set, in which the Album Artist is Clapton but the Artist for each song might be the Yardbirds, Cream, Blind Faith, and so on). You can also use this field for Artist name formatted differently; for example, the Artist field could have the artist as *Bob Dylan* and the Album Artist as *Dylan, Bob*. You can then change the list view options (as I describe in Chapter 11) to include the Album Artist field as a column for sorting the song list.

Editing fields for a single item

Although the track information grabbed from the Internet is enough for identifying a song in your iTunes library, some facts — such as composer credits — might not be included. Adding composer credits is usually worth your effort because you can then search and sort by composer and create playlists based on the composer. Videos (movies, TV shows, and music videos), podcasts, and audio books might also have information in their fields that you want to change or have blank fields that could use some helpful information.

To get a look at (and edit) what Gracenote CDDB has provided about an item select the item and then choose File⇨Get Info (or press ⌘-I on a Mac or Ctrl-I in Windows). You see the item's information dialog, as shown in Figure 12-3.

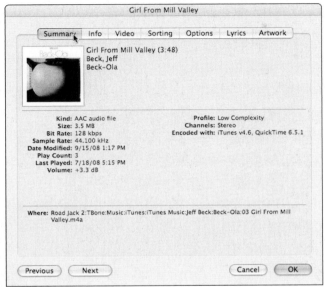

Figure 12-3:
A song's information dialog.

When you select one item, its information dialog appears and your edits affect only one item; when you select multiple items, the Multiple Item Information dialog appears and your edits affect multiple items.

A selection's information dialog offers the following tabs:

- ✔ **Summary:** The Summary tab (as shown in Figure 12-3) offers useful information about the media file format and location on your hard drive, the file size, and the digital compression method (along with bit rate, sample rate, and other settings).

- ✔ **Info:** The Info tab allows you to change the name, artist, composer, album, genre, year, and other information. You can also add comments, as shown in Figure 12-4.

- ✔ **Video:** The Video tab lets you enter information to describe the video. The information fields are set up for TV shows, including the title of the show, episode number and ID, and season number, but you can skip them for movies and music videos and just add a description.

- ✔ **Sorting:** The Sorting tab allows you to add information to fields for additional choices while sorting your library content. For example, you can add a different name for the artist in the Sort Artist field to the right of the Artist field, such as *Dylan, Bob* for *Bob Dylan*. Information from the Info tab appears on the left side, and you can add an alternative sort field on the right side. You can even add a Show field for the title of a concert or some other use. Choose View⇨View Options to select a sort field as a List view option, and then you can sort your content in List view by using the sort fields.

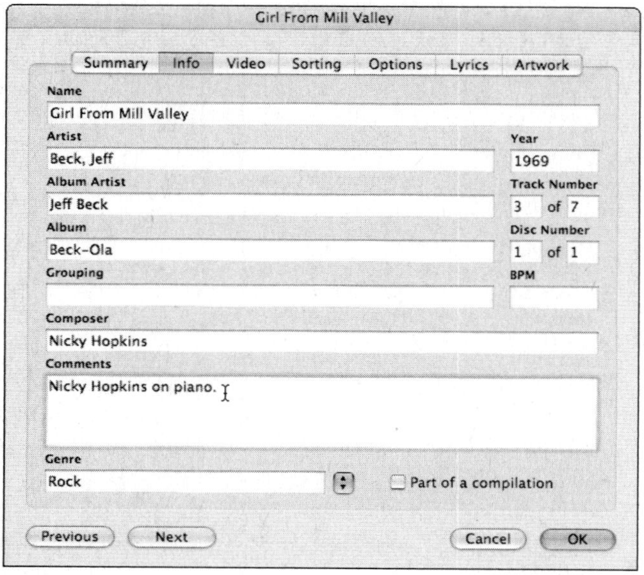

Figure 12-4:
View and
edit infor-
mation from
the Info tab.

✔ **Options:** The Options tab, as shown in Figure 12-5, offers the following:

- *Volume Adjustment:* You can set the volume for a song, video, podcast, or audio book in advance so that it always plays at that volume (or lower, if your overall iTunes or iPod/iPhone volume is set lower). Drag the slider to the right to increase the volume adjustment up to 100% (twice the usual volume); drag the slider to the left to decrease the volume adjustment to –100% (half the usual volume). For more details on setting the volume in advance, see Chapter 13.

- *Equalizer Preset:* Choose an equalizer preset for an item. See Chapter 13 for details on using the Equalizer in iTunes, and Chapter 16 on how you can use an Equalizer preset to control how an item sounds on your iPod or iPhone.

- *Media Kind:* Set (or change) the type of media. For example, after importing a video, you can change its Media Kind to movie, TV show, or music video.

- *Rating:* Assign up to five stars to an item as a rating. (See how in the next section.)

- *Start Time and Stop Time:* Set the start and stop times for an item. You can use these options to cut unwanted intros and outros of a song (such as announcers, audience applause, and tuning up), or to skip opening credits or commercials of movies. You can also use it in conjunction with the Convert feature to split an item (or, in the parlance of record label executives and artists, split a track) into multiple items (tracks).

Visit this book's companion Web site for details on setting start and stop times and using the iTunes equalizer.

- *Remember Playback Position:* Set this option for an item so that when you select and play the item, iTunes resumes playing it from where you left off. This option is usually turned on for audio books, movies, and TV shows.

- *Skip When Shuffling:* Set this option for an item to be skipped from Party Shuffle.

- *Part of a Gapless Album:* Set this option for an item to be played back without a gap between songs. (See Chapter 8 to find out about the gaps between songs.)

✔ **Lyrics:** The Lyrics tab offers a text field for typing or pasting lyrics (or any text). Some songs in the iTunes Store are supplied with lyrics — you can find them here.

TIP

You can view lyrics on an iPod touch or iPhone by starting a song and then, while the song is playing, tapping the song's album cover. To see lyrics on an iPod nano or iPod classic, start playing a song and then press the Select button several times until you see the lyrics. On an iPod nano, the first press shows the scrubber bar, the second shows ratings, the third shows the Shuffle slider, and the fourth shows the lyrics. If you press the Select button too many times, the iPod returns to the Now Playing display.

✔ **Artwork:** The Artwork tab allows you to add or delete artwork for the item. See the upcoming section "Adding Cover Art."

Figure 12-5:
Add a rating
to a song
from the
Options tab.

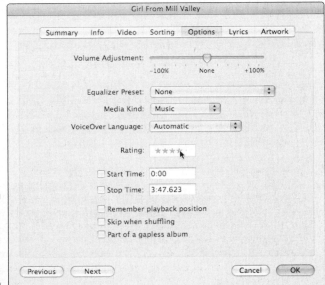

If you follow the careers of certain guitarists, vocalists, or session musicians, you can sort your music in List view by something other than the given artist for the album. First, provide a new entry for the Sort Artist or Sort Album Artist fields on the Sorting tab, and then choose that field as a view option so that you can sort on it. For example, I like to use the Sort Artist field for the leader, lead guitarist, or lead singer in a band, or a session player or special guest (such as Nicky Hopkins, who played keyboards on a variety of albums by different bands including The Who, The Rolling Stones, and The Beatles). After entering *Nicky Hopkins* into the Sort Artist field for the songs, I can choose View⇨View Options and select Sort Artist for a column heading. I can then sort the List view by clicking the new Sort Artist heading to find all recordings featuring Nicky Hopkins.

You can apply the entry of a sort field on the Sorting tab to all the tracks of the same album or to all tracks by the same artist, album artist, composer, or show. After changing the sort field for an item on the Sorting tab, select the item in List view, Control-click (Mac) or right-click (Windows) the item to display the contextual menu, and then choose Apply Sort Field. Click Yes to make the change.

To move through an album one item at a time when using Get Info (without closing and reopening the information dialog), click the Previous or Next buttons in the lower-left corner of the dialog.

Adding a rating

iTunes allows you to rate your content. The cool thing about ratings is that they're *yours*. You can use ratings to mean anything you want. For example, you can rate songs based on how much you like them, whether your mother would listen to them, or how they blend into a work environment. You can also rate videos based on your watching habits, as well as audio books and podcasts.

To add a rating to a content item, click the Options tab (refer to Figure 12-5) and drag inside the My Rating field to add stars. The upper limit is five stars (for the best). You can also select the item and choose File⇨Rating to assign a rating to an item, or display a Ratings column in List view to assign ratings. (See Chapter 11 for details on changing the view options.)

You might have noticed the My Top Rated playlist in the Source pane. This playlist is an example of a *smart playlist* — a playlist that updates when ratings are changed. The My Top Rated playlist plays all the top-rated songs in your library. You can find out more about playlists in Chapter 14.

Adding Cover Art

iTunes displays the cover art for your albums, videos, movies, podcasts, audio books, and TV shows in the Cover Flow browser. (See Chapter 11 for details.) All current iPod models and the iPhone, and even Apple TV, all display the cover art. So it makes sense to get the art, especially because it's free!

Items that you buy from the iTunes Store typically include an image of the album, book, or box cover art or a photo of the artist that serves as cover art. You can see the artwork in the lower-left corner of the iTunes window by clicking the Show/Hide Artwork button, (the rightmost button in the row of four buttons at the bottom of the iTunes window on the left side). The artwork changes for each item or album that you select or play. You can toggle between displaying the cover art of the item playing to the cover art of a selected item by clicking the right arrow (or the words `Now Playing`) above the cover art view in iTunes. Toggle back to displaying the cover art of the now-playing item by clicking the right arrow again (or the words `Selected Item`).

To fill your library automatically with cover art for the CDs you ripped, get yourself an iTunes Store account if you don't already have one. Log in to your account and then choose Advanced⇨Get Album Artwork. iTunes grabs the cover art not only for iTunes Store purchases, but also for CDs you ripped — provided that the albums are also available in the iTunes Store.

To download cover art for ripped CDs automatically after ripping them (without having to manually choose Advanced⇨Get Album Artwork each time), choose iTunes⇨Preferences on a Mac or Edit⇨Preferences in Windows, click the Store tab, and select the Automatically Download Missing Album Artwork option.

You can also get your cover art from other places that sell CDs, such as Amazon.com, or you can even scan them from the actual CDs. The optimal size for cover art is 300 x 300 pixels. Save it in a graphics format that iTunes (and its underlying graphics technology, *QuickTime*) understands — JPEG, GIF, PNG, TIFF, or Photoshop. With a Web browser, you can visit Web pages to scout for suitable art; just Control-click (Mac) or right-click (Windows) an image to download and save the image on your hard drive. With Safari on a Mac and some browsers (such as Firefox) in Windows, you can drag the image directly from the Web browser window into the iTunes art pane.

To add artwork to one or more items, select it (or them) in your iTunes library and do one of the following:

✔ **Drag the artwork's image file from a Desktop folder into the artwork viewing area (the lower-left corner of the iTunes window).**

To add artwork for an entire album (rather than just individual songs) or season of TV shows, first select the album or season in the Column Browser or select all the items in List view. Then drag the image file into the artwork viewing area.

✔ **Add artwork to a single item through the information window.**

Choose File⇨Get Info and then click the Artwork tab in the Get Info dialog. Click the Add button, browse your hard drive or network for the image file, select the file, and then click the OK button.

✔ **Add artwork for multiple items in the Multiple Item Information dialog.**

Choose File⇨Get Info after selecting the items, enable the Artwork field (select its check box), and then drag a graphics file for the cover art from a Desktop folder to the Artwork well. Click the Yes button for the warning message to change the artwork.

See the section "Editing multiple items at once," earlier in this chapter, to find out more about using the Multiple Item Information dialog.

To remove the artwork from an item, view the artwork in a larger window or resize the artwork, choose File⇨Get Info, and then click the Artwork tab. You can add a different image with the Add button, delete images with the Delete button, or resize images with the size slider.

Chapter 13

Playing Content in iTunes

In This Chapter

▶ Adjusting your computer volume

▶ Playing songs on your stereo through a wireless AirTunes connection

▶ Playing songs, podcasts, and audio books in iTunes

▶ Playing videos in iTunes

*I*f you like to entertain folks by spinning tunes and playing videos at home or at parties, iTunes could easily become your media jockey console. With iTunes, your computer is a mean multimedia machine that can mix sounds, photos, and videos. And even if you've never mastered a stereo system beyond adjusting the bass, treble, and volume, you can quickly and easily fine-tune the sound in iTunes, and even adjust the volume and equalizer settings for each song, video, audio book, and podcast.

But that's not all: You can also use iTunes to play video on your computer's display, or you can send it to a larger television or display monitor — even a video projector — to get a bigger picture. And if you've integrated Apple TV with your home audio system and television, you can use iTunes to feed music and video to Apple TV wirelessly, as I describe in this chapter.

To find out more about Apple TV, visit this book's companion Web site.

Changing the Computer's Output Volume

You can control the volume and other characteristics of the sound coming from your computer's speakers, headphones, or external speakers. Even if you connect your computer to a home audio system with its own volume and equalizer controls, it's best to get the volume correct at the source — your computer and iTunes — and then adjust the output volume as you please on your audio system or external speaker unit.

You control the volume by using your computer system's audio controls. iTunes also controls the volume, but that control is within the limits of the computer's volume setting. For example, if you set your computer's volume to half and set iTunes volume to full, you get half volume because the computer limits the volume to half. If you set your computer volume at half and also reduce the iTunes volume to half, you actually get *one-quarter* volume — half the computer's setting. After the sound leaves your computer, you can adjust it further with the volume controls of your stereo system or external speakers.

The appropriate volume depends entirely on your preferences for hearing music, audio books, or video soundtracks. In general, though, the maximum level of output from your computer is preferable when connecting to a stereo system or speakers with volume controls. After setting your computer to the maximum volume, adjust the iTunes volume or your stereo or speaker volume (or both) to get the best sound. When using the computer's speakers or headphones, the computer's volume and the iTunes volume are the only volume controls that you have, so after adjusting the volume on your computer to the maximum level (or lower if you prefer), adjust the iTunes volume.

Adjusting the sound on a Mac

The Mac was built for sound from the very start. Making and playing music have been part of the Mac culture since the day that Steve Jobs introduced an audience to the original Mac with sound coming from its small speaker. (It played synthesized speech and simple tones, but it was the first personal computer with built-in sound.)

Today's Macs come with built-in or external speakers and at least one headphone/line-out connection that you can use to connect external speakers or a stereo system. Mac OS X lets you configure output speakers and control levels for stereo speakers and multichannel audio devices.

If you use external speakers, headphones, or a stereo system, make sure that you connect these devices properly before adjusting the volume.

To adjust the volume on your Mac, follow these steps:

1. **Choose System Preferences from the Apple menu or the Dock and then click the Sound icon.**

   Otherwise, press Option and a volume control key on your keyboard simultaneously as a shortcut. You can have iTunes open and playing music while you do this.

2. **In the Sound preferences window that opens, click Output and select the sound output device.**

If you have headphones or external speakers attached to the headphones connection on your Mac, a Headphones option appears in the list of sound output devices, as shown in Figure 13-1. The External Speakers or Internal Speakers option may also appear for speakers connected through a line-out connection or built into the Mac.

3. **Adjust the volume.**

You can do any of the following:

- Drag the slider to adjust the volume while you listen to music.

- Select the Mute check box to silence your Mac.

- Drag the Balance slider to put more music in the left or right channel.

4. **Close the Preferences window, either by choosing System Preferences⇨Quit System Preferences, clicking the red button in the upper-left corner of the window, or pressing ⌘-Q.**

The Sound preferences window isn't like a dialog: When you change settings, you can hear the effect immediately without having to click OK. (There isn't an OK button, anyway.)

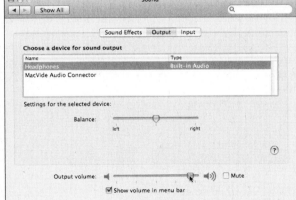

Figure 13-1:
Adjusting the sound output volume on a Mac with headphones attached.

Adjusting the sound in Windows

Windows 7, Windows Vista, Windows XP, and Windows 2000 let you configure output speakers and control levels for stereo speakers and multichannel audio devices.

Use the Sounds and Audio Devices Properties dialog to change the volume. To open this dialog, choose Start⇨Control Panel, click the Sounds and Audio Devices icon, and then click the Volume tab.

As shown in Figure 13-2, the Sounds and Audio Devices Properties dialog offers the Device Volume slider, which you drag to set the volume. You can also silence your PC by selecting the Mute check box.

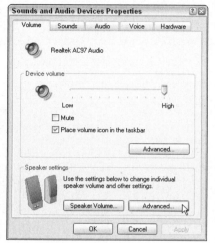

Figure 13-2:
Adjust
the sound
output
volume on
a Windows
PC.

If you select the Place Volume Icon in the Taskbar option and your sound card supports changing the volume with software, a sound icon appears in the notification area of Windows. You can then change the volume quickly without having to open the Sounds and Audio Devices Properties dialog. Simply click the speaker icon and drag the slider that pops up. For more information about adjusting sound on a PC, see *PCs For Dummies,* 11th Edition, by Dan Gookin (published by Wiley).

Using AirTunes or Apple TV for Wireless Stereo Playback

You want to play the music in your iTunes library, but your stereo system is across the room or in another room, and you don't want to extend wires to the stereo system. What you need is a wireless connection from your computer to your stereo system.

You can use an Apple AirPort Wi-Fi network in your home — such as AirPort Express by itself, or Apple TV with AirPort Extreme or Time Capsule. AirPort Express and Apple TV work with Apple's AirTunes technology, which lets you play your iTunes music through your stereo or powered speakers in any room of your house, without wires. The only catch is that your computer must be within range of the Wi-Fi network or connected by an Ethernet cable.

Apple's AirPort technology provides Wi-Fi networking for any AirPort-equipped Mac or wireless-capable PC that uses a Wi-Fi–certified IEEE 802.11b, 802.11g, or 802.11n wireless card or offers built-in Wi-Fi. For more about AirPort, see *Mac OS X Snow Leopard All-in-One For Dummies,* by Mark L. Chambers (published by Wiley).

If you already have a wireless network in place, you can add AirPort Express without changing anything. The AirPort Express wirelessly links to your existing wireless network without requiring any change to the network. You can even use several AirPort Express units — one for each stereo system or set of powered speakers, in different rooms.

All by itself, AirPort Express creates a Wi-Fi network. You can attach your Internet cable modem or other Ethernet network to AirPort Express to link your ready-made Wi-Fi network to the outside world. You can also take AirPort Express on the road to use in hotel rooms to share an Internet connection among wireless computers.

To use AirTunes and AirPort Express, follow these steps:

1. **Follow the instructions to install the software supplied with AirPort Express.**

2. **Connect your stereo or a set of powered speakers to the AirPort Express audio port.**

   You can use an optical digital or analog audio cable. (Both are included in the AirPort Express Stereo Connection Kit available from the Apple Store.) Which cable you use depends on whether your stereo or set of powered speakers has an optical digital or analog connection.

3. **Plug AirPort Express into an electrical outlet.**

   Use the AC plug that came with AirPort Express or the power extension cord included in the AirPort Express Stereo Connection Kit. AirPort Express turns on automatically when connected to an electrical outlet. The status light glows yellow while AirPort Express is starting up. When it is fully up and running, the light turns green.

4. **On your computer, set your iTunes preferences to look for speakers connected wirelessly with AirTunes.**

   a. *Choose iTunes⇨Preferences (Mac) or Edit⇨Preferences (Windows).*

   b. *Click the Devices tab to show the Devices pane.*

c. *Select the Look for Remote Speakers Connected with AirTunes check box in the Devices pane, as shown in Figure 13-3.*

You also have these options in the Devices pane:

- *To control volume from a stereo:* Select the Disable iTunes Volume Control for Remote Speakers check box to control speakers separately (a setting you should use if connecting to a stereo with a volume control).

- *To control volume from iTunes:* Leave this option deselected (the default) to control the volume from within iTunes.

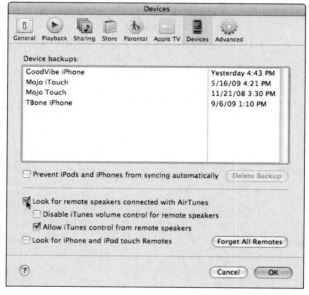

Figure 13-3: Select the option to look for remote speakers connected to your computer using AirTunes.

After selecting the option to look for AirTunes-connected speakers, the Speakers pop-up menu appears in the lower-right corner of the iTunes window. *Note:* The menu will probably be set to Computer, the default option.

5. Choose AirTunes-Equipped Network from this new pop-up menu.

The Speakers pop-up menu includes the computer itself as well as any available wireless AirTunes networks, as shown in Figure 13-4. You can select the AirTunes network to play music ("Express Buddy" in Figure 13-4). From that point, iTunes plays music through the AirTunes network rather than through the computer. To get back to playing music through speakers connected to the computer (or through the computer's built-in speakers), choose Computer from the Speakers pop-up menu.

Figure 13-4:
Choosing
the AirTunes
network
"Express
Buddy"
from the
Speakers
menu.

Choosing Airport Express "Express Buddy"

The AirPort Express is small enough to fit in the palm of your hand, and it travels well because all it needs is a power outlet. You can take your laptop and AirPort Express to a friend's house or party, connect the AirPort Express to the stereo system and a power outlet, and then use your laptop anywhere in its vicinity to play DJ. You can even use portable powered speakers in a hotel room without wires and use a hotel room's LAN-to-Internet access with an AirPort Express to connect your wireless computer and other wireless computers in the room to the Internet.

To play music through speakers connected to your Apple TV, choose Apple TV from the Speakers pop-up menu, as shown in Figure 13-5. You can use any computer with iTunes to play its library content (audio *and* video) through Apple TV to your home entertainment system without your having to synchronize that library's content — meaning that you don't have to change the content that is already synchronized with your Apple TV. That way, if you invite a friend over with her laptop, you can quickly play any tune in her laptop's library without changing the synchronized content from your computer. You can play anything in an iTunes library, even if your Apple TV is already filled with synchronized content.

To find out how to synchronize your Apple TV, visit this book's companion Web site.

Figure 13-5:
Choosing
Apple TV on
a wireless
network to
play music
and video.

If you set up your Apple TV to work with an Apple AirPort-based network, you can choose the Multiple Speakers option in the Speakers pop-up menu (refer to Figure 13-5) and play your iTunes content through both the computer and Apple TV speakers at the same time.

Playing Songs

When you've found a song you want to play (see Chapter 11 for browsing and searching details), simply select it in the List pane and then click the Play button. The Play button toggles to a Pause button while the song plays.

When the song finishes, iTunes continues playing the songs in the list in sequence until you click the Pause button (which then toggles back into the Play button) or until the song list ends. This setup is useful if you select an album, but not so great if you select a song at random and don't want to hear the next one. (Fortunately, you can arrange songs in playlists so that they play back in exactly the sequence you want; see Chapter 14 for details.)

You can skip to the next or previous song by pressing the right- or left-arrow key, respectively, or by clicking the Forward or Back button next to the Play button. You can also double-click another song in the list to start playing it.

Press the spacebar to perform the same function as the Play button; press the spacebar again to pause.

If you want to see the rest of your computer screen while playing music, you can minimize the iTunes screen to just the playback controls. On a Mac, choose Window➪Zoom (or click the green button in the upper-left corner of the window); choose it again (or click the green button again) to zoom back out to full size. On a Windows PC, choose View➪Switch to Mini Player (or press Ctrl-M); click the screen button (the middle button on the left side of the Mini Player) or press Ctrl-M to zoom back out to full size.

Grooving with the iTunes DJ

Playlists, as I describe in Chapter 14, are great for organizing music in the order that you want to play it, but you can have iTunes serve up songs at random. iTunes DJ (formerly Party Shuffle) is a dynamic playlist that automatically generates a semirandom selection in a list that you can modify on the fly. With iTunes DJ, you might even find songs in your library you forgot about or rarely play. iTunes DJ always throws a few rarely played songs into the mix.

To use iTunes DJ, follow these steps:

1. **Select iTunes DJ in the Playlists section of the Source pane.**

   The iTunes DJ track list appears in place of the List pane, with the Source pop-up, Settings, and Refresh buttons at the bottom, as shown in Figure 13-6.

2. **Choose a source from the Source pop-up menu below the track list.**

   You can select Music (refer to Figure 13-6) to use the entire music portion of your library, or select any playlist as the source for music (including a smart playlist; see Chapter 14 for details). If you select a playlist, iTunes DJ limits its choices to songs from that playlist.

3. **Click the Settings button, and set the following options in the Settings dialog as shown in Figure 13-7:**

   - *Recently Played Songs:* Choose how many songs should remain in the Party Shuffle list after they're played. You can drag already-played songs (even though they're grayed out after playing) to a spot later in the list to play them again.

   - *Upcoming Songs:* Choose how many songs should be listed as *upcoming* (not yet played). By displaying upcoming songs first, you can decide whether to rearrange the list or delete songs from the Party Shuffle playlist before they're played.

- *Play Higher Rated Songs More Often:* Select this option to have iTunes add more high-rated songs to the random list. Using this option, you weight the randomness in favor of higher-rated songs. See Chapter 12 to find out how to add ratings to songs.

- *Allow Guests to Request Songs with Remote for iPhone or iPod touch:* Select this option to let your guests use Apple's Remote app for the iPod touch or iPhone to connect to your iTunes library and request songs, which are added to the iTunes DJ playlist. You can enter a welcome message for your guests that appears in Remote, and if you also select the Enable Voting check box, your guests can use Remote to vote on songs — songs with more votes are automatically promoted to the top of the iTunes DJ list. You can restrict access to a specific playlist or other source in the Source pane (such as Genius playlists) by selecting the Restrict Requests to Source option and choosing a source from the pop-up menu. (For example, I chose the My Top Rated playlist in Figure 13-7.) You can control access via Remote by selecting the Require Password check box and entering a password.

4. **(Optional) If you don't like the order of songs, you can rearrange them. If you dislike any songs, you can remove them.**

   You can rearrange the order of songs in the iTunes DJ playlist by dragging songs to different positions in the list. Remove songs by selecting them in the iTunes DJ playlist and pressing Delete/Backspace (or choosing Edit➪Delete). Don't worry — the songs aren't deleted from your library, just from the iTunes DJ playlist.

iTunes DJ Settings

Display: 10 ⬍ recently played songs

20 ⬍ upcoming songs

☑ Play higher rated songs more often

☑ Allow guests to request songs with Remote for iPhone or iPod touch

Welcome Message:

☑ Restrict requests to source: 🎵 My Top Rated ⬍

Guests will only be allowed to request songs that are in this source.

☑ Enable voting

Guests can vote to control when songs play.

☐ Require password:

(?) (Cancel) (OK)

Figure 13-7:
Change the
iTunes DJ
settings.

5. **Play the iTunes DJ playlist by selecting the first song (or any song) and then clicking the Play button or pressing the spacebar.**

   You can start playing the first song or any song on the list. (When you pick a song in the middle to start playing, the songs before it are grayed out to show that they won't play.)

6. **Add, delete, or rearrange songs, even while iTunes DJ plays.**

   While the iTunes DJ list plays, you can add songs in one of two ways:

   • *Open iTunes DJ in a separate window by double-clicking iTunes DJ in the Source pane.* You can then drag songs from the main iTunes window — either from the Music portion of your library (select Music in the Library section of the Source pane) or from a playlist in the Source pane — directly into position in the iTunes DJ track list.

   • *Without opening iTunes DJ in a separate window, you can switch to the music portion of your library or a playlist and drag the song over iTunes DJ in the Source pane.* When you add a song to iTunes DJ, it shows up at the end of the track list. You can then drag it to a new position.

   You can add one or more albums to the iTunes DJ track list by dragging the albums; the songs play in album order. You can also add all the songs by an artist by dragging the artist's name. iTunes DJ acts like a dynamic playlist — you add, delete, and change the order of songs on the fly.

Cool DJs mix the iTunes DJ window with other open playlist windows. Just double-click the playlist item in the Source pane to open it in a separate window. You can then drag songs from different playlist windows to the iTunes DJ window while iTunes DJ plays, adding songs in whatever order you want in real time.

If you have songs in your library that you never, *ever* want to have appear in your iTunes DJ playlist, select the song, choose File⇨Get Info, click the Options tab, and select the Skip When Shuffling option. With this option on, the song is skipped when shuffling playback *and* when using iTunes DJ. You can skip entire albums by selecting the album, choosing File⇨Get Info, clicking Yes to the warning dialog, and choosing Yes from the Skip When Shuffling pop-up menu. (You can select an entire album quickly by showing the browser — choose View⇨Show Column Browser — and selecting the album name in the Album column.)

Cross-fading song playback

You can often hear a song on the radio fade out while another song immediately fades in over the first song's ending — a *cross-fade*. With iTunes, you can smoothly transition from the ending of one song to the beginning of the next one. Ordinarily, iTunes is set to have a short cross-fade of one second (the time after the fade-out of the first song to the fade-in of the second), but you can adjust that if you like.

What's totally cool is that you can cross-fade two songs in iTunes even if they're from different sources. The songs could be in your library, in a shared library, on CD, or even on one (or more) iPods connected to your computer and playing through iTunes. You can play DJ at a party with a massive music library on a laptop and enlarge that library with one or more iPods and any number of CDs, and have the songs cross-fade.

You can change the cross-fade by choosing iTunes⇨Preferences on a Mac or Edit⇨Preferences in Windows and then clicking the Playback button. The Playback preferences dialog appears, as shown in Figure 13-8.

In the Playback preferences dialog, select the Crossfade Songs check box and then increase or decrease the cross-fade by dragging the slider. Each notch in the slider represents one second. The maximum amount of cross-fade is 12 seconds. With a longer cross-fade, you get more overlap from one song to the next; that is, the second song starts before the first one ends. To turn off the cross-fade, deselect the Crossfade Songs check box.

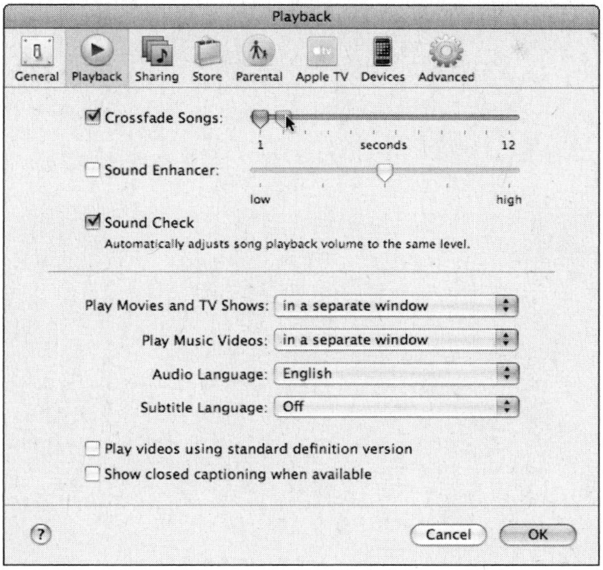

Figure 13-8:
Set the cross-fade between songs and other playback options.

Playing Podcasts

A podcast transfers audio or audio/video episodes, such as weekly broadcasts, automatically to your iTunes library from the Internet or through the iTunes Store (as I describe in episodic detail in Chapter 8). Podcasts that you subscribe to appear in the List pane when you select the Podcasts option in the Library section of the Source pane. You can add podcast episodes to your library by subscribing to them in the iTunes Store (see Chapter 7) or on a Web site (see Chapter 8).

To play the most recent podcast episode, select the Podcasts item in the Library section of the Source pane, select a podcast in any view, and then click the Play button. To play a specific podcast episode, follow these steps:

1. **Select the Podcasts item in the Library section of the Source pane and choose List or Cover Flow view.**

2. **Select a podcast in the List view or in the list under the Cover Flow view, and then click the triangle to see its episodes.**

   The triangle rotates, and a list of episodes appears beneath the podcast, as shown in Figure 13-9 (using List view).

3. **Select the podcast and then click the Play button.**

   You can use the iTunes playback controls to fast-forward or rewind the podcast or play it from any point. The blue dot next to a podcast means that you haven't yet played it. As soon as you start listening to a podcast, the dot disappears.

Figure 13-9:
Open a podcast to see its episodes.

When you play a podcast, iTunes remembers your place when you stop listening to it, just like it remembers when you place a bookmark in an audio book or pause during a movie — even after quitting and restarting iTunes. iTunes resumes playing from that playback position when you return to the podcast to play it.

Some podcasts are enhanced to include chapter marks and photos. When you play an enhanced podcast in iTunes, a Chapters menu appears on the iTunes menu bar. Choose this menu to display the podcast's chapter marks, artwork, and chapter start times.

If the podcaster embedded a photo in an audio podcast file or included a link to a video from the file, the photo or video content appears in the Artwork pane.

Although you can drag a podcast into a playlist to include it in that playlist, you can also drag a podcast to the Source pane to create a new playlist, as long as you drag it to an empty space in the Playlist section of the Source pane (and not into another playlist). The new playlist takes on the name of the podcast. You can also add other podcasts to the new playlist and rename the playlist. For more information about playlists, see Chapter 14.

Playing Audio Books

You can store and play audio books, articles, and spoken-word titles just like songs in iTunes, and you can download titles from the iTunes Store (as I describe prolifically in Chapter 7). Choose Audiobooks in the Library section of the Source pane to see them.

To play an audio book, select it just like you would a song (see details on browsing and listing content in Chapter 11) and then click the Play button. You can use the iTunes playback controls to fast-forward or rewind the audio book or play it from any point.

Audio books from the iTunes Store are enhanced to include chapter marks. When you play any of these audio books in iTunes, the Chapters menu appears on the iTunes menu bar, just like it does for a podcast with chapters. Choose the Chapters menu to display and select the audio book's chapter marks.

Playing Videos

iTunes is versatile when it comes to playing videos — the TV shows, movies, video podcasts, and music videos you downloaded from the iTunes Store (see Chapter 7) as well as the video files you imported into iTunes from other sources (see Chapter 8).

To watch a video in iTunes, select it in your library (see details on browsing and listing movies, TV shows, and videos in Chapter 11) and then click the Play button. Use the iTunes Previous/Rewind, Play/Pause, and Forward/Next buttons to control playback and the iTunes volume slider to control the volume, just like with songs.

By default, the video appears in the Artwork pane in the lower-left corner of the iTunes window, as shown in Figure 13-10. If the Artwork pane isn't visible, playing the video makes it appear. You can also make the Artwork pane appear or disappear by clicking the Show/Hide Artwork button.

To watch a video in a separate window, click the video while it plays in the Artwork pane. A separate window appears that includes a transparent QuickTime controls pane with buttons for controlling video playback, as shown in Figure 13-11. Click the Play button at the center of the pane to play or pause, and then drag the slider to move forward or backward through the video. Click the Rewind or Fast Forward button on either side of the Play button in the controls pane to move backward or forward through a video. Click the red "close window" button in the upper-left corner to close the window.

Figure 13-10:
A video appears in the Artwork pane. Ugh, too small!

Figure 13-11:
Drag the QuickTime playback slider to move forward or backward through a video.

The transparent QuickTime controls pane disappears while the video plays, but you can make it reappear at any time by moving the cursor to the bottom center of the video window. The controls pane also offers a volume control slider to set the audio volume of the video, and the Full-Screen Video button to change the video display to full-screen. (See the section "Playing a video full-screen," later in this chapter.)

You can resize the separate video window by dragging the lower-right corner of the window. You can also choose fixed window sizes by choosing them from the View menu. For example, choose View⇨Video Size⇨Half Size to display the video window at half the actual size, or choose View⇨ Video Size⇨Double Size to display the window at twice the size. Choose View⇨ Video Size⇨Actual Size to set the window back to the actual size of the video picture.

Changing video playback preferences

To change your iTunes preferences for playing movies, TV shows, and music videos, choose iTunes⇨Preferences (Mac) or Edit⇨Preferences (Windows), and click the Playback tab (refer to Figure 13-8). You can choose the following options separately for movies/TV shows and for music videos:

✔ In the Artwork Viewer, as described above and shown in Figure 13-10.

✔ In a Separate Window, as described above and shown in Figure 13-11.

✔ In the iTunes Window, as shown in Figure 13-12, with a transparent QuickTime controls pane that offers buttons for controlling video playback. Click the Play button at the center of the QuickTime controls pane to play or pause, and then drag the slider to move forward or backward through the video. Click the Rewind or Fast Forward button on either side of the Play button in the controls pane to move backward or forward through a video. Click the circled X to stop playing the video and return to the normal iTunes window.

✔ Full Screen or Full Screen (with Visuals), which fills the entire computer display. See the next section, " Playing a video full-screen" for details.

Playing a video full-screen

After choosing the Full Screen option from the Play Movies and TV Shows pop-up menu and/or the Play Music Videos pop-up menu as described in the previous section (refer to Figure 13-8), those videos fill the screen when they play, with a transparent QuickTime controls pane offering buttons for controlling video playback.

Figure 13-12:
Click the circled X to stop playing the video inside the iTunes window.

Some videos look good when displayed full-screen, but others may not. Videos purchased from the iTunes Store look fine, but video from other sources may look pixilated at full-screen resolution.

To change from watching a video in a separate window to a full-screen view, click the Full-Screen Video button in the transparent QuickTime controls pane (refer to Figure 13-11). This button doesn't appear unless you're playing a video in a separate window. You can also choose View⇨Video Size⇨Fit to Screen.

When you're playing a video in full-screen view, the following controls are available:

- ✔ **Esc (Escape):** Press to stop full-screen playback and return to the iTunes window.

- ✔ **Spacebar:** Press to pause playback. (Pressing the spacebar again resumes playback.)

- ✔ **Your mouse or pointing device:** Simply move these to display the transparent QuickTime controls pane and then click the Full-Screen Video button (now with its arrows pointing inward) to stop full-screen playback and return to the iTunes window.

A cool party trick is to seamlessly mix music videos and music with visuals. (See Chapter 6 to find out about displaying visuals.) To display a mixed playlist of music and videos (see Chapter 14 to create playlists), choose iTunes⇨Preferences (Mac) or Edit⇨Preferences (Windows). Then click the Playback tab and choose the Full Screen (with Visuals) option from the Play

Music Videos pop-up menu (or even the Play Movies and TV Shows pop-up menu, if you include these in your playlist). When you play the mixed music-video playlist, iTunes automatically shows full-screen video for your videos and full-screen visuals for your music, seamlessly moving from one to the other.

For many, the computer display is just fine for viewing videos full-screen. However, if you want to connect your PC to a television, the easiest way is through Apple TV. Apple TV lets you connect an HD-compatible television and audio system wirelessly (or by wired Ethernet) to any computer running iTunes in the network and store content for playback.

To find out more about Apple TV and details about connections to home video and stereo equipment, visit this book's companion Web site.

Adjusting the Sound

Some songs are just too loud. I don't mean too loud stylistically, as in thrash metal with screeching guitars; I mean too loud for your ears when you're wearing headphones or so loud that the music is distorted. And some songs are just too soft; you have to increase the volume to hear them and then lower the volume to listen to louder songs. Videos, podcast episodes, and audio books can also vary greatly from loud to soft. To remedy these problems, you can set the volume in advance for these items. You can also sound-check your entire music library to bring it in line, volume-wise.

Setting the volume in advance

With songs, audio books, podcast episodes, and videos that you already know are too loud (or too soft), consider setting the volume for those items in advance so that they always play with the desired volume adjustment. You can even set the volume for entire albums or podcasts.

To adjust the overall volume of a particular item in advance so that it always plays at that setting, perform the following steps:

1. **Select one or more items in your iTunes library.**

   To set the volume in iTunes for multiple songs, you can select an entire album in Browse view or you can select all the songs. To set the volume for a whole podvcast, select it instead of individual episodes.

2. **Choose File⇨Get Info.**

   The information dialog appears.

3. **Click the Options tab.**

   Drag the Volume Adjustment slider left or right to adjust the volume lower or higher, as shown in Figure 13-13. You can do this while playing the file.

4. **Click the OK button to finish.**

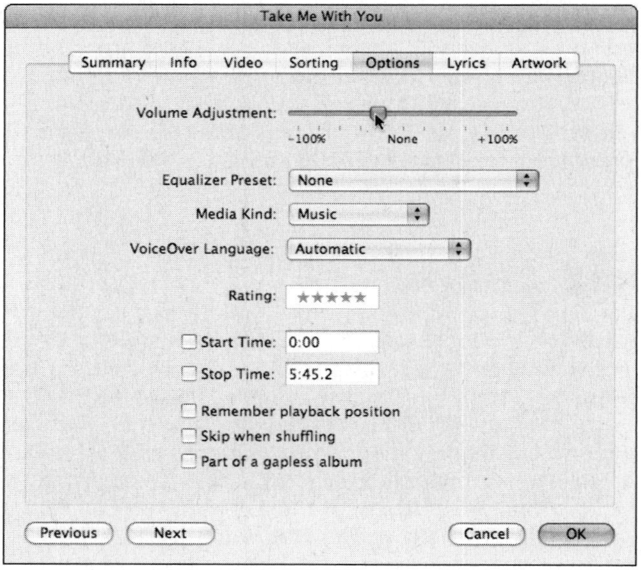

Figure 13-13:
Adjust the volume setting for a song here.

Equalizing the sound

The Beach Boys were right when they sang "Good Vibrations" because that's what music is — the sensation of hearing audible vibrations conveyed to the ear by a medium, such as air. Musicians measure pitch by the *frequency* of vibrations. When you increase the bass or treble, you're actually increasing the volume, or intensity, of certain frequencies. iTunes provides an equalizer to fine-tune the sound spectrum frequencies in a more precise way than with bass and treble controls. It increases or decreases specific frequencies of the sound to raise or lower highs, lows, and midrange tones.

You can use the iTunes equalizer (EQ) to customize playback for different musical genres, listening environments, or speakers. iTunes comes with more than 20 EQ presets of the most commonly used settings, including ones for specific music genres, such as classical and rock.

To choose an equalizer preset for a song, video, podcast, or audio book, select the item in the iTunes library, choose File⇨Get Info, and click the Options tab (refer to Figure 13-13). Click the Equalizer Preset pop-up menu to assign an EQ preset, and click the OK button. If something is playing, you hear the effect in the sound immediately after choosing the preset.

For even finer control, you can open the iTunes Equalizer window by choosing Window⇨Equalizer. You can then adjust frequencies by clicking and dragging sliders that look like mixing-board faders. You can also see what a preset actually does to the frequencies by clicking the Equalizer window's pop-up menu to select the same preset by name. The faders in the equalizer show you exactly what the preset does.

Find out more about tweaking the sound with the equalizer by visiting the Tips section of my Web site (www.tonybove.com).

Sound-checking and enhancing the volume

Because music CDs are manufactured inconsistently, discrepancies occur in volume. Some CDs play louder than others; occasionally, even individual tracks on a CD might vary.

You can standardize the volume level of all the songs in your iTunes library with the Sound Check option. This option has the added benefit of applying the same volume adjustment when you play the songs back on your iPod or iPhone, as I describe in Chapter 16.

To enable Sound Check, follow these steps:

1. **Drag the iTunes volume slider to set the overall volume for iTunes.**

   The volume slider is located in the upper-left corner of the iTunes window, to the right of the Play button.

2. **Choose iTunes⇨Preferences (Mac) or Edit⇨Preferences (Windows).**

   The iTunes Preferences dialog appears.

3. **Click the Playback tab.**

   The Playback preferences appear (refer to Figure 13-8).

4. **Select the Sound Check box.**

   iTunes sets the volume level for all songs according to the level of the iTunes volume slider.

5. **Click the OK button.**

   The Sound Check option sets a volume adjustment based on the volume slider on all the songs so that they play at approximately the same volume.

The operation runs in the background while you do other things. If you quit iTunes and then restart it, the operation continues where it left off when you quit. You can switch Sound Check on or off at any time.

You can also improve the depth of the sound by enhancing high and low frequencies. Audiophiles and sound purists would most likely use the equalizer to boost frequencies, but you can use this brute-force method to enhance the sound. Follow these steps:

1. **Choose iTunes⇨Preferences (Mac) or Edit⇨Preferences (Windows).**

   The iTunes Preferences dialog appears.

2. **Click the Playback tab.**

   The Playback preferences appear (refer to Figure 13-8).

3. **Select the Sound Enhancer check box and adjust the slider:**

   • *Increase the sound enhancement.* Dragging the Sound Enhancer slider to the right (toward High) is similar to pressing the loudness button on a car stereo or the equivalent of boosting the treble (high) and bass (low) frequencies in the equalizer.

   • *Decrease the high and low frequencies.* Drag the slider to the left toward Low.

The middle setting is neutral, adding no enhancement — the same as disabling Sound Enhancer by deselecting its check box.

Chapter 14

Organizing iTunes Content with Playlists

In This Chapter

▶ Creating a playlist of songs and albums

▶ Adding podcast episodes and videos to playlists

▶ Creating and editing smart playlists

▶ Creating a Genius playlist

*T*he ability to play any set of songs in a specific order is one of the joys of using iTunes and iPods. A *playlist* is a list of the items that you want, organized in the sequence that you want to play them. For example, you can make a playlist of love songs from different albums for a romantic mood, or surf songs for a trip to the beach.

You can also organize playlists for different operations, such as copying to your iPod, iPhone, or Apple TV or burning a CD. I create playlists that combine songs from different albums based on themes or similarities. For example, I have a jazz playlist for cruising around with my iPhone in the city at night, a classic rock playlist for jogging with my iPod shuffle in the morning and hanging out in coffee shops with my iPod nano, a playlist of short films mixed with TV shows for a long airplane ride with my iPod touch, and a playlist of rain songs to celebrate rainy days.

You can create as many playlists of songs, audio books, podcast episodes, and videos as you want, in any order that you like. The items and their files don't change, nor are they copied. iTunes simply creates a list of the item names with links to the actual items and their files.

You can even create a *smart playlist,* which automatically includes items in the playlist based on the criteria you set up and also removes items that don't match the criteria. The information included in iTunes (see Chapter 12) is very useful for setting up the criteria. For example, you can define the criteria for a smart playlist to automatically include songs from a particular artist or songs that have the highest rating or fit within a particular musical genre.

Creating Playlists

Playlists are important for managing your content library. For example, you need to create a playlist in order to burn a CD (as I show in Chapter 15), and you may want to synchronize your iPod or iPhone using playlists (as I describe in Chapter 9). They can also make it easier to find items you like without searching the entire library for them. You can create playlists of individual songs or entire albums. You can also include audio books, TV shows, videos, podcast episodes, and Web radio stations in playlists.

To create a playlist, follow these steps:

1. **Click the Add Playlist button (in the lower-left corner of the iTunes window under the Source pane) or choose File⇨New Playlist.**

   This step creates a new, untitled playlist in the Playlists section of the Source pane named, appropriately enough, *untitled playlist,* highlighted and ready to rename.

2. **Give the playlist a new descriptive name.**

   You can begin typing a new name and press Return (or just click somewhere else) to save the name. (If the playlist name wasn't highlighted first, click once to select it and then click the name again so that the text cursor appears; doing so highlights the playlist name, making it ready for you to type the new name.)

   After you type the new name, iTunes automatically sorts it into alphabetical order in the Playlists section of the Source pane (underneath the preset smart playlists).

3. **Select a source, such as Music or Audiobooks, in the Library section of the Source pane and then drag items from the library to the playlist.**

   Drag one item at a time or drag a group of items, dropping them onto the playlist name in the Source pane. The initial order of items in the playlist is based on the order in which you drag them to the list. You can add all the podcast episodes to a playlist by dragging the podcast name, or you can open it to reveal its episodes (see Chapter 13 for details) and drag separate episodes to the playlist rather than the entire podcast.

4. **Select the playlist in the Playlists section of the Source pane to play it.**

   After selecting a playlist, the items in the playlist appear in the List pane. Select any item in the playlist to start playing from that item to the end of the playlist, and click the Play button.

To rearrange the list of items in the playlist, see the section "Rearranging and managing playlists," later in this chapter.

To open a playlist in a new window, double-click the icon next to the playlist name in the Source pane. You can then browse your music library and drag items from your music library to the separate playlist window.

To create a playlist quickly, select the group of items in the List pane that you want to make into a playlist. Choose File➪New Playlist from Selection, or drag the selection to an area between playlists in the Source pane. You can then type a name for the new playlist that appears.

Making a playlist of an album is simple. Select the Music option in the Library section of the Source pane, and then select an album — either in Grid or Cover Flow view, or in List view using the Column Browser (choose View➪Show Column Browser). Drag the selected album to an area between playlists in the Playlists section of the Source pane. Or, select the album and then choose File➪New Playlist from Selection. iTunes automatically creates a new playlist named after the album. You can create a playlist with all of a podcast's episodes the same way: choose Podcasts in the Source pane and select the podcast that you want to make into a playlist, and then choose File➪New Playlist from Selection.

You might want to play several albums back to back without having to select each album to play it. For example, you might want to use an iPod on that long drive from London to Liverpool to play The Beatles' albums in the order they were released (or perhaps in the reverse order, following The Beatles' career from London back to Liverpool). To create a playlist of entire albums in a particular order, drag each album to the same playlist in the order you want to play them. Each time you drag an album, iTunes automatically lists the songs in the proper track sequence for each album. The albums are listed in the playlist in the order that you dragged them.

You can mix videos with songs and other items in a playlist. For example, you can mix songs and music videos, songs and a video documentary, or just a selection of TV shows, music, podcasts, movies, and audio books for an entire day's worth of entertainment. However, if you transfer the playlist to an iPod that doesn't play video, the iPod skips the videos.

Rearranging and managing playlists

To rearrange the items in a playlist, follow these steps:

1. **Select the playlist in the Playlists section of the Source pane.**

   After selecting a playlist, the items in the playlist appear in the List pane.

2. **Drag items in the List pane to rearrange the list.**

   - *To move an item (such as a song) up the list and scroll at the same time,* drag it over the up arrow in the first column.

- *To move an item down the list and scroll,* drag it to the bottom of the list.

- *To move a group of items at once,* press Shift and select a range of items (or press ⌘ on a Mac or Ctrl in Windows while clicking to select specific songs) and then drag them into a new position.

Besides dragging items, you can also rearrange a playlist by sorting it: Just click one of the column headings, such as Name, Time, or Artist.

You can drag items from one playlist to another. Only links are copied, not the actual files.

You can rename a playlist at any time by clicking its name twice and typing a new one. Also, in case you forget which items are in which playlists, you can see all the playlists that include a particular item. In List view, press Control on a Mac and click the item; in Windows, right-click the item and choose Show in Playlist from the contextual menu. The playlists that include the item are listed in the submenu.

You can organize playlists into folders in the Source pane. Choose File⇨New Playlist Folder to create a folder in the Playlists section. Then drag playlist names and drop them over the new folder — just like how you treat files and folders in your operating system. Folders are useful for grouping playlists that are similar in content or function. For example, I created a different folder that corresponds to each of my iPods to organize the playlists I use to synchronize with those iPods. (See Chapter 9 to read about iPod synchronization.) You can include smart playlists in folders as well as regular playlists.

Deleting items from a playlist

You can delete items from playlists while keeping the items in your library. When you delete an item from a playlist, the item is simply deleted from the list — not from the library. You can also delete entire playlists without harming the content in the library. *Note:* You'll need to switch to the Library section of the Source pane (Music, Movies, TV Shows, and so on) if you want to delete items permanently from your library.

To delete an item from a playlist, select the playlist in the Playlists section of the Source pane and then select the item. Press Delete/Backspace or choose Edit⇨Delete. In the warning dialog that appears, click the Remove button to remove the selected item from the list.

The one way you can completely delete an item from your library from within a playlist is by selecting the item and pressing ⌘-Option-Delete (Mac) or Ctrl-Alt-Backspace (Windows).

To delete a whole playlist, select the playlist in the Playlists section of the Source pane and then press Delete/Backspace or choose Edit➪Delete.

Using Smart Playlists

Under iTunes DJ (near the top of the Playlists section of the Source pane), you can find *smart playlists,* which are indicated by a gear-in-a-document icon. iTunes comes with a few sample smart playlists, such as My Top Rated and Recently Added, and you can create your own. Smart playlists add items to themselves based on prearranged criteria, or *rules.* For example, when you rate your content items, My Top Rated changes to reflect your new ratings. You don't have to set up anything because My Top Rated and Recently Added are already defined for you.

Of course, smart playlists are ignorant of your taste in music or video. You have to program them with rules by using the song information in iTunes (see Chapter 12 about adding or editing song information, including ratings). For example, you can create a smart playlist that uses the Year field to grab all the songs from 1966. This list, in no particular order, might include The Beatles ("Eleanor Rigby"), Frank Sinatra ("Strangers in the Night"), The Yardbirds ("Over Under Sideways Down"), and Ike and Tina Turner ("River Deep, Mountain High") — a far-out playlist, no doubt, but not necessarily what you want. You can use other fields of information that you entered (such as ratings, artist name, or composer) to fine-tune your criteria. You can also use built-in functions, such as *Play Count* (the number of times the item was played) or *Date Added* (the date the item was added to the library).

Creating a smart playlist

To create a new smart playlist, choose File➪New Smart Playlist. The Smart Playlist dialog appears (as shown in Figure 14-1), offering the following choices for setting criteria:

✔ **Match the Following Rule:** From the first pop-up menu (refer to Figure 14-1), you can choose any of the categories used for information, such as Artist, Composer, or Last Played. From the second pop-up menu, you can choose an operator, such as the greater-than or less-than operator. The selections that you make in these two pop-up menus combine to create a rule, such as `Year is greater than 1966` or, as in Figure 14-1, `Composer contains` (the words) `Woody Guthrie`.

You can also add multiple conditions by clicking the + button (on the right) as shown in Figure 14-2. You then decide whether to match all or any of these conditions. The Match *xx* of the Following Rules option is enabled by default when you set one or more rules.

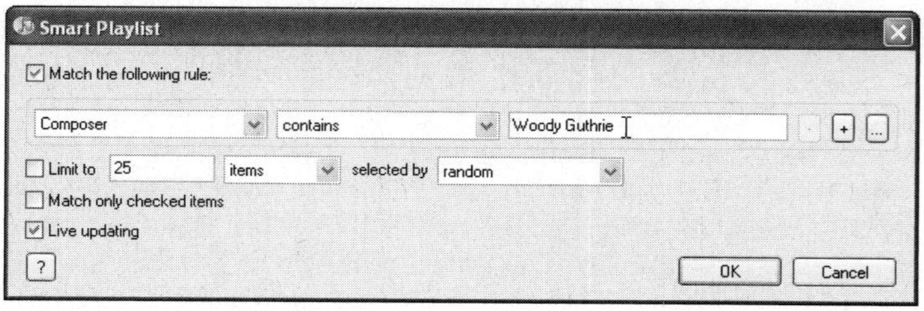

Figure 14-1:
Set the first
match rule
for a smart
playlist.

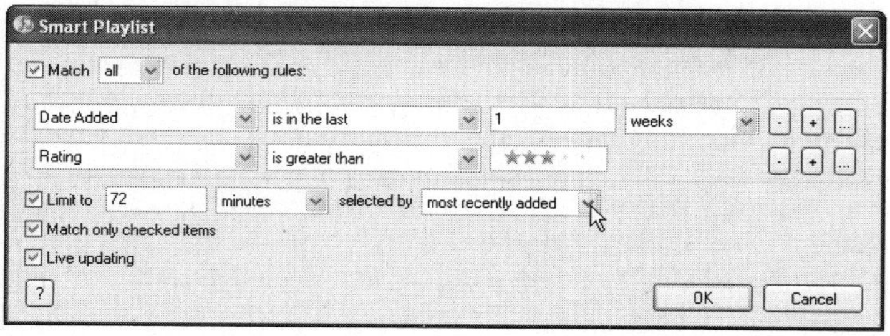

Figure 14-2:
Use multiple
conditions
and a time
limit for a
smart
playlist.

> ✔ **Limit To:** You can limit the smart playlist to a specific *duration,* measured by the number of songs (items), time, or size in megabytes or gigabytes, as shown in Figure 14-2. You can have items selected by various methods, such as random, most recently played, and so on.

> ✔ **Match Only Checked Items:** This option selects only those songs or other items in the library that have a check mark beside them, along with the rest of the criteria. Selecting and deselecting items is an easy way to fine-tune your selection for a smart playlist.

> ✔ **Live Updating:** This allows iTunes to continually update the playlist while you play items, add or remove items from the library, change their ratings, and so on.

After setting up the rules, click the OK button. iTunes creates the playlist, noted by a gear-in-a-document icon and the name *untitled playlist* (or whatever phrase you used for the first condition, such as the album or artist name). You can click in the playlist field and then type a new name for it.

A smart playlist for recent additions

Setting up rules gives you the opportunity to create playlists that are smarter than the ones supplied with iTunes. For example, I created a smart playlist with criteria (as shown in Figure 14-2) that does the following:

✔ Includes any item added to the library in the past week that also has a rating greater than three stars.

✔ Limits the playlist to 72 minutes to be sure that it fits on a 74-minute audio CD, even with gaps between the songs. It also refines the selection to the most recently added if the entire selection becomes greater than 72 minutes.

✔ Matches only selected items.

✔ Performs live updating.

Editing a smart playlist

To edit a smart playlist, select it from the Playlists section of the Source pane and choose File➪Edit Smart Playlist. Or, you can Control-click (Mac) or right-click (Windows) the playlist and then choose Edit Smart Playlist from the contextual menu. Either way, the Smart Playlist window appears with the criteria for the smart playlist.

For example, to modify the smart playlist so that items with a higher rating are picked, simply add another star or two to the My Rating criteria.

You can also choose to limit the playlist to a certain number of items selected by various methods, such as random, most recently played, and so on.

Adding a Touch of Genius

If you select a song and click the Genius button, iTunes takes a look at your selection and creates a playlist of songs that go along with it. That's genius!

The Genius sidebar (which I describe in glorious detail in Chapter 6) works with Apple's iTunes Store content to match your tastes to other iTunes users using a technique called *collaborative filtering*. The Genius feature analyzes the music in other people's iTunes libraries — people who also have the same song you selected (if they also turn on the Genius feature in iTunes). All this information is shared anonymously. The only music Genius knows, however, is the music available in the iTunes Store.

For the Genius feature to work, you need an iTunes Store account (see Chapter 7), and you must turn on Genius to enable iTunes to scan your music library and catalog your iTunes collection. The scanning process may take a few minutes or (for very large collections) a few hours, but you can continue using iTunes while it scans your music.

To turn on Genius, click the Turn on Genius button in the Genius sidebar, enter your Apple ID and password for your iTunes Store account, and click the Continue button.

You can also turn on the Genius feature by choosing Store⇨Turn On Genius, and turn if off by choosing Store⇨Turn Off Genius. If you add new music, you can tell iTunes to immediately update the Genius feature with new information by choosing Store⇨Update Genius.

Creating a Genius playlist

To create a Genius playlist, select a song in the List pane and click the Genius button (the button with the atom icon) at the lower-right corner of the iTunes window. iTunes displays the Genius playlist based on the selected song. You can limit the number of songs for the Genius playlist by clicking the Limit To pop-up menu in the top row of buttons on the right side of the List pane, as shown in Figure 14-3.

You can refresh the Genius playlist with a new batch of songs based on the selected song by clicking the Refresh button in the top row of buttons (refer to Figure 14-3). When you refresh a Genius playlist, you lose the previous version of that playlist.

To save a Genius playlist, click the Save Playlist button in the right corner of the top row of buttons. The playlist is saved with the Genius icon using the name of the selected song and listed in the Playlists section of the Source pane at the top, above smart playlists. You can revisit this Genius playlist and refresh it, or change its song limit. You can also rearrange the songs in the Genius playlist by dragging them. To sort the songs, click the column headers in the List pane — just like other playlists.

You can synchronize your saved Genius playlists with your iPod or iPhone (see Chapter 9 for details). Synchronized Genius playlists on the iPod or iPhone contain the same songs that appeared in the iTunes version of the playlist. See Chapter 16 for details on using Genius playlists with iPods and iPhones.

Figure 14-3:
Limit the
number of
songs for
the Genius
playlist.

Genius button

Playing Genius mixes

The Genius of iTunes is that it can take into consideration everything in
your library and, comparing your library to other libraries, come up with
an interesting mix of songs. To give you a taste of what's possible with the
Genius feature, check out Genius Mixes.

Start by selecting Genius Mixes in the Genius section of the Source pane
(Genius must already be turned on as described earlier in this section).

iTunes compiles a set of Genius mixes based on your library, as shown in
Figure 14-4. Each square represents a separate mix. As you hover over a
square, a play button appears; click the play button to play the mix.

You may be surprised at how well the Genius feature serves up appropriate
mixes. Apple has improved the Genius feature by collecting more data from
millions of iTunes users. You are one, so you should be proud that you have
contributed to Genius!

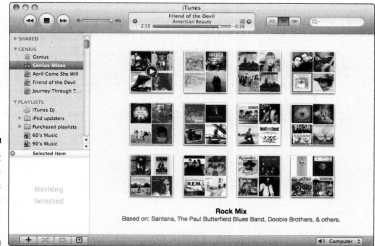

Figure 14-4:
Generate
Genius
mixes from
your entire
library.

Chapter 15

Gimme Shelter for My Media

In This Chapter

▶ Choosing the format and settings for burning a disc

▶ Burning an audio CD, an MP3 CD, or a data DVD

▶ Locating and backing up files in the iTunes library

▶ Backing up your entire iTunes library

*Y*ou might think that your digital content is safe, stored as-is, on your iPod, iPhone, Apple TV, and hard drive. However, demons in the night are working overtime to render your hard drive useless — and at the same time, someone left your iPod out in the rain, your iPhone can't phone home, and your Apple TV is on the fritz.

Copyright law and common sense prohibit you from using copyrighted content and then selling it to someone else. However, with iTunes, you're allowed to make copies of music, videos, audio books, and podcasts that you own for personal use, including copies for backup purposes.

This chapter boils down everything you need to know about burning your own discs to make copies of your content. I burn audio CDs or MP3 CDs to make safety copies of songs I buy from the iTunes Store. I also like to custom-mix songs from different artists and albums onto an audio or MP3 CD.

I burn data DVDs to back up my video files — and I also copy my entire iTunes library to another hard drive as a backup, as I describe in this chapter. This operation is very important, especially if you've purchased items that don't exist anywhere else in your collection but on your computer. That way, even if your hard drive fails, you still have your iTunes library.

To find out how to consolidate media files into one library, how to manage multiple iTunes libraries for easier synchronization with multiple devices, and how to move a library from one computer to another (such as a PC to a Mac or vice versa), visit this book's companion Web site.

You should not rely on your iPod, iPhone, or Apple TV as your sole music storage device or as a backup for your iTunes library. Although purchases you make with your iPod touch or iPhone *are* copied back to your iTunes library, you can't copy any other content from your iPod, iPhone, or Apple TV to your computer via iTunes. It's a one-way trip from iTunes *to* your iPod, iPhone, or Apple TV because record labels and video distributors don't want indiscriminate copying, and Apple has complied with these requests. You can, however, use *third-party utility programs* (not supported by Apple) to copy content both ways.

To find out more about third-party utility programs for managing your iPod or iPhone, visit the Tips section of my Web site (www.tonybove.com).

The iTunes Store uses Apple FairPlay technology for some content (such as commercial movies and TV Shows), which protects the rights of copyright holders while also giving you some leeway in using the copyrighted content. But you can still copy the media files freely so that backup is easy and straightforward on either a Mac or a PC.

Do not violate copyright law. You're allowed to copy content for your own use, but you cannot legally copy content for any other purpose. Consult a lawyer if you're in doubt.

Burning Your Own Discs

Once upon a time, when vinyl records were popular, rock radio disk jockeys (who didn't like disco) held disco-meltdown parties. People were encouraged to throw their disco records onto a pile to be burned or steamrolled into a vinyl glob. I admit that I shamelessly participated in one such meltdown. However, this section isn't about that. Rather, *burning* a disc is the process in which the CD drive recorder's laser heats up points on an interior layer of the disc to record information.

Using recordable CDs and DVDs

If you have a CD-R, CD-RW, or DVD-R drive (such as the Apple SuperDrive for a Mac) and a blank CD-R (*R* stands for *recordable*), you can burn music, audio books, and audio podcast episodes on audio CDs that play in most CD players. You can fit up to 74 minutes of music on a high-quality audio-format CD-R; most can go as high as 80 minutes.

Blank audio CD-Rs (I'm talking discs now and not drives) are available in stores that carry consumer electronics. You can also get them online from the Apple Store (not the music store — the store that sells computers and accessories). Choose iTunes⇨Shop for iTunes Products (Mac) or Help⇨Shop for iTunes Products (Windows) to reach the Apple Store online.

You can also burn an audio CD-R of song files in the MP3 format, which is useful for backing up a music library or making discs for use in MP3 CD players. You can play MP3 files burned on a CD-R in MP3 format on any MP3 disc player, on combination CD/MP3 players, on many DVD players, and (of course) on computers that recognize MP3-formatted CDs (including computers with iTunes). An MP3-formatted CD-R can hold more than 12 hours of music. You read that right — *12 hours on one disc.* This is why *MP3 discs* are popular: because they are essentially CD-Rs with MP3 files stored on them.

If you have a DVD burner, such as an Apple SuperDrive, you can burn *data discs* in the DVD-R or DVD-RW format to use with other computers. This approach is suitable for making backup copies of media files (or any data files). A DVD-R can hold about 4,700,000,000 bytes (more than 4GB).

Creating a disc burn playlist

To burn a CD (actually a CD-R, but most people refer to recordable CD-R discs as *CDs*), you must first define a playlist for the CD. (See Chapter 14 to find out how to create a playlist.) You can use songs encoded in any format that iTunes supports; however, you get higher-quality music with the uncompressed AIFF and WAV formats or with the Apple Lossless format. (You can back up your library to DVD without creating a playlist, as I describe in the section "Backing up to DVD-Rs or CD-Rs," later in this chapter.)

If your playlist includes music purchased from the iTunes Store in the older protected AAC-encoding format (before 2009), some rules might apply. You can burn seven copies of the same playlist containing protected songs to an audio CD, but no more. As of this writing, all music you purchase in the store is in the newer unprotected iTunes Plus format, with no limit on burning discs.

You can get around this limitation by creating or using a new playlist, copying the protected songs to the new playlist, and then burning more CDs with the new playlist.

Calculating how much music to use

When you create an audio CD playlist, you can calculate how many songs can fit on the CD by totaling the durations of the songs. You can see the size of a playlist by selecting it; the bottom of the iTunes window shows the number of songs, the duration of the songs, and the amount in megabytes for the selected playlist. Click the duration to see a more precise total time for the playlist, as shown in Figure 15-1.

Figure 15-1: Click the duration of the playlist below the List pane to see the total time.

In Figure 15-1, the selected playlist takes about 1.1 hours (1:08:54, to be precise) to play, so it fits on a standard audio CD. (The 15 songs take up only 65.3MB of hard drive space; they were purchased from the iTunes Store.)

A one-hour playlist of AIFF-encoded music, which occupies over 600MB of hard drive space, also fits on a standard audio CD. You calculate the amount you can fit on a standard audio CD using the duration, not the hard drive space occupied by the music files. Although a CD holds between 650MB and 700MB (depending on the disc), the music is stored in a special format known as CD-DA (or Red Book) that fills byte sectors without error-correction and checksum information. Thus, you can fit about 90MB more — 740MB total — of AIFF-encoded music on a 650MB disc. I typically put 1.1 hours (about 66 minutes) of music on a 74-minute or an 80-minute CD-R, leaving minutes to spare.

Always use the actual duration in hours, minutes, and seconds to calculate how much music you can fit on an audio CD — either 74 or 80 minutes for blank CD-Rs. I recommend leaving at least one extra minute to account for the gaps between songs.

You do the *opposite* for an MP3 CD or a data DVD. Use the actual megabytes to calculate how many song files can fit on a disc — up to 700MB for a blank CD-R. You can fit lots more music on an MP3 CD-R because you use MP3-encoded songs rather than uncompressed AIFF songs.

If you have too many songs in the playlist to fit on a CD, iTunes gives you the option to cancel the burn operation, or to burn as many songs in the playlist as will fit on the CD (either audio or MP3). Then it asks you to insert another CD to continue burning the remaining songs in the playlist.

Importing music for an audio CD-R

Before you rip an audio CD of songs that you want to burn to an audio CD-R, you might want to change the import settings (as I describe in Chapter 8). Use the AIFF, WAV, or Apple Lossless encoders for songs from audio CDs if you want to burn your own audio CDs with music at its highest quality. You can also burn MP3-encoded songs on an audio CD, but the quality is not as good as with AIFF, WAV, or Apple Lossless.

AIFF is the standard digital format for uncompressed sound on a Mac, and you can't go wrong with it. *WAV* is basically the same thing for Windows. The Apple Lossless encoder provides CD-quality sound in a file size that's about 55 to 60 percent of the size of an AIFF- or WAV-encoded file. Both the AIFF encoder and the WAV encoder offer the same custom settings for sample rate, sample size, and channels, which you can set by choosing Custom from the Settings pop-up menu in the Importing section of the Advanced pane of iTunes Preferences. You can choose the automatic settings, and iTunes detects the proper sample rate, size, and channels from the source. Apple Lossless is always set to automatic.

The songs you purchase from the iTunes Store are supplied in an unprotected format encoded in AAC that carries no restrictions. (The format is also known as iTunes Plus.) However, you may still have songs in the older protected AAC format in use up until 2009. You can't convert the protected format to anything else, but you can still burn the songs onto CDs, and the quality of the result on CD is acceptable. Audio books also come in a protected format that can't be converted by iTunes, but you can burn them onto CDs with acceptable quality.

The AAC encoder creates an audio file that is similar in audio quality to one created by the MP3 encoder but takes up less space; both are acceptable to most CD listeners. I think AAC offers a decent trade-off of space and quality and is suitable (although not as good as AIFF or Apple Lossless) for burning to an audio CD.

For a complete description of these encoders, visit this book's companion Web site.

Switching import encoders for MP3 CD-Rs

MP3 discs are essentially CD-Rs with MP3 files stored on them. Consumer MP3 CD players are readily available in consumer electronics stores, including hybrid models that play both audio CDs and MP3 CDs.

You can fit 8–12 hours of stereo music on an MP3 CD with the MP3 format — the amount varies depending on the encoding options and settings you choose. For example, you might be able to fit up to 20 hours of mono (monaural) recordings because they use only one channel and carry less information. On the other hand, if you encode stereo recordings at high bit rates (above 192 bits per second), you may fit up to 9 hours.

You can use only MP3-encoded songs to burn an MP3 CD-R. Any songs not encoded in MP3 are skipped and not burned. Audible books and commercial spoken-word titles are typically provided in an audio format that uses security technologies, including encryption, to protect purchased content; however, you can include anything that is encoded in MP3, including audio books from other sources. But you can't burn an MP3 CD-R with Audible files; any Audible files in a burn playlist are skipped when you burn an MP3 CD-R.

Burning a disc

Burning a CD is a simple process, and getting it right the first time is a good idea because when you burn a CD-R, it's done — right or wrong. You can't erase content and reuse a CD-R. Fortunately, CD-Rs are inexpensive, so you won't be out more than a few cents if you burn a bad one. (Besides, they're good as coasters for coffee tables.)

Follow these steps to burn a disc:

1. **Select the playlist and then click the Burn Disc button.**

   The Burn Disc button appears in the lower-right corner of the iTunes window whenever you select a playlist (refer to Figure 15-1). After clicking Burn Disc, the Burn Settings dialog appears, as shown in Figure 15-2.

2. **Select options in the Burn Settings dialog and click the Burn button.**

   See the following section for instructions on selecting these important options.

3. **Insert a blank disc (label side up).**

   iTunes immediately checks the media and begins the burn process, displaying a progress bar and the names of the songs burning to the disc.

If you chose the MP3 CD format, iTunes skips over any songs in the playlist that aren't in this format.

When iTunes finishes burning the disc, iTunes chimes, and the disc is mounted on the Desktop.

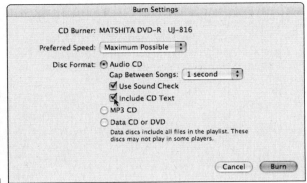

Figure 15-2:
Choose burn
settings
before burn-
ing the disc.

4. **Eject the newly burned disc from your drive and then test it.**

5. **Don't delete your burn playlist yet.**

    You can read why in the later section "Troubleshooting burns."

Burning takes several minutes. You can cancel the operation at any time by clicking the X next to the progress bar, but canceling the operation isn't like undoing the burn. If the burn has already started, you can't use that CD-R or DVD-R again.

If the playlist has more music than can fit on the disc using the chosen format, iTunes asks whether you want to create multiple audio CDs with the playlist. If you choose to create multiple audio CDs, iTunes burns as many full songs as possible from the beginning of the playlist and then asks you to insert another disc to burn the rest. To calculate the amount of music in a playlist, see the earlier section "Calculating how much music to use."

Spoken-word fans: Audible audio books with chapter markers are burned onto a CD with each chapter as a separate track.

Choosing your burn settings

Set the following options in the Burn Settings dialog to ensure that you burn your CD right the first time (refer to Figure 15-2):

✔ **Preferred Speed:** Choose a specific recording speed or the Maximum Possible option from the Preferred Speed pop-up menu. iTunes typically detects the rating of a blank CD-R and adjusts the recording speed to fit. However, if your blank CD-Rs are rated for a slower speed than your burner or if you have problems creating CD-Rs, you can change the recording speed setting to match the CD's rating.

✔ **Disc Format:** The disc format is perhaps the most important choice you have to make. Decide whether you're burning an audio CD (CD-R), an MP3 CD (CD-R), or a Data CD (CD-R) or DVD (DVD-R or DVD-RW). Your choice depends on what type of player you're using or whether you're making a data backup of files rather than a disc that plays in a player. Choose one of the following:

  • *Audio CD:* Burn a normal audio CD of up to 74 or 80 minutes (depending on the type of blank CD-R) using any iTunes-supported music files, including songs bought from the iTunes Store. Although connoisseurs of music might use AIFF- or WAV-encoded music to burn an audio CD, you can also use songs in the AAC and MP3 formats.

  • *MP3 CD:* Burn an MP3 CD with songs encoded in the MP3 format. No other formats are supported for MP3 CDs.

  • *Data CD or DVD:* Burn a data CD-R, CD-RW, DVD-R, or DVD-RW with music files. You can use any encoding formats for the songs. *Important:* Data discs won't play on most consumer CD players: They're meant for use with computers. However, data discs are good choices for storing backup copies of music bought from the iTunes Store.

✔ **Gap between Songs:** You can add an appropriate gap between songs, just like commercial CDs. With this option enabled, you can set the gap time as well. You can choose from a gap of 0 to 5 seconds, or None. I recommend leaving the menu set to the default setting of 2 seconds for playlists of studio-recorded songs, and None for concerts and songs recorded live. Albums and song selections that you set to be gapless (see Chapter 8) will likewise be gapless if you set the Gap between Songs option to None.

✔ **Use Sound Check:** Musicians do a sound check before every performance to check the volume of microphones and instruments and their effect on the listening environment. The aptly named Use Sound Check option in the Burning preferences dialog turns on the Sound Check feature to balance your tunes, volume-wise.

Note: This option, for audio CDs only, works regardless of whether you're already using the Sound Check option in the Playback preferences for iTunes playback as described in Chapter 13. You can select this option for burning without ever changing the preferences for iTunes playback.

✔ **Include CD Text:** Selecting this option adds the artist and track name text to the CD for certain CD players (often, in-car players) that can display the artist and track name while playing a CD.

Studying Files in an iTunes Library

If you like to keep your records properly filed, you'll love iTunes and its nice, neat file-storage methods. For all content items, iTunes creates a folder named for the artist and subfolders within the artist folder named for each album. These folders are stored in the iTunes Media folder unless you change your storage preferences. Note, however, that if you updated a previous version of iTunes that used the iTunes Music folder, iTunes continues to use the self-same iTunes Music folder.

Finding the iTunes library

The default method of storing content in the iTunes library is to store all media files — including music, videos, podcasts, and audio books — in the `iTunes Media` folder (or iTunes Music folder if you updated from a previous version of iTunes), which is inside the `iTunes` folder. With this method, media files that you drag to the iTunes window are copied into the `iTunes Media` folder (without deleting the original files). The `iTunes` folder also has folders for mobile applications and album artwork. So that's easy — everything is inside the `iTunes` folder.

iTunes maintains a separate `iTunes` folder (with a separate `iTunes Media` folder) in each home folder (Mac) or user folder (PC). If you share your computer with other users who have home folders, each user can have a separate iTunes library on the same computer (and, of course, a separate iPod that synchronizes with it). You need only one copy of the iTunes program.

On a Mac, iTunes stores your content library in your home folder's `Music` folder. The path to this folder's default location is

```
your home folder/Music/iTunes/iTunes Media
```

On a Windows PC, iTunes stores your content library in your user folder. The path to this folder's default location is

```
your user folder/My Documents/My Music/iTunes/iTunes Media
```

Locating a media file

You can find the location of any media file by selecting the item (such as a song or video), choosing File➪Get Info, and then clicking the Summary tab of the information dialog that appears. You can see the file type next to the Kind heading of the Summary tab. The Where section tells you where the song is, as shown in Figure 15-3.

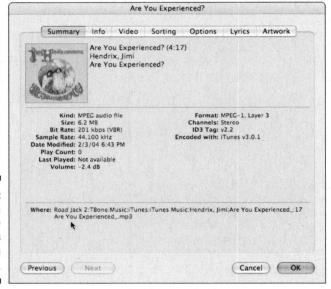

Figure 15-3:
Locate a media file from its information dialog.

If you access shared libraries on a network, you probably have content you can display in iTunes that isn't actually in your library but is part of a shared library or playlist on a network. In those situations, when you look at the Summary tab of the information dialog for an item in a shared library, the Where section doesn't appear. For more information about sharing iTunes libraries over a network, visit this book's companion Web site.

You can also open the folder that contains the media file for any item. Select the item in List, Grid, or Cover Flow view. Then, on a Mac, choose File➪Show in Finder (or press ⌘-R); in Windows, choose File➪Show in Windows Explorer (or press Ctrl-R). iTunes gives control to the operating system, which displays the folder that contains the media file. You can show the file if it's on your hard drive but not if it's in a shared library on another computer.

Copying media files

You can easily store the music that you rip from your CDs in other locations: After the music becomes digital, you can copy it endlessly with no subsequent loss in quality. You can copy media files to other hard drives and computers without any restrictions on copying — just keep in mind that protected items, such as movies and TV shows you purchased from the iTunes Store, have some playback restrictions (see Chapter 7 for iTunes Store details).

To copy the media file for an item to another hard drive or folder (such as a song or video), you can drag the item directly from the iTunes window to the other hard drive or folder.

You can also copy the files and folders from the iTunes Media folder to other hard drives or other computers using the operating system's copying function. For example, on a Mac, you can use the Finder to copy content files. Windows PCs offer several methods, including using Windows Explorer, to copy files. For example, copying an entire album, or every song by a specific artist, is easy — just drag the folder to its new home folder on another hard drive.

Backing Up an iTunes Library

Backups? You don't need no stinkin' backups!

Yes, you do, so think twice about not making them! I know: Backing up your files can be inconvenient and can eat up the capacity of all your external hard drives. Still, it must be done. And fortunately, it's easy to do, either manually as described in this section, or automatically with a system backup utility such as Apple's Time Machine.

With iTunes, you can copy your library to another hard drive on your computer or to another computer. You can burn as many data DVDs as needed to store all the files.

Backing up to DVD-Rs or CD-Rs

Apple provides a handy wizard that walks you through backing up your iTunes library, playlists, and iTunes Store purchases to CD-Rs or DVD-Rs. You can choose to back up the entire library, perform *incremental backups* (only items added or changed since the last backup), or save only store purchases. Choose File⇨Library⇨Back Up to Disc and then choose one of the following:

- ✔ **Back Up Entire iTunes Library and Playlist:** This might take a stack of DVD-Rs (or a truckload of CD-Rs), but it's worth doing if you have no other way to back up your library.

- ✔ **Back Up Only iTunes Store Purchases:** This is an essential procedure, because if you lose these files, you have to repurchase them. You can use CD-Rs or DVD-Rs.

- ✔ **Only Back Up Items Added or Changed Since Last Backup:** Use this method to copy only items that were added or changed since your last backup.

To restore your iTunes library from a stack of backup DVD-Rs or CD-Rs, open iTunes and insert the first disc. Then follow the instructions that appear automatically after inserting the disc.

Backing up to another hard drive

To copy your entire library to another hard drive, locate the iTunes folder on your computer (see the section "Finding the iTunes library," earlier in this chapter). Drag this folder to another hard drive or backup device, and you're all set. This action copies everything, including the playlists in your library.

The copy operation might take some time if your library is huge. Although you can interrupt the operation anytime, the newly copied library might not be complete. Finishing the copy operation is always best.

If you restore the backup copy to the same computer with the same names for its hard drive, the backup copy's playlists work fine. *Playlists* are essentially lists of songs in the XML (eXtensible Markup Language) format, with pathnames to the song files. If the hard drive name is different, the pathnames won't work. However, you can import the playlists back into iTunes by choosing File➪Library➪Import Playlist, and then browsing for and selecting the iTunes Media Library.xml file (or iTunes Music Library.xml file for previous versions of iTunes) inside the iTunes folder, which realigns the playlist pathnames to the new hard drive.

For a complete description of how to copy your iTunes library to other computers and hard drives, including from Mac to PC or vice versa, visit this book's companion Web site.

Part IV

Playing It Back on Your iPod or iPhone

The 5th Wave   By Rich Tennant

"You ever notice how much more streaming media there is than there used to be?"

In this part . . .

Part IV is all about playing content with your iPod or iPhone, including music, videos, podcasts, audio books, and photos.

- Chapter 16 shows you how to locate and play songs. I show you how to find songs, shuffle and repeat songs and albums, and create playlists right on your iPod or iPhone. I also describe how to set the volume and tweak the sound.

- Chapter 17 describes how to locate and play videos, including movies, TV shows, and YouTube videos. You can skip forward or backward, scale the picture to fit the display, and bookmark your favorite sections. I also show you how to play podcasts and audio books.

- Chapter 18 is all about synchronizing photo albums with your iPod or iPhone, zooming in to photos, sharing them with friends, and putting on a slide show.

Chapter 16

The Songs Remain the Same

In This Chapter

▶ Locating songs by artist, album, or playlist

▶ Repeating and shuffling songs and albums

▶ Creating and saving On-The-Go and Genius playlists

▶ Playing an iPod shuffle

▶ Tweaking the sound on your iPod or iPhone

▶ Changing the volume level and volume limit

*E*ven though the iPod and iTunes have irrevocably changed the entertainment industry and how you enjoy music, one thing remains the same: You still play songs. You just play them with more *panache* on your iPod or iPhone.

You can pick any song that you want to hear at any time. You can also shuffle through songs to get an idea of how wide your music choices are or to surprise yourself or others. Browse by artist and album, select a playlist, and even create playlists on the fly — this chapter explains it all, for any iPod or iPhone. *Note:* If you have an iPod shuffle, everything you need to know is in the section "Playing an iPod shuffle."

Locating Songs on your iPod or iPhone

With so many songs on your iPod or iPhone, finding a particular song by its title may take longer than finding it another way — like finding a needle in a haystack or even trying to find "Needle in a Haystack" by The Velvelettes. It may be faster to locate albums by cover art or to find songs by searching for artist (or composer), genre, album, or playlist. You can browse your music any number of ways without interrupting the music you're playing.

Going with the Cover Flow

Cover Flow (also called the *cover browser*) lets you flip through your cover art to select music alphabetically by artist. The iPod classic, iPod nano, iPod touch, and iPhone (as well as some earlier sixth-generation models) can display the cover art for albums.

To browse music by cover art with an iPod touch, choose Music from the Home screen; on an iPhone, choose iPod from the Home screen. Then turn the iPod touch or iPhone quickly to view it horizontally. This movement changes the display to landscape mode and displays the cover browser, as shown in Figure 16-1.

Figure 16-1:
Cover Flow:
the cover
browser
(on an iPod
touch).

Slide your finger across the album covers to scroll swiftly through the music library, or tap to the right or left of the cover art in the foreground to move forward or backward an album cover at a time.

Tap the Play button in the lower-left corner (shown in Figure 16-1) to start playing the first song in the foreground album; the Play button turns to a Pause button so that you can tap it again to stop playback. Tap the *i* button in the lower-right corner (or tap the foreground cover art) to list the songs in that album. Then you can tap a song to start playing it.

The Cover Flow browser is also available on the iPod classic and iPod nano models. Choose Music from the main menu on an iPod classic and then choose Cover Flow from the Music menu. Rotate an iPod nano 90 degrees to the left or the right, and the Cover Flow browser appears automatically. (You can also choose Cover Flow from the Music menu.)

To browse by cover art on an iPod nano or iPod classic, scroll the click wheel clockwise to move forward or counterclockwise to move backward through album covers. You can also press the Fast Forward or Rewind buttons to step forward or backward in your library one cover at a time. Press the Select button in the middle of the click wheel to select the album in the foreground; a list of songs appears. Use the click wheel to scroll the list of songs and then press the Select button to select a highlighted song.

Choosing artists and albums

You can quickly and easily locate a song by looking up either the song's artist or its album. Your iPod or iPhone organizes music by artist and then within each artist by album.

To browse music by artist on an iPod touch, choose Music from the Home screen; on an iPhone, choose iPod from the Home screen. Next, tap the Artists icon along the bottom row of the Music or iPod screen. A scrollable list of artists appears, with an alphabet listed vertically along the right side, as shown in Figure 16-2 — flick your finger down to see the very top, which shows the search field.

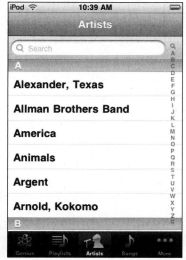

Figure 16-2: Locate an artist.

Tap any letter in the alphabet shown on the right to scroll the list directly to that letter. Tap an artist name to see a list of albums or songs by that artist. (You see multiple albums if more than one album is available — tap the album name to select the album.) Tap a song title to start playing the song. To search, tap inside the search field in the top, and start typing in the onscreen keyboard that appears. Suggestions appear below matching what you type — you can tap a suggestion to go right to it.

To browse music by album title on an iPod touch or iPhone, tap the More icon along the bottom of the iPod screen, which displays a list of options including Albums, and then tap Albums. The albums appear in a scrollable list with the album cover on the left side and an alphabet listed vertically along the right side, as shown in Figure 16-3 — flick your finger down to see the very top, which shows the search field.

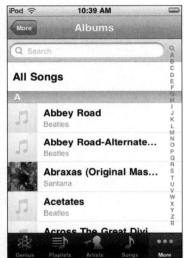

Figure 16-3:
Browse by
album title.

Slide your finger up and down the alphabet to scroll quickly, or tap any letter in the alphabet to scroll the list directly to that letter. Tap an album title or its cover art to see a list of songs in the album. Tap a song title to start playing the song.

Follow these steps with an iPod classic or iPod nano (or earlier models) to locate a song by artist and then by album:

1. **Choose Music from the iPod main menu.**

2. **From the Music menu that appears, choose Artists.**

   To be more selective, you can browse by genre first. Choose Genres and then choose a genre from the Genres menu to get a list of artists that have songs in that genre (in alphabetical order by artist name).

3. **Select an artist from the Artists menu.**

   The artist names are listed in alphabetical order by last name or the first word of a group. Scroll the Artists menu until the artist name is highlighted and then press the Select button. The artist's menu of albums appears. (You can also select All Albums at the top of the Artists menu to go directly to the Albums menu.)

4. **Choose All Songs or the name of an album from the artist's menu.**

   You can find All Songs at the top of the artist's menu; it should already be highlighted. Press the Select button to choose it or scroll until an album name is highlighted; then press the Select button. A song list appears after you choose either an album or All Songs.

5. **Select a song from the list.**

   The songs in the album list are in *album order* (the order that they appear on the album); in the All Songs list, songs are listed in album order for each album.

To choose an album directly on an iPod nano or iPod classic, choose Albums from the Music menu. The Albums menu appears, displaying albums in alphabetical order. Choose an album from the Albums menu. Then select a song from the list.

Choosing playlists

When you synchronize your iPod or iPhone with your entire iTunes library, your iTunes playlists are included. Well, that makes sense, doesn't it? You can choose to synchronize your iPod or iPhone with only specified playlists, as I describe in Chapter 9.

To browse music by playlist on your iPod touch or iPhone, tap Music on the iPod touch Home screen or iPod on the iPhone Home screen, and tap the Playlists icon along the bottom row of the Music or iPod screen. A scrollable list of playlists appears. Tap a playlist title to see a list of songs in the playlist and tap a song title to start playing the song.

Follow these steps to locate a playlist on your iPod classic or iPod nano (or earlier models):

1. **Choose Music from the iPod main menu.**

2. **From the Music menu, choose Playlists.**

3. **From the Playlists menu that appears, choose a playlist.**

Playlists are listed in alphabetical order. Scroll the Playlists menu to highlight the playlist name and then press the Select button. A list of songs in the playlist appears.

4. **Select a song from the list.**

The songs in the playlist are in *playlist order* (the order defined for the playlist in iTunes). Scroll up or down the list to highlight the song you want.

Choosing song titles and more

To locate songs by title on an iPod touch or iPhone, tap Music on the iPod touch Home screen or iPod on the iPhone Home screen, and tap the Songs icon along the bottom row of the Music or iPod screen. A scrollable list of songs appears with an alphabet listed vertically along the right side — flick your finger down to see the very top, which shows the search field. Slide your finger up and down the alphabet to scroll quickly, or tap any letter in the alphabet to scroll the list directly to that letter. To search, tap inside the search field in the top, and start typing in the onscreen keyboard that appears. Suggestions appear below matching what you type — you can tap a suggestion to go right to it. Tap a song title to start playing the song.

You can also find music by composer or genre on an iPod touch or iPhone by tapping the More icon along the bottom row of the Music or iPod screen. You can then select Composers to see an alphabetical list of composers or Genres to see all the genres of the songs. Tap either a composer or a genre to see a list of songs.

Follow these steps with an iPod classic or iPod nano (or earlier models) to locate a song by its title:

1. **Choose Music from the iPod main menu.**

2. **From the Music menu that appears, choose Songs.**

3. **Select a song from the Songs menu.**

The songs are listed in alphabetical order by title. Scroll the Songs menu until the song title is highlighted and then press the Select button.

Controlling Song Playback

To play a song on an iPod touch or iPhone, tap the song title (or the Play button in Cover Flow). On an iPod nano, iPod classic, or older model, scroll the list as previously described to highlight the song title and then press either the Select button or the Play/Pause button to play the selected song.

When the song finishes, the iPod or iPhone plays the next song in the sequence that appeared in the list you chose it from. For example, if you chose a song on the Songs screen of an iPod touch or iPhone or the Songs menu of an iPod nano or iPod classic, the next song would be the next one in sequence on the Songs screen or menu. If you chose the last song in an album on the Albums screen or menu, the iPod or iPhone stops after playing it. If you chose a song from a playlist, the next song would be the next one in the playlist, and after playing the last song, it also stops playing, as with an album. (See the section "Repeating songs," later in this chapter, to find out how to repeat albums and playlists.)

Controlling playback on an iPod touch or iPhone

Whenever you play a song on an iPod touch or iPhone, you see the album cover associated with the song on the Now Playing screen. You also see the buttons for playback control — Previous/Rewind, Play/Pause, and Next/Fast Forward. (See Figure 16-4.) Slide your finger along the volume slider at the bottom of the display to change the volume.

Figure 16-4:
The Now Playing screen on an iPod touch.

Tap the Next/Fast Forward button once to play the next song in sequence, and tap the Previous/Rewind button once at the beginning of a song, or twice during the song, to play the previous song. You can fast-forward through a song by touching and holding down the Next/Fast Forward button, and you can rewind a song by touching and holding down the Previous/Rewind button.

You can tap the bullet-list button in the upper-right corner if you want to display a list of the album's contents. You can then tap the title of another song on the album to start playing that song.

To return to menus and make other selections when playing a song, tap the left-arrow button in the upper-left corner of the display.

Tap underneath the left-arrow button or the album title while a song is playing to show more buttons and the scrubber bar for navigating through the song, as shown in Figure 16-5 — and if lyrics are available in the iTunes information, they also appear.

To skip to any point in a song, use your finger to drag the playhead along the scrubber bar. To finely scrub through a song, after dragging the playhead, slide your finger down the screen (toward the physical Home button) to slow the scrubbing.

To start a song over from the beginning, drag the playhead on the scrubber bar all the way to the left or tap the Previous/Rewind button once.

If you're viewing another content menu on the iPod touch or iPhone, tap Now Playing at the upper-right corner of the display to go directly to the Now Playing display.

Controlling playback on an iPod classic or iPod nano

While a song is playing, the artist name and song name appear on the Now Playing screen. Color-display iPods also display the album cover, and the iPod classic and iPod nano models show a progress bar as well.

To adjust the volume on an iPod nano or iPod classic, scroll the click wheel when you see the progress bar. On older iPod models, press the Select button once to show the progress bar. For more info, see the later section "Adjusting and Limiting the Volume."

Back Genius Shuffle

Repeat Scrubber List

Figure 16-5:
Tap under
the album
title to show
more
buttons, the
scrubber
bar, and
lyrics on an
iPod touch.

Play/Pause Volume

Previous/Rewind Fast/Fwd

To pause playback, press the Play/Pause button while a song is playing. To stop playing a song, press the Play/Pause button again (the same button).

To skip to any point in a song, press the Select button to reveal the scrubber bar (on older models, press the Select button twice). Scroll the click wheel to move the playhead across the scrubber bar forward (to the right) or backward (to the left) in the song.

Press the Select button multiple times on an iPod nano or iPod classic to cycle through the options: scrubber bar, Genius Start button, rating bullets, shuffle settings, and lyrics (if you typed them in for the song, as I describe in Chapter 12, or if they were included with a downloaded song). After the rating bullets appear, scroll the click wheel to add a rating to the song. For details on the Genius feature, see the section "Consulting the iTunes Genius," and to find out how to shuffle, see the section "Shuffling song order," both later in this chapter.

Press the Next/Fast Forward button once to play the next song in sequence, and press the Previous/Rewind button once at the beginning of a song, or twice during the song, to play the previous song. You can fast-forward through a song by pressing and holding down the Next/Fast Forward button, and rewind a song by pressing and holding down the Previous/Rewind button.

To start a song over from the beginning, move the playhead on the scrubber bar all the way to the left or press the Previous/Rewind button once.

While playing a song, you can browse the album or its artist as well as assign the song to an On-The-Go playlist or Genius playlist. Press and hold the Select button, and a menu appears with the following choices: Start Genius, Add to On-The-Go, Browse Album, Browse Artist, and Cancel. Scroll the click wheel to choose an option.

To return to the menus and make other selections when playing a song on an iPod classic or iPod nano, press the Menu button or press and hold the Select button until a menu appears on top of the cover art.

You can cross-fade songs on an iPod nano or iPod classic, just like in iTunes (as I describe in Chapter 13). A *cross-fade* creates a smooth transition from the ending of one song to the beginning of the next one. To set your iPod nano or iPod classic to cross-fade songs, choose Settings➪Playback➪Audio Crossfade from the main menu and press Select to turn it on. (Press Select again to turn it off.)

Repeating songs

If you want to drive yourself crazy repeating the same song over and over, your iPod or iPhone is happy to oblige. (You might want to try repeating "They're Coming to Take Me Away, Ha-Haaa" by Napoleon XIV, a favorite from the old *The Dr. Demento Show* radio broadcasts — and perhaps they will come to take you away.) More than likely, you'll want to repeat a playlist or album, which you can easily do.

On an iPod touch or iPhone, tap underneath the left-arrow button or the album title while a song is playing. The Repeat and Shuffle buttons appear, along with the scrubber bar and lyrics, directly below the top row of buttons. (Refer to Figure 16-5.)

Ordinarily when a song finishes, the iPod touch or iPhone plays the next song in the sequence that appeared on the Playlists, Artists, Songs, or Albums screen you chose it from. When it reaches the end of that list, it stops — if you chose the last song in an album on the Albums screen, the iPod touch stops after playing it. But if you tap the Repeat button once while the songs are playing, the entire sequence repeats. If you chose an album, the album repeats; if you chose a playlist, the playlist repeats.

After you tap Repeat once to repeat the sequence of songs, the Repeat button shows blue highlighting. Tap the Repeat button again to repeat only the current song — the button changes to include a blue-highlighted numeral 1. Tap it once more to return to normal playback.

You can set your iPod classic or iPod nano (or older models) to repeat a single song, or to repeat all the songs in the selected album or playlist, by following these steps:

1. **Locate and play a song.**

2. **While the song plays, press the Menu button repeatedly to return to the main menu and then choose the Settings menu.**

3. **Scroll the Settings menu until Repeat is highlighted.**

   The Repeat setting displays Off, One, or All next to it.

4. **Press the Select button until the setting changes to One to repeat one song or All to repeat all the songs in the album or playlist (or Off to turn Repeat off).**

   If you press the button more than you need to, keep pressing until the setting you want reappears. The button cycles among the Off, One, and All settings.

You can also press the Previous/Rewind button to repeat a song.

Shuffling song order

Maybe you want your song selections to be surprising and unpredictable, and you want your iPod or iPhone to read your mind. You can *shuffle* song playback to play in random order, just like an automated radio station without a disk jockey or program guide.

On an iPod touch or iPhone

When you are playing a song or a song is paused, you can just shake your iPod touch or iPhone, and it shuffles the songs in the album you are playing. By default, your iPod touch or iPhone is set to shuffle when shaken (not stirred). To turn this feature off, choose Settings⇨Music from the iPod touch Home screen or Settings⇨iPod from the iPhone Home screen, and tap On for the Shake to Shuffle option to turn it off. (Tap Off to turn it on.)

You can also set your iPod touch or iPhone to shuffle songs across your library. The shuffle algorithm is as random as it gets (not taking into account a fundamental tenet of chaos theory that says a pattern will emerge). When an iPod touch or iPhone creates a shuffle, it reorders the songs (like shuffling a deck of cards) and then plays them in the new order.

To turn your iPod touch or iPhone into a random song player, choose Music from the iPod touch Home screen or iPod from the iPhone Home screen, and tap the Songs icon at the bottom of the display. The song list appears, with Shuffle at the top of the list. Tap Shuffle to turn on Shuffle.

You can also set the iPod touch or iPhone to shuffle songs within an album or playlist after starting the album or playlist. Start playing a song in the album or playlist and then tap underneath the left-arrow button or the album title while a song is playing. The Repeat and Shuffle buttons appear, along with the scrubber bar, directly below the top row of buttons (refer to Figure 16-5). Tap the Shuffle button to shuffle songs within the currently playing album or playlist.

You can also set an iPod touch or iPhone to shuffle any album or playlist *before* playing it. First, select the playlist or album; then tap Shuffle at the top of the list of songs for that playlist or album.

Want to repeat an entire album or playlist but still shuffle the playing order each time you hear it? Start playing a song in the album or playlist and then set your iPod touch or iPhone to repeat all the songs in the album or playlist as described in the section "Repeating songs," earlier in this chapter. Then set the iPod touch or iPhone to shuffle the songs as described in this section.

On an iPod nano or iPod classic

To turn your iPod classic or iPod nano (or older model) into a random song player, choose Shuffle Songs from the main menu.

To shuffle songs in an album or a playlist with an iPod classic or iPod nano (or older model), or to shuffle albums, follow these steps:

1. **Choose Settings from the main menu and scroll to Shuffle.**

   The Shuffle setting displays Off next to it.

2. **Press the Select button once (Off changes to Songs) to shuffle the songs in the next album or playlist you play. Press Select again (Songs changes to Albums) to shuffle the albums without shuffling the songs within each album.**

   When you set Shuffle to Songs, the iPod classic or iPod nano shuffles songs within the currently playing playlist or album, or if nothing is playing, the next album or playlist you choose to play. When you set Shuffle to Albums, it plays all the songs on the currently playing album (or the next album you play) in order and then randomly selects another album in the list and plays through it in order.

   If you press the Select button more than you need to, keep pressing until the setting you want reappears. The button cycles among the Off, Songs, or Albums settings.

While playing a song or while a song is paused, you can shake an iPod nano so that its motion detector switches to a random song. Whenever you shake it, the iPod nano shuffles again to another random song. Shaking to shuffle doesn't change your shuffle settings — it just immediately shuffles songs. Shaking to shuffle is disabled when you put the Hold switch in the Hold position (so that you don't keep changing songs as you jog or exercise strenuously) or if the iPod nano display is off. You can also disable it by choosing Settings⇨Playback⇨Shake from the main menu and then press the Select button until the Shake setting displays `Off`. To turn it on, choose Settings⇨Playback⇨Shake from the main menu and press the Select button until the Shake setting displays `Shuffle`.

Playing an iPod shuffle

Speaking of shuffling, the *iPod shuffle* is a special iPod designed with song shuffling foremost in mind — it offers no display or menus for selecting specific songs or albums by title. The idea is to use iTunes to put songs, audio books, and podcasts — as well as playlists of these elements — on the iPod shuffle (as I describe in Chapter 9), clip it to your clothes or something, put the Apple-supplied earbuds in your ears, and listen while controlling playback with the earbud's remote controller. The VoiceOver feature tells you the name of the song you're playing (as well as your battery status) and lets you choose from a spoken menu of playlists.

Starting playback

The iPod shuffle has a three-position switch on the top for playing songs in playlist order, for shuffling songs randomly, and for turning it off. To start playing songs, plug the earbuds into the iPod shuffle and place them in your ears, and slide the three-position switch from Off to Play in Order (the icon with arrows chasing each other in a closed loop) or Shuffle (the icon showing arrows crossed).

Playback starts as soon as you turn the three-way switch away from Off — to indicate this, the iPod shuffle status light blinks green once. However, if the iPod shuffle is already playing before you plug in your earbuds, playback may stop. To start playback, press the center button on the remote controller or toggle the three-way switch to Off and back to Play in Order or Shuffle.

You can use any set of headphones with your iPod shuffle — attach them and slide the three-position switch from Off to Play in Order or Shuffle. To turn off playback, slide the three-position switch back to Off. The only difference is that you don't have a remote controller to control playback or adjust the volume.

Controlling playback

To pause playback, press the earbud remote controller's center button once. The iPod shuffle status light blinks green for 30 seconds.

To go forward to the next track, press the center button twice quickly (the status light blinks green once). To fast-forward through the current track to the next track, press the center button twice, but on the second press, keep holding it down.

To go back to the previous track, press the center button three times quickly within the initial six seconds of the current track (the status light blinks green once); to go to the beginning of the current track, press the center button three times *after* the initial six seconds. To rewind through the current track to its beginning and then to the previous track, press the center button three times, but on the third press, keep holding it down.

If you set the three-position switch to Play in Order, going backward or forward navigates in the order the songs were copied to the iPod shuffle or the order within each playlist. However, if you set the position switch to Shuffle, the playing order is randomized first. Then going backward skips backward within the shuffle order, and going forward skips forward within the shuffle order. For example, suppose your iPod shuffle plays the 14th song, then the 5th song, and then the 20th song. In that case, pressing the center button three times quickly within the first six seconds of the 20th song takes you back to the 5th song, and pressing it three times again takes you back to the 14th song. From there, pressing the center button twice quickly skips through the songs in the same order again: the 14th song, the 5th song, and then the 20th song.

Using VoiceOver to choose playlists

If you installed the VoiceOver kit and enabled VoiceOver for your iPod shuffle in iTunes when you set it up (as I describe in Chapter 2), you can hear the iPod shuffle talk back to you. Specifically, you can hear song titles and artist names, a menu of playlists for you to choose from, and the status of your battery charge.

VoiceOver for your iPod shuffle is enabled by default, but you can turn it on or off by connecting your iPod shuffle to your computer for synchronizing it, as I describe in Chapter 9. The Summary page of the iPod shuffle sync options appears, as shown in Figure 16-6. Under Voice Feedback, select the Enable VoiceOver check box to turn it on (or deselect it to turn it off). You also have the option to choose the language you want from the Language pop-up menu. This sets the language for spoken messages and playlist names, as well as many of the song titles and artist names. Finally, click the Apply button to apply these settings.

To hear the title and artist of the song, press and hold the center button. If you press the center button twice quickly to go to the next track, the next message plays as well.

To hear the playlist menu, press and hold the center button until you hear a tone and then release it to hear the names of playlists. The playlist menu announces the current playlist (if one is playing), "All Songs," any other playlists in alphabetical order, any podcasts, and finally any audio book titles. As you listen to the playlist menu, you can press the plus (+) or minus (–) button to move forward or backward in the playlist menu. After hearing the playlist, podcast, or audio book title you want, press the center button once to select it. If you don't want to choose anything from the playlist menu, you can exit by pressing and holding the center button.

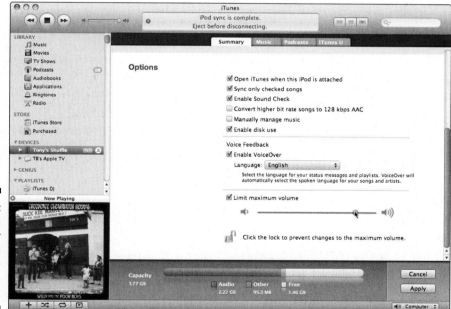

Figure 16-6: Enabling VoiceOver for an iPod shuffle while syncing it.

If you've synced an iPod shuffle loaded with the VoiceOver kit with iTunes, iTunes adds a new option to the Options tab of the Get Info dialog: VoiceOver Language. You can use it to pick a different language for specific songs. After selecting the songs in iTunes, choose File⇨Get Info, click the Options tab, and then choose a language from the VoiceOver Language pop-up menu. Click the OK button to finish.

Ordering Playlists On-The-Go

You can create a temporary, *On-The-Go* playlist, queuing the songs in the order you want, right on your iPod touch, iPod nano, iPod classic, or iPhone. The selections appear automatically in a playlist appropriately called *On-The-Go,* on the Playlists menu. This option is particularly useful for picking songs to play right before driving a car. (Hel-*lo!* You shouldn't be messing with your iPod or iPhone while driving.)

Selecting and playing songs for an On-The-Go playlist

Follow these steps with an iPod touch or iPhone to select songs for your On-The-Go playlist:

1. **Choose Music from the iPod touch Home screen or iPod from the iPhone Home screen.**

   The Music or iPod screen appears with the Playlists and other icons along the bottom of the display.

2. **Tap the Playlists icon and choose On-The-Go from the Playlists list.**

   The Songs list appears with a plus (+) sign next to each song, as well as an Add All Songs option at the top, as shown in Figure 16-7. If you have only several dozen albums, this list isn't too long, and you can skip to Step 4. If you have a lot more music, narrow your search with Step 3.

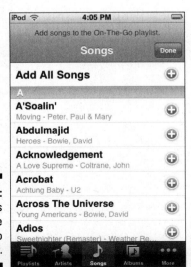

Figure 16-7:
Add songs to the On-The-Go playlist.

3. **(Optional) Tap Playlists, Artists, Songs, or More to narrow your search for songs to add to the On-The-Go playlist.**

   Tap an icon along the bottom row (see Figure 16-7) to browse your iPod touch or iPhone library — tap Playlists to select songs from playlists or entire playlists, tap Artists to browse artists, or tap Songs to select songs. On an iPod touch, tap Albums to select from albums or tap More to select songs from compilations, to browse by genre, or to select audio books or podcast episodes. On an iPhone, tap More to select songs from albums or compilations, to browse by genre, or to select audio books or podcast episodes.

4. **Tap the plus (+) sign next to a song you want to add to the On-The-Go playlist, or tap the plus sign next to Add All Albums to add all the albums of an artist found in Step 3.**

   As you tap the plus sign for a song, the song is included in the On-The-Go playlist, and it turns gray in the list so that you know it has already been selected. You can tap Add All Albums as an alternative if you want to add all the songs for a particular artist — first browse for that artist in Step 3.

5. **Repeat Steps 3 and 4, adding songs in the order you want them to be played.**

   You can continue to add songs to the list. Your iPod touch or iPhone keeps track of the On-The-Go playlist until you clear it (as I describe in the section "Clearing an On-The-Go playlist," later in this chapter) or synchronize it, as I describe in Chapter 9.

6. **Tap the Done button when you're finished adding songs.**

   The Done button appears in the upper-right corner while you select songs, just waiting for you to finish. After touching Done, you return to the list of songs in the On-The-Go playlist, as shown in Figure 16-8.

7. **To start playing the On-The-Go playlist, tap any song.**

   Scroll up or down the list (see Figure 16-8) to choose a song, and tap the song title to play the playlist starting from that song. You can tap Shuffle to shuffle the songs in the playlist.

The songs in the playlist are in *playlist order* (the order you added them). You can change that order by tapping the Edit button (see Figure 16-8), which displays the Edit screen with a Move icon (three horizontal bars, like half of an I-Ching symbol) on the far right side of each song. Drag the Move icon for a song to move it up or down the list. Then tap the Done button at the top of the Edit screen.

You can also add entire playlists, entire albums, or everything by an artist to the On-The-Go playlist. In Step 4, tap the Playlists, Artists, or Album icon on an iPod touch (or the More icon followed by the Albums selection on an iPhone) to show one of those menus and then select a playlist, album, or artist. Finally, tap All Songs at the top of the list of song selections.

Figure 16-8:
The
On-The-Go
playlist
ready to
play (or be
cleared).

To select and then play items in your On-The-Go playlist for an iPod classic, iPod nano, or older iPod, follow these steps:

1. **Locate and highlight a song, album title, or audio book.**

2. **Press and hold the Select button until the menu appears, and choose Add to On-The-Go. On older models, press and hold Select until the title flashes.**

3. **Repeat Steps 1 and 2, adding items in the order you want them to be played.**

   You can continue to add items to the list of queued items in the On-The-Go playlist at any time. Your iPod keeps track of the On-The-Go playlist until you clear it, save it, or synchronize your iPod.

4. **To play the On-The-Go playlist, scroll the Music menu until Playlists is highlighted and then press the Select button.**

5. **On the Playlists menu that appears, scroll to highlight On-The-Go at the bottom of the menu, and press the Select button.**

   A list of songs in the On-The-Go playlist appears.

6. **Select a song from the list and press the Select button.**

   The songs in the playlist are in *playlist order* (the order you added them). Scroll up or down the list to highlight the song you want, and press the Select button to play the playlist starting from that song.

Deleting items from an On-The-Go playlist

When you delete listed items, they disappear from the On-The-Go playlist but they are still in your iPod or iPhone; only the playlist is changed.

To delete an item from an On-The-Go playlist in your iPod touch or iPhone, follow these steps:

1. **Choose Music from the iPod touch Home screen or iPod from the iPhone Home screen.**

   The Music or iPod menu appears with the Playlists and other touch buttons along the bottom of the display.

2. **Touch the Playlists button and choose On-The-Go from the Playlists list.**

   The list of items in the playlist appears.

3. **Touch the Edit button in the upper-left corner of the display.**

   Circled minus (–) signs appear in front of each song title.

4. **Scroll the list to find the item you want to delete.**

5. **Touch the minus (–) sign next to the song to delete; then touch the Delete button.**

   The red Delete touch button appears after you touch the circled minus sign.

6. **Repeat Steps 4 and 5 to find and delete each item from the playlist.**

   When you delete items, they disappear from the On-The-Go playlist one by one.

To delete an item from an On-The-Go playlist in your iPod classic or iPod nano, follow these steps:

1. **Select the On-The-Go playlist.**

   If you don't see the iPod main menu, repeatedly press the Menu button to return to the main menu. Choose Music from the main menu, scroll the Music menu until Playlists is highlighted, and then press the Select button. The Playlists menu appears. Scroll to On-The-Go and press the Select button, and the list of items in the playlist appears.

2. **Locate and highlight the item you want to delete.**

3. **Press and hold the Select button until the menu appears, and choose Remove from On-The-Go. On older models, press and hold Select until the title flashes.**

4. **Repeat Steps 2 and 3 for each item you want to delete from the playlist.**

   When you delete items, they disappear from the On-The-Go playlist one by one.

Clearing an On-The-Go playlist

After creating the On-The-Go playlist, it remains defined in your iPod or iPhone until you clear it.

It turns out that when you synchronize your iPod or iPhone with your iTunes library, the On-The-Go playlist is automatically copied to your iTunes library and then cleared. (You can rename the playlist there, just like any other playlist — see Chapter 14.)

You can also clear the On-The-Go playlist completely in one step on an iPod touch or iPhone: just tap the Clear button. (See Figure 16-8.)

To clear the On-The-Go playlist in an iPod nano or iPod classic, follow these steps:

1. **Choose Music⇨Playlists⇨On-The-Go from the main menu.**

2. **Select Clear Playlist in the list of items in the playlist.**

   The Clear menu appears, showing the Clear Playlist and Cancel options.

3. **Select the Clear Playlist option.**

   All the items disappear from the On-The-Go playlist. If you don't want to clear the playlist, select the Cancel option.

Consulting the iTunes Genius

The Genius button for creating Genius playlists in iTunes (wisely laid out for all to see in Chapter 14) has also been incorporated into the iPod nano, iPod classic, iPod touch, and iPhone to create Genius playlists. You can also listen to your Genius Mixes in your iTunes library on your iPod nano, iPod touch, or iPhone.

For Genius to work, it has to recognize the song you select and you need to have enough songs on your iPod or iPhone that are (basically) similar. As for the mechanics of it all, you do need to set up an account in the iTunes Store if you don't already have one (see Chapter 7) and then enable the Genius feature in iTunes as I describe in Chapter 14. Finally, you have to synchronize your iPod or iPhone as described in Chapter 9 so that the Genius is activated. (You can also add Genius playlists along with other playlists in iTunes to your iPod or iPhone while syncing.)

To create a Genius playlist on an iPod touch or iPhone, choose Music from the iPod touch Home screen or iPod from the iPhone Home screen and follow these steps:

1. **Locate and start playing a song to base the Genius playlist on.**

   The Now Playing screen appears when the song is playing.

2. **Tap the Now Playing screen to see the control buttons.**

   Tap underneath the left-arrow button or the album title while a song is playing. The Repeat, Genius, and Shuffle buttons appear underneath the scrubber bar directly below the top row of buttons. (Refer to Figure 16-5.) The Genius button is the one in the center sporting the atom icon.

3. **Tap the Genius button.**

   The Genius playlist appears, as shown in Figure 16-9, with New, Refresh, and Save buttons at the top. You can flick your finger to scroll the list. The Genius playlist can be as long as 25 songs. Tap any song to start playing the playlist from that song.

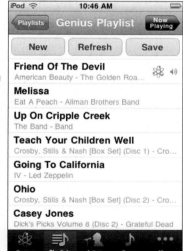

Figure 16-9: The Genius playlist created from the song "Friend of the Devil" by the Grateful Dead.

4. **(Optional) Refresh the Genius playlist by tapping Refresh.**

   Refreshing a playlist changes it to include different songs based on the same song you played (depending on how many similar songs you have in your iPod touch or iPhone).

5. **Save the Genius playlist by tapping Save.**

   The playlist is saved in the Playlists section of your iPod touch or iPhone using the title of the song it is based on. The playlist is copied back to your iTunes library when you sync your iPod touch or iPhone. That's all you need to do — the next steps are optional.

If you subsequently refresh a saved Genius playlist before syncing, the saved playlist is refreshed and you lose the previous version of it.

6. **(Optional) Create a new Genius playlist by tapping New and then selecting a new song to base it on.**

   After touching New, the song list appears for selecting a song. Choose a song, and your iPod touch or iPhone creates a new Genius playlist and starts playing the song, displaying the Now Playing screen.

7. **(Optional) After Step 6, return to the Genius playlist by tapping the left-arrow button in the upper-left corner of the Now Playing screen.**

You can refresh any Genius playlist, whether you created it in iTunes and synced to your iPod touch or iPhone, or you created it directly on your iPod touch or iPhone. Select the playlist and tap Refresh at the top of the list (or tap Delete to delete the list).

You can set an iPod touch or iPhone to create a Genius playlist based on a song before you actually start playing the song itself. Just choose Music from the iPod touch Home screen or iPod from the iPhone Home screen, and then tap Playlists in the lower-left corner of the display. Tap Genius at the top of the list of playlists, and a list of songs appears. Select a song, and your iPod touch or iPhone creates a Genius playlist based on it and then starts playing the song you selected. To return to the Genius playlist, tap the left-arrow button in the upper-left corner of the Now Playing screen.

To create a Genius playlist on an iPod nano or iPod classic, follow these steps:

1. **Locate and start playing a song to base the Genius playlist on.**

   The Now Playing screen appears when the song is playing.

2. **Press and hold the Select button until a menu appears on top of the Now Playing screen.**

3. **Choose Start Genius and press the Select button.**

   The new Genius playlist appears, with Refresh and Save Playlist at the top of the list. Scroll the list to see all the songs, and select any song to start playing the playlist associated with that song.

4. **(Optional) Refresh the Genius playlist by selecting Refresh at the top of the Genius playlist.**

   Refreshing a playlist changes it to include different songs based on the same song you played (depending on how many similar songs you have in your iPod).

5. **(Optional) Save the Genius playlist by selecting Save Playlist (under Refresh at the top of the Genius playlist).**

   The playlist is saved in the playlists section of your iPod using the title of the song it is based on. The playlist syncs automatically with your iTunes library the next time you connect your iPod and sync it (as I describe in Chapter 9).

   If you subsequently refresh a saved Genius playlist, the saved playlist is refreshed and you lose the previous version of it.

Genius Mixes are generated by iTunes from songs in your library that go great together. (See Chapter 14 to learn how to apply the touch of Genius.) Genius Mixes are synced automatically if you sync everything to your iPod touch, iPhone, or iPod nano, or you can sync specific Genius Mixes as playlists — see Chapter 9 to learn how to sync by playlist.

To play your Genius Mixes from your iTunes library on an iPod nano, choose Music⇨Genius Mixes from the main menu. You can use the Next/Fast-forward or Previous/Rewind buttons to browse the Genius Mixes — the dots at the bottom of the Genius Mixes screen indicate how many Genius Mixes are synced to your iPod nano. To start playing a Genius Mix, press the Play/Pause button or the Select button when you see its screen. Genius Mixes play just like playlists.

To play them on your iPod touch, choose Music from the Home screen and tap the Genius icon in the lower left corner. On an iPhone, choose iPod from the Home screen and tap the Genius icon in the lower left corner. You can flick with your finger left or right to browse the Genius Mixes — the dots at the bottom of the Genius Mixes screen indicate how many Genius Mixes are synced to your iPod touch or iPhone. To start playing a Genius Mix, tap the Play arrow in the middle of the screen for a Genius Mix. Genius Mixes play just like playlists.

Adjusting and Limiting the Volume

Because an iPod or iPhone can be quite loud when set to its highest volume, I recommend turning down the volume before using headphones.

To adjust the volume on an iPod touch or iPhone, follow these steps:

1. **Play something (like music).**

2. **While the content is playing, tap the lower portion of the display and slide your finger on the volume slider.**

After tapping the lower portion of the display while playing something, the volume slider with a silver knob appears on the iPod touch or iPhone screen at the bottom underneath the playback controls. (Refer to Figure 16-4.) Use your finger to slide the knob to the right to increase the volume or to the left to decrease the volume.

To adjust volume for an iPod classic or iPod nano, follow these steps:

1. **Play something.**

2. **While the content is playing, change the volume by scrolling the click wheel.**

   A volume bar appears in the iPod display to guide you. Scroll with your thumb or finger clockwise to increase the volume or counterclockwise to decrease the volume.

To adjust the volume for an iPod shuffle, press the Volume Up (+) or Volume Down (– button on the earbud remote.

You can also limit the highest volume for your iPod or iPhone to be lower than the actual maximum. This limit can help protect your hearing while you're listening to content from sources with different volume levels.

To limit the volume to be lower than the actual maximum volume on an iPod touch or iPhone, follow these steps:

1. **Choose Settings from the Home screen.**

2. **Choose iPod from the Settings screen of an iPhone or Music from the Settings screen of an iPod touch.**

3. **Choose Volume Limit from the iPod Settings (iPhone) or Music Settings (iPod touch) screen.**

   A volume slider appears with a silver knob.

4. **Slide your finger on the volume slider to limit the volume.**

   Slide the knob with your finger to the right to increase the volume or to the left to decrease the volume.

5. **Tap the iPod button (iPhone) or the Music button (iPod touch) in the upper-left corner of the display to set the limit and return to the previous menu, or if you want, tap the Lock Volume Limit button to lock the volume limit.**

   If you accept the new limit without locking it, you get to skip the next step; you're done. The lock is useful for locking the volume limit so that others can't change it (such as your children). However, it also means that you have to enter the volume limit code to unlock the iPod touch or iPhone to change the volume limit.

6. **Set the volume limit code for locking the volume limit.**

   If you tapped the Lock Volume Limit button to lock the volume limit, your iPod touch or iPhone displays four squares for entering a code number. Tap the calculator-style number pad to type numbers for your code and be sure to make up a code that you can remember! (If you don't want to enter a code, tap the Cancel button in the upper-left corner.)

To limit the volume to be lower than the actual maximum volume on an iPod shuffle, connect it to your computer for synchronizing, as I describe in Chapter 9. The Summary page of the iPod shuffle sync options appears (refer to Figure 16-6). Select the Limit Maximum Volume check box and drag the volume slider underneath this option to set the maximum volume. Finally, click the Apply button to apply the new setting.

Tweaking the Sound

You can do some tweaking of the sound quality in your iPod or iPhone in addition to the usual sound adjustments you make in iTunes (which I describe in amplified detail in Chapter 13). You can use the same Sound Check option provided in iTunes to standardize the volume level of all the songs. You can also use the iPod or iPhone equalizer to choose presets for different musical genres, listening environments, or speakers.

Peaking with the Sound Check

To enable Sound Check to work in your iPod or iPhone, first follow the steps in iTunes described in Chapter 13 to sound-check your iTunes library. After syncing your iPod or iPhone with the sound-checked library (as I describe in Chapter 9), you can take advantage of the volume leveling in your iPod or iPhone.

To turn on Sound Check in an iPod touch or iPhone, choose Settings⇨Music from the iPod touch Home screen or Settings⇨iPod from the iPhone Home screen. Tap the Off button next to the Sound Check option to turn it on. Tap On to turn it back off.

To turn on Sound Check in an iPod nano or iPod classic, choose Settings⇨Playback⇨Sound Check⇨On from the main menu. To disable it, choose Settings⇨Playback⇨Sound Check⇨Off.

To turn on Sound Check in an iPod shuffle, connect it to your computer for synchronizing, as I describe in Chapter 9. The Summary page of the iPod shuffle sync options appears (refer to Figure 16-6). Select the Enable Sound Check option, and click the Apply button to apply the new setting. After the iPod shuffle syncs with the iTunes library, the songs in your iPod shuffle are sound-checked.

All things being equal (ized)

You can use the iPod or iPhone built-in equalizer presets to improve or enhance the sound coming through a particular stereo system and speakers. With the equalizer presets, you can customize playback for different musical genres, listening environments, or speakers.

The iPod or iPhone equalizer uses a bit more battery power when it's on, so you might have less playing time.

To set an equalizer preset on an iPod touch or iPhone, choose Settings⇨ Music from the iPod touch Home screen or Settings⇨iPod from the iPhone Home screen, and tap EQ to display a list of presets. You can scroll the list of presets and tap a preset to select it — a check mark appears next to it after you select it. The equalizer is set to Off until you select one of the presets.

To select an iPod equalizer preset on an iPod classic or iPod nano, choose Settings⇨Playback⇨EQ from the main menu to display a list of presets. You can scroll the list of presets and press Select to select one. The equalizer is set to Off until you select one of the presets.

Each equalizer preset offers a different balance of frequencies designed to enhance the sound in certain ways. For example, Bass Booster increases the volume of the low (bass) frequencies; Treble Booster does the same to the high (treble) frequencies.

To see what a preset actually does to the frequencies, choose Window⇨ Equalizer in iTunes to open the iTunes equalizer; then select the same preset by name. The faders in the equalizer show you exactly what the preset does.

Find out how to assign standard iTunes presets or your own custom presets to specific songs, audio books, podcast episodes, and videos — and use those presets when playing these items back on your iPod or iPhone — by visiting the free tips section of my Web site (www.tonybove.com).

Chapter 17

Bring Videos, Books, and Podcasts

. . . .

In This Chapter

▶ Playing movies and TV shows on your iPod or iPhone

▶ Playing YouTube videos

▶ Playing podcasts and audio books

▶ Listening to the iPod nano's FM radio

. . . .

*T*he Buggles sang "Video Killed the Radio Star," but both coexist quite nicely on your iPod or iPhone, which is not only a fantastic music player (and the current iPod nano can even play FM radio), but also a terrific video player, with crisp, clear picture quality. Video appears horizontally on an iPod touch, iPod nano, or iPhone screen (in what's known as *landscape mode*), and if you rotate it 180 degrees to the opposite horizontal position, the video adjusts accordingly. All the controls you expect in a DVD player are right on the screen at the touch of a finger.

You can also play audio books and podcasts on this multimedia machine. The iTunes Store offers an amazing selection of TV shows, movies, audio books, and podcasts. (See Chapter 7.) This chapter shows you how to control video playback, skip forward or backward, and scale the picture to fit your screen. It also shows you how to watch YouTube videos on your iPod touch or iPhone.

Everything's Coming Up Videos

Movies, TV shows, and music videos are easy to locate and play. Videos you purchase from the iTunes Store are ready to use, but videos you bring in from other sources may have to be converted first by iTunes for use on your iPod or iPhone. You can tell whether a video needs to be converted by selecting the video in iTunes and checking the Advanced menu: the Create iPod or iPhone version option is grayed out. To convert a video, select the video in iTunes and choose Advanced⇨Create iPod or iPhone Version.

To find out more about why videos need to be converted and how to prepare your own videos and convert imported videos for use with an iPod or iPhone, visit the free tips section of my Web site (www.tonybove.com).

To locate and play a video on your iPod touch or iPhone, follow these steps:

1. **Tap Videos on the iPod touch Home screen, or tap iPod on the iPhone Home screen and then tap the Videos icon at the bottom of the screen.**

2. **Scroll the Videos screen to see the sections for Movies, TV Shows, Music Videos, and Podcasts (video podcasts only).**

   The video titles are listed in alphabetical order within these sections.

3. **Tap the title of an item to play it.**

To play a video on an iPod classic or iPod nano, follow these steps:

1. **Choose Videos from the main menu to select a movie, TV show, or imported video. Choose Music from the main menu to select a music video.**

2. **Scroll the menu until the title is highlighted and then press the Select button to play your selection.**

   Hold the iPod nano horizontally to view the picture. If you rotate the iPod nano to the opposite horizontal position, the video adjusts accordingly.

Videos are automatically set to remember the playback position when you pause them. (See how to pause in the next section.) This feature lets you pause a video or TV episode in iTunes while you synchronize your iPod or iPhone. After syncing, you can continue playing the video or episode on your iPod or iPhone from where you paused. This feature also works the opposite way: If you start playing a video on your iPod or iPhone and then pause, and then you sync it with iTunes, the video retains the playback position so that you can continue playing it in iTunes from where you paused.

Playback at your fingertips on an iPod touch or iPhone

To control playback on an iPod touch or iPhone, tap the screen to show the video controls (as shown in Figure 17-1). You can tap again to hide them.

Tap the Play/Pause button while a video is playing to pause the playback. To raise or lower the volume, drag the volume slider. (See Figure 17-1.) To stop watching a video before it finishes playing, tap the Done button in the upper-left corner of the display or press the physical Home button.

Figure 17-1:
Tap the
screen
to use
playback
controls.

Play/Pause   Volume

Previous/Rewind   Next/Fast Forward

You can fast-forward through a video by touching and holding down the Next/Fast Forward button, and you can rewind a video by touching and holding down the Previous/Rewind button.

To skip to any point in a video, drag the playhead along the scrubber bar. To start a video over from the beginning, drag the playhead on the scrubber bar all the way to the left or tap the Previous/Rewind button (if the video doesn't contain chapters).

 If the video contains chapters, you can skip to the previous or next chapter by tapping the Previous/Rewind or Next/Fast Forward button. To start playing at a specific chapter, tap the bullet-list button that appears in the upper-right corner.

If a video offers an alternative audio language or subtitles, a Subtitles button appears. Tap the Subtitles button and then choose a language from the Audio list or a language from the Subtitles list, or tap On to turn off subtitles.

 You can delete a video directly from your iPod touch or iPhone by flicking left or right across the video selection in the Videos menu and then tapping the Delete button that appears. Your video is still in iTunes but is deleted from the iPod touch or iPhone — but remember, you can sync it again and copy the video back to it (as I explain in Chapter 9). If you delete a rented movie from the iPod touch or iPhone, it's deleted permanently.

Scaling the picture on an iPod touch or iPhone

Videos are displayed in landscape mode in widescreen format on an iPod touch or iPhone. You can also scale the video picture to fill the screen or to fit within the screen. Tap the Scale button (the one with two arrows facing away from each other — refer to Figure 17-1) or double-tap the video picture itself to switch from one to the other.

Filling the screen may crop the sides or top and bottom to give you a larger view of the center of the picture. Fitting to the screen assures that the entire picture is shown, but you may see black bars on the sides or top and bottom.

Playback under your thumb on an iPod nano or classic

The video playback controls on an iPod classic or iPod nano work the same way as with songs — you use precisely the same buttons, in other words. Scroll the click wheel to adjust the volume as you would for a song (as I describe in Chapter 16).

To pause playback, press the Play/Pause button while a video is playing. To start again, press Play/Pause again.

To skip to any point in a video, press the Select button to reveal the scrubber bar. Scroll the click wheel to move the playhead across the scrubber bar forward (to the right) or backward (to the left) in the video.

Press the Next/Fast Forward button once to play the next video in sequence (such as the next episode of a TV show), and press the Previous/Rewind button once at the beginning of a video, or twice during the video, to play the previous video in sequence. You can fast-forward through a video by pressing and holding down the Next/Fast Forward button, and rewind a video by pressing and holding down the Previous/Rewind button. If the video contains chapters, you can skip to the previous or next chapter by pressing the Previous/Rewind or Next/Fast Forward button — but remember, this trick works only if the original video was set up to contain chapters. To start a video over from the beginning, move the playhead on the scrubber bar all the way to the left, as previously described, or press the Previous/Rewind button once.

To return to menus and make other selections on an iPod classic or iPod nano, press the Menu button.

YouTube on Your iPod touch or iPhone

With the iPod touch or iPhone, the newest and most popular videos in YouTube are right in your hand. All you need to do is connect to the Internet — by Wi-Fi with an iPod touch, or by Wi-Fi or 3G with an iPhone. (See Chapter 4 to set up Wi-Fi.) You can search for and play videos, bookmark favorites for later playback, and share videos with others by e-mail.

Tap YouTube on the Home screen to run the YouTube app. If this is your first visit to the YouTube app, the Featured screen appears, as shown in Figure 17-2 (left side). Otherwise, the screen you were viewing when you last used the app appears.

Figure 17-2:
YouTube:
Featured
videos (left)
and most-
viewed
videos for
today, for
this week,
and for all
time (right).

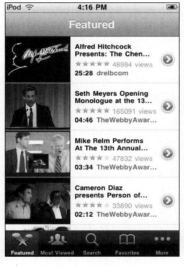

You can tap icons along the bottom of the display to get to other screens, such as Most Viewed, as shown in Figure 17-2 (right side), which offers buttons at the top for today's most-viewed videos, the faves for this week, and all the most-viewed videos.

After you've saved your favorites as bookmarks (see the section "Bookmarking and sharing," later in this chapter), you can go right to your favorite videos by tapping the Favorites icon. Tap the More icon to see even more screens, including Top Rated (the best of the best), Most Recent (the most recent videos added), and History (all the videos you've played so far). You can also tap the Sign In button to sign in to your YouTube account and access the My Videos section of your account.

The History screen offers a Clear button so that you can clear your history at any time.

Running down a stream: Playback control

Tap a selection to play the video. YouTube *streams* the video to your iPod touch or iPhone — sending it bit by bit — so that you can start playing it immediately.

Tap the video picture to see the controls (see Figure 17-3, left side), which are exactly like the video controls described in the previous section. The progress of the downloaded stream appears in the scrubber bar. Even though you can play the video as it streams, you might want to pause it for a few seconds so that more of the stream is downloaded. You can then play the video without any hiccups (depending, of course, on the speed and stability of your connection).

Figure 17-3:
YouTube controls for video playback, bookmarking, and sharing (left) and for searching for videos (right).

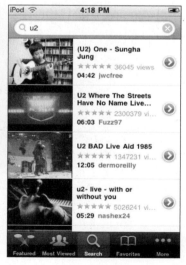

Bookmarking and sharing

YouTube offers a couple of handy buttons on its videos (see Figure 17-3, left side, for both buttons):

✓ **Bookmark button (a book icon):** This button appears to the left of the Previous/Rewind button, and you can use it to bookmark the video so that you can easily find it on the Favorites screen.

> ✔ **Share button (an envelope icon):** This button is located to the right of the Next/Fast Forward button. Tap it to bring up the e-mail sending screen to share the video with others via e-mail — see Chapter 20 for details on how to fill out the e-mail message.

Tap the Bookmark button to save a bookmark for the video — the video selection appears in the Favorites screen (tap the Favorites icon in the bottom row). (The Bookmark button is gray rather than white if the video is already bookmarked.)

You can also bookmark or share the video without playing it — in case the material disgusts you or you don't have time for it — and you can view information about the video as well as related video selections, to clue you into its content *before* playing it. Tap the right-arrow button on the right side of each selection (refer to Figure 17-2, right side) to see information about the video and to use the Bookmark or Share buttons.

To delete entries from your Favorites screen (especially those news stories that have gone stale), tap the Favorites icon at the bottom of the display to show your bookmarked favorites; then tap the Edit button in the upper-right corner of the screen. The Favorites screen changes to include circled minus (–) signs next to the video selections. To delete a bookmarked video selection, tap the circled minus sign, which rotates and displays a Delete button over the selection; then tap the Delete button. To cancel deletion, tap the rotated circled minus sign again. Tap the Done button in the upper-right corner of the Favorites screen to finish editing.

Searching for videos

To search for the videos on YouTube that everyone's talking about, tap the Search icon in the bottom row of icons. Then tap the Search Entry field that appears at the top of the screen. The on-screen keyboard pops up, ready for your search term. (For instructions on using the on-screen keyboard, see Chapter 3.)

If the entry field already has a search term, tap the circled *x* in the right corner of the field to clear its contents. Then tap out the letters of the search term using the on-screen keyboard and tap the Search key on the keyboard. Immediately after tapping Search, video selections from YouTube appear below, as shown in Figure 17-3, right side (in which I type just **u2** to get the latest U2 music videos).

You can scroll this list by dragging up and down. If a video selection appears that satisfies your search, tap it to play it without further ado.

One Chapter at a Time: Audio Books and Podcasts

Audio books are, naturally, organized into chapters or parts. Podcasts are also organized into parts, called *episodes,* and both play the same way. The audio book title or podcast name and episode appear on your iPod or iPhone display along with its cover — similar to a book or album cover.

After syncing your audio books and podcast episodes (as I describe in glorious detail in Chapter 9), you can play them on your iPod or iPhone. Audio books and podcasts are automatically set to remember the playback position when you pause. If you pause playback on your iPod or iPhone and then sync with iTunes, you can resume playback at that position on either the iPod or iPhone, or in iTunes.

Finding and playing on an iPod touch or iPhone

Tap Music on the iPod touch Home screen or iPod on the iPhone Home screen, and then tap the More icon at the lower-right corner of the Music or iPod screen to see the More screen.

For the literary-minded, tap Audiobooks on the More screen and then scroll the Audiobooks screen to select and play an audio book. Tap an audio book on the Audiobooks screen that appears and then tap a chapter or part to play it, starting from that point. The audio book chapters or parts are listed in proper order for each book.

For a podcast, tap Podcasts on the More screen and then scroll the Podcasts screen to select and play a podcast episode. Podcasts are organized by podcast name (which is like an album name), and episodes are listed within each podcast in the order that they were released (by date). A blue dot appears next to any podcast that has unplayed episodes.

You control the playback of an audio book or podcast episode exactly the same way as a song (see Chapter 16) — you can pause playback by tapping the Play/Pause button and so on. You can control video podcasts the same way you control videos. (See the section "Everything's Coming Up Videos," earlier in this chapter.)

Finding and playing on an iPod nano or iPod classic

Podcasts, naturally, have their own menu on an iPod nano or iPod classic. They're organized by podcast name (which is like an album name), and podcast episodes are listed within each podcast in the order that they were released (by date).

To play a podcast episode, choose Podcasts from the iPod classic or iPod nano main menu. Scroll the Podcasts menu until the podcast name is highlighted and press the Select button; then scroll and select an episode. A blue dot appears next to any podcast that has unplayed episodes.

To play an audio book, choose Music from the iPod classic or iPod nano main menu, and then Audiobooks from the Music menu. The audio book episodes (collections of chapters) are listed in the proper order for each book. Scroll the list of audio book episodes until the one you want is highlighted and then press the Select button to play it.

Playing the FM Radio in an iPod nano

The current iPod nano model includes an FM radio that displays station and song information for radio stations that support RDS (Radio Data System). If the station supports iTunes Tagging, you can also tag any songs you hear for later purchase from the iTunes Store. You can also pause a radio broadcast, and resume playing it from the same point up to 15 minutes later.

Connect your earbuds or headphones to your iPod nano first, because the iPod nano uses the earbud or headphone cord as the FM radio antenna. Also, the radio doesn't play through the iPod nano speaker— only through the earbuds or headphones.

To hear the radio, choose Radio from the iPod nano main menu. The radio screen appears with a station already selected — if you don't see the radio dial underneath the station's number, press the Select button until it appears. You can scroll the click wheel to tune to a station while you listen for a signal, or press the Next/Fast-forward or Previous/Rewind buttons to jump from station to station. Press and hold Next/Fast-forward or Previous/Rewind to scan stations and hear a five-second preview of each station. To stop scanning and listen to the current station, press the Select button.

To save a station as a favorite, Press and hold the Select button until a menu appears, scroll to highlight Add to Favorites, and then press the Select button. After saving one or more favorite stations, pressing Next/Fast-forward or Previous/Rewind while tuning takes you to the next or previous favorite station.

After you tune to a station, the progress bar replaces the radio dial. (Press the Select button to switch between the progress bar and the radio dial.) The progress bar fills up as you continue to listen to the station. To pause the broadcast while the radio is playing, press the Play/Pause button. The actual time you paused appears above the progress bar. As Live Pause continues, a yellow triangle appears for your pause point in the progress bar, and the progress bar continues to fill up — showing the time that's passed since you paused. Press Play/Pause again to resume the broadcast from the point you paused.

You can navigate back and forth along the progress bar. To skip forward or back in one-minute intervals, press the Next/Fast-forward or Previous/Rewind buttons. To fast-forward or rewind, press and hold Next/Fast-forward or Previous/Rewind, or scroll the click wheel. The progress bar displays as completely filled when Live Pause reaches the 15-minute limit. You can still navigate back and forth through the 15 most recent minutes, as long as your pause isn't cleared. Anything older than 15 minutes is cleared to make room for the continuing broadcast. If you pause without resuming for 15 minutes, your iPod nano goes to sleep and clears your paused radio.

To disable Live Pause, press Menu from the Radio screen, highlight and select Live Pause, and then press the Select button to select Off. To enable Live Pause again, select On.

Tagging a song that strikes your fancy for later purchase from the iTunes Store is a great idea, but it only works with stations that support iTunes Tagging. To tag a song you hear, press and hold the Select button until a menu appears. Highlight Tag in the menu and press the Select button. Tagged songs are marked with a tag icon next to the song title, and they appear in the Radio menu under Tagged Songs (press the Menu button while the radio is playing to see the Radio menu).

The next time you sync your iPod nano to iTunes, your tagged songs are synced to iTunes and removed from the iPod nano. You can preview and purchase these tagged songs by clicking Tagged in the Store section of the Source pane, and then click the View button for the song you want. To preview the song, double-click it or click the preview button. To buy the song, click the Buy button.

To turn the FM Radio off and clear paused radio, press the Menu button and choose Stop Radio (which appears only if the radio is on). You can also display the most recently played songs on a station that supports RDS by pressing Menu and then choosing Recent Songs.

Chapter 18

Your Pocket Picture Player

In This Chapter

▶ Synchronizing photo albums

▶ Viewing photos and slide shows

▶ Taking pictures and shooting videos with an iPhone

▶ Shooting videos with an iPod nano

▶ Sharing your photos and video clips

*T*he world is awash in pictures, from photos and video clips to cartoon images, graphics, and famous paintings. In this chapter, I refer to everything you can *see* as a picture — whether it be a photo, graphic image, shot of a computer or iPod touch or iPhone screen, or a recorded video clip (a moving picture).

If you like to carry pictures around with you, you're going to love the iPod or iPhone as a player for viewing pictures. And if you like to send and receive pictures by e-mail, you're going to love the fact that you can use your iPod touch or iPhone to share them with others. This chapter shows you how.

Syncing with Photo Albums and Folders

After importing photos from cameras into your computer, and importing image files from other sources, you can organize them into albums or collections. On a Mac, you can use iPhoto (version 4.0.3 or newer) or Aperture. On a Windows PC, you can use Adobe Photoshop Album (version 2.0 or newer) or Adobe Photoshop Elements (version 3.0 or newer).

You can then set up your iPod or iPhone to sync with your entire photo library or with specific albums in your library so that any changes you make to the library or to those albums are copied to the iPod or iPhone. In addition, any pictures you collect from e-mails on your iPod touch or iPhone are synced back to the photo library on your computer.

If you don't have iPhoto or one of the Adobe products, you can store your pictures in their own folder on your hard drive (such as the Pictures folder in your home folder on a Mac or the My Pictures folder in your My Documents folder in Windows). You can then use iTunes to transfer pictures from this folder, treating the folder as a single photo album. If you have subfolders in this folder iTunes copies the subfolder assignments as if they were album assignments.

To find out more about organizing pictures into albums, visit the free tips section of my Web site (`www.tonybove.com`).

Transferring pictures to your iPod or iPhone

To copy pictures from your computer to your iPod or iPhone using iTunes, follow these steps:

1. **Connect your iPod or iPhone to your computer and then select its name in the Devices section of the iTunes Source pane.**

   iTunes displays the Summary page (under the Summary tab of the synchronization pages) to the right of the Source pane. (See Chapter 9 for details.)

2. **Click the Photos tab.**

   The Photos sync options appear, as shown in Figure 18-1. (On a Mac, you'll see iPhoto selected to sync photos from.)

3. **Select the Sync Photos From check box and then pick the source of your pictures from the pop-up menu: a photo application, the Pictures (Mac) or My Pictures (PC) folder, or the Choose Folder option.**

   Pick your application (such as iPhoto on a Mac or Adobe Photoshop Album in Windows) from the pop-up menu to synchronize with its library. If you don't use these applications, pick the Pictures folder on a Mac or the My Pictures folder on a PC, or pick Choose Folder to browse your hard drive or other storage media and select the folder containing pictures. After selecting the folder, click Choose (Mac) or OK (Windows).

4. **If you chose a photo application that organizes pictures by album, collection, events, or faces (such as iPhoto), or if you stored pictures in subfolders in your Pictures or My Pictures folder, select one of the following options below the Sync Photos From check box:**

   • *All Photos Albums, and Faces:* Copies all pictures and albums (or collections) from the library or folder selected in Step 3.

   • *Selected Albums, Events, and Faces, and Automatically Include:* Select this option to be more specific about which albums, events, and/or faces to sync, and to include recent events automatically — you can choose how many recent events or events from the last month or several months from the pop-up menu, or choose All Events or No Events. (In Figure 18-1, I chose The Most Recent Event.) After selecting this option, you can then make selections in the Albums, Events, and Faces columns.

- *Events column:* If you chose a photo application that organizes pictures by events (such as iPhoto), you can select the check box next to each name (or date, if no name) of an event to synchronize.

- *Albums column:* Lets you choose which photo albums from the library (or subfolders from the folder) selected in Step 3 you want to copy. The idea here is to scroll the list box to see all the albums or collections in your library (or subfolders in your folder) and then select the check box next to each one you want to copy. (In Figure 18-1, you can see that I decided to copy the albums named John and Jimi 2 from my iPhoto library.)

- *Faces column:* If you chose a photo application that organizes pictures by faces (such as iPhoto), you can select the check box next to each face's name. (In Figure 18-1, you can see that I decided to copy all pictures with Jimi Bove's face and John Bove's face from my iPhoto library.)

5. **Click the Apply button to apply changes, and click the Sync button if synchronization hasn't already started automatically.**

   iTunes copies the photo library or albums you selected to your iPod or iPhone (and deletes all other pictures from the iPod or iPhone except those saved in Saved Images or in Camera Roll)

Syncing saved pictures with iTunes

You can save pictures that you receive via e-mail on your iPod touch or iPhone, photos you record with your iPhone, videos you shoot with your iPhone 3GS, and videos you shoot with your iPod nano in a special photo album — Saved Images (for image captures and e-mailed pictures you save) or Camera Roll (for photos and videos you shoot). (I describe how to save pictures from e-mails later in this chapter.)

To synchronize these saved pictures back to your computer, connect your iPod touch or iPhone to your computer as you normally would to sync it (as described in Step 1 of the previous section).

On a Mac, iPhoto pops up automatically — click the Import All button, or select the pictures you want and click the Import Selected button. After importing the pictures into the iPhoto library, iPhoto asks whether you want to delete the originals from the iPod touch or iPhone. Click Delete Originals to delete the pictures from the iPod touch or iPhone (they're safe in your photo library now) or click Keep Originals to save them — in case you want to e-mail them or upload them to social networks from your iPod touch or iPhone.

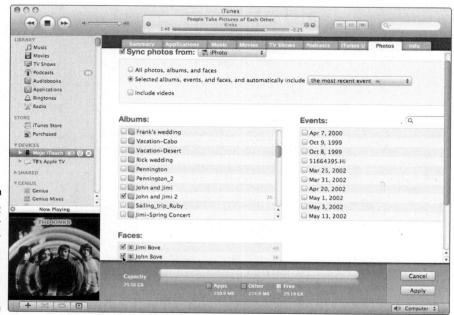

Figure 18-1: Sync your iPod or iPhone with photos (iPod nano shown).

On a Windows PC, iTunes can be set up to sync with Adobe Photoshop Album or Photoshop Elements (as I describe in the previous section) and will automatically transfer the pictures (including video clips). If you don't use those applications, follow the instructions that came with your photo application to import the pictures, or use the Microsoft Scanner and Camera Wizard, to save the pictures to a folder of your choice.

To import recorded videos to your computer from an iPod nano, the iPod nano must be enabled for disk use — select the iPod nano in the Device section of the Source pane, click the Summary tab, and select the Enable Disk Use option. In addition to appearing in iTunes, your iPod nano from this point on also appears on your computer as an external hard drive, with the same name you gave it during initial setup. Your recorded videos are stored in the DCIM folder on your iPod nano, and you can simply drag them to your computer. To clear space on your iPod nano after you've copied your recorded videos to your computer, delete them from the DCIM folder.

Viewing Pictures and Slideshows

You might remember the old days when you carried fading, wallet-sized photo prints, or worse, a deck of slides that required a light box or projector to show them to others. You can now dispense with all that because all you need is your iPod or iPhone.

Slide shows are an especially entertaining way of showing pictures because you can include music as well as transitions between them. You can display your slide show on the iPod or iPhone, or on a television by connecting your iPod or iPhone to the TV using the Universal Dock, Component AV Cable, or Composite AV Cable from Apple (available in the Apple Store).

To find out how to connect your iPod or iPhone to televisions, stereos, video monitors, and video equipment, visit this book's companion Web site.

Viewing pictures on an iPod touch or iPhone

To view pictures on your iPod touch or iPhone, follow these steps:

1. **Tap Photos on the Home screen.**

   The Photo Albums screen appears, as shown in Figure 18-2 (left side), with a list of photo albums. On an iPod touch, the list includes Saved Photos if you've saved pictures from e-mail messages. On an iPhone, the list includes Camera Roll for saved pictures from e-mails and for new photos shot with the iPhone Camera (and video clips shot with the iPhone 3GS Camera).

2. **Tap a photo album's name (or the arrow to the right of the name), or tap Photo Library to see all pictures.**

   Thumbnail images appear, as shown in Figure 18-2 (right side). The Photo Library choice displays thumbnails of *all* the pictures in your iPod touch or iPhone (except the Camera Roll or Saved Images albums). Selecting an album displays thumbnails of only the pictures assigned to that album.

3. **Flick your finger to scroll the thumbnails and tap a thumbnail to select a picture.**

   You might have several screens of thumbnails. Flick your finger to scroll the thumbnails and tap one to select it and view it.

To view a picture in landscape orientation, rotate the iPod touch or iPhone sideways. The picture automatically changes to fit the new orientation and expands to fit the screen if the picture itself is in landscape orientation.

To zoom into the picture to see more detail, double-tap the area you want to zoom into. Double-tap again to zoom out. You can also zoom into an area by unpinching with two fingers, and zoom out by pinching. To pan around a picture, drag it with your finger.

To move to the next picture in the library, flick horizontally across the picture with your finger. You can flick across to go backward or forward through the album or the entire library.

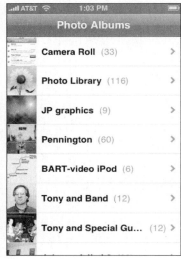

Figure 18-2:
Tap a photo album or the entire photo library (left) and then tap a thumb-nail image (right).

Options   Play

Tap the full-screen picture to show or hide the navigation controls, as shown in Figure 18-3. You can see the next or previous pictures in the album or library by tapping the Previous or Next buttons that appear when you tap the picture.

To set up a slide show, follow these steps:

1. **Choose Settings➪Photos from the Home screen.**

   The Photos Slideshow settings screen appears.

2. **Tap the Play Each Slide For option to set the duration of each slide.**

   You can select ranges from 2 to 20 seconds.

3. **Tap the Transition option to pick a transition to use between photos in the slide show.**

   The Wipe Across transition is my favorite, but you can select Cube, Dissolve, Ripple, or Wipe Down. Tap the Photos button to return to the Photos Slideshow settings screen.

4. **Select the other options as appropriate for your slide show:**

   • *Repeat:* Repeats the slide show.

   • *Shuffle:* Shuffles photos in the slide show in a random order.

5. **Tap the Settings button to return to the Settings screen or press the physical Home button to return to the Home screen.**

Figure 18-3:
Photo
navigation
controls.

Options Previous   Next

To play a slide show, follow these steps:

1. **Tap Photos on the Home Screen, and tap an album on the Photos screen or tap Photo Library.**

2. **To start the show, tap the Play/Pause button at the bottom of the thumbnail images. (Refer to Figure 18-2, right side.)**

3. **Use the navigation buttons to move back and forth in your slide show.**

   Tap any picture to see the navigation controls (refer to Figure 18-3) to move to the next or previous picture.

4. Press the physical Home button to stop the slide show.

The Home button returns you to the Home screen. You can also stop a slide show by tapping the picture.

Viewing pictures on an iPod nano or iPod classic

To view pictures (photos and images, but not video clips) on your iPod nano or iPod classic, follow these steps:

1. Choose Photos from the main menu.

The Photos menu appears with All Photos and Settings choices at the top, followed by a list of photo albums and/or events in alphabetical order.

2. Choose All Photos or an album or event name.

The All Photos choice displays thumbnail images of all the pictures in your iPod. Selecting an album or event displays thumbnail images of only the pictures assigned to that album or event.

3. Scroll the click wheel to highlight the thumbnail you want and then press the Select button to select the picture.

You might have several screens of thumbnails. Scroll the click wheel to scroll through the thumbnails. When you select a thumbnail, your iPod displays the picture.

To view a picture in landscape orientation on an iPod nano, rotate the iPod nano sideways. The picture automatically changes to fit the new orientation and expands to fit the screen if the picture itself is in landscape orientation.

Press the Previous/Rewind button to see the previous picture in the album or library, or the Next/Fast Forward button to see the next picture. Press the Play/Pause button to start a slide show (see the section "Setting up a slide show," later in this chapter). Press Menu to return to the thumbnails, and press Menu again to return to the Photos menu.

To set up a slide show, follow these steps:

1. Choose Photos⇨Settings from the main menu.

2. Choose Times per Slide from the Settings menu to set the duration of each slide.

You can select ranges from 2 to 20 seconds. Or, you can select Manual to set the slide show to advance to the next slide when you click the Next/Fast Forward button.

3. **Pick your music by choosing Music from the Settings menu and then choose a playlist.**

   You can choose any playlist in your iPod for your slide show, including On-The-Go and Now Playing. iPhoto lets you assign an iTunes playlist to an iPhoto album, and that assignment is saved in your iPod. If you copy the playlist to your iPod, it's automatically assigned to the slide show.

4. **Select a transition to use between photos in the slide show by choosing Transitions from the Settings menu.**

   Wipe Across is my favorite, but you can select Cross Fade, Fade to Black, Zoom Out, or Wipe Center. Choose Random if you want to use a different (and random) transition for each photo change. Choose Off for no transition. After you choose a transition, the Settings menu appears again.

5. **Set the iPod to display the slide show by choosing TV Out from the Settings menu.**

   You have three choices for TV Out:

   - *On* displays the slide show on a television. While the slide show plays on your TV, you can also see the slides as large thumbnails on your iPod, along with the photo number within the album or library, and the Next and Previous icons.

   - *Ask* displays a screen requesting that you select TV Off or TV On; you make the choice each time you play a slide show.

   - *Off* displays the slide show with full-size images on the iPod.

6. **(Optional) Select other preferences from the Settings menu:**

   - *Repeat:* Repeats the slide show.

   - *Shuffle Photos:* Shuffles photos in the slide show in a random order.

   - *TV Signal:* Changes your television signal to PAL for European and other countries that use PAL as their video standard. NTSC (also referred to humorously as "never the same color") is the U.S. standard.

To play a slide show, follow these steps:

1. **Choose Photos from the main menu.**

2. **Choose an album in the Photos menu, or All Photos.**

3. **To start the show, press the Play/Pause button.**

   You can also start a slide show when viewing a single picture by pressing the Select button.

4. **If you previously set TV Out to Ask (as described in the previous section), choose TV On or TV Off for your slide show.**

   • *TV On* displays the slide show on a television (through the video-out connection). You can also see the slides as large thumbnails on the iPod.

   • *TV Off* displays the slide show with full-size images on the iPod.

5. **Use the playback buttons to navigate your slide show.**

   If you set Time per Slide to Manual, press Next/Fast Forward to move to the next picture and press Previous/Rewind to return to the previous picture.

   If you set Time per Slide to a specific duration, use Play/Pause to pause and play the slide show.

6. **Press the Menu button to stop the slide show.**

   Pressing the Menu button returns you to the Photos menu.

Shooting Videos with an iPod nano

So you think those nifty portable video cameras are so cute? Check out the current model iPod nano: You can shoot high-quality video with sound, and even apply special video effects. You can, of course, watch what you record on your iPod nano, and then transfer the video to your computer to edit and share.

To find out how to shoot photos with an iPhone (and shoot videos with an iPhone 3GS), visit the free tips section of my Web site (www.tonybove.com).

Turn your current model iPod nano around, and you'll find the lens and microphone on the back. It points outward so that you use the display as a viewfinder to see the video you're shooting. Be careful not to block the lens or microphone with your fingers — hold the iPod nano on its edges when recording for best results.

To use iPod nano as a video camera, choose Video Camera from the main menu. The screen turns into a viewfinder, and you can shoot video in landscape or portrait mode by rotating the iPod nano. When you're ready to begin shooting, press the Select button. Press it again to stop recording. While you are recording, a blinking red light appears in the upper right corner of the display, next to the recording time.

You can apply special effects only *before* recording — the Pod nano can't add or remove effects after recording, and you can't change video settings while recording. To shoot video with special effects, choose Video Camera from the main menu, and then Press and hold the Select button to display the video effects palette. Scroll the click wheel to highlight the effects, and press the Select button to select the one that's highlighted. The viewfinder screen appears with the selected effect — which is fun for viewing the world through the viewfinder. Press the Select button again to start shooting with the special effect, and press it again to stop recording. When you press the Menu button to leave the Video Camera screen, the special effect changes back to Normal.

Your recording time depends on the how much space you have in your iPod nano, and how long your battery can last. A recorded video can be up to 2GB in size. Once a recorded video takes up 2GB of space, recording stops. To resume recording, press the Select button.

The iPod nano saves your recorded videos in the Camera Roll. To watch what you just recorded, press Menu from the Video Camera viewfinder to show the Camera Roll. Select a video by its date and time, and press the Select button to play it. Your recorded videos can also be played from the Videos menu — choose Videos➪Camera Videos, select a video from the list, and then press the Select button to play it.

To delete a recorded video on your iPod nano, choose Videos➪Camera Videos and then select a video from the list to delete. Press and hold the Select button until a menu appears, scroll the click wheel to highlight Delete or Delete All, and then press Select. It's a good idea to remove any recorded videos you don't want to save, because they take up a lot of space.

To sync your recorded videos with your computer, see "Syncing saved pictures with iTunes" earlier in this chapter.

Sharing Pictures with an iPod touch or iPhone

What good is it to collect pictures without sharing them with other people? You can share pictures in your iPod touch or iPhone by sending one or more in an e-mail, uploading as many as you want to social networks, and sharing entire photo albums using MobileMe. With an iPhone 3G or 3GS, you can also send pictures using MMS (if supported by your carrier). And with an iPhone 3GS, you can record video clips and share them the same way, using e-mail or MMS. You can also upload video clips to YouTube or your MobileMe gallery.

Sending a picture by e-mail

To send an image in an e-mail, tap Photos on the Home screen, tap a photo album or Photo Library, and choose the image for viewing (refer to Figure 18-2). Then tap the picture to see the navigation controls (refer to Figure 18-3).

Tap the Options button in the lower-left corner of the screen to see the Options menu, as shown in Figure 18-4, and then tap the Email Photo button to e-mail a photo or the Email Video button (not shown) to e-mail a video clip. If you have MMS support with your iPhone carrier, you also see buttons to send the photo or video by MMS.

Figure 18-4: Choose the option to e-mail the photo.

The New Message screen appears in the Mail app for e-mail or in the Messages app for MMS messages on an iPhone. The photo or video clip is embedded in the message. You can tap in the message field to enter text. Then fill in the To and Subject fields, as described in Chapter 20.

You can also use the Options menu to assign the photo to a contact in your Contacts list (see Chapter 21 for details) or use the image as the iPod touch or iPhone wallpaper (see Chapter 4). If you've set up a photo gallery on MobileMe to share with others, you can include any picture or video clip in this published gallery so that others can immediately see it. Choose Send to MobileMe in the Options menu, and select the gallery to include the picture or video clip.

Selecting and copying multiple pictures

To select more than one picture (photo, image, or video clip) to copy and paste into another app or to share by e-mail, tap Photos on the Home screen and tap a photo album or Photo Library (refer to Figure 18-2, left side). Then tap the Options button in the lower-left corner of the thumbnail images (refer to Figure 18-2, right side).

The Select Photos screen appears, showing the same thumbnails. Tap each thumbnail on the Select Photos screen, as shown in Figure 18-5 (left side), to select each image. As you tap each thumbnail, a check mark appears in the thumbnail to indicate that it is part of the selection.

The Share and Copy buttons appear at the bottom as you make a selection. To e-mail the selected pictures, tap the Share button and then tap Email. The Mail app launches and starts a new e-mail message that includes all the selected images (see Chapter 20 for details on sending e-mails).

To copy the pictures to another app or paste them into an existing message, tap the Copy button. You can paste the pictures into any app that accepts pasted pictures — such as a saved e-mail draft message in Mail. Touch and hold to mark an insertion point in the e-mail message (which brings up the keyboard), and the Select/Select All/Paste bubble appears, as shown in Figure 18-5 (right side). Tap Paste to paste the images into the message.

You can also receive pictures from others by e-mail. (See Chapter 20 for details on how to check your e-mail.) A down-arrow button appears within a message that contains an attached picture. Tap the down-arrow button to download the picture to your iPod touch or iPhone.

After the download completes, tap the picture in the e-mail message, and the Save Image and Cancel buttons appear. Tap the Save Image button to save the picture in your iPod touch or iPhone photo library (in the Saved Images album) or tap Cancel to cancel. If the message has more than one picture (such as three), you can tap a button to save them all.

Figure 18-5:
Select
pictures
for copying
or sharing
(left), and
paste the
pictures
into a draft
e-mail mes-
sage (right).

Capturing a screen shot

You too can capture shots of the iPod touch or iPhone screen and display them in a book or Web site, just as I have. No matter what application you're running, quickly press and release the Sleep/Wake and physical Home buttons at the same time. The iPod touch or iPhone screen flashes (and if your volume is up, you can hear a shutter click). This indicates that the screen was saved in the Saved Images album on an iPod touch or the Camera Roll album on an iPhone — choose the album in Photos to see the picture. You can take as many screen shots as you like. The next time you sync your iPod touch or iPhone to your computer, your photo application (such as iPhoto) launches to receive these new pictures.

Part V
Touching the Online World

The 5th Wave   By Rich Tennant

"Other than this little glitch with the landscape view, I really love my iPhone."

In this part . . .

This part takes the concept of playing media to an entirely new level by providing access to the world of online content. Now you can use your iPod touch or iPhone to touch Web sites around the world, download songs, check your e-mail, and even monitor your stock portfolio.

✔ Chapter 19 spins the Web and shows you how to surf Web pages with Safari on your iPod touch or iPhone. You find out how to search with Google or Yahoo! and interact with Web services to do everything from checking live news feeds to making travel reservations.

✔ Chapter 20 shows you how to turn your iPod touch or iPhone into a lean, clean e-mail machine. You can check e-mails from multiple e-mail accounts, send messages, and manage your e-mail settings.

✔ Chapter 21 puts you in contact with your Contacts, helps you manage your Calendar, and connects you with the most popular social networks on the planet — Facebook, MySpace, and Twitter. The weather becomes more predictable, your stocks proudly show their charts, and the Earth itself reveals its secrets in satellite and map views.

Chapter 19

Surfin' Safari

In This Chapter

▶ Browsing the Web with your iPod touch or iPhone

▶ Navigating, scrolling, and zooming into Web pages

▶ Saving and using Web page bookmarks

▶ Saving Web site icons to your Home screen

The World Wide Web makes the world go 'round a whole lot faster than ever before. I browse the Web for many different kinds of content and services. It's gotten to the point where I now use the Web to make travel, restaurant, and entertainment reservations, and I purchase everything online, from music, videos, books, and clothing to electronics equipment, garden supplies, groceries, and furniture. I get to track my shipments and purchases, review the latest news, check up on the blogs of my friends and associates, read novels, view slide shows and movies posted on the Internet, and even scan text messages from cell phones — all thanks to the Internet.

I can do all this using the Safari browser on an iPod touch or iPhone with an Internet connection, so I rarely need a laptop when I travel. I can also search using Google or Yahoo! — both services are built into Safari, and I can always browse any other search site. An iPod touch or iPhone can join AirPort and other Wi-Fi networks at home, at work, or at Wi-Fi hotspots around the world, as I describe in Chapter 4, to connect to the Internet. An iPhone can also use the Edge network, and an iPhone 3G or iPhone 3GS can also use a 3G network.

Take a Walk on the Web Side with Safari

Safari on the iPod touch or iPhone not only lets you browse through Web sites, but also lets you add bookmarks and icons to your Home screen for convenient access. (You can also synchronize those bookmarks with your computer's Web browser, as I describe in Chapter 10.)

Go URL own way

It's a snap to browse any Web site. Just tap out the site's address on the on-screen keyboard. (For instructions on using the on-screen keyboard, see Chapter 3.)

The Web site address is known as a URL (*Uniform Resource Locator*) and usually begins with `http://www.` followed by the name of the Web site or other characters (such as `http://www.apple.com` or `http://www.tony bove.com/tonytips`). However, you can leave off the `http://www.` part and just go with the rest of the characters of the URL (`apple.com` or `tony bove.com/tonytips`).

For the blow-by-blow account, check out the following steps:

1. **Tap Safari on the Home screen.**

   The iPod touch or iPhone displays the last Web page you visited or a blank page, with the rectangular URL entry field at the upper-left corner and an oval search-entry field in the upper-right corner, as shown in Figure 19-1, left side. (If you don't see these two entry fields side by side, tap the status bar at the top of the screen to jump to the top of the Web page.)

2. **Tap the URL field.**

   The on-screen keyboard appears. Above that is an entry field for typing the URL.

3. **If the entry field already has a URL, tap the circled *x* in the right corner of the field to clear its contents.**

4. **Tap out the URL for the Web page using the on-screen keyboard.**

   Immediately as you start typing the characters of the URL, you see a list of suggested Web sites in your bookmarks or history list that match the characters you typed so far (as shown in Figure 19-1, right side). You can scroll the suggested list by dragging up and down. If the Web site you want appears, tap it to go directly to the site without further ado. Otherwise, keep typing the URL, including the extension — the keyboard includes a .com button, next to the Go button, for your convenience.

5. **Tap the Go button on the keyboard (or tap Cancel to cancel).**

   When you tap the Go button, the keyboard closes and the message `Loading` appears in the status bar. Then the Web page loads from the Internet, if the page exists. If you mistyped the URL or the page doesn't exist, you get the message `Safari can't open the page because it can't find the server`. Tap OK and start again from Step 2.

   To cancel entering a URL, tap the Cancel button in the upper-right corner of the screen (refer to Figure 19-1, right side).

URL entry   Search entry

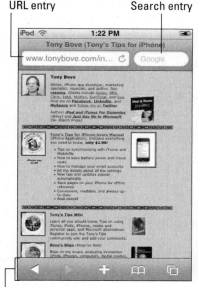 

Figure 19-1:
The URL
and search
fields (left).
Start
entering the
URL and
suggestions
appear
(right).

Navigation bar

 To stop a Web page from loading if you change your mind, tap the *x* on the right side of the URL entry field. This *x* turns into a circular arrow after the page is loaded. To reload an already-loaded Web page to refresh its contents, tap the circular arrow.

Hanging loose with your bookmarks

If you already have bookmarks saved in your iPod touch or iPhone, you can go directly to your favorite bookmarked pages. (To add bookmarks to your iPod touch or iPhone, you can sync bookmarks from your computer's Web browser, as described in Chapter 10, and you can also save bookmarks of pages you visit with your iPod touch or iPhone, as described in the section "Bookmarking as You Go," later in this chapter.)

Follow these steps:

1. **Tap Safari on the Home screen.**

   Your iPod touch or iPhone displays the last Web page you visited or a blank page. A navigation bar sporting various icons and buttons appears along the bottom, as shown in Figure 19-2.

2. **Tap the Bookmarks icon — the one that looks like an open book — on the navigation bar.**

The Bookmarks screen appears with the special History folder that records your page visits, and other Bookmark-related folders (such as Bookmarks Bar and Bookmarks Menu, provided with the Safari application on Macs and PCs). You can scroll this list by dragging up and down.

3. Tap a folder to view its contents.

For example, tapping Bookmarks Menu opens the folders and bookmarks from the Bookmarks Menu section of Safari on your Mac or PC. Tapping Bookmarks Bar opens the folders and bookmarks in the Bookmarks Bar section. Tapping History opens the history of the Web pages you've visited.

4. Tap a bookmark to load the Web page.

Folders have a folder icon to the left of their names, and actual bookmarks have an open-page icon next to their Web page names. Tap a folder to reveal its contents, and tap a bookmark to load a Web page.

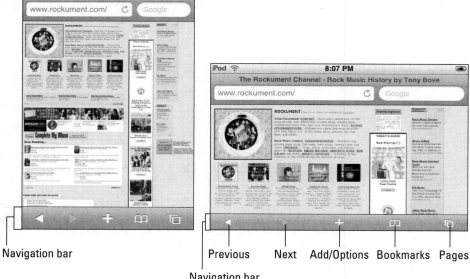

Figure 19-2:
Use the navigation bar to navigate Web pages and to open and save bookmarks.

Navigation bar

Previous   Next   Add/Options   Bookmarks   Pages

Navigation bar

As shown in Figure 19-2, you can rotate the iPod touch or iPhone sideways to view Web pages in landscape (horizontal) orientation and then double-tap to zoom in or out — Safari automatically fits sections of Web pages (such as columns of text) to fill the screen for easy reading. You can also spread with two fingers to control the amount of zooming.

Pearl diving with Google or Yahoo!

If you've done any Web surfing at all, you already know all there is to know about search engines. They're simply *the* tool for finding Web sites. The two most popular search engines out there — Google and Yahoo! — are built into Safari on your iPod touch or iPhone.

Google is set up to be your default Web search engine, but you can quickly change that. To choose Yahoo! (or to go back to Google), tap Settings➪Safari➪Search Engine and tap Yahoo! or Google. Turning on one search engine turns off the other one.

Follow these steps to search with Google or Yahoo! from within Safari:

1. **Tap Safari on the Home screen.**

   The last Web page you visited or a blank page appears. You can find the URL entry field in the upper-left corner and the oval search-entry field, with Google or Yahoo! in gray, in the upper-right corner (refer to Figure 19-1, left side). (If you don't see these two entry fields side by side, tap the status bar at the top of the screen to jump to the top of the Web page.)

2. **Tap the oval search-entry field.**

   The keyboard appears. Above that is the search-entry field (with a magnifying glass icon).

3. **Tap inside the search-entry field.**

4. **Tap out the letters of the search term using the keyboard.**

   Immediately as you start typing characters, you see a list of suggested bookmarks in your bookmarks folder or history list. You can scroll this list by dragging up and down.

5. **If a bookmark appears that satisfies your search, tap it to go directly to the Web page without further ado. Otherwise, keep typing the search term.**

6. **Tap the Google or Yahoo! button at the lower-right corner of the keyboard.**

   Doing so closes the keyboard and displays the search results. (*Note:* The Google or Yahoo! button replaces the Go button on the keyboard when searching.)

Let Your Fingers Do the Surfing

After you've found the Web page you want, you can use your fingers to navigate its links and play any media it has to offer. You can also bounce around from previous to next pages in your browsing session, open multiple pages, zoom into pages to see them clearly, and scroll around the page to see all its sections while zooming.

Scrolling and zooming

To zoom into a Web page in Safari, spread two fingers apart on the screen (unpinch). To zoom back out, bring your fingers together (pinch).

Double-tap the display to zoom into any part of the page. You can also double-tap a column to automatically zoom in so that the column fills the display. Double-tap again to zoom back out.

To scroll around the page, touch and drag the page. (If you happen to touch a link, drag the link so that you don't follow it.) You can drag up, down, or sideways to see the entire Web page, or you can flick your finger up or down to quickly scroll the page. Use two fingers to scroll within the frame on a Web page or one finger to scroll the entire page.

To jump to the top of a Web page, tap the status bar at the top of the screen.

All of these gestures work the same way in either portrait or landscape orientation. To view a Web page in landscape orientation, rotate the iPod touch or iPhone sideways. Safari automatically reorients and expands the page. To set it back to portrait, rotate it again.

It's all touch and go

To follow a link on a Web page, tap the link. Text links are usually underlined (sometimes in blue). Many images are also links that you can tap to navigate to another page or use to play media content.

If a link leads to a sound or movie file supported by the iPod touch or iPhone, Safari launches the player for the sound or movie; if the link points to YouTube, the YouTube app launches to play the video. (See Chapter 16 for sounds and Chapter 17 for videos.)

You can see the link's destination — without following it — by touching and holding down on the link until the destination address appears (next to your finger). You can touch and hold an image to see whether it has a link.

To move to the previous page in your browsing sequence, tap the left-arrow button in the left side of the navigation bar at the bottom of the screen. (Refer to Figure 19-2.) Safari replaces the current page with the previous one. If you've just started browsing and this is the first page you've opened, the left-arrow button is grayed out.

To move to the next page, tap the right-arrow button (to the right of the left-arrow button) in the navigation bar at the bottom of the screen. (Refer to Figure 19-2.) Safari replaces the current page with the next one in the browsing sequence. This button is grayed out unless you've navigated backward to some previous page.

You can always go back to any of the pages you visited by tapping the Bookmarks button on the navigation bar and then tapping History. To clear your History list on your iPod touch or iPhone, tap Clear.

Surfing multiple pages

Although you can open Web pages one at a time and switch back and forth between them, you can also open several pages and start a new browsing sequence with each page, just like opening separate browser windows or tabs.

Some links automatically open a new page instead of replacing the current one, leaving you with multiple pages open. Safari displays the number of open pages inside the Pages icon in the right corner of the navigation bar at the bottom of the screen. If there's no number on the icon, it means only one page is open.

To open a separate page, tap the Pages icon on the right side of the navigation bar at the bottom of the screen; then tap the New Page button. Safari brushes aside the existing page to display a new one. You can then use your bookmarks, enter a Web page URL, or search for a Web page. (If you change your mind and don't want to open a new page, tap the Done button to cancel.)

To close a separate page, tap the Pages icon on the right side of the navigation bar to display the page thumbnail images and then tap the red circled *x* in the upper-left corner of the Web page thumbnail for the page you want to close. The page disappears.

To switch among open pages, tap the Pages icon to display the page thumbnail images, as shown in Figure 19-3, and flick left or right to scroll the images. When you get to the thumbnail image of the page you want, touch it!

Figure 19-3:
Switch
among open
Web pages.

Interacting with pages

Many Web pages have pop-up menus for making choices. For example, the NextBus Stop Selector site (www.nextmuni.com) offers pop-up menus for selecting the state, the transit agency, and the bus line. To make choices for a pop-up menu, tap the menu. Safari displays a list of possible choices for that pop-up menu (such as a list of bus lines). Choose one by tapping it; you can also flick to scroll the list of choices.

After choosing an option, tap the Done button to finish with that pop-up menu. You can also tap the Previous or Next button to move to the previous or next pop-up menu.

Entering text into a Web site — such as reservation information, passwords, credit card numbers, search terms, and so on — is as easy as tapping inside the text field. Safari brings up the keyboard for typing the text. You may want to rotate the iPod touch or iPhone sideways to view Web pages in landscape (horizontal) orientation so that the keyboard is wider and easier to use.

You can move to the next or previous text field by tapping the Next or Previous button at the top of the keyboard, or by tapping inside another text field. To finish typing with the keyboard, tap the Done button. If you don't like what you typed, use the Backspace key to delete it before tapping Done.

After you finish filling out all the required text fields on the page, tap Go on the keyboard (or tap Search, which some pages use rather than Go). If the Web page is a form, tapping Go automatically submits the form. Some Web pages offer a link for submitting the form, which you must tap to finish entering information.

Copying text

You may want to copy one or more paragraphs of text from a Web page to paste into another app (such as Notes) or into an e-mail message. Although you can e-mail a link to a Web page (as I show in the section "Sending a Web link by e-mail," later in this chapter), you may want to copy a section of text and then paste the section into the message itself.

To copy a section of text from a Web page, touch and hold somewhere within the section (also known as a "long tap"). Safari automatically highlights the section with selection handles on either end and displays the Copy bubble. (See Figure 19-4.) Tap Copy to copy the selection.

Figure 19-4: Copy a selected section of text on a Web page.

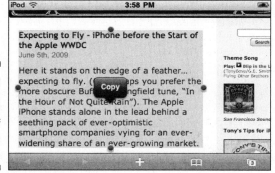

If you zoomed into the Web page and the "long tap" selects only a single word, try zooming out first (pinching) and then trying the "long tap" (touch and hold) again. You can also make a more precise selection by dragging one of the handles. A rectangular magnifier appears for dragging the handle precisely. When you remove your finger to stop dragging, the Copy bubble appears.

For details on pasting the selected text into apps such as Notes or into an e-mail message, see Chapter 3.

Bookmarking as You Go

The best way to keep track of Web pages you've visited and want to visit again is to create bookmarks for the pages. You can then quickly go back to that page by selecting the bookmark. The bookmarks in your iPod touch or iPhone synchronize with your Safari bookmarks on your Mac, or with your Safari or Internet Explorer bookmarks on your PC, as I describe in Chapter 10.

Saving a bookmark

Follow these steps to save a bookmark:

1. **Browse to the Web page you want.**

2. **Tap the plus (+) sign in the middle of the navigation bar (refer to Figure 19-2).**

   The special options menu appears with the Add Bookmark, Add to Home Screen, Mail Link to This Page, and Cancel buttons.

3. **Tap the Add Bookmark button to add a bookmark.**

   The name of the Web site appears in the title field, ready for editing, along with the on-screen keyboard. Below that is the actual URL for the Web page, and below that, the Bookmarks folder.

4. **(Optional) Edit the bookmark's title.**

   Before saving a bookmark, you can edit its title with the on-screen keyboard. Tap the circled *x* on the right side of the title field to clear its contents, or use the Backspace key on the keyboard to erase backward from the end of the title, and type the new title.

5. **(Optional) Choose a bookmark folder.**

   Before saving a bookmark, you can choose a bookmark folder for saving it; otherwise, Safari saves the bookmark in the topmost level of bookmarks. Tap Bookmarks to see the list of bookmark folders — you can flick to scroll the list quickly or drag it slowly. Select a bookmark folder by touching it.

6. **Tap the Save button to save the bookmark or tap Cancel to cancel.**

   The Save button appears in the upper-right corner of the display, and the Cancel button appears in the upper-left corner.

You can also edit your bookmarks and bookmark folders. Tap the Bookmarks button on the navigation bar and choose the folder to edit or the folder that has the bookmark you want to edit. Then tap the Edit button in the lower-left corner of the screen. The Edit Bookmarks display appears, with circled minus (–) signs next to the bookmark folders.

You can then do any of the following:

✔ To make a new folder within the selected folder, tap New Folder. If you want to create a new folder at the topmost level, first tap the Bookmarks button in the upper-left corner to go back to the topmost Bookmarks list, tap the Edit button, and then tap New Folder.

✔ To delete a bookmark or folder, tap next to the bookmark or folder and then tap Delete.

✔ To reposition a bookmark or folder, drag next to the item you want to move.

✔ To edit the name of a bookmark or folder, tap the bookmark or folder and use the on-screen keyboard to type the new title. (Tap the circled *x* in the title field to clear its contents first, if you want.)

✔ To change where a bookmark or folder is stored, tap the Bookmark Folder field for the selected bookmark or folder and then tap a new folder to hold the folder chosen for editing.

Tap the Done button in the lower-left corner of the Edit Bookmarks display to finish editing.

Sending a Web link by e-mail

As I describe in Chapter 20, your iPod touch or iPhone can send e-mail as well as receive it, as long as it's connected to the Internet. And if you want to share a Web page you just found with your friend, the steps are simple:

1. **Browse to the Web page and then tap the plus (+) sign in the middle of the navigation bar at the bottom of the screen. (Refer to Figure 19-2.)**

   A special options menu magically pops up from the bottom with the Add Bookmark, Add to Home Screen, and Mail Link to This Page buttons, along with a Cancel button.

2. **Tap the Mail Link to This Page button.**

   Keep in mind that you must have already set up an e-mail account on your iPod touch or iPhone, as I describe in Chapter 10.

   An e-mail message appears, ready for you to finish composing. The Subject field is already filled in with the Web page name, and the link itself is already inserted in the body of the message. The To and Cc fields are left blank — ready for you to fill in.

3. **Tap the circled plus (+) sign on the right side of the To field to select a name from your Contacts list, or use the on-screen keyboard to enter the e-mail address.**

   See Chapter 20 for details on sending an e-mail.

4. **Tap Send at the upper-right corner of the display to send the message.**

Bringing It All Back Home

You can add Web thumbnail icons for your favorite Web pages to the Home screen so that you can access the page with one touch. Web icons appear on the Home screen along with the icons of other apps. (Discover how to rearrange the icons and add multiple screens to the Home screen in Chapter 3.)

Follow these steps to add a Web site to your Home screen:

1. **Browse to the Web page you want.**

2. **Tap the plus (+) sign in the middle of the navigation bar.**

   The special options menu appears, with Add Bookmark, Add to Home Screen, Mail Link to This Page, and Cancel buttons.

3. **Tap the Add to Home Screen button.**

   The name of the Web site appears in the title field, ready for editing, along with the keyboard. The icon to be added to the Home screen — a thumbnail image of the site or a graphic image defined by the site for this purpose (usually a logo) — appears to the left of the title field.

4. **(Optional) Edit the Web icon's title.**

   Before saving a Web icon to the Home screen, you can edit its title with the keyboard. Tap the circled *x* on the right side of the title field to clear its contents, or use the Backspace key on the keyboard to erase backward from the end of the title and then type the new title.

5. **Tap the Add button to add the Web site icon, or tap Cancel to cancel.**

   The Add button appears in the upper-right corner of the display, and the Cancel button appears in the upper-left corner.

Chapter 20

The Postman Always Beeps Once

In This Chapter

▶ Checking and sending e-mail with an iPod touch or iPhone

▶ Changing message settings and sending options

▶ Setting the Push and Fetch features for optimal e-mail retrieval

*Y*our e-mail is just a touch away. The Mail app on your iPod touch or iPhone can display richly formatted messages, and you can send as well as receive photos and graphics, which are displayed in your message along with the text. You can even receive Portable Document Format (PDF) files, Microsoft Word documents, and Microsoft Excel spreadsheets as attachments and view them on your iPod touch or iPhone.

The Mail app can work in the background to retrieve your e-mail when your iPod touch is connected to Wi-Fi or your iPhone is connected to Wi-Fi or 3G. If you signed up for Apple's MobileMe service (formerly the .Mac service, now www.me.com), as I describe in illustrious detail in Chapter 10, your iPod touch or iPhone receives e-mail the instant it arrives in the mailbox on the MobileMe service. Services such as MobileMe, Microsoft Exchange, and Yahoo! Mail *push* e-mail messages to your iPod touch or iPhone so that they arrive immediately, automatically. You get a single beep when your mail has arrived (unless you turned off the New Mail sound effect, as I describe in Chapter 4).

Other types of e-mail services let you *fetch* e-mail from the server — when you select the account in Mail on your iPod touch or iPhone, Mail automatically starts fetching the e-mail, and you can browse your e-mail accounts or even use other apps while Mail fetches messages. You can also tell Mail to fetch more messages by tapping the Fetch (circular arrow) icon in the lower-left corner of the Mail, Mailboxes, or message screens.

Checking E-Mail

 You know that you have unread e-mail if the Mail icon on the Home screen shows a number — this is the number of unread messages in your inboxes. As e-mail is pushed (or fetched), this number increases until you read the messages. Tap the Mail icon to start the Mail app.

If you've set up an e-mail account, a list of mailboxes appears for that account, as shown in Figure 20-1 (left side). If you've set up more than one e-mail account, Mail displays the Accounts screen, listing the e-mail accounts you synchronized with your iPod touch or iPhone (see Figure 20-1, middle). Tap an account on the Accounts screen to view the mailboxes for that account (see Figure 20-1, right side). (See Chapter 10 for details on synchronizing, setting up, deleting, and changing settings for e-mail accounts.)

Figure 20-1:
A MobileMe account's mailboxes (left); multiple e-mail accounts (middle), and the mailbox (Inbox) of an AOL e-mail account (right).

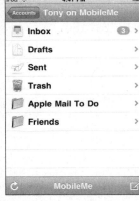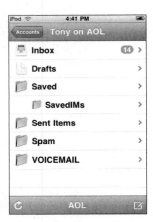

Next, tap Inbox in the list of mailboxes. A list of incoming message headers appears, as shown in Figure 20-2, with the sender's name, subject, and the first sentence or two of each message, along with a blue dot if the message hasn't been read yet.

The message is the medium

Tap a message header to read the message. You can scroll the message by flicking or dragging your finger, and zoom into and out of the message by unpinching and pinching with your fingers. You can also zoom directly into a column in the message by double-tapping the message, and zoom out by double-tapping it again.

Figure 20-2: Check out your incoming messages. A blue dot indicates an unread message.

If the e-mail includes an attachment, a button appears within the message showing the icon of an attached file and a right arrow, as shown in Figure 20-3 (left side) — to view the attachment, just tap the right arrow. If the format of the attached file is one of the supported formats (which include files that have the extensions .doc, .docx, .htm, .html, .pdf, .txt, .xls, and .xlsx), Mail downloads and opens the attachment as shown in Figure 20-3 (right side). If not, Mail displays a document icon with the name of the file — but you can't open it.

You can see all the recipients of a message (except Bcc, or *blind carbon copy,* recipients) by opening the message and tapping the blue word Details in the upper-right corner of the message. Tap a name or e-mail address that appears to see the recipient's contact information. Tap Hide to hide the recipients.

You can add the sender or recipient to your Contacts list on your iPod touch or iPhone by tapping the name or e-mail address. A screen appears with the Email, Create New Contact, and Add to Existing Contact buttons. Tap Create New Contact to create a new contact (or tap Add to Existing Contact if you want to add the information to an existing contact). Tap the Email button to send an e-mail to that recipient's address. (See the "Sending E-Mail" section, later in this chapter.)

Links appear in a message underlined in blue, and pictures embedded in the message may also have links. Tapping a link can take you to a Web page in Safari, open a map in Maps, or open a new preaddressed e-mail message in Mail. To return to your e-mail, press the physical Home button and tap Mail on the Home screen.

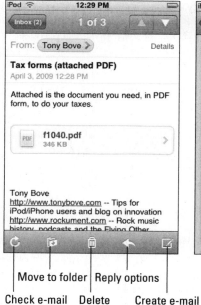

Figure 20-3:
The e-mail
message
appears
with an
attachment
(left side);
tap the right
arrow to
view the
attachment
(a PDF file).

Move to folder | Reply options

Check e-mail | Delete | Create e-mail

Attached PDF file

You can mark a message as unread so that it stays in your Inbox: Open the message, tap the blue word Details in the upper-right corner, and tap the blue Mark as Unread text next to the blue dot inside the message. The message is marked as unread — a blue dot appears next to the message header in the mailbox list until you open it again.

Deleting a message

To delete an open message, tap the Trash icon at the bottom center of the message display. Mail deletes the message from your iPod touch or iPhone (but *not* from your computer or mail server unless it's set up that way — see Chapter 10 for details on setting up e-mail accounts) and then displays the next message in sequence. You can also move to the previous or next message by tapping the up and down arrows in the upper-right corner.

You can also delete a message without opening it. In the list of message headers, drag your finger across a message header and tap the Delete button that appears.

To delete a list of messages quickly, choose the mailbox (such as Inbox) and tap the Edit button in the upper-right corner of the screen. The messages appear with empty circles next to them. Tap each message so that a check mark appears in the empty circle. After checking off the messages to delete, tap the Delete button in the lower-left corner.

Sending E-Mail

You can use the Mail app to reply to any message instantly and send e-mail to any e-mail address in the world. You can even send a message to a group of people without having to select each person's e-mail address.

To send an e-mail, follow these steps:

1. **Tap Mail on the Home screen.**

   The Accounts screen appears if you've set up more than one e-mail account, and you should look at Step 2; otherwise, the mailboxes appear for your account, and you can skip to Step 3.

2. **(Optional) Choose an e-mail account from the Accounts screen for sending the e-mail.**

   You can skip this step if you have only one e-mail account. If you have several e-mail accounts on your iPod touch or iPhone, you can select one of them or you can use the default account for sending e-mail. (See the next section in this chapter to set the default account.) You can also defer this decision until Step 6.

3. **Tap the pencil-document icon in the lower-right corner of the Mail screen.**

   The New Message screen appears, as shown in Figure 20-4, along with the keyboard. If you have multiple accounts set up on your iPod touch or iPhone, the default account for sending e-mail appears in the From field, as shown in Figure 20-4.

4. **Enter the recipient's e-mail address in the To field.**

   If your recipient is listed in your Contacts, tap the circled plus (+) sign in the To field (see Figure 20-4) and choose a contact to add the contact's e-mail address to the To field. You can repeat this process to add multiple e-mail addresses to the To field from your contacts.

   If your recipient isn't listed in your Contacts or if you don't know whether the recipient is listed, tap the To field entry and use the keyboard to type one or more e-mail addresses (and use a comma to separate each address). As you type an e-mail address, addresses that match from your Contacts list appear below. Tap one to add it to the To field.

Figure 20-4:
The New
Message
screen.

5. **(Optional) Add more addresses to the Cc or Bcc field.**

   You can add e-mail addresses to the Cc (carbon copy) and Bcc (blind carbon copy) fields to copy others. Whereas Cc addresses appear on messages received by recipients, indicating that they were copied on the message, Bcc addresses don't appear on messages received by recipients — they're like stealth readers. Tap the Cc/Bcc letters to expand the message to include the Cc and Bcc fields; then enter addresses the same way you do in Step 4.

6. **(Optional) Change the From address.**

   You can change the e-mail address for the sender to one of your e-mail accounts. The default e-mail account for sending e-mail is already selected; tap the From field (refer to Figure 20-4) to display a pop-up menu of e-mail accounts and then tap an e-mail account to use as the sender's account.

7. **Enter the e-mail subject.**

   Tap the Subject entry field (refer to Figure 20-4) to type a subject with the keyboard; then tap underneath the Subject field to type a message. Press Return on the keyboard when you're finished.

8. **Tap Send in the upper-right corner of the display (refer to Figure 20-4) to send the message.**

You can also forward and reply to any message you receive. Open the message and tap the curled left-arrow button that appears in the lower-left side of the message display. Then tap Reply to reply to the sender of the message, Reply All to reply to all the recipients as well as the sender (but not the Bcc recipients), or Forward to forward the message to someone else (or Cancel to go back to the message). The New Message screen appears with the keyboard so that you can type your reply or add a message to the one you're forwarding. Tap Send to send the reply or forwarded message.

When you reply to a message, files or images attached to the initial message aren't sent with the reply. When you tap Forward to forward a message, a pop-up menu with the Include and Don't Include buttons appears for a message with an attachment. Tap Include to include the attachment in the forwarded message, or tap Don't Include to forward the message without the attachment.

To save a message as a draft so that you can work on it later, start typing the message as described in the preceding steps, but before tapping Send, tap Cancel in the upper-left corner of the display (refer to Figure 20-4). Then, from the menu that appears, tap Save to save the message in your Drafts mailbox or tap Don't Save to discard the message (or Cancel to go back to typing the message). You can find the saved message in the Drafts mailbox of the same e-mail account. Tap the message to add to it or change it and then send it.

To send one or more photos in a message, tap Photos on the Home screen and select them as described in Chapter 18.

Message Settings and Sending Options

To change your e-mail message settings and sending options, choose Settings⇨Mail, Contacts, Calendars from the Home screen. In the Mail, Contacts, Calendars settings screen that appears, use your finger to scroll down to the Mail section to change your e-mail message settings and sending options, as shown in Figure 20-5.

In the Mail section, you can change global settings for messages in all accounts. To set the number of messages you can see at once in a mailbox, tap Show and then choose a setting. You can choose to see the most recent 25, 50, 75, 100, or 200 messages. (To download additional messages when you're in Mail, scroll to the bottom of your Inbox and tap Download More.)

Figure 20-5:
The Mail
section
of Mail,
Contacts,
and
Calendars
settings.

If you think you have shaky fingers and might delete a message by mistake, you can set Mail to confirm that you want to delete a message first before deleting. Tap the Off button to turn on the Ask before Deleting option. (Tap it again to turn it off.) If Ask before Deleting is on, Mail warns you first when you delete a message, and you have to tap Delete to confirm the deletion.

What you see is what you got

You can also set how many lines of each message are previewed in the message list headers. Choose Preview (refer to Figure 20-5) and then choose to see any amount from zero to five lines of each message. To set a minimum font size for messages, tap Minimum Font Size and then choose Small, Medium, Large, Extra Large, or Giant.

If you want to see all the images in your e-mails and don't mind waiting for the images to download, turn on the Load Remote Images option. If you leave it off, your messages appear faster but you have to touch each image icon to download and see each image.

If you care about whether a message was sent directly to you or whether you were sent it as a Cc copy (which still might make it important, but at least you know), you can set whether Mail shows the To and Cc labels in message lists. Tap the Off button for the Show To/Cc Label option to turn it on. (Tap it again to turn it off.) If the Show To/Cc Label option is on, you see To or Cc in the list next to each message.

Return to sender, address unknown

For those who are obsessive about making sure that e-mails are sent — and you know who you are — Mail can send you a copy of every message you send. Tap the Off button to turn on the Always Bcc Myself option. (Tap it again to turn it off.) The Bcc refers to *blind carbon copy,* and it means that your message is sent and copied back to you without your e-mail address appearing in the recipient's list.

You can add a *signature* to your messages that can include any text — not your real, handwritten scrawl but rather a listing of your name, title, phone number, favorite quote, or all of these — to personalize your e-mails. Tap Signature (refer to Figure 20-5) and then type a signature with the on-screen keyboard. The signature remains in effect for all future e-mails sent from your iPod touch or iPhone.

To set the default e-mail account for sending messages, tap Default Account (refer to Figure 20-5) and then choose an e-mail account. Your iPod touch or iPhone will use this account whenever you start the process of sending a message from another application, such as sending a photo from Photos or tapping the e-mail address of a business in Maps.

For details on synchronizing e-mail accounts automatically from iTunes or MobileMe, as well as for setting up an account, changing account settings, and deleting accounts manually on your iPod touch or iPhone, see Chapter 10.

If Not Push, Then Fetch

The Push and Fetch options control how your iPod touch or iPhone receives e-mail. You can set these options for all accounts and specifically for each account.

MobileMe, Microsoft Exchange, and Yahoo! Mail e-mail accounts can *push* messages *to* your iPod touch or iPhone so that they arrive immediately after arriving at the account's e-mail server. With other types of accounts, the Mail app *fetches* messages *from* the account's e-mail server — either on a time schedule or manually. (If manually, you select the account before the Mail app retrieves the e-mail.) Push accounts (such as MobileMe e-mail) can be set to either push or fetch.

You can turn the Push feature on or off as you please. Keeping it on uses more battery power because the iPod touch or iPhone receives messages immediately when it's connected to the Internet. When you turn the Push feature off, Mail fetches the e-mail from the accounts instead, and you can set the timetable for fetching, or set fetching to manual.

For optimal battery life, turn Push off and set Fetch to Manually so that Mail fetches only when you tap the e-mail account to read or send e-mail. Pushing e-mail as it arrives, or fetching e-mail often, uses up a considerable amount of battery power; doing both drains the battery even more quickly.

To turn Push on or off, choose Settings➪Mail, Contacts, Calendars from the Home screen and tap Fetch New Data. The Fetch New Data screen appears. Tap the On button for Push to turn it off (and vice versa).

If you like, set a timetable for fetching e-mail automatically so that you don't have to think about it. Choose a time interval on the Fetch New Data screen — pick Every 15 Minutes, Every 30 Minutes, or Hourly. You can also pick Manually so that Mail fetches only when you tap the e-mail account to read or send e-mail.

You can also set Push or Fetch settings for individual accounts. Scroll the Fetch New Data screen to the bottom and touch Advanced. The Advanced screen appears. Each account in the list shows Push or Fetch, depending on whether the account offers push e-mail. Tap the account to change its settings separately.

Setting Push to Off or setting Fetch to Manually on the Fetch New Data screen overrides the individual account settings.

Chapter 21

Using Applications on Your iPod or iPhone

In This Chapter

▶ Checking your calendar and entering events

▶ Entering and sorting your contacts

▶ Using the Maps app to find locations on an iPod touch or iPhone

▶ Keeping track of stocks and weather on an iPod touch or iPhone

▶ Recording voice memos

▶ Connecting to social networks on an iPod touch or iPhone

*A*s John Lennon once sang, "Life is what happens to you when you're busy making other plans." And while life happens to you in real time, you can consult your iPod or iPhone calendar to view your appointments, look up friends in your list of contacts, and record voice memos on what to do next. On an iPod touch or iPhone, you can change appointments in the calendar and contact your contacts, as I describe in this chapter.

The iPod classic and iPod nano are supplied with "extras" (in the Extras menu) such as Calendars, Contacts, and Voice Memos, as well as "click wheel" Games, and you can find more in the iTunes Store that you can download. The iPod touch and iPhone, on the other hand, can run many thousands of apps available in the App Store. (See Chapter 7 for details on downloading from the iTunes Store and App Store.) This chapter shows you how to use the Calendars, Contacts, and Voice Memos extras on an iPod classic or nano, as well as how to use the Calendar and Contacts apps supplied with your iPod touch or iPhone.

Your iPod touch or iPhone can also find almost anything on Earth, even itself, and show the location on a map or satellite picture. And although you can't harness the forces of nature, or even the influences that drive Wall Street, you can use your iPod touch or iPhone to make better guesses about the weather and the stock market — find out how in this chapter.

To socialize and stay in contact with friends, relatives, and associates, you can use social networks such as Facebook and MySpace to share photos, thoughts, links, and profile information. The App Store offers social networking apps that link you directly to these networks and to messaging sites such as Twitter. You'll find all this and more in this chapter on your social life with iPod touch.

To find out how to sync your iPod classic or nano with "click wheel" Games from the iTunes Store, and to play those games, visit this book's companion Web site.

Checking Your Calendar

The calendar in your iPod or iPhone isn't just for looking up dates (though it's quite good at that). If you see a blank calendar, it means that you need to synchronize your iPod or iPhone with your calendar files from iCal (Mac) or Outlook (Windows), or from MobileMe, as I describe in Chapter 10.

On an iPod touch or iPhone, tap Calendar on the Home screen. Here's what happens:

- ✔ **If this is your first visit to the Calendar app and you've synchronized multiple calendars to your iPod touch or iPhone,** a list of your calendars appears (see Figure 21-1, left side). Tap All at the top to view all calendars merged into one or tap a specific calendar to see only that calendar. The calendar appears in a monthly view by default (see Figure 21-1, right side).
- ✔ **If you opened Calendar before,** the app shows the calendar and view opened previously.

Tap any day to see the events on that day, which are displayed below the calendar view in a list.

Tap the List, Day, or Month button to change the calendar view to a list of events, a full day of scheduled appointments, or a month view, respectively. If you roam around from day to day or month to month, tap the Today button in the lower-left corner of the display to see the calendar for today.

On an iPod nano or iPod classic, choose Extras⇨Calendars. If you've synchronized multiple calendars, a list of calendars appears with All Calendars at the top. Press the Select button to select All Calendars for a merged view of all your calendars, or scroll the click wheel and press the Select button to select a specific calendar. You can then scroll the click wheel to go through the days of the calendar. Select an event to see its details. Press the Next and Previous buttons to skip to the next or previous month. To see your To-Do list, choose Extras⇨Calendars⇨To Do's.

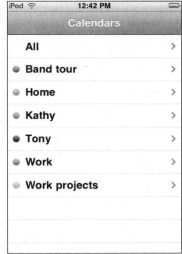 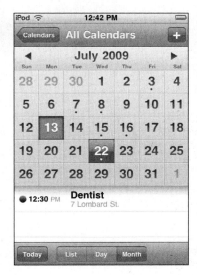

Figure 21-1:
The
Calendar
app's list of
calendars
(left) and
monthly
view (right).

A change is gonna come (iPod touch or iPhone)

Change happens, and you'll want to change your schedule or even add new events as you learn about them. Although you can enter appointments and events on your computer and sync them with your iPod touch or iPhone, as I point out in Chapter 10, you can also enter and change appointments and events directly in your iPod touch or iPhone and keep changes and additions synced with your computer.

To add an event, follow these steps:

1. **Open the Calendar app as described earlier.**

   The Calendar app opens. Either the Calendar screen appears (refer to Figure 21-1, right side), or if you have multiple calendars, the list of calendars appears (refer to Figure 21-1, left side) — in which case you need to tap a calendar to see the Calendar screen.

2. **Tap the plus (+) sign in the upper-right corner of the Calendar screen.**

   The Add Event screen appears, as shown in Figure 21-2 (left side).

3. **Tap the Title/Location button, and enter the event's title and location using the on-screen keyboard.**

   The Title and Location fields appear along with the on-screen keyboard, as shown in Figure 21-2 (right side).

Figure 21-2:
Add an
event in
Calendar
(left) and
give it a title
and location
(right).

4. **Tap Save in the upper-right corner to save the entry (or Cancel in the upper-left corner to cancel the entry).**

   The Add Event screen appears again for selecting more options, as shown in Figure 21-3 (left side).

5. **Tap the Starts/Ends button to enter the starting and ending times and dates.**

   The Start & End screen appears, as shown in Figure 21-3 (right side), with a slot-machine-style number wheel to select the date and time.

6. **Tap the Starts button and select the date and time, or tap the Off button for All-Day to turn on the All-Day option.**

   Slide your finger up and down the slot-machine-style number wheel to select the date and time. If you turn on the All-Day option, the number wheel changes to show only dates; select a date for the all-day event and skip the next step.

7. **Tap the Ends button, and select the date and time as you did in Step 6.**

8. **Tap Save in the upper-right corner to save the entry (or Cancel in the upper-left corner to cancel the entry).**

   The Add Event screen appears again for selecting more options (refer to Figure 21-3, left side).

9. **(Optional) Set the event to repeat by tapping Repeat and selecting a repeat time; then tap Save (or Cancel).**

   You can set the event to repeat every day, every week, every two weeks, every month, or every year (or Never, to not repeat). After you tap Save or Cancel, the Add Event screen appears again for selecting more options.

Figure 21-3:
Tap Starts/
Ends (left)
and enter
starting
and ending
dates and
times (right).

10. **(Optional) Set an alert for a time before the event by tapping Alert and choosing an alert time; then tap Save (or Cancel).**

    You can set the alert to occur from five minutes to two days before the event. You can also set a second alert time in case you miss the first one. After you tap Save or Cancel, the Add Event screen appears again for selecting more options.

11. **(Optional) If you have multiple calendars synced with your iPod touch or iPhone, you can change the calendar for the event by tapping Calendar and choosing a calendar.**

    The Calendars screen appears with a list of your calendars. Tap a calendar's name to choose it. After you tap Save or Cancel, the Add Event screen appears again for changing event options.

12. **(Optional) Enter notes about the event by tapping Notes and using the on-screen keyboard to type notes.**

    The Notes field appears along with the keyboard so that you can type your notes. After you tap Save or Cancel, the Add Event screen appears again for changing event options.

13. **Tap Done in the upper-right corner of the Add Event screen to save the event (or Cancel in the upper-left corner to cancel the event).**

    The new event now appears in your calendar in the lower portion of the Calendar screen when you select the day (refer to Figure 21-1, right side).

To edit an event, tap the event in the lower portion of the Calendar screen and then tap Edit in the upper-right corner of the Event screen. The event information appears and is ready for editing or deleting. To edit the event information, follow Steps 3–13 in this section.

The Delete Event button appears at the bottom of the event information only when you're editing an event. After tapping Delete Event, a warning appears to confirm the deletion — tap Delete Event again or tap Cancel. The Calendar screen appears.

Yesterday's settings (and today's)

If the calendar events you synced from your computer include alarms, you can turn on your iPod classic or iPod nano calendar alarm so that it beeps for those events. Choose Extras⇨Calendars⇨Alarms. Select Alarms once to set the alarm to Beep, select Alarms twice to set it to None (so that only the message for the alarm appears), or select it a third time to set it to Off. (The Alarms choices cycle from Beep to None to Off and then back to Beep.) For details on setting alarms, see Chapter 4.

On an iPod touch or iPhone, you can set alerts for meeting invitations and choose how many weeks of events to sync back to (to clear out old events). Choose Settings⇨Mail, Contacts, Calendars from the Home screen and then scroll the Mail, Contacts, Calendars settings screen to the Calendars section, as shown in Figure 21-4 (left side).

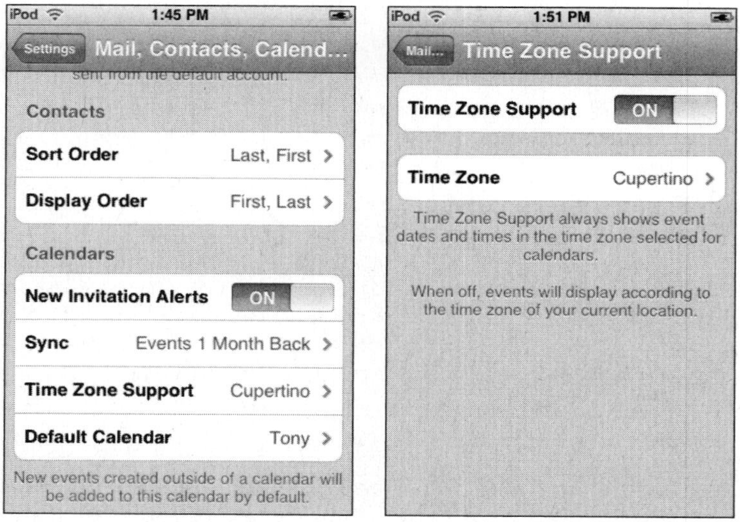

Figure 21-4: The Contacts and Calendars sections for settings (left) and the Time Zone setting (right).

iPod 🔋	1:45 PM	📷
Settings	Mail, Contacts, Calend...	

sent from the default account.

Contacts

Sort Order	Last, First >
Display Order	First, Last >

Calendars

New Invitation Alerts	ON
Sync	Events 1 Month Back >
Time Zone Support	Cupertino >
Default Calendar	Tony >

New events created outside of a calendar will be added to this calendar by default.

iPod 🔋	1:51 PM	📷
Mail...	Time Zone Support	

Time Zone Support	ON

Time Zone	Cupertino >

Time Zone Support always shows event dates and times in the time zone selected for calendars.

When off, events will display according to the time zone of your current location.

To set the option for how far back in time to sync your calendar events, tap Sync and choose a period of time (such as Events 2 Weeks Back).

If you have a Microsoft Exchange account set up with Calendars enabled, you can receive and respond to meeting invitations from others in your organization that also use Exchange. To set a sound as an alert for receiving a meeting invitation, tap the Off button for New Invitation Alerts to turn it on.

You can also turn time zone support on or off. When time zone support is on, event dates and times are displayed in the time zone of the city you selected. When time zone support is off, events are displayed in the time zone of your current location as determined by the network time. You might want to turn it on and select your home city so that dates and times are displayed as if you were in your home city, rather than where you actually are. For example, if you live in San Francisco and you're visiting New York, turning on time zone support and selecting San Francisco keeps the dates and times in your calendars on San Francisco time. Otherwise, they would switch to New York time.

To turn on time zone support, tap Time Zone Support, and on the Time Zone Support screen (refer to Figure 21-4, right side), tap Off to turn on time zone support (or tap On to turn it off). Then tap Time Zone and enter the name of a major city. As you type, city names are suggested based on what you've typed. Select the city to return to the Time Zone Support screen and then tap the Mail button in the upper-left corner to return to the settings screen — or, if you're finished making changes, press the physical Home button to leave settings altogether and return to the Home screen.

You can set your iPod touch or iPhone to play a beeping sound for your calendar alert. Choose Settings➪General➪Sounds and tap the Off button for Calendar Alerts to turn it on. (Tap it again to turn it off.)

Using Your Contacts

The bits of information that you're most likely to need on the road are people's names, addresses, and phone numbers. An iPod or iPhone can store that stuff (in the Contacts format) right alongside your music. To see how to sync your personal contacts info on your computer with the info on your iPod or iPhone, check out Chapter 10.

To view contacts on an iPod touch or iPhone, tap the Contacts icon on the Home screen. The All Contacts screen appears. If you've organized contacts into groups, you can tap the Groups button in the upper-left corner of the screen to show the Groups screen, and then tap a group to see just that group, or tap All Contacts to return to the All Contacts screen.

The contact list is sorted automatically in alphabetical order by last name (in bold) but displayed so that the first name comes first, as shown in Figure 21-5 (left side). Scroll the list of contacts with your finger or tap a letter of the alphabet along the right side to go directly to names that begin with that letter. Then tap a contact to see that person's info screen.

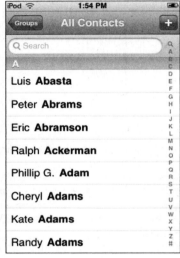

Figure 21-5: Scroll the alphabetical list or tap a letter along the right side (left) or search by typing part of a name (right).

The contact's info screen shows all the information about reaching that contact. Tap an e-mail address to bring up the Mail app and send an e-mail to that contact. Tap a Web site address to load that page into Safari. Tap a physical address (with a street address) to bring up the Maps app and locate the contact on the map.

To view a contact on an iPod classic or iPod nano, choose Extras⇨Contacts from the main menu. If you've organized contacts into groups, a list of groups appears, with All Contacts at the top. Press the Select button to select All Contacts, or scroll the click wheel and press the Select button to select a group. You can then scroll the list of contacts and select a contact. The contact list is sorted automatically in alphabetical order by first name and then last name, or by last name followed by first name.

Orders to sort and display

You can change which way the contacts sort so that you can look up people by their first names (which can be time-consuming with so many friends named Elvis).

On an iPod touch or iPhone, choose Settings➪Mail, Contacts, Calendars from the Home screen and then scroll the Mail, Contacts, Calendars settings screen to the Contacts section (refer to Figure 21-4, left side). Tap Sort Order and then tap one of these options:

- ✔ **First, Last:** Sorts the contact list by first name, followed by the last name, so that *Brian Jones* sorts under the letter *B* for *Brian* (after *Brian Auger* but before *Brian Wilson*).

- ✔ **Last, First:** Sorts the contacts by last name, followed by the first name, so that *Brian Jones* sorts under the letter *J* for *Jones*. (*Jones, Brian* appears after *Jones, Alice* but before *Jones, Norah*.)

On an iPod nano or iPod classic, choose Settings➪General➪Sort Contacts and then press the Select button in the scrolling pad for each option:

- ✔ **First:** Sorts the contact list by first name, followed by the last name.
- ✔ **Last:** Sorts the contacts by last name, followed by the first name.

You can also change the way contacts are listed on an iPod touch or iPhone — with either their first names followed by their last names or their last names followed by their first names — regardless of how you sort them. Choose Settings➪Mail, Contacts, Calendars and then scroll the Contacts, Calendars settings screen to the Contacts section (refer to Figure 21-4, left side). Tap Display Order and then tap one of these options:

- ✔ **First, Last:** Displays the contacts list by first name and then last name, as in *Paul McCartney*.

- ✔ **Last, First:** Displays the contacts list by last name followed by a comma and the first name, as in *McCartney, Paul*.

Soul searchin' on an iPod touch or iPhone

Can't remember the person's full name or last name? You can search for any part of a person's name in Contacts on an iPod touch or iPhone by tapping the Search entry field at the very top of the list of contacts. The search-entry field appears with the keyboard (see Figure 21-5, right side), and suggestions appear as you type.

Tap a suggested name to view the Contacts record for that person. You can then edit or delete the contact information.

Adding, editing, and deleting contacts on an iPod touch or iPhone

You meet people all the time, so why not enter their information immediately? You can enter new contacts, edit existing contacts, and even delete contacts directly on your iPod touch or iPhone, and keep your contacts in sync with your computer. (For sync info, see Chapter 10.)

To add a contact, follow these steps:

1. **Tap the Contacts icon on the Home screen.**

2. **Tap the plus (+) sign in the upper-right corner of the Contacts display.**

   The New Contact screen appears, as shown in Figure 21-6 (left side).

3. **Tap the First Last button and enter the contact's first and last name, as well as the company name, using the keyboard.**

   The First, Last, and Company fields appear on the Add Name screen (see Figure 21-6, right side) along with the keyboard.

4. **Tap Save in the upper-right corner of the Add Name screen to save the name (or Cancel in the upper-left corner to cancel the name).**

   The New Contact screen appears again for selecting more options (refer to Figure 21-6, left side).

Figure 21-6:
Add a new contact (left) and enter the contact's name (right).

5. **Tap the Add New Phone button and enter the phone number and label for the number.**

   The Add Phone screen appears with a numeric keyboard for typing the number. Tap the field under the number to select a label for the type of phone (mobile, home, work, main, home fax, and so on).

   To enter a pause in a phone number (sometimes required for extensions or code numbers), tap the +*# button and tap Pause, which inserts a comma representing the pause. Each pause lasts two seconds; you can enter as many as you need.

6. **Tap Save in the upper-right corner of the Add Phone screen to save the phone number (or Cancel in the upper-left corner to cancel the entry).**

   The New Contact screen appears again for adding more information.

7. **Tap the Add New Email button to add an e-mail address using the on-screen keyboard and select a label for the type of e-mail address.**

   The Add Email screen appears with a field to enter the information, a button to set the label describing it, and the on-screen keyboard.

8. **Tap Save in the upper-right corner to save the entry (or Cancel in the upper-left corner to cancel the entry).**

   The New Contact screen appears again for adding more information.

9. **(Optional) Repeat Steps 7 and 8 with the Add New URL button to add a new URL (Web site address) for the contact.**

10. **Tap Add New Address on the New Contact screen, and add street (or P.O. Box) information, city, state, zip code, and country.**

    The keyboard appears with two entry fields for Street and one each for City, State, and Zip. Tap the country button to set the country and the label button (set to home) for the type of address.

11. **Tap Save in the upper-right corner to save the address (or Cancel in the upper-left corner to cancel it).**

    The New Contact screen appears again for adding more information.

12. **(Optional) Tap Add Field to add more fields to the contact. When you're done, tap Save (or Cancel).**

    You can add a prefix, middle name, suffix, phonetic first and last names, nickname, job title, department, birthday, date, or note. Tap each field, and use the keyboard to type in the information. Tapping Save or Cancel returns you to the New Contact screen.

13. **(Optional) Add a photo.**

    To add a photo, tap Add Photo in the upper-left corner of the New Contact screen. A pop-up menu appears with Take Photo (iPhone only), Choose Existing Photo, or Cancel. The Take Photo option takes you to the Take Picture screen, where you can tap the camera shutter button to take a picture. (See Chapter 18 for details on taking pictures.) The Choose Existing Photo option takes you to the Photos app, where you can tap a photo album and then tap a photo. Finally, tap Set Photo (or Cancel).

14. **Tap Save in the upper-right corner of the New Contact screen to save the contact information (or Cancel in the upper-left corner to cancel the contact information).**

To edit a contact, tap the contact to see the contact's Info screen and then tap Edit in the upper-right corner of the Info screen to show the circled minus (–) sign and plus (+) sign buttons.

You can edit or delete any information for a contact while leaving the rest of the information intact. Tap any field to edit the information in that field. Tap the circled minus (–) sign next to the information to reveal a Delete button. Tap the Delete button to delete the information, or tap the circled minus sign again to leave it alone.

To change a photo, tap the existing photo in the upper-left corner of the Info screen. A pop-up menu appears for you to tap Take Photo (iPhone only), Choose Existing Photo, Edit Photo, Delete Photo, or Cancel. Tap Choose Existing Photo to choose a photo from the Photo app library, as described in Step 13 earlier.

Tap Done in the upper-right corner of the Info screen to finish editing and return to the contact information.

To delete a contact entirely, tap Edit, scroll down to the bottom, and then tap Delete Contact. Remember, if you do this, the contact will also be deleted from your contact list on your computer when you sync your iPod touch or iPhone.

Earth, Wind, and Finance on Your iPod touch or iPhone

You can use the Maps app to find any location on Earth and obtain driving directions — without having to ask someone out on the street. Your iPod touch or iPhone offers Location Services to nail down the unit's physical location, and it offers that information to the Maps app and any other app that needs it, so you can instantly find out where you are in the world.

Your iPod touch or iPhone also runs apps that can connect to the Internet — such as the Weather and Stocks apps to display the most recent information. You can personalize the Stocks app to reflect your exact portfolio, and you can add cities to the Weather app to check conditions before you travel to them.

Consulting Maps

The Maps app provides street maps, satellite photos, and hybrid street-satellite views of locations all over the world. It also offers detailed driving directions from any location to just about any other location — unless you can't get there from here.

Tap Maps on the Home screen and a map appears, as shown in Figure 21-7 (left side), ready for zooming, scrolling, or searching specific locations. To find out where you are, tap the Compass icon in the lower-left corner of the map screen. A dialog appears, asking whether Maps can use your current location; tap OK to use it. The map then changes to show your general location with a compass-like circle representing your approximate physical location, as shown in Figure 21-7 (right side). This circle continues to shrink as Maps retrieves more-accurate information.

You can zoom in to the map by double-tapping the map with one finger or unpinching with your fingers. To zoom out, pinch with your fingers or double-tap with two fingers. You can also drag the map to pan around it and see more areas.

To find a location and see a map, tap the search-entry field at the top of the Maps screen (refer to Figure 21-7, left side). The keyboard appears so that you can enter information. You can find any location by its address or closest landmark, or you can find the physical address of a friend: Type the name of someone in your contacts list or an address, an intersection, the name of a landmark or of a general area, or a zip code.

Search entry   Bookmarks

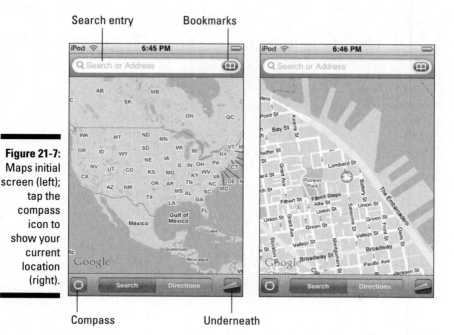

Figure 21-7:
Maps initial
screen (left);
tap the
compass
icon to
show your
current
location
(right).

Compass   Underneath

For example, to search for a friend, start typing the person's name. If the letters you type match any names with street addresses in your Contacts list, Maps offers them up as suggestions. Tap a suggested name to look up that person's home or business address.

To search for a landmark, an intersection, a zip code, or a type of business, type as much as you know into the Search field — such as **94111 pizza** for a pizza shop in the 94111 zip code. If the landmark is well known, type its name, as shown in Figure 21-8 (left side). Then tap the Search key on the keyboard. A red pin appears to mark the location you've searched for on the map (see Figure 21-8, right side), with a label showing the address.

To clear the entry from the Search field quickly, tap the *x* on the right side of the field. You can then type a new search term.

Figure 21-8: Type a search term and tap the Search button (left) to see the location (right).

If you search for the name of a business or type of business *after* searching for your own location, Maps is smart enough to locate the closest ones. Multiple pins appear on the map, showing the location of each business.

To bookmark a location after searching for it, tap the circled right arrow on the right side of the pin's label (refer to Figure 21-8, right side) to open the Info screen, as shown in Figure 21-9 (left side). You can then mark the spot with a bookmark that includes a name and description or do other things such as get directions. Tap the Add to Bookmarks button on the Info screen, which brings up the keyboard so that you can type a name for the location, as shown in Figure 21-9 (right side). Tap Save in the upper-right corner of the Add Bookmark screen to save the bookmark (or Cancel to cancel the bookmark). Tap Map in the upper-left corner of the Info screen to go back to the map.

To go directly to a bookmarked location, tap the Bookmarks icon to the right of the search-entry field (refer to Figure 21-7) and then tap a location, or tap the Done button in the upper-right corner to return to the map.

Figure 21-9:
The Info
screen
for the
location
(left) for
saving a
bookmark
(right).

Do you want to see what the location looks like? You can change the view of the location to show a satellite image (if available), a hybrid of street view and satellite, or a list of bookmarked locations. Tap the Underneath button — the curled-page icon in the lower-right corner (refer to Figure 21-7, left side) — to see a menu underneath the map. Then tap Satellite to view a satellite image of the site. You can zoom in to the image the same way you zoom in to the map. You can also view a hybrid of satellite image and street map — tap the Underneath button and then tap Hybrid in the menu underneath the map.

To get driving directions from one location to another, you first need to search for or pinpoint a location and then tap Directions at the bottom of the map screen (refer to Figure 21-8, right side).

For example, if you want to get directions from your current location to a bookmarked location, first find your physical location on the map by tapping the compass icon in the lower-left corner of the map screen (refer to Figure 21-7, right side). Then tap Directions, and in the Directions screen that appears, your current location already occupies the Start field. Tap the Bookmarks icon in the End field and select a bookmarked location for the End field, as shown in Figure 21-10 (left side).

You can tap a pin on a map to see the Info screen for that location, and then tap Directions to Here or Directions from Here to get directions. The Directions screen appears, with the first location selected as either the Start or End. You can also type entries for both the Start and End fields by tapping those fields and using the keyboard.

After setting your Start and End locations, tap Route in the lower-right corner of the keyboard (refer to Figure 21-10, left side) to mark the route on the map. Alternatively, you can tap Clear in the upper-left corner to reenter your Start and End fields, or Cancel in the upper-right corner to cancel getting directions.

You can switch the entry for Start to End (or vice versa) by tapping the looped arrow button to the left of the Start and End fields. Using this button, you can get directions one way; then tap the button to reverse the Start and End fields to get directions for the way back.

As shown in Figure 21-10 (right side), the route on the map in the Overview screen is purple, with pins marking the start and end locations. Touch the car icon at the top of the Overview screen to see driving directions and the approximate driving time. If traffic data is available, the driving time is adjusted accordingly, but don't expect miracles — the information depends on data collected and services provided by third parties, not by Apple, and traffic patterns change. You can also touch the bus icon to see public transit directions, or the walking-man icon to see walking directions.

To view directions one step at a time on the map, tap Start in the upper-right corner of the Overview screen (refer to Figure 21-10, right side) to see the first leg of the journey. Then tap the right-arrow button in the upper-right corner of the first leg's screen to see the next stretch. You can also tap the left-arrow button in any of the step-by-step directions to go back a step. The Maps app patiently walks you through your entire journey.

Figure 21-10:
Set the start
and end
locations
(left) and tap
Directions
(right).

To view all the legs of your journey in a list, tap the Underneath icon in the lower-right corner of the display and tap List. Then tap any location in the list to see a map showing that leg of the trip.

Riding the storms with Weather

The Weather app provided with your iPod touch or iPhone looks up the current temperature and weather conditions, and it provides a six-day forecast for any city of your choice. Weather isn't the only app that does this — you can try other apps such as The Weather Channel, WeatherBug, or AccuWeather (all free).

To use Weather, tap Weather on the Home screen. In daytime, the weather screen is light blue, and at night, it's dark purple. What makes Weather useful is your ability to add your own cities — as many as you need — so that you can look up the weather in multiple locations instantly.

To add a city, follow these steps:

1. **Tap the *i* button in the lower-right corner of the weather display for your city, as shown in Figure 21-11 (left side).**

2. **Tap the plus (+) sign in the upper-left corner of the Weather screen (Figure 21-11, center).**

   A location field appears with the on-screen keyboard (Figure 21-11, right side).

3. **Enter the city's name or zip code — as you type, suggestions appear below in a list.**

4. **Choose one of the suggestions or continue typing the city name or zip code and then tap Search.**

The city you chose appears in the list of cities on the Weather screen, with a circled minus (–) sign next to it on the left and three horizontal gray bars on the right.

At this point, you can add more cities by tapping the plus (+) sign in the upper-left corner again. You can also reorder the list of cities by dragging the three gray bars next to a city to a new place in the list.

To delete a city, tap the circled minus sign next to the city name (refer to Figure 21-11, center) to show the Delete button. Then tap the Delete button to delete it (or tap the circled minus sign again to leave it alone).

Figure 21-11:
Tap the *i*
button in
Weather
(left) to view
the list of
cities (cen-
ter) and to
add another
city (right).

Tap the Done button in the upper-right corner of the Weather screen to finish adding cities and see the weather display for your city.

To switch from one city to the next, flick your finger over the city weather display horizontally or tap the tiny white buttons at the bottom of the city weather display (refer to Figure 21-11, left side).

Tapping your money maker with Stocks

You can check your financial stocks, funds, and indexes with your iPod touch or iPhone as long as it's connected to the Internet. (Whether the news is good or bad, you can quickly e-mail your broker — see Chapter 20.)

Tap Stocks on the Home screen. The Stocks app displays a few stocks and indexes you may be interested in (such as Apple and Google), and it shows updated quotes (although quotes may be delayed by up to 20 minutes). Scroll the Stocks list by dragging or flicking it with your finger.

Swipe the lower section of the Stocks screen to see either a summary, a graph (as shown in Figure 21-12, left side), or the latest news. To see a current graph of the stock, swipe the lower section to the center and tap the 1d (one day), 1w (one week), 1m (one month), 3m (three months), 6m (six months), 1y (one year), or 2y (two years) button above the graph in the stock reader. Tap the change number next to each stock to switch to show the percentage change, the market capitalization, or the change in price.

Of course, you'll want to add your portfolio to Stocks. To add a stock, index, or fund to watch, here's what you do:

1. **Tap the *i* button in the lower-right corner of the stock reader, as shown in Figure 21-12 (left side).**

2. **Tap the plus (+) sign in the upper-left corner of the Stocks screen (Figure 21-12, center).**

   The Add Stock field appears with the keyboard (Figure 21-12, right side).

3. **Enter the stock symbol or company name (or index or fund name).**

   As you type, suggestions appear below in a list.

4. **Choose one of the suggestions or continue typing the symbol or name and then touch Search.**

The stock, fund, or index you chose appears in the list on the Stocks screen, with a circled minus (–) sign next to it on the left and three horizontal gray bars on the right.

Figure 21-12:
Touch the
i button in
Stocks (left)
to view the
list (center)
and to add
another
stock, fund,
or index
(right).

At this point, if you want to add more stocks, funds, or indexes, tap the plus (+) sign in the upper-left corner again. To reorder a list of stocks, drag the three gray bars next to a stock to a new place in the list.

To delete a stock, tap the circled minus sign next to the stock name (refer to Figure 21-12, center) to show the Delete button. Then tap the Delete button to delete it (or tap the circled minus sign again to leave it alone).

Tap the Done button in the upper-right corner of the Stocks screen to finish adding stocks and see the stock reader.

Recording Voice Memos

An iPod touch can record audio through an external microphone (such as the Apple Earphones with Remote and Mic), while an iPhone can use either the external mic or its built-in mic. An iPod nano can record voice memos using its built-in mic on the back next to the video camera, or using an iPod nano–compatible microphone. An iPod classic can record voice memos using the optional Apple Earphones with Remote and Mic or an iPod classic-compatible microphone. You can find external mics for purchase at the Apple Store.

Voice memos can be up to two hours long. If you record for more than two hours, your iPod or iPhone automatically starts a new voice memo to continue your recording. After syncing with iTunes (as I describe in Chapter 9), the voice memos appear in the Music section of your iTunes library and in the Voice Memos playlist (created for you if you don't already have one).

Recording on an iPod touch or iPhone

The Voice Memos app lets you record audio through an external microphone (such as the Apple In-Ear Headphones with Remote and Mic) connected to an iPod touch or iPhone, or through the internal microphone of an iPhone. You can then send recordings to others by e-mail (or by text message on an iPhone, if your account with your carrier supports MMS), or sync them back to your computer's iTunes library.

To start recording, tap the Voice Memos app on the Home screen and then tap the red dot button on the left side of the VU meter on the microphone recording screen. (You can also press the center button on the control capsule of the Apple In-Ear Headphones to start recording.) The red dot changes to a Pause button, as shown in Figure 21-13 (left side), and the list button on the right side of the VU meter changes to a Stop button. Tap the Pause or Stop button to stop recording.

Tap the list button on the right side of the VU meter to see the Voice Memos screen with your list of recordings, as shown in Figure 21-13 (middle). Select a recording, and you can then tap Share to send it by e-mail, or Delete to delete it. After tapping Share, tap Email Voice Memo to open a new e-mail message with the recording (or tap Cancel). See Chapter 20 for details on sending an e-mail.

You can also tap the Play/Pause button on the left of the recording to play it, and tap the right arrow on the far right side of the recording to open the Info screen for that recording, as shown in Figure 21-13 (right side).

Figure 21-13: Record your voice (left), select a saved recording (middle), and open the Info screen (right).

The Info screen also lets you trim the recording so that it's shorter — tap Trim Memo to view the playback timeline, as shown in Figure 21-14, and tap along the timeline to set a stop time. Then tap Trim Voice Memo (or Cancel to cancel).

Touch Voice Memos in the upper-left corner of the Info screen to return to the Voice Memos screen, and tap Done in the upper-right corner to return to the microphone recording screen.

Figure 21-14: Trim your voice recording before sharing it.

Recording on an iPod nano or iPod classic

The Voice Memos Extra in your iPod nano or iPod classic lets you record voice memos through an external mic or, in the case of the iPod nano, through the internal mic. (Be careful not to block the mic, which is on the back.) To record voice memos with an iPod classic, first connect the Apple Earphones with Remote and Mic, or connect an external mic to the Dock connection — you won't see a Voice Memos menu item if you've never connected a mic to the iPod classic.

To start recording with an iPod nano, choose Extras➪Voice Memos from the main menu — the Record screen appears, showing a microphone. Press the Play/Pause button or the Select button to begin recording, and press it again to pause recording. After pausing, you can select Resume to continue recording, or just press Play/Pause again. To finish, press the Menu button, and then highlight Stop and Save and press the Select button. Your saved recording is listed by date and time.

To start recording with an iPod classic, choose Voice Memos➪Start Recording from the main menu. Recording starts immediately. Press the Play/Pause button to pause recording. After pausing, you can select Resume to continue recording, or Stop and Save to stop and save it. Your saved recording is listed by date and time.

You can set a chapter mark in your voice memo on an iPod nano to go back to that section quickly. While recording, press the Select button whenever you want to set a chapter mark. During playback, you can go directly to the next chapter by pressing the Next/Fast-forward button. Press Previous/Rewind once to go to the start of the current chapter, and twice to go to the start of the previous chapter.

To play or delete a recording on an iPod nano, choose Extras➪Voice Memos, press the Menu button, select Voice Memos, and then choose a recording. Select Play and then press the Select button to start playing the recording, or Delete to delete the recording. When you sync your voice memos with your iTunes library, they are automatically deleted from your iPod nano.

To play a recording on an iPod classic, choose Extras➪Voice Memos and then select the recording. When you sync your voice memos with your iTunes library, they are automatically deleted from your iPod classic.

A Day in the Social Life on an iPod touch or iPhone

Connecting socially on a digital network isn't new — I connected to friends way back in the pre-Internet dark ages by using exotic-sounding networks such as Usenet, bulletin board systems (BBS), The Source, CompuServe, the WELL (Whole Earth 'Lectronic Link), and EIES (Murray Turoff's server-based Electronic Information Exchange Service). What's new is that more sophisticated social networks have appeared and gone mainstream very quickly, with MySpace, Facebook, and Twitter leading the pack.

You can use your iPod touch or iPhone to stay in touch with your connections on these and many other social networks on the Internet — viewing and typing messages, chatting, uploading and sharing photos, joining groups, and so on.

Ain't it good to know you've got a Facebook friend

Facebook is the fastest-growing free-access social networking site as of this writing, with more than 200 million active users worldwide. If you're one of them (as I am), you already know that you can add friends, send them messages, and update your personal profile with photos, videos, links, and all sorts of Facebook widgets that extend the service's functions. Although you can do all this using a browser on your computer and using Safari on your iPod touch or iPhone, the site itself is far too cumbersome for easy access that way. What's needed is a "baby Facebook" on the iPod touch or iPhone.

And that's exactly what Facebook for iPhone is: This app — which also runs on the iPod touch — lets you check your friends' status updates and photos, start a conversation in Facebook Chat, and upload images from your iPod touch or iPhone.

 After downloading the Facebook app (see Chapter 7 for details on downloading apps from the App Store), tap Facebook on the Home screen and then log in to your Facebook account, as shown in Figure 21-15 (left side). Your Facebook home screen appears, as shown in Figure 21-15 (center), showing your news feed. Tap the multiple-squares button in the upper left corner to see the Facebook icons for all of the app's features, as shown in Figure 21-15 (right side). If you have any messages in your Inbox, a number appears on top of the Inbox icon (refer to Figure 21-15, right side).

Figure 21-15:
Log in
to your
Facebook
account
(left) to
see your
Facebook
home
news feed
(center)
and more
choices
(right).

After logging in, the Facebook app remembers your username and password so that you don't have to type them to log in again. (Of course, that means if anyone grabs your iPod touch or iPhone, they'll have access to your Facebook account — use a passcode to lock up your iPod touch or iPhone, as I describe in Chapter 4, so that no one can use it without the passcode.) If you don't want the Facebook app to remember your login info, tap the Logout button in the upper-right corner of Facebook's icons screen (refer to Figure 21-15, right side).

Along the bottom of the Facebook screen are the Home icon for returning to the Home screen, the profile icon (with your first name) for showing your profile, the Friends icon to access a list of your Facebook friends, and the Inbox icon to check your messages. You can also Chat to chat directly with any of your friends who are online.

The Facebook app even lets you upload and share photos: Tap the the Photos icon and add a new album (type its name and description). You can then tap the Camera icon in the upper right corner of the album's screen, and choose Take Photo to snap a photo (iPhone only) or Choose From Library to pick a photo from your iPod touch or iPhone photo albums.

MySpace odyssey

So MySpace, owned by Fox Interactive Media, was the most popular mainstream social networking site until Facebook came along. Today, it's the number-two service, and it's still an awesomely huge network. MySpace focuses on music, movies, and TV shows — just about every band in the universe has a MySpace page, and it's easy to add music to your profile.

You can use Safari on your iPod touch or iPhone to access MySpace, but like most social networks, the home page you see is far too cumbersome for easy access that way. The MySpace Mobile for iPhone app is much easier to use and works fine on your iPod touch as well. It lets you send and receive messages, check status updates and photos, stay up to date on bulletins, and upload images from your iPod touch or iPhone.

 After downloading the MySpace app (see Chapter 7 for app downloading details), tap MySpace on the Home screen and log in to your MySpace account, as shown in Figure 21-16 (left side). As you log in, you can turn on the Remember Me option so that after logging in, the MySpace app remembers your username and password so that you don't have to log in again.

After you log in, your MySpace Home screen appears, as shown in Figure 21-16 (right side), with menu selections for viewing and editing your profile, checking the status and mood messages from your friends, checking friend updates, adding comments, reading bulletins, reading blogs, and changing your settings.

Figure 21-16: Log in to your MySpace account (left) to see your MySpace Home screen (right).

Along the bottom of the MySpace screen are the Home icon for returning to the Home screen, the Mail icon to check your messages, the Requests icon to view and respond to requests, the Friends icon for a list of your MySpace friends, and the Photos icon to upload photos to your MySpace page. To add photos, tap the Photos icon to see the photos already on your MySpace page and then tap the Add Photos button. You can then snap a photo (iPhone only) or pick a photo from your iPod touch or iPhone photo albums.

Dedicated follower of Twitter

The most talked-about newcomer to the social network scene is Twitter, a free social messaging utility for staying connected with people in real time. With Twitter, you can post and receive messages that are 140 characters or less — called *tweets*. All public tweets are available to read on the public timeline, or you can read just the ones posted by the Twitter members you follow. You can post a tweet that can be read by all your followers and by anyone reading the public tweets.

Members use Twitter to organize impromptu gatherings, carry on a group conversation, or just send a quick update to let people know what's going on. Companies use Twitter to announce products and carry on conversations with their customers. You can use Safari on your iPod touch or iPhone to access Twitter, but there are alternatives that offer a better Twitter experience on your iPod touch or iPhone.

For example, you can use the Twitter for iPhone Web service (http://twitterforiphone.com) with your iPod touch or iPhone to easily flip through all your messages with the flick of a finger. Twitter for iPhone offers a menu, as shown in Figure 21-17 (left side), for checking recent posts, updating your status, sending direct messages and replies to others on Twitter, browsing friends, and adding new friends (called *followers*).

 The App Store has several apps for accessing Twitter, but my favorite as of this writing is Twitterific — the free version includes advertising (see Figure 21-17, right side), but a premium version is also available without ads. The free version of Twitterific does all the basic stuff you'd expect a Twitter client for an iPod touch or iPhone to do: You can read messages from people you follow, post messages of your own, and get alerted to private direct messages and public replies.

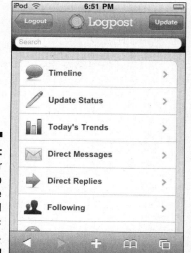

Figure 21-17:
Twitter for iPhone Web service (left) and Twitterific (right).

And wherever you go, "tweetness follows." Twitterific taps into the location services of your iPod touch or iPhone so that with your permission, it can let your followers know where you are and let you know when your followers are posting from a nearby location. You can set options for viewing messages, optimize the interface for left-handed operation, and use its own mini-browser to view linked Web pages without having to quit the app and run Safari. You can also copy a link to the last-opened Web page in Safari on your iPod touch or iPhone into a tweet — a very useful trick if you like to include Web links with your tweets. Tweet dreams!

Part VI
The Part of Tens

The 5th Wave — By Rich Tennant

"Okay, the view's just up ahead. Everyone switch to 'America the Beautiful' on your iPhone playlist."

In this part . . .

1n this part, you find two chapters chock-full of information.

✔ Chapter 22 offers ten common iPod and iPhone recovery steps that everyone must take at one time or another, including powering on and off, resetting settings, resetting the system, updating the software, and restoring the iPod or iPhone to its original factory condition.

✔ Chapter 23 offers the top ten tips not found elsewhere in the book, including tips on keeping your battery juiced, your screen clean, and your songs rated.

Chapter 22

Ten Steps to Recovery

In This Chapter

▶ Resetting your iPod or iPhone

▶ Updating iPod or iPhone software

▶ Restoring your iPod or iPhone settings

▶ Restoring an iPod or iPhone to its original factory condition

his no-nonsense chapter may not be fun, but it's necessary. Humans aren't perfect, and neither are the machines they make. If your iPod or iPhone stops working as it should, or an iPod touch or iPhone app causes it to freeze up, you can turn to this chapter.

This chapter also covers updating the firmware and software on your iPod or iPhone. (*Firmware* is software encoded in hardware.) All software devices need to be updated now and then — it's a good thing because new versions fix known bugs and add improvements.

Finally, I describe how to restore your iPod or iPhone to its factory default condition. Restoring to factory condition is a drastic measure that erases any music or information, but it usually solves a software glitch when nothing else does.

Powering Up and Unlocking

To turn on an iPod nano or iPod classic, press any part of the click wheel. To turn on an iPod touch or iPhone, press either the Sleep/Wake button or the physical Home button.

If an iPod nano or iPod classic refuses to turn on, check the position of the Hold switch — on the top of a current-model iPod classic or iPod nano (or on the bottom next to the dock connection on older iPod nano models). The Hold switch locks the iPod buttons so that you don't accidentally activate them. Slide the Hold switch to the left, hiding the orange layer, to unlock the buttons. (If you see the orange layer underneath one end of the Hold switch, the switch is still in the locked position.)

The "hold" switch for an iPod shuffle is actually the three-position switch (or the on-off switch on older models). Slide the three-way switch to expose the green layer underneath to turn on your iPod shuffle.

Rather than a hold button, iPod touch and iPhone models display the message `Slide to unlock` — slide your finger across this message to unlock your iPod touch or iPhone.

If you previously set a passcode for the iPod or iPhone (see Chapter 4), you must enter the passcode; otherwise you need to attach the iPod or iPhone to the computer you used to set up and synchronize it, or completely restore the iPod or iPhone to its original factory condition, as I describe later in this chapter.

Keep in mind that starting up an iPod touch or iPhone that was completely turned off takes quite a bit of power — more than if it woke from sleep. If you do turn it off, plug it into AC power or your computer before turning it back on.

Powering Down

Your iPod or iPhone should be set to go to sleep automatically, unless you change the settings.

The iPod nano or iPod classic lets you set its backlight to turn off automatically by choosing Settings⇨General⇨Backlight and picking the amount of time to remain on (or choosing Always On). This is similar to putting it to sleep.

You can set your iPod touch or iPhone to automatically go to sleep by choosing Settings⇨General⇨Auto-Lock and choosing the amount of time before sleeping (or choosing Never, to prevent automatic sleep).

You can force an iPod classic or iPod nano to power off by pressing the Play/Pause button.

To force your iPod touch or iPhone to go to sleep, press the Sleep/Wake (On/Off) button on the top. To turn it off completely so that it has to start its system again from scratch, press and hold the Sleep/Wake button on top for a few seconds until a red slider appears on the screen that says `Slide to power off` and then slide your finger across the slider to turn it off.

Stopping a Frozen App

Apple is not perfect, and neither are the many thousands of developers who create the apps that run on an iPod touch or iPhone, and the "extra" or click-wheel games on an iPod nano or iPod classic.

If your iPod touch or iPhone freezes while running an app, press and hold the Sleep/Wake button on top for a few seconds until a red slider appears on the screen that says `Slide to power off` — then press and hold the physical Home button until the application quits. If that doesn't work, see the previous section in this chapter.

If your iPod nano or iPod classic itself freezes, you need to reset its system — see the next section.

Resetting Your iPod or iPhone System

Sometimes problems arise with electronics and software that cause your iPod or iPhone to stop working properly. You can usually fix the problem by resetting it and restarting the iPod or iPhone system from scratch — just like resetting a computer. Resetting the system does *not* restore the iPod or iPhone to its original factory condition, nor does it erase anything — your content and settings remain intact.

Before resetting the system, you may want to connect the iPod or iPhone to a power outlet by using the AC power adapter. You can reset your iPod or iPhone without connecting it to power if it has enough juice in its battery. However, if you have access to power, it makes sense to use it because the reset operation uses power, and starting up your iPod or iPhone from scratch again also uses power.

To reset the iPod touch or iPhone, press and hold the Sleep/Wake button and the physical Home button at the same time for at least ten seconds, ignoring the red slider that says `Slide to power off`, until the Apple logo appears.

To reset the iPod nano or iPod classic, follow these steps:

1. **Toggle the Hold switch.**

   Slide the Hold switch to the right, exposing the orange layer, to lock the buttons, and then slide it back to unlock.

2. **Press the Menu and Select buttons simultaneously and hold for at least six seconds or until the Apple logo appears; then release the buttons when you see the Apple logo.**

The appearance of the Apple logo signals that your iPod is resetting itself, so you no longer have to hold down the buttons.

Release the Menu and Select buttons as soon as you see the Apple logo. If you continue to press the buttons after the logo appears, the iPod displays the low battery icon, and you must connect it to a power source before using it again.

To reset the iPod shuffle, first disconnect it from your computer (if you haven't already done so) and then slide the three-position switch to the Off position. The green stripe under the switch should not be visible. Wait five seconds and then switch the slider back to the Shuffle Songs or Play in Order position.

After resetting, everything should be back to normal, including your music and data files.

Resetting iPod or iPhone Settings

Perhaps someone played a practical joke on you and set your iPod language to German (and you don't understand German). Or maybe a fee-based hotel Wi-Fi network has captured your iPod touch or iPhone and won't let go. Sometimes you need to reset your settings and preferences.

You can reset all your iPod nano or iPod classic settings, or all or part of your iPod touch or iPhone settings, while leaving your content and personal information intact. On an iPod touch or iPhone, you can also erase all content and reset network settings.

To reset iPod nano or iPod classic settings, choose Settings⇨Reset Settings and select Reset (or Cancel to cancel). This resets all the items on the Settings menu to their default settings.

To see your resetting options on an iPod touch or iPhone, choose Settings⇨General⇨Reset from the Home screen. The Reset screen appears, as shown in Figure 22-1.

You have several options for resetting:

✔ **Reset All Settings:** To return your iPod touch or iPhone to its original condition with no preferences or settings while still keeping your content and your personal information (including contacts, calendars, e-mail accounts, and apps with their data) intact, tap Reset All Settings.

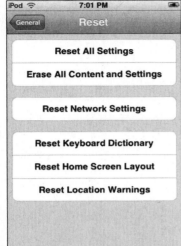

Figure 22-1:
Options for
resetting
iPod touch
settings and
clearing all
content.

✔ **Erase All Content and Settings:** To erase *everything,* first connect the iPod touch or iPhone to your computer or a power adapter and then tap Erase All Content and Settings. This operation can take hours! It wipes out everything by overwriting the data. You can't use the iPod touch or iPhone until it finishes. It may be easier and faster to do a full restore from iTunes, as I describe in the section "Restoring to Factory Condition," later in this chapter.

✔ **Reset Network Settings:** You can reset your network settings so that your previously used networks are removed from the Wi-Fi list. This type of reset is useful if you can't find any other way to stop a Wi-Fi network from connecting automatically to your iPod touch or iPhone — just tap Reset Network Settings, and you're automatically disconnected from any Wi-Fi network. (Wi-Fi is turned off and then back on.) For more details about choosing Wi-Fi networks, see Chapter 4.

✔ **Reset Keyboard Dictionary:** To reset the keyboard dictionary, tap this button. This erases all words that have been added to the dictionary. (Words are added when you reject words suggested by the keyboard and type the word — see Chapter 3 for details.)

✔ **Reset Home Screen Layout:** If you rearranged the icons on your Home screen (as I describe in Chapter 3), you may want to set them back to their original positions. To reset your Home screen to the default arrangement, tap Reset Home Screen Layout.

✔ **Reset Location Warnings:** Location warnings are requests by apps to use the Location Services. The iPod touch or iPhone stops displaying these warnings the second time you tap OK. If you want to start displaying the warnings again, tap Reset Location Warnings.

Checking the Software Version

You should always keep your iPod or iPhone updated with new versions of the system software that controls it. iTunes automatically checks for updates of this software and lets you update your iPod or iPhone without affecting the music or data stored on it.

Make sure that you use the newest version of iTunes. To check for the availability of an updated version for Windows, run iTunes and choose Help⇨Check for iTunes Updates.

If you use a Mac and you enabled the Software Update option in your System Preferences, Apple automatically informs you of updates to your Apple software for the Mac, including iTunes, Safari, iCal, and Address Book. All you need to do is select which updates to download and then click the Install button to download them. iTunes includes updates for all iPod and iPhone generations and can detect which model you have.

To determine which version of the system software is installed on your iPod touch or iPhone, choose Settings⇨General⇨About from the Home screen; on an iPod nano or iPod classic, choose Settings⇨About from the main menu. Next to the word *Version* is information that describes the software version installed.

Updating the Software

iTunes tells you whether your iPod or iPhone has the newest software installed. Connect the iPod or iPhone to your computer, select it in the iTunes Source pane (in the Devices section) and you'll see the Summary page appear to the right of the Source pane. The Version section of the page tells you whether your iPod or iPhone software is up to date and when iTunes will check for new software.

If an update is available, a dialog appears to ask permission to download it. Go ahead and click the OK button to update the software; you'll be glad you did because Apple often includes new features and battery-saving upgrades. After updating the software, iTunes continues syncing with the iPod or iPhone until it is finished.

Restoring to Factory Condition

You can restore your iPod or iPhone to its original factory condition. This operation erases its storage and returns the iPod or iPhone to its original settings. It's the last resort for fixing problems, and it's the only choice if you intend to change the computer you're using for syncing your iPod or iPhone.

To restore an iPod or iPhone, follow these steps for both the Mac and Windows versions of iTunes:

1. **Connect the iPod or iPhone to your computer.**

   iTunes opens automatically.

2. **Select the iPod or iPhone in the Devices section of the Source pane, and click the Summary tab if it isn't already selected.**

   The Summary pane appears to the right of the Source pane.

3. **Click the Restore button.**

   An alert dialog appears to confirm that you want to restore the iPod or iPhone.

4. **Click the Restore button again to confirm the restore operation.**

   A progress bar appears, indicating the progress of the restore operation. iTunes notifies you when the restore is finished.

Setting Up and Syncing

After the restore operation finishes (as previously described), iTunes displays the setup screen for a newly minted iPod or iPhone — the restore operation makes it like new again.

In the setup screen, as described in Chapter 2, you can give your iPod nano or iPod classic a new name.

For an iPod touch or iPhone, iTunes provides the options to restore the settings from a previously backed-up iPod touch or iPhone, or to set it up as new. If you choose to set it up as new, you can give your iPod touch or iPhone a new name and set the automatic options, as I describe in Chapter 2. See the next section in this chapter if you want to restore from a backup.

To replace content and apps that were erased by the restore operation, sync your iPod or iPhone with your computer's iTunes library, as I describe in Chapter 9, and with personal information (contacts, calendars, notes, e-mail accounts, and bookmarks), as I describe in Chapter 10. You also need to resync your pictures, as I describe in Chapter 18.

Restoring Settings from a Backup (iPod touch and iPhone)

iTunes provides protection and backs up your iPod touch or iPhone settings so that you can restore them. This backup comes in handy if you want to apply the settings to a new iPod touch or iPhone, or to one that you had to restore to its factory condition.

Whenever you sync your iPod touch or iPhone, iTunes automatically copies all the settings you use to customize your iPod touch or iPhone and its apps, including Wi-Fi network settings, the keyboard dictionary, and settings for contacts, calendars, and e-mail accounts.

To restore your settings, connect your new or restored iPod touch or iPhone to the same computer and copy of iTunes you used before so that iTunes remembers the backup settings. iTunes should open automatically. (If it doesn't, open iTunes manually.) As you start the setup process, iTunes gives you the choice of restoring the settings from a previously backed-up iPod touch or iPhone, or setting up the iPod touch or iPhone as new. Choose the option to restore the settings and then click the Continue button to finish setting up your iPod touch or iPhone. If you choose to set it up as new, follow the step-by-step instructions in Chapter 2 for setting it up.

To delete the backed-up settings for an iPod touch or iPhone, open iTunes and choose iTunes⇨Preferences (on a Mac) or Edit⇨Preferences (on a Windows PC). Click the Devices tab, select the iPod touch or iPhone in the Device backups list, and then click Remove Backup. You don't need to connect the iPod touch or iPhone to do this.

Chapter 23

Ten Tangible Tips

In This Chapter

▶ Keeping your battery juiced and your screen clean

▶ Rating your songs

▶ Deleting apps, videos, and podcasts from your iPod touch or iPhone

▶ Using international keyboards on an iPod touch or iPhone

*T*his book is filled with tips, but I've put ten truly handy ones in this chapter that just didn't fit in elsewhere but which can help make your iPod or iPhone experience a completely satisfying one.

Saving the Life of Your Battery

Follow these simple rules to extend your battery life:

✔ Don't keep an iPod or iPhone in a snug carrying case when charging — that snug case can cause overheating.

✔ Top it off with power whenever it's convenient.

✔ Set your iPod touch or iPhone to automatically go to sleep by choosing Settings➪General➪Auto-Lock from the Home screen.

✔ Set the iPod nano or iPod classic backlight to turn off automatically by choosing Settings➪General➪Backlight and picking the amount of time to remain on (or choosing Always On).

Everything else you need to know is in Chapter 1.

Keeping Your Screen Clean

If the iPod or iPhone display has excessive moisture on it from humidity or wet fingers, wipe it with a soft, dry cloth. If it's dirty, use a soft, slightly damp, lint-free cloth — an inexpensive eyeglass cleaning cloth sold in vision-care stores or pharmacies is a good choice. By no means should you use window cleaners, household cleaners, aerosol sprays, solvents, alcohol, ammonia, or abrasives — they can scratch or otherwise damage the display. Also, try not to get any moisture in any of the openings, as it could short out the device.

Getting Healthy with Nike

Use your iPod touch, iPhone, or iPod nano as a workout companion with Nike+ running shoes and a Nike + iPod Sport Kit. The kit's sensor fits inside your Nike+ shoe under the insole. A receiver is provided for the iPod nano and first-generation iPod touch (current-generation iPod touch and iPhone models include a receiver).

When you have the kit and the shoes, activate the app on your iPod touch or iPhone — choose Settings➪Nike + iPod and tap Off for the Nike + iPod option to turn it on. To activate the kit on your iPod nano, choose Nike + iPod from the main menu.

You can track your pace, time, and distance from one workout to the next, and you can pick songs and playlists to match. You can even sync your workout data with Nikeplus.com, see all your runs, and share motivation with runners across the world.

Rating Your Songs

Ratings are useful — the Shuffle and Genius features are influenced by ratings, and you can define smart playlists with ratings to select only rated songs so that you can avoid the clunkers and spinal tappers. In fact, when you try to put a music library on your iPod or iPhone that's larger than the device's capacity, iTunes decides which songs to synchronize based on — you guessed it — *ratings*.

iTunes lets you rate your songs, but so does your iPod or iPhone. You can rate any song on your iPod or iPhone as you listen to it. Ratings you assign on your iPod or iPhone are automatically resynchronized to your iTunes library when you connect your iPod or iPhone again.

To assign a rating to a song, start playing the song on your iPod or iPhone (see Chapter 16 for details). The Now Playing screen should appear. On an iPod nano or iPod classic, press the Select button three times, cycling through the scrubber bar and Genius Start button to reach the rating bullets; then scroll the click wheel to give the song zero to five stars.

On an iPod touch or iPhone, follow these steps to rate your songs:

1. **Tap the List button to display a list of the album or playlist contents.**

   The List button is in the upper-right corner.

2. **Tap the title of any song in the track listing or leave selected the song that's playing.**

3. **Drag across the ratings bar at the top of the track listing to give the song zero to five stars.**

The upper limit is five stars (for the best).

Deleting Apps from Your iPod touch or iPhone

You can turn off the synchronization of certain apps in your iTunes library before syncing your iPod touch or iPhone to iTunes, as I describe in Chapter 9, so that the apps disappear from your iPod touch or iPhone. But you can also delete apps directly from your iPod touch or iPhone.

Touch and hold any icon on the Home screen until all the icons begin to wiggle (as if you're about to rearrange them or add Home screens). To delete an app, tap the circled *x* that appears inside the app's icon as it wiggles. The iPod touch or iPhone displays a warning that deleting the app also deletes all its data; tap Delete to go ahead and delete the app and its data, or tap Cancel to cancel.

To stop the icons from wiggling, press the physical Home button on the device, which saves any changes you made to your Home screens.

Deleting Videos and Podcasts from Your iPod touch or iPhone

Need more room on your iPod touch or iPhone? You can delete a video or podcast episode directly from your iPod touch or iPhone by flicking left or right across the video or podcast episode selection and then tapping the Delete button that appears.

Your video or podcast episode is deleted from your iPod touch or iPhone only. When you sync your iPod touch or iPhone with iTunes, the video or podcast episode is copied back to your iPod touch or iPhone unless you change your sync settings or switch to manually managing music and videos, as I describe in Chapter 9. ***Note:*** If you delete a rented movie from an iPod touch or iPhone, it's gone forever (or until you rent it again).

Measuring Traffic in Maps

The Maps app supplied with the iPhone and iPod touch not only shows you the route to take, but in some areas, it can also show you traffic patterns so that you can avoid the jams. The traffic data is constantly updated and aggregated from a variety of Internet sources by Google. It is available for more than 30 major U.S. cities, including New York, Los Angeles, San Francisco, and Washington.

To use Maps, tap Maps on the Home screen. The Maps app appears (refer to Chapter 21). You can obtain directions first, as I describe in Chapter 21, or just display any location on the map that has highways. To show traffic information, tap the Underneath button (the curled-page icon in the lower-right corner) to see a menu underneath the map and then tap Show Traffic.

When the map shows traffic, highways are color-coded according to the flow of traffic:

- Green for highways moving faster than 50 miles per hour (mph)
- Yellow for 25–50 mph
- Red for less than 25 mph

If you don't see color-coded highways, you may need to zoom out to see highways and major roads.

To stop showing the traffic, tap the Underneath button and then tap Hide Traffic.

Turning On International Keyboards on Your iPod touch or iPhone

You can turn on keyboards for different languages and use them simultaneously. To turn on international keyboards, choose Settings➪General➪Keyboard from the Home screen and then tap International Keyboards (scroll the list to find it). The international keyboards appear, as shown in Figure 23-1 (left side).

Figure 23-1:
Turn on international keyboards (left), switch languages on the keyboard (middle), and draw Chinese characters (right).

You can turn on any of the keyboards you need — tap Off to turn each one on. To access languages with more than one keyboard, such as Japanese, tap Japanese first and then tap the specific keyboard layout (QWERTY or Kana).

You can then switch keyboards while typing information by tapping the globe icon, as shown in Figure 23-1 (middle), that appears to the right of the 123 key when more than one international keyboard is turned on. The language of the newly active keyboard appears briefly on the spacebar.

Each time you tap the globe icon, the keyboard layout switches to the next language you've turned on, in the order that they appear in the international keyboards list.

To use the Japanese Kana keyboard, use the keypad to select syllables. For more syllable options, tap the arrow key and select another syllable or word from the window. With the Japanese QWERTY keyboard, you can use the QWERTY layout to input code for Japanese syllables. As you type, suggested syllables appear, and you can tap the syllable to choose it.

Drawing Chinese Characters

The iPod touch and iPhone offer keyboards for both Traditional and Simplified Chinese, with Handwriting and Pinyin layouts for both. Turn on international keyboards as described in the preceding section and tap Chinese (Simplified) or Chinese (Traditional). Then tap Off to turn on Handwriting or Pinyin. (You can turn both on.)

For the Handwriting layouts, use the touchpad to enter Chinese characters with your finger. (Refer to Figure 23-1, right side.)

As you draw character strokes, matching characters appear in a list, with the closest match at the top. When you choose a character, its related characters appear in the list as additional choices.

For Simplified Pinyin, use the QWERTY keyboard to enter Pinyin for Chinese characters; as you type, suggested Chinese characters appear. Tap a character to choose it or continue entering Pinyin to see more character options.

Stopping a Wi-Fi Network from Joining

Your iPod touch or iPhone remembers your Wi-Fi connections and automatically uses one when it detects it within your range. If you've used multiple Wi-Fi networks in the same location, it picks the last one you used. (For details on choosing a Wi-Fi network, see Chapter 4.)

But if your iPod touch or iPhone keeps picking up a Wi-Fi network that you can't properly join, such as a private network that requires a password you don't know or a commercial network that charges for access, you can tell your iPod touch or iPhone to *forget* this particular network, rather than turning off Wi-Fi itself. This is very useful if a paid service has somehow gotten hold of your iPod touch or iPhone and won't let you move on to other Web pages without typing a password.

Choose Settings⇨Wi-Fi from the Home screen and tap the circled right-arrow (>) button next to the selected network's name. The network's information screen appears. Tap the Forget This Network button at the top of the screen so that your iPod touch doesn't join it automatically. Then tap the Wi-Fi Networks button in the upper-left corner to return to the Wi-Fi Networks screen. You can always select this network manually, and you can still continue to use other Wi-Fi networks.

Index

Numerics

8GB model of iPod touch, 12
1-Click, buying media from iTunes
    Store with, 117
16GB model of iPod touch, 12
32GB model for iPod touch, 12

• A •

AAC format
  playlist for burning discs in, 243
  ripping a CD on iTunes, 133
accent marks, typing, 49
advance, setting volume in, 225–226
AIFF format
  playlist for burning discs in, 243
  ripping a CD on iTunes, 133
AirPort Express, 210–214
AirTunes, 210–214
alarms
  in Calendar application, 332
  setting, 63–66
albums
  browsing songs by, 184–185
  deleting, 193
  playlists of, 231
  searches by, 256–257
alerts, 332, 333
App Store, 122–123
App Store icon, 44
Apple Lossless format
  playlist for burning discs in, 243
  ripping a CD on iTunes, 133
Apple TV
  converting video for use with, 142
  music played through speakers
      connected to, 213–214
  playing videos, 225
applications
  browsing, 186–187
  browsing and downloading, 126–127
    deleting, 193, 367
    frozen apps, stopping, 359
    updating, 127
artists
    browsing songs by, 184–185
    burning discs, artist and track name text
        included in, 247
    deleting, 193
    searches by, 255–258
attachments, email, 319
audio books
    browsing in iTunes library, 185
    browsing in iTunes Store, 112–113
    deleting, 193
    displayed in List View (iTunes), 188
    finding, 286–287
    on iPhone, 286
    on iPod classic, 287
    on iPod nano, 287
    on iPod touch, 286
    overview, 286
    playing, 221, 286–287
audio CDs, burning, 240–241, 246
Auto Kit (Belkin), 83
Auto-Capitalization option for keyboard
    (iPhone and iPod touch), 54
Auto-Correction option for keyboard
    (iPhone and iPod touch), 54
Autofill, 159–160
automatic synchronization, preventing, 150
automatically retrieving song information
    from the Internet, 196
AUX (auxiliary) input, 82

• B •

backlight, adjusting, 72
backups
    burning your own discs for, 240–247
    to CD-Rs, 249–250
    copyright issues, 240
    to DVD-Rs, 249–250
    to hard drive, 250

backups *(continued)*
  incremental backups, performing, 249
  for iTunes library, 249–250
  overview, 239–240, 249
  restoring settings from, 364
battery
  calibrating, 26
  charge cycle for, 26
  draining, 25
  extending life of your, 365
  overview, 23
  power specifications for, 23
  recharging, 24–25
  replacing, 25
  saving power, tips for, 25–28
  status light for, 24–25
Bcc (blind carbon copy), 325
Belkin
  Auto Kit, 83
  TuneDok, 83
black check mark in List View (iTunes), 188
blind carbon copy (Bcc), 325
bone conduction, 80
bookmarks
  for location, 341–342
  in Safari, 307–308, 314–315
  synchronization with iTunes, 165
  for videos, 284–285
Bose SoundDock Portable digital music
    system, 80
box, looking through and saving your, 18
brightness, adjusting, 72–73
broadcast icon in List View (iTunes), 188
browsing
  album, browsing songs by, 184–185
  applications, 186–187
  apps, browsing and downloading,
    126–127
  artist, browsing songs by, 184–185
  audio books, 112–113, 185
  content in iTunes, 180–182
  cover art, 182–183
  games, 186–187
  movies, 112–114, 186
  music videos, 112–114
  podcasts, 185–186
  podcasts, browsing and downloading, 126

  podcasts, browsing and subscribing
    to, 114–116
  songs, browsing and downloading,
    124–126
  songs and albums in iTunes Store,
    108–110
  TV shows, 112–114, 186
  videos, 186
  Web sites, 306–307
burning discs
  artist and track name text, including, 247
  audio CDs, 240–241, 246
  backups, burning your own discs for,
    240–247
  data CDs, 246
  described, 240
  disc format settings, 246
  DVDs, 241, 246
  gap between songs, adding, 246
  MP3 CDs, 241, 246
  playlist for, 241–244
  recording speed, 246
  settings for, 245–247
  sound check before, 246
  steps for, 244–245
buying media from iTunes Store
  downloads, resuming interrupted,
    120–121
  with 1-Click, 117
  overview, 116–117
  redeeming gift certificates and prepaid
    cards, 121–122
  with Shopping Cart, 117–119

• *C* •

calculating what will fit on CD, 242–243
Calculator icon, 44
Calendar application
  alarms, 332
  alerts, 332, 333
  events, adding, 329–331
  events, deleting, 332
  events, editing, 331–332
  meeting invitations in, 333
  overview, 328–329

synchronization with iTunes, 165, 167
syncing, 332
time zone support for, 333
Calendar icon, 44
calibrating battery, 26
Camera icon, 44
caps lock option for keyboard (iPhone and iPod touch), 48, 54
car stereo system
  cassette player adapter, using, 82–83
  integrating an iPod or IPhone with your, 84
  options for, 81–82
  overview, 81
carrying cases, 86–87
cassette player adapter, using, 82–83
CD-R drive as requirement for iPod/iPhone, 20
CD-Rs
  backup for iTunes library to, 249–250
  importing music for an audio CD-R, 243
CDs played in iTunes
  overview, 97–98
  rearranging tracks, 98–99
  repeating an entire CD, 99
  skipping tracks, 99
  visual effects, displaying, 99–101
Celebrity Playlists, 111
Chambers, Mark L. (*Mac OS X Snow Leopard All-in-One For Dummies*), 4, 211
charge cycle for battery, 26
chasing arrows in List View (iTunes), 188
checking email, 318–321
Chinese characters, drawing, 370
Chopper, 46
city added to Weather application, 344
Classic Visualizer, 100
cleaning iPod touch, 40
clearing On-The-Go playlists, 272
Clock icon, 44
clocks
  creating, 61–62
  removing, 61
cloud computing, 162
collaborative filtering, 235

columns in List View (iTunes), customizing, 189–190
Compass icon, 44
contacts
  adding, 336–338
  deleting, 338
  editing, 338
  first name, sorting by, 335
  last name, sorting by, 335
  overview, 333–334
  photos, adding, 338
  searching, 335
  sorting, 334–335
  synchronization with iTunes, 163–165, 167
  viewing, 333–334
Contacts icon, 44
content indicators in List View (iTunes), 188
content information
  editing, 198–204
  entering, 197
  links, 105
converting videos, 142, 279
copying
  everything at once, 148–150
  items directly to your iPod/iPhone, 157–158
  media files in iTunes library, 248–249
  text, 51–53
copyright issues, 240
cover art
  adding, 205–206
  browsing by, 182–183
  deleting, 206
  downloading, 206
  in iTunes Store, 183
  searches by, 254–255
cover browser, 95
Cover Flow
  overview, 182–183
  searches by, 254–255
cross-fading song playback, 218–219
current item playing on iTunes, showing, 192
current location, showing your, 339–340

customization
  email, 323–325
  List View (iTunes), 189–190
cutting text, 51–53

● *D* ●

data CDs, 246
date and time
  alarms, setting, 63–66
  creating clocks, 61–62
  on iPhone, 58–59
  on iPod classic, 59–60
  on iPod nano, 59–60
  on iPod touch, 58–59
  multiple time zones, displaying clocks
    with, 61–62
  removing clocks, 61
  sleep timer, 68–69
  stopwatch, using, 67–68
  timers, using, 66
deleting
  apps, 367
  cities in Weather application, 345
  confirmation before deleting email, 324
  contacts, 338
  content in iTunes library, 193–194
  email, 320–321
  items on your iPod/iPhone, 158–159
  podcasts, 368
  stock/index/fund, 346
  videos, 285, 368
deselecting items before synchronization
  with iTunes, 151
Devices, 93
disc format settings for burning discs, 246
displaying content in List View (iTunes),
  187–190
Dock Connector, 20–21
docks, 18
downloading
  apps, browsing and downloading,
    126–127
  apps from App Store, 123
  cover art, 206
  podcasts, browsing and downloading, 126

resuming interrupted downloads, 120–121
songs, browsing and downloading, 1
  24–126
draining battery, 25
driving directions, finding, 342–344
duplicate items in iTunes library, showing,
  192–193
DVD-R drive as requirement for iPod/
  iPhone, 20
DVDs
  backup for iTunes library to, 249–250
  burning discs, 241, 246
  calculating what will fit on, 243

● *E* ●

editing
  contacts, 338
  smart playlists, 235
  text, 49–51
editing content information on iTunes
  of multiple items, 199–200
  overview, 198
  ratings, adding, 204
  of single items, 200–204
8GB model of iPod touch, 12
Eject button, 94
email
  attachments, 319
  blind carbon copy (Bcc), 325
  checking, 318–321
  customizing, 323–325
  deleting, 320–321, 324
  deleting, confirmation before, 324
  fetching messages, 325–326
  images in, 324
  links in, 319
  mail accounts, changing, 174–175
  mail accounts, deleting, 175
  mail accounts, setting up, 172–174
  notes made on keyboard (iPhone and
    iPod touch), sending, 48
  overview, 317
  pushing messages, 325–326
  reading, 318–320
  recipients, 319

replying to, 323
saving, 323
saving a picture attached to an, 301–302
sending, 321–323
sending a Web link by, 315
sending pictures by, 299–300
sent messages, receiving a copy of
    your, 325
settings for, 323–325
signatures, 325
synchronization with iTunes, 166–167
unread, 318, 320
enhanced podcasts, 220
enhancing the volume, 228
equalizer presets
    for iPhone, 277
    for iPod classic, 278
    for iPod nano, 278
    for iPod touch, 277
    overview, 202
    volume adjustments in iTunes, 226–227
erasing all content and settings, 361
events
    adding, 329–331
    deleting, 332
    editing, 331–332
Exchange ActiveSync protocol, 162
exclamation point in List View
        (iTunes), 188
eXtensible Markup Language (XML), 138

• F •

Facebook application, 350–351
factory condition, restoring to, 363
fast-forwarding
    playback in iPod shuffle, 266
    videos, 281, 282
fetching messages, 325–326
file formats
    AAC format, ripping a CD on iTunes, 133
    AAC format, playlist for burning
        discs in, 243
    AIFF format, playlist for burning
        discs in, 243
    AIFF format, ripping a CD on iTunes, 133

Apple Lossless format, playlist for
    burning discs in, 243
Apple Lossless format, ripping a CD on
    iTunes, 133
MP3 format, burning discs in, 241
MP3 format, ripping a CD on iTunes, 133
for photos, 292
WAV format, playlist for burning
    discs, 243
WAV format, ripping a CD on iTunes, 133
finding
    albums, 256–257
    artists, 255–258
    audio books, 286–287
    contacts, 335
    cover art, 254–255
    Cover Flow, 254–255
    iTunes library, 247
    playlists, 257–258
    podcasts, 286–287
    songs on iPhone, 253–258
    songs on iPods, 253–258
    title of song, 258
    videos, 280
    videos in YouTube, 285
firmware, 357
first name
    artists in iTunes Store listed
        alphabetically by, 110
    sorting contacts by, 335
font size, setting, 74
frozen apps, stopping, 359
full-screen
    playing videos on iTunes on, 223–225
    visual effects on, 100–101

• G •

games, browsing, 186–187
gap between songs, adding, 246
Gapless Album option, 134–135
Genius button (iTunes), 96
Genius playlists
    creating, 236, 273–274
    on iPhone, 274
    on iPod classic, 274–275

Genius playlists *(continued)*
  on iPod nano, 274–275
  on iPod touch, 274
  limiting number of songs on, 237
  overview, 235–236, 272
  refreshing, 236, 274
  saving, 236
  synchronizing, 236
Genius sidebar (iTunes), 97, 102
Global Positioning System (GPS), 74
Google Earth application, 347
Gookin, Dan *(PCs For Dummies, 11th Edition)*, 210
Gracenote CDDB, 97, 197
green check mark in List View (iTunes), 188

• H •

hard drive
  backup for iTunes library to, 250
  removing items from library but keeping on, 193, 194
headphones, finding, 18
hertz, 80
home page (iTunes Store), 106
Home screen
  adding a Web site to your, 316
  resetting, 361

• I •

images
  contacts, adding photos to, 338
  email, saving a picture attached to an, 301–302
  email, sending pictures by, 299–300
  file formats for, 292
  on iPhone, viewing, 293–294
  on iPod classic, viewing, 295
  on iPod nano, viewing, 295
  on iPod touch, viewing, 293–294
  MobileMe, sharing pictures on, 302
  multiple pictures, selecting and copying, 300–301

organizing, 289–290
  overview, 289–290
  screen shots, capturing, 302
  sharing, 299–302
  slideshows, 295–299
  syncing, 292
  transferring to iPod/iPhone, 290–292
  viewing, 293–295
iMix playlists, 111
import preferences and settings, changing, 130–133
importing music for an audio CD-R, 243
incremental backups, performing, 249
installation
  of iTunes on Macintosh, 33–35
  of iTunes on Windows PC, 29–32
  of QuickTime on Windows PC, 29
integrating an iPod or IPhone with your car stereo system, 84
interacting with Web pages, 312–313
international keyboard, 369
Internet connection as requirement for iPod/iPhone, 20
i-P23 speaker systems (Sonic Impact), 81
iPhone
  accessories included with, 18
  Alarm icon, 43
  alarms, setting, 63–64
  audio books on, 286
  battery for, 23–28
  Battery icon, 43
  cleaning, 40
  clocks, creating, 61
  controlling playback, 280–281
  date and time on, 58–59
  dock, 42
  equalizer presets, 277
  erasing all content and settings, 361
  fingers, touching and gesturing with your, 45
  Genius playlists, 274
  Home screen, 40–42
  Home screen, resetting, 361
  Home screen pages, rearranging, 45–46
  icons available, list of, 43–44
  iTunes, setup for, 35–38

iTunes Store on, 124–127
keyboard, 47–54
keyboard dictionary, resetting, 361
location warnings, resetting, 361
Lock icon, 43
mail accounts, 172–175
models, 16
motion sensing by, 46
Network activity icon, 43
network settings, resetting, 361
OK to disconnect message, 38
online, 75–76
on/off for, 22, 358
overview, 10, 16–17
passcode for, 70, 358
photos, viewing, 293–294
Play icon, 43
podcasts on, 286
powering down, 358
requirements for, 19–20
resetting, 359
scaling picture on, 282
Search screen, 42
searching for songs on, 253–258
settings, resetting, 360–361
shuffling song order, 263–264
sleep timer, 69
Slide to unlock message, 40
slideshows, playing, 298
slideshows, setting up, 296–297
song playback on, 258–260
Sound Check, 277
status bar, 43
stopwatch, using, 67–68
timers, using, 66
videos, locating and playing, 280
volume, 275, 276
VPN icon, 43
Wi-Fi icon, 43
wiggling icons, 45–46
iPhone 3G, 16
iPhone 3GS, 16–17
iPhoto, 289
iPod classic
  alarms, setting, 64–66
  audio books on, 287
  buttons on, 55–56

clocks, creating, 62
date and time on, 59–60
described, 11
equalizer presets, 278
Extras option, 55
Genius playlists, 274–275
Music option, 54
Now Playing option, 55
On-The-Go playlists, 270
overview, 13
passcode for, 70
photos, viewing, 295
Photos option, 55
podcasts on, 55, 287
powering down, 358
resetting, 359–360
scrolling on, 54
settings, resetting, 360
Settings option, 55
shuffling song order, 55, 264–265
sleep timer, 69
slideshows, playing, 298–299
slideshows, setting up, 297–298
song playback, 260–262
Sound Check, 277
stopwatch, using, 68
turning on, 357–358
using, 54–56
videos, controlling playback, 282
videos, locating and playing, 280
Videos option, 54
volume, 275
iPod icon, 44
iPod nano
  alarms, setting, 64–66
  audio books on, 287
  buttons on, 55–56
  clocks, creating, 62
  date and time on, 59–60
  described, 11
  equalizer presets, 278
  Extras option, 55
  Genius playlists, 274–275
  Music option, 54
  Now Playing option, 55
  On-The-Go playlists, 270

iPod nano *(continued)*
overview, 14
passcode for, 70
photos, viewing, 295
Photos option, 55
podcasts on, 287
Podcasts option, 55
powering down, 358
resetting, 359–360
scrolling on, 54
settings, resetting, 360
Settings option, 55
Shuffle Songs option, 55
shuffling song order, 264–265
sleep timer, 69
slideshows, playing, 298–299
slideshows, setting up, 297–298
song playback, 260–262
Sound Check, 277
stopwatch, using, 68
turning on, 357–358
using, 54–56
videos, controlling playback, 282
videos, locating and playing, 280
Videos option, 54
volume, 275
iPod shuffle
described, 11
fast-forwarding playback, 266
overview, 15–16, 265
pausing playback, 266
playlists, using VoiceOver to choose, 266–267
random selection of songs for, 37
resetting, 360
rewinding playback, 266
shuffling song order, 266
song playback, 265–267
Sound Check, 277
starting playback, 265
turning on, 358
USB cable for, 20
VoiceOver feature for, 15, 266–267
volume, 275
iPod touch
Alarm icon, 43
alarms, setting, 63–64

apps for, 13
audio books on, 286
Battery icon, 43
cleaning, 40
clocks, creating, 61
date and time on, 58–59
described, 11
dock, 42
8GB model, 12
equalizer presets, 277
fingers, touching and gesturing with your, 45
Genius playlists, 274
Home screen, 40–42
Home screen pages, rearranging, 45–46
icons available, list of, 43–44
iTunes Store on, 124–127
keyboard, 47–54
Lock icon, 43
mail accounts, 172–175
models, 12
motion sensing by, 46
Music icon, 44
Network activity icon, 43
online, 75–76
overview, 12–13
passcode for, 70, 358
photos, viewing, 293–294
Play icon, 43
podcasts on, 286
powering down, 358
scaling picture on, 282
Search screen, 42
shuffling song order, 263–264
16GB model, 12
sleep timer, 69
Slide to unlock message, 40
slideshows, playing, 298
slideshows, setting up, 296–297
song playback, 259–260
Sound Check, 277
status bar, 43
stopwatch, using, 67–68
32GB model, 12
timers, using, 66
turning on, 358
videos, controlling playback, 280–281
videos, locating and playing, 280

Videos icon, 44
volume, 275, 276
VPN icon, 43
Wi-Fi icon, 43
iPod-ready automobiles, 84
iPods. *See also specific iPods*
  accessories included with, 18
  battery for, 23–28
  erasing all content and settings, 361
  Home screen, resetting, 361
  iTunes, setup for, 35–38
  keyboard dictionary, resetting, 361
  location warnings, resetting, 361
  models, comparison of, 11–12
  network settings, resetting, 361
  OK to disconnect message, 38
  on/off for, 21–22
  overview, 10
  requirements for, 19–20
  resetting, 359–360
  searching for songs on, 253–258
  settings, resetting, 360–361
  song playback on, 258–265
iTunes. *See also* synchronization with
    iTunes
  audio books, playing, 221
  browsing content in, 180–182
  CDs played in, 97–101
  content information, editing, 198–204
  content information, entering, 197
  cover art, adding, 205–206
  cover browser, 95
  Cover Flow view, 182–183
  equalizer, 226–227
  equalizer preset, 202
  Genius button, 96
  Genius playlists, 235–237
  Genius sidebar, 97, 102
  installation, 29–35
  iPhone setup for, 35–38
  iPod setup for, 35–38
  launching, 32, 34, 93
  List pane, 94, 95, 180, 181
  minimizing, 215
  music added to, 129–138
  music files, adding, 137–138

  opening, 93
  overview, 92–93
  photos, syncing, 292
  photos transferred to iPod/iPhone,
    290–292
  player buttons, 96
  playlist buttons, 96
  podcasts, adding, 138–142
  podcasts, playing, 219–220
  rating content on, 204
  rating your songs, 366–367
  as requirement for iPod/iPhone, 19
  ripping a CD, 129–138
  Search field, 96
  Setup Assistant, 32, 34–35
  Show/Hide artwork button, 96
  Show/Hide Genius Sidebar button, 96
  sizing, 97
  song information retrieved from the
    Internet, 196–197
  songs, playing, 214–219
  Source pane, 93–94, 180
  Speakers pop-up menu, 96
  Status pane, 96
  version, checking for updated, 362
  version, using up-to-date, 29, 33
  videos, playing, 221–225
  videos added to iTunes library, 142–143
  View buttons, 96
  visual effects in, 99–101
  volume, 207–208
  volume, adjusting, 225–228
  Volume control, 96
  what you can do with, 92–93
iTunes DJ, 215–218
iTunes icon, 44
iTunes installation
  on Macintosh, 33–35
  options for, 31
  on Windows PC, 29–32
iTunes library
  albums, browsing songs by, 184–185
  albums, deleting, 193
  applications, browsing, 186–187
  applications, deleting, 193
  artist, browsing songs by, 184–185

iTunes library *(continued)*
  artists, deleting, 193
  audio books, browsing, 185
  audio books, deleting, 193
  backup for, 249–250
  copying media files in, 248–249
  cover art, browsing by, 182–183
  current item playing, showing, 192
  deleting content in, 193–194
  duplicate items, showing, 192–193
  finding, 247
  games, browsing, 186–187
  locating media files in, 247–248
  media file for content item, finding, 192
  movies, browsing, 186
  multiple items, deleting, 194
  options in, 180
  playlists, deleting songs from, 193
  podcasts, browsing, 185–186
  podcasts, deleting, 193, 194
  removing items from library but keeping
    on hard drive, 193, 194
  restoring, 250
  ringtones, deleting, 193
  songs, deleting, 193
  TV shows, browsing, 186
  TV shows, deleting, 194
  versions of songs, deleting, 193
  videos, browsing, 186
  videos, deleting, 193
  Web radio stations, deleting, 193
iTunes Plus format, 104
iTunes Store
  App Store, 122–123
  audio books, browsing, 112–113
  browsing songs and albums, 108–110
  buying media from, 116–122
  Celebrity Playlists, 111
  collaborative filtering, 235
  content links, 105
  cover art in, 183
  downloads, resuming interrupted,
    120–121
  first name, artists listed alphabetically
    by, 110

  Genius playlists, 235–237
  home page, 106
  iMix playlists, 111
  movies, browsing, 112–114
  music videos, browsing, 112–114
  opening, 105
  overview, 104–106
  podcasts, browsing and subscribing to,
    114–116
  power searching, 111–112
  preferences, changing, 119–120
  setting up an account, 106–108
  synchronization with, 146
  TV shows, browsing, 112–114
iTunes Store on iPod touch/iPhone
  apps, browsing and downloading,
    126–127
  apps, updating, 127
  overview, 124
  podcasts, browsing and downloading, 126
  songs, browsing and downloading,
    124–126
iTunes Visualizer, 100

• K •

keyboard, international, 369
keyboard (iPhone and iPod touch)
  accent marks, typing, 49
  Auto-Capitalization option for, 54
  Auto-Correction option for, 54
  caps lock, enabling, 48
  caps lock option for, 54
  copying text, 51–53
  cutting text, 51–53
  dictionary, resetting, 361
  editing text on, 49–51
  emailing notes made on, 48
  numbers, typing, 48–49
  options for, 53–54
  overview, 47
  pasting text, 51–53
  saving notes made on, 48
  shortcut option for, 54
  symbols, typing, 48–49

typing into Notes app, 47–48
word suggestions, 49–51
Kincaid, Bill (developer of iTunes), 1

• L •

labeling your Voice Memos recording, 348
Labyrinth, 46
landmarks, finding, 339–340
last name, sorting contacts by, 335
launching iTunes, 32, 34, 93
Leonhard, Woody (*Windows Vista All-in-One Desk Reference For Dummies*), 4
Light Bike, 46
limiting number of songs on Genius playlists, 237
links
  in email, 319
  in Safari, 310–311
List pane (iTunes), 94, 95, 180, 181
List View (iTunes)
  audio books displayed in, 188
  black check mark in, 188
  broadcast icon in, 188
  chasing arrows in, 188
  columns in, customizing, 189–190
  content indicators in, 188
  customization of, 189–190
  displaying content in, 187–190
  exclamation point in, 188
  green check mark in, 188
  music videos displayed in, 188
  orange waveform in, 188
  podcasts displayed in, 188
  searching content in, 191–192
  songs displayed in, 188
  sorting content in, 190–191
  speaker in, 188
  TV shows displayed in, 188
live updating for smart playlists, 234
locating media files in iTunes library, 247–248
Location Services, using, 74
location warnings, resetting, 361
lyrics, 203

• M •

Mac OS X Snow Leopard All-in-One For Dummies (Chambers), 4, 211
Macintosh
  iTunes installation on, 33–35
  MobileMe, setting up, 168–169
  organization, applications for, 162
  as requirement for iPod/iPhone, 19
  volume, 208–209
mail accounts
  changing, 174–175
  deleting, 175
  setting up, 172–174
Mail app, 317
Mail icon, 44
managing playlists, 232
manually managing your music and videos
  Autofill, using, 159–160
  copying items directly to your iPod/iPhone, 157–158
  deleting items on your iPod/iPhone, 158–159
  overview, 156–157
  song information retrieved from the Internet, 196
  steps for, 156–157
  synchronization with iTunes, 156–160
Maps application
  bookmarking a location, 341–342
  current location, showing your, 339–340
  driving directions, finding, 342–344
  landmarks, finding, 339–340
  overview, 339
  satellite image of location, showing, 342
  searching, 339–341
  traffic data on, 368
  zooming in, 339
Maps icon, 44
MARWARE, 83
maximum volume, limiting volume to be lower than actual, 276
media file for content item, finding, 192
meeting invitations in Calendar application, 333
Microsoft Exchange, 325

minimizing iTunes, 215
MobileMe
  cloud, overwriting data in, 170–172
  described, 162
  mail account, setting up, 172–174
  setting up on Macintosh, 168–169
  setting up on Windows (Microsoft), 170
  sharing pictures on, 302
  synchronization with, 167–172
motion sensing by iPod touch, 46
movies. *See also* videos
  browsing, 186
  synchronization with iTunes, 154–155
MP3 CD
  burning, 246
  calculating what will fit on, 243
  switching import encoders for, 244
MP3 format
  burning discs in, 241
  ripping a CD on iTunes, 133
multiple items
  deleting, 194
  editing content information on iTunes of, 199–200
multiple pages, surfing, 311–312
multiple pictures, selecting and copying, 300–301
multiple time zones, displaying clocks with, 61–62
music videos
  browsing, 112–114
  displayed in List View (iTunes), 188
MySpace application, 351–352

• N •

navigating with Safari, 310–311
network settings, resetting, 361
new window, opening a playlist in a, 231
Nike+ iPod Sport Kit, 366
Notes icon, 44
notes synchronized with iTunes, 166
numbers, typing on keyboard (iPhone and iPod touch), 48–49

• O •

1-Click, buying media from iTunes Store with, 117
on/off
  for iPhones, 22
  for iPods, 21–22
On-The-Go playlists
  clearing, 272
  deleting items from, 271–272
  for iPod classic, 270
  for iPod nano, 270
  overview, 268
  playing songs, 269
  selecting songs for, 268–269
  song order, changing, 269
orange waveform, 188
organization
  applications for, 162
  of photos, 289–290
  of playlists, 232
output volume, changing computer's, 207–210

• P •

Party Shuffle. *See* iTunes DJ
Pass the Pigs, 46
passcode
  for iPhone, 70, 358
  for iPod classic, 70
  for iPod nano, 70
  for iPod touch, 70, 358
  overview, 69
  setting, 70–71
  unlocking, 71
pasting text, 51–53
pausing
  playback in iPod shuffle, 266
  videos, 280, 282
PC as requirement for iPod/iPhone, 19
PCs For Dummies, 11th Edition (Gookin), 210
personal information synchronized with iTunes, 163–167

personal settings
  backlight, adjusting, 72
  brightness, adjusting, 72–73
  font size, setting, 74
  Location Services, using, 74
  overview, 71–72
  restrictions, setting, 75
  sound effects, setting, 73–74
  wallpaper, setting, 73
Phone icon, 44
Photos icon, 44
physical location, using your, 74
pictures
  contacts, adding photos to, 338
  email, saving a picture attached to an, 301–302
  email, sending pictures by, 299–300
  file formats for, 292
  on iPhone, viewing, 293–294
  on iPod classic, viewing, 295
  on iPod nano, viewing, 295
  on iPod touch, viewing, 293–294
  MobileMe, sharing pictures on, 302
  multiple pictures, selecting and copying, 300–301
  organizing, 289–290
  overview, 289–290
  screen shots, capturing, 302
  sharing, 299–302
  slideshows, 295–299
  syncing, 292
  transferring to iPod/iPhone, 290–292
  viewing, 293–295
playback, song
  on iPhone, 258–260
  on iPod classic, 260–262
  on iPod nano, 260–262
  on iPod shuffle, 265–267
  on iPod touch, 259–260
  on iPods, 258–265
  overview, 258–259
  repeating songs, 262–263
  shuffling song order, 263–265
player buttons (iTunes), 96
playing
  audio books, 286–287
  podcasts, 286–287

  slideshows, 298–299
  songs on On-The-Go playlists, 269
  videos, 280
playing songs on iTunes
  cross-fading song playback, 218–219
  with iTunes DJ, 215–218
  overview, 214–215
playing videos on iTunes
  on full-screen, 223–225
  options for, 223
  overview, 221–223
  preferences, changing, 223
  separate window, watching a video in a, 222–223
playlist buttons (iTunes), 96
playlist for burning discs
  AAC format for, 243
  AIFF format for, 243
  Apple Lossless format for, 243
  calculating what will fit on CD, 242–243
  DVD, calculating what will fit on, 243
  importing music for an audio CD-R, 243
  MP3 CD, calculating what will fit on, 243
  MP3 CD, switching import encoders for, 244
  overview, 241
  WAV format for, 243
playlists
  of albums, 231
  Autofill used to create random, 160
  creating, 230–233
  deleting, 233
  deleting items from, 232
  deleting songs from, 193
  Genius, 235–237, 272–275
  iTunes DJ, using, 215–218
  managing, 232
  new window, opening a playlist in a, 231
  On-The-Go, 268–272
  organizing, 232
  overview, 229
  podcasts added to, 220
  quick creation of, 231
  rearranging, 231–232
  renaming, 232
  searches by, 257–258
  smart, 229, 233–235

playlists *(continued)*
  synchronization with iTunes, 151–153
  using VoiceOver to choose, 266–267
plug-ins for visualizers, 101
podcasts
  adding, 138–142
  browsing, 185–186
  browsing and downloading, 126
  browsing and subscribing to, 114–116
  deleting, 193, 194, 368
  described, 12
  displayed in List View (iTunes), 188
  enhanced, 220
  finding, 115, 286–287
  on iPhone, 286
  on iPod classic, 287
  on iPod nano, 287
  on iPod touch, 286
  overview, 114, 286
  playing, 116, 219–220, 286–287
  playlists, adding to, 220
  subscribing to, 116
  synchronization with iTunes, 153–154
podcasts added to iTunes library
  overview, 138–139
  scheduling podcast updates, 141–142
  subscribing to podcasts, 139–140
  updating podcasts, 140
Pope Benedict XVI, 9
power accessories, 87
power adapters, 18
power converter kits, 87
power searching in iTunes Store, 111–112
power specifications for battery, 23
power supply
  Dock Connector, 20–21
  overview, 20
powered hub, 21
powering down, 358
preferences
  iTunes Store, 119–120
  playing videos on iTunes, 223
presets, equalizer
  for iPhone, 277
  for iPod classic, 278
  for iPod nano, 278
  for iPod touch, 277

overview, 202
volume adjustments in iTunes, 226–227
ProClip, 83
pushing messages, 325–326

● *Q* ●

quick creation of playlists, 231
QuickTime
  described, 30, 142
  installation on Windows PC, 30
  as requirement for iPod/iPhone, 20

● *R* ●

rating
  content on iTunes, 204
  your songs on iTunes, 366–367
reading email, 318–320
Really Simple Syndication (RSS)
    technology, 138
rearranging
  playlists, 231–232
  tracks in iTunes, 98–99
recharging battery, 24–25
recipients for email, 319
recordable CDs, 240–241
recordable DVDs, 241
recording speed for burning discs, 246
recording with Voice Memos
    application, 348
redeeming gift certificates and prepaid
    cards in iTunes Store, 121–122
refreshing Genius playlists, 236, 274
renaming playlists, 232
repeating an entire CD, 99
repeating songs, 262–263
replaceable alkaline batteries, 87
replacing battery, 25
replying to email, 323
resetting
  iPhone, 359
  iPod classic, 359–360
  iPod nano, 359–360
  iPod shuffle, 360
  iPods, 359–360

your settings, 360–361
your system, 359–360
restoring
    to factory condition, 363
    iTunes library, 250
    settings from backups, 364
restrictions, setting, 75
rewinding playback, 266
ringtones, deleting, 193
ripping a CD on iTunes
    AAC encoder, using, 133
    AIFF encoder, using, 133
    Apple Lossless encoder, using, 133
    Gapless Album option, 134–135
    import preferences and settings,
        changing, 130–133
    MP3 encoder, using, 133
    overview, 129–130
    steps for, 136–137
    WAV encoder, using, 133
Robbin, Jeff (developer of iTunes), 1
RSS (Really Simple Syndication)
    technology, 138
rules for smart playlists, 233–235

• S •

Safari
    bookmarks, 307–308, 314–315
    browsing Web sites, 306–307
    email, sending a Web link by, 315
    Home screen, adding a Web site to
        your, 316
    interacting with Web pages, 312–313
    links, 310–311
    multiple pages, surfing, 311–312
    navigating with, 310–311
    overview, 305
    scrolling in, 310
    searching with Google, 309
    searching with Yahoo!, 309
    text, copying, 313
    text entered into Web sites, 312–313
    URLs, entering, 306–307
    zooming in, 310
Safari icon, 44

satellite image of location, showing, 342
saving email, 323
saving notes made on keyboard (iPhone
    and iPod touch), 48
saving power, tips for, 25–28
scaling videos, 282
scheduling podcast updates, 141–142
screen, cleaning your, 366
screen shots, capturing, 302
scrolling in Safari, 310
Search field (iTunes), 96
searches
    by album, 256–257
    by artist, 255–258
    audio books, 286–287
    contacts, 335
    by cover art, 254–255
    by Cover Flow, 254–255
    with Google, 309
    iTunes library, 247
    in List View (iTunes), 191–192
    Maps application, 339–341
    by playlist, 257–258
    podcasts, 286–287
    for songs on iPhone, 253–258
    for songs on iPods, 253–258
    by title of song, 258
    videos, 280
    videos in YouTube, 285
    with Yahoo!, 309
selecting songs for On-The-Go playlists,
    268–269
selecting what to sync, 150–156
sending email, 321–323
sent messages, receiving a copy of your, 325
separate window, watching a video in a,
    222–223
setting passcode, 70–71
setting up
    iTunes Store account, 106–108
    restored iPhone, 363–364
    restored iPods, 363–364
    slideshows, 296–298
settings, resetting
    iPhone, 360–361
    iPod classic, 360

settings, resetting *(continued)*
  iPod nano, 360
  iPods, 360–361
Settings icon, 44
Setup Assistant (iTunes), 32, 34–35
sharing
  photos, 299–302
  videos, 284–285
Shopping Cart, buying media from iTunes
    Store, 117–119
shortcut option for keyboard (iPhone and
    iPod touch), 54
Show/Hide artwork button (iTunes), 96
Show/Hide Genius Sidebar button
    (iTunes), 96
shuffling song order
  described, 263
  on iPhone, 263–264
  on iPod classic, 264–265
  on iPod nano, 264–265
  on iPod shuffle, 266
  on iPod touch, 263–264
signatures in email, 325
Silver Rattle, 46
single items, editing content information
    on iTunes of, 200–204
16GB model of iPod touch, 12
sizing iTunes, 97
skipping to points in videos, 281, 282
skipping tracks in iTunes, 99
sleep timer, 68–69
slideshows
  on iPhone, playing, 298
  on iPhone, setting up, 296–297
  on iPod classic, playing, 298–299
  on iPod classic, setting up, 297–298
  on iPod nano, playing, 298–299
  on iPod nano, setting up, 297–298
  on iPod touch, playing, 298
  on iPod touch, setting up, 296–297
  overview, 295
  playing, 298–299
  setting up, 296–298
smart playlists
  creating, 233–234
  editing, 235
  live updating, 234

naming, 234
  overview, 233
  rules for, 233–235
social networks
  Facebook application, 350–351
  MySpace application, 351–352
  overview, 349
  Twitter, 352–354
software, updating, 362
software version, checking, 362
song information retrieved from the
    Internet
  automatic, 196
  Gracenote CDDB, 197
  manual, 196
  overview, 196
song lyrics, 203
song order for On-The-Go playlists,
    changing, 269
song playback
  on iPhone, 258–260
  on iPod classic, 260–262
  on iPod nano, 260–262
  on iPod shuffle, 265–267
  on iPod touch, 259–260
  on iPods, 258–265
  overview, 258–259
  repeating songs, 262–263
  shuffling song order, 263–265
songs
  browsing and downloading, 124–126
  deleting, 193
  displayed in List View (iTunes), 188
  on iPod/iPhone, searching, 253–258
  playing, 214–219
sorting contacts, 334–335
sorting content in List View (iTunes),
    190–191
Sound Check
  before burning discs, 246
  enabling, 227–228, 277
  for iPhone, 277
  for iPod classic, 277
  for iPod nano, 277
  for iPod shuffle, 277
  for iPod touch, 277
sound effects, setting, 73–74

SoundJam MP, 1
Source pane (iTunes window)
  Devices, 93
  Eject button, 94
  Library, 93
  overview, 93–94, 180
  Playlists, 94
  Store, 93
space needed for synchronization with
    iTunes, 149
speaker in List View (iTunes), 188
speaker systems, 79–81
Speakers pop-up menu (iTunes), 96
splitter cable, 81
start times, 202–203
starting playback for iPod shuffle, 265
status light for battery, 24–25
Status pane (iTunes), 96
stereo system, wireless connection to,
    210–214
stereo-in connection, 82
Stocks application
  adding a stock/index/fund, 346
  deleting a stock/index/fund, 346
  overview, 345
Stocks icon, 44
stop times, 202–203
stopping a network from joining Wi-Fi
    network, 370
stopwatch, using, 67–68
streaming video to iPod/iPhone from
    YouTube, 284
sublibraries created for synchronization
    with iTunes, 150
subscribing to podcasts, 139–140
subtitles in videos, 281
switching between cities in Weather
    application, 345
symbols, typing on keyboard (iPhone and
    iPod touch), 48–49
synchronization with iTunes
  automatic synchronization, preventing, 150
  of bookmarks, 165
  of calendars, 165, 167
  of contacts, 163–165, 167
  copying everything at once, 148–150

deselecting items before, 151
of e-mail accounts, 166–167
manually managing your music and
    videos, 156–160
of movies, 154–155
of notes, 166
overview, 146–148
of personal information, 163–167
of playlists, 151–153
of podcast episodes, 153–154
selecting what to sync, 150–156
space needed for, 149
steps for, 146–148
sublibraries created for, 150
of TV shows, 154–156
syncing
  Calendar application, 332
  Genius playlists, 236
  photos, 292

● **T** ●

Tap Tap Revenge, 45
text
  copying, 313
  entered into Web sites, 312–313
third-party utility programs, 240
32GB model for iPod touch, 12
time and date
  alarms, setting, 63–66
  creating clocks, 61–62
  on iPhone, 58–59
  on iPod classic, 59–60
  on iPod nano, 59–60
  on iPod touch, 58–59
  multiple time zones, displaying clocks
      with, 61–62
  removing clocks, 61
  sleep timer, 68–69
  stopwatch, using, 67–68
  timers, using, 66
time zone support for Calendar
    application, 333
timers, using, 66
title of song, searches by, 258
traffic data on Maps application, 368

trimming your recording in Voice Memos application, 349
TuneDok (Belkin), 83
turning on/off
  iPhone, 22, 358
  iPod classic, 357–358
  iPod nano, 357–358
  iPod shuffle, 358
  iPod touch, 358
  iPods, 21–22, 357–358
TV shows
  browsing in iTunes library, 186
  browsing in iTunes Store, 112–114
  deleting, 194
  displayed in List View (iTunes), 188
  synchronization with iTunes, 154–156
tweets, 352–354
Twitter, 352–354
Twitter for iPhone Web service, 353
Twitterific, 353–354
typing into Notes app, 47–48

• U •

unlocking passcode, 71
unpinching, 39
unread email messages, 318, 320
updating podcasts, 140
upright position, dock used to keep iPod/iPhone in, 21
URL (uniform resource locator)
  described, 306
  entering into Safari, 306–307
USB 2.0, 21
USB cable for iPod shuffle, 20
USB (Universal Serial Bus) connection
  described, 18
  high-powered, 19
  as requirement for iPod/iPhone, 19

• V •

version of iTunes
  checking for updated, 362
  using up-to-date, 29, 33
versions of songs, deleting, 193

videocasts, 114
videos. *See also* YouTube
  added to iTunes library, 142–143
  browsing, 186
  browsing videos in iTunes Store, 112–114
  converting, 279
  deleting, 193, 281, 368
  fast-forwarding, 281, 282
  finding, 280
  on iPhone, scaling picture, 282
  on iPhone, controlling playback, 280–281
  on iPhone, locating and playing, 280
  on iPod classic, controlling playback, 282
  on iPod classic, locating and playing, 280
  on iPod nano, controlling playback, 282
  on iPod nano, locating and playing, 280
  on iPod touch, scaling picture, 282
  on iPod touch, controlling playback, 280–281
  on iPod touch, locating and playing, 280
  overview, 279
  pausing, 280, 282
  playing, 280
  playing in Apple TV, 225
  playing in iTunes, 221–225
  scaling, 282
  skipping to points in, 281, 282
  subtitles in, 281
View buttons (iTunes), 96
viewing
  contacts, 333–334
  photos, 293–295
visual effects in iTunes, 99–101
visualizers
  Classic Visualizer, 100
  full-screen visual effects, 100–101
  iTunes Visualizer, 100
  overview, 99
  plug-ins, 101
vodcasts, 114
Voice Memos application
  labeling your recording, 348
  overview, 347–348
  recording with, 348
  trimming your recording, 349
Voice Memos icon, 44

VoiceOver feature for iPod shuffle, 15,
266–267
volume
changing computer's output volume,
207–210
on iPhone, 275, 276
on iPod classic, 275
on iPod nano, 275
on iPod shuffle, 275
on iPod touch, 275, 276
on Macintosh, 208–209
maximum volume, limiting volume to be
lower than actual, 276
overview, 207–208
for specific items, 202
on Windows (Microsoft), 209–210
volume adjustments in iTunes
advance, setting volume in, 225–226
enhancing the volume, 228
equalizer presets, 226–227
overview, 207–208, 225
Sound Check, enabling, 227–228

• *W* •

wallpaper, setting, 72–73
WAV format
playlist for burning discs, 243
ripping a CD on iTunes, 133
Weather application
adding a city, 344
deleting a city, 345
overview, 344
switching between cities, 345
using, 344
Weather icon, 44
Web radio stations, deleting, 193
Web sites
Home screen, adding a Web site to
your, 316
scrolling, 310
text, copying, 313
text entered into, 312–313
zooming in, 310
Weberka, Peter *(Windows XP Gigabook For
Dummies)*, 4

Wi-Fi network
choosing, 77–78
overview, 75–77
stopping a network from joining, 370
turning off, 76
turning on, 76
Wi-Fi (wireless fidelity), 11
wiggling icons, 45–46
Windows PC
iTunes installation on, 29–32
MobileMe, setting up, 170
organization, applications for, 162
QuickTime installation on, 29
volume, 209–210
*Windows Vista All-in-One Desk Reference
For Dummies* (Leonhard), 4
Windows XP Gigabook For Dummies
(Weberka), 4
wireless connection to stereo system,
210–214
wireless music adapter
overview, 85
recommendations for, 85–86
using, 85
word suggestions with keyboard (iPhone
and iPod touch), 49–51

• *X* •

Xhake Shake, 46
XML (eXtensible Markup Language), 138

• *Y* •

Yahoo! Mail, 325
Yahtzee Adventures, 46
YouTube
bookmarking videos, 284–285
deleting videos, 285
overview, 283
searching videos, 285
sharing videos, 284–285
streaming video to iPod/iPhone from, 284
YouTube icon, 44

● *Z* ●

zooming in
  Maps application, 339
  Safari, 310
  Web sites, 310